TRANSFORMING EARLY ENGLISH

Transforming Early English shows how historical pragmatics can offer a powerful explanatory framework for the changes medieval English and Older Scots texts undergo, as they are transmitted over time and space. The book argues that formal features such as spelling, script and font, and punctuation – often neglected in critical engagement with past texts – relate closely to dynamic, shifting socio-cultural processes, imperatives and functions. This theme is illustrated through numerous case studies in textual recuperation, ranging from the reinvention of Old English poetry and prose in the later medieval and early modern periods, to the eighteenth-century 'vernacular revival' of literature in Older Scots.

JEREMY J. SMITH is Glasgow University's Professor of English Philology, a Fellow of the Royal Society of Edinburgh, and an Honorary Fellow of the Association for Scottish Literary Studies. His publications reflect his wide interests, which range from English historical linguistics and book history to the language of Robert Burns.

STUDIES IN ENGLISH LANGUAGE

The aim of this series is to provide a framework for original studies of English, both present-day and past. All books are based securely on empirical research, and represent theoretical and descriptive contributions to our knowledge of national and international varieties of English, both written and spoken. The series covers a broad range of topics and approaches, including syntax, phonology, grammar, vocabulary, discourse, pragmatics and sociolinguistics, and is aimed at an international readership.

Already published in this series

Daniel Schreier and Marianne Hundt (eds.): *English as a Contact Language*
Bas Aarts, Joanne Close, Geoffrey Leech and Sean Wallis (eds.): *The Verb Phrase in English: Investigating Recent Language Change with Corpora*
Martin Hilpert: *Constructional Change in English: Developments in Allomorphy, Word Formation, and Syntax*
Jakob R. E. Leimgruber: *Singapore English: Structure, Variation, and Usage*
Christoph Rühlemann: *Narrative in English Conversation: A Corpus Analysis of Storytelling*
Dagmar Deuber: *English in the Caribbean: Variation, Style and Standards in Jamaica and Trinidad*
Eva Berlage: *Noun Phrase Complexity in English*
Nicole Dehé: *Parentheticals in Spoken English: The Syntax–Prosody Relation*
Jock O. Wong: *The Culture of Singapore English*
Marianne Hundt (ed.): *Late Modern English Syntax*
Irma Taavitsainen, Merja Kytö, Claudia Claridge and Jeremy Smith (eds.): *Developments in English: Expanding Electronic Evidence*
Arne Lohmann: *English Coordinate Constructions: A Processing Perspective on Constituent Order*
Nuria Yáñez-Bouza: *Grammar, Rhetoric and Usage in English: Preposition Placement 1500–1900*

Anita Auer, Daniel Schreier and Richard J. Watts (eds.): *Letter Writing and Language Change*
John Flowerdew and Richard W. Forest: *Signalling Nouns in English: A Corpus-Based Discourse Approach*
Jeffrey P. Williams, Edgar W. Schneider, Peter Trudgill and Daniel Schreier (eds.): *Further Studies in the Lesser-Known Varieties of English*
Jack Grieve: *Regional Variation in Written American English*
Douglas Biber and Bethany Gray: *Grammatical Complexity in Academic English: Linguistics Change in Writing*
Gjertrud Flermoen Stenbrenden: *Long-Vowel Shifts in English, c. 1050–1700: Evidence from Spelling*
Zoya G. Proshina and Anna A. Eddy (eds.): *Russian English: History, Functions, and Features*
Raymond Hickey (ed.): *Listening to the Past: Audio Records of Accents of English*
Phillip Wallage: *Negation in Early English: Grammatical and Functional Change*
Marianne Hundt, Sandra Mollin and Simone E. Pfenninger (eds.): *The Changing English Language: Psycholinguistic Perspectives*
Joanna Kopaczyk and Hans Sauer (eds.): *Binomials in the History of English: Fixed and Flexible*
Alexander Haselow: *Spontaneous Spoken English: An Integrated Approach to the Emergent Grammar of Speech*
Christina Sanchez-Stockhammer: *English Compounds and Their Spelling*
David West Brown: *English and Empire: Language History, Dialect, and the Digital Archive*
Paula Rodríguez-Puente: *The English Phrasal Verb, 1650–present: History, Stylistic Drifts, and Lexicalisation*
Erik R. Thomas (ed.): *Mexican American English: Substrate Influence and the Birth of an Ethnolect*
Thomas Hoffmann: *English Comparative Correlatives: Diachronic and Synchronic Variation at the Lexicon–Syntax Interface*
Nuria Yáñez-Bouza, Emma Moore, Linda van Bergen and Willem B. Hollmann (eds.): *Categories, Constructions, and Change in English Syntax*
Raymond Hickey (ed.): *English in the German-speaking World*
Axel Bohmann: *Variation in English World-wide: Registers and Global Varieties*
Raymond Hickey (ed.): *English in Multilingual South Africa: The Linguistics of Contact and Change*
Jeremy J. Smith: *Transforming Early English: The Reinvention of Early English and Older Scots*

Earlier titles not listed are also available

TRANSFORMING EARLY ENGLISH

The Reinvention of Early English and Older Scots

JEREMY J. SMITH
University of Glasgow

CAMBRIDGE
UNIVERSITY PRESS

University Printing House, Cambridge CB2 8BS, United Kingdom

One Liberty Plaza, 20th Floor, New York, NY 10006, USA

477 Williamstown Road, Port Melbourne, VIC 3207, Australia

314-321, 3rd Floor, Plot 3, Splendor Forum, Jasola District Centre, New Delhi - 110025, India

103 Penang Road, #05-06/07, Visioncrest Commercial, Singapore 238467

Cambridge University Press is part of the University of Cambridge.

It furthers the University's mission by disseminating knowledge in the pursuit of education, learning and research at the highest international levels of excellence.

www.cambridge.org
Information on this title: www.cambridge.org/9781108414852
DOI: 10.1017/9781108333474

First published 2020
First paperback edition 2022

A catalogue record for this publication is available from the British Library

Library of Congress Cataloging in Publication data
NAMES: Smith, J. J. (Jeremy J.), author.
TITLE: Transforming early English : the reinvention of early English and older Scots / Jeremy J. Smith.
DESCRIPTION: Cambridge, United Kingdom ; New York, NY : Cambridge University Press, 2020. | Series: Studies in English language | Includes bibliographical references and index. | Contents: Prologue : snatched from the fire : the case of Thomas Percy – On historical pragmatics – Inventing the Anglo-Saxons – 'Witnesses preordained by God' : the reception of Middle English religious prose – The great tradition : Langland, Gower, Chaucer – Forging the nation : reworking older Scottish literature – On textual transformations : Scott and beyond.
IDENTIFIERS: LCCN 2019042282 (print) | LCCN 2019042283 (ebook) | ISBN 9781108420389 (hardback) | ISBN 9781108333474 (ebook)
SUBJECTS: LCSH: English language – History. | Historical linguistics.
CLASSIFICATION: LCC PE1075 .S46 2020 (print) | LCC PE1075 (ebook) | DDC 427/.02–dc23
LC record available at https://lccn.loc.gov/2019042282
LC ebook record available at https://lccn.loc.gov/2019042283

ISBN 978-1-108-42038-9 Hardback
ISBN 978-1-108-41485-2 Paperback

For Elaine
And In Memoriam R.M.H.

Contents

Preface

This book argues that the functionalist approach known as *historical pragmatics* offers a powerful explanatory paradigm for the formal changes medieval English and Scots texts undergo as they are transmitted in writing over time and space.

Although I hope that the book offers something new both in terms of general insights, and for those interested in the particular illustrative case studies discussed, its overall argument has been long in the making. It derives from conversations, beginning in the late 1970s, with three especially remarkable scholars: Christian Kay, Malcolm Parkes and Michael Samuels. All are sadly no longer with us. My colleague Christian introduced me many years ago to pragmatics as an approach to the study of texts, and I cannot put a value on our friendship and her innumerable kindnesses; her death in 2016 was a huge blow to everyone who knew her. Malcolm, inter alia an inspirational conversationalist, was wont to say that 'the greatest mistake a paleographer makes is to forget the nature of the text being copied'. This axiom has stuck with me for the last forty years, and its emphasis on the relationship of textual form to socio-cultural function is central to this book's argument. And Michael's sustained and profoundly principled focus on the importance of the human element in linguistic and philological study has been a key influence on my thinking.

Other friends and colleagues have been crucial in helping me develop my initial, inchoate thoughts, although all remaining flaws are entirely my responsibility. Merja Kytö, my general editor, and Irma Taavitsainen have been engaged with every aspect of the book from the outset, and I am deeply grateful for their enthusiastic input. I owe a very special debt to John Thompson, whose thoughtful and supportive comradeship has been an inspiration throughout, and to Ian Johnson and Crawford Gribben, all of whom have collaborated with me in the larger and continuing *Textual Afterlives* research programme of which this book is a part. Tim Machan gave me some invaluable encouragement and feedback for which I am extremely grateful, and I am also particularly indebted to Wendy Scase, who gave meticulous comments on a late draft, and whose forthcoming monograph on medieval English writing-systems in relation to socio-cultural functions is highly relevant to its concerns. My colleague Katie Lowe has been, as ever, encouraging in multiple ways, as has my long-term collaborator at Stavanger, Merja Stenroos. Dauvit Broun, Gerry Carruthers, Isabel de la Cruz Cabanillas, Maria José Esteve Ramos, Frank Ferguson, Simon Horobin, David Jasper, Joanna Kopaczyk, Nigel Leask, Linne Mooney, Veronica O'Mara, Murray Pittock, Andrew Prescott and Alison Wiggins have helped me with generous support, and with detailed references and comments. My graduate students (past and present) have always demonstrated that the supervisory process is one of mutual learning. In the specific context of this book, however, I should like to thank the following: Juulia Ahvensalmi, Fraser Dallachy, Laura Esteban Segura, Danni Glover, George Head, Lauren McClelland, Imogen Marcus, Manon Thuillier, Gillian Weir, Graham Williams, Hiroshi Yadomi and the late Vanessa Yuille, and above all Lena Leitner, Francesca Mackay, Diane Scott and David Selfe.

I am also conscious of debts – some from many years ago – for points of information and/or orientation to Richard Beadle, Michael Benskin, the late Norman Blake, Julia Boffey, Rolf Bremmer, Rhona Brown, Graham Caie, Thomas Clancy, Michael Clanchy, Claudia Claridge, Margaret Connolly, John Corbett, Orietta da Rold, Marina Dossena, the late Ian Doyle, Martha Driver, Tom Duncan, Siân Echard, Tony Edwards, Liz Elliott, Mel Evans, Julia Fernandez Cuesta, Sue Fitzmaurice, Douglas Gifford, Vincent Gillespie, Claire Graf, Johanna Green, the late Jeremy Griffiths, Ralph Hanna, Kate Harris, Theo van Heijnsbergen, John Hines, Carole Hough, Anne Hudson, Elspeth Jajdelska, Claire Jones, Andreas Jucker, Kathy Kerby-Fulton, Colin Kidd, Pam King, John Kirk, Meg Laing, Craig Lamont, Charles Lock, Angelika Lutz, Caroline Macafee, Derrick McClure, Alasdair MacDonald, the late Angus McIntosh, Mike MacMahon, Martti Mäkinen, Willy Maley, Sally Mapstone, Rob Maslen, Charlotte Methuen, Robert Millar, Alastair Minnis, Haruko Momma, Colette Moore, Kylie Murray, Sabina Nedelius, Roibeard O Maolalaigh, Päivi Pahta, Noel Peacock, Derek Pearsall, Matti Peikola, Ryan Perry, Sue Powell, Ad Putter, Susan Rennie, the late Matti Rissanen, Jane Roberts, Beth Robertson, Alicia Rodriguez Alvarez, Nieves Rodriguez Ledesma, Nicola Royan, Elisabeth Salter, Cathy Shrank, Rosie Shute, Jennifer Smith, Scott Spurlock, the late Eric Stanley, Estelle Stubbs, Louise Sylvester, Toshi Takamiya, Jacob Thaisen, Kjetil Thengs, Elaine Treharne, Sebastiaan

Verweij, Dan Wakelin, Ron Waldron, Keith Williamson, and Laura Wright. I should also like to thank Marc Alexander and Alice Jenkins, my line managers in 2017–19, for their unstinting encouragement.

I am indebted to audiences at the following locations where I have presented on matters relating to this project: Aberdeen, Alcala de Henares, Belfast, Cambridge, Castellon de la Plana (Morella), Edinburgh, Florence, Glasgow, Helsinki, Hull, Kalamazoo, London, Manchester, Newcastle, Oviedo, Oxford, Seville, Sheffield, South Bend (Notre Dame), St Andrews, Stavanger, Uppsala, and Zurich.

I am very grateful to the following libraries both for access to/information about their collections, and for their online resources: Glasgow University Library above all (especially Julie Gardham, Bob Maclean, Niki Russell and the team in Special Collections, always so helpful and knowledgeable); the Beinecke Library, Yale; the Bodleian Library, Oxford; the British Library, London; Cambridge University Library; the Royal Library, Copenhagen; Edinburgh University Library; Exeter Cathedral Library; the Folger Shakespeare Library, Washington, DC; the Huntington Library, San Marino, California; Lambeth Palace Library, London; Lichfield Cathedral Library; the Linen Hall Library, Belfast; London University Library; the library of Longleat House; the Mitchell Library, Glasgow; the National Library of Scotland, Edinburgh (especially Helen Vincent); the Parker Library, Corpus Christi College, Cambridge; the Pierpont Morgan Library, New York; the Pepys Library, Magdalene College, Cambridge (especially Catherine Sutherland); the library of Petworth House, Kent; Princeton University Library; Queen's University Library, Belfast (especially Michael O'Connor and Deirdre Wildy); the Arni Magnusson Institute, Reykjavík; St John's College Library, Cambridge (especially Kathryn McKee); the library of Sidney Sussex College, Cambridge (especially Nicholas Rogers); the library of the Society of Antiquaries; the library of Trinity College, Cambridge; the library of Trinity College, Oxford; the library of University College, Oxford; the Biblioteca Capitolare, Vercelli; Waseda University Library, Tokyo; the Royal Library, Windsor Castle; Worcester Cathedral Library. I am grateful to several of these libraries for permission to publish the plates that are an important part of the book.

Versions of parts of the book have been published elsewhere, although all have been substantially revised. Part of Chapter 2 appeared as 'The evolution of Old and Middle English texts' in Machan (2017); parts of Chapter 3 appeared first as 'Mapping the language of the Vernon Manuscript', in Scase (2013a), and as 'The afterlives of Nicholas Love', in

Studia Neophilologica, Smith (2017b); and part of Chapter 5 appeared first as 'Textual afterlives: Barbour's *Bruce* and Hary's *Wallace*', in Kirk and Macleod (2013). I am grateful to the editors for their forbearance in allowing me to rework this material.

I am greatly indebted to institutions and other bodies who have supported this project: All Souls College, Oxford, who elected me to a Visiting Fellowship in 2010, enabling me, while completing other tasks, to formulate the key research questions addressed in this book; the Royal Society of Edinburgh, who supported John, Ian, Crawford and myself in a related workshop programme in 2010–11; and above all the Leverhulme Trust, whose extremely generous award of a Research Fellowship for 2017–19 made it possible for me to write this book. The Trust's emphasis on personal vision, as well as on support for academics whose research has been held back by lengthy periods in managerial or administrative roles, has been particularly appreciated. And I have been exceptionally lucky with my publishers: Helen Barton at Cambridge University Press has been encouraging and positive from the outset of the project, and I am hugely grateful for the skills and professionalism of her team, most notably Isabel Collins, Bethany Johnson and Chris Jackson.

I owe more than I can say to my wife, Elaine Higgleton, and to our daughter, Amy Smith. To them, as ever, all my love.

A Note on the Transcriptions

As in a previous publication (Smith 2012a), the many transcribed texts used for illustration in this book are edited diplomatically directly from the manuscripts and early printed editions concerned. These transcriptions follow, with some minor modifications, principles laid down by Grant Simpson for transcribing the handwriting of Scottish documents: the 'purpose of the transcripts . . . is to show the reader as exactly as possible what the writing in each document was intended to represent' (Simpson 1998: 47). Thus the following editorial principles are adopted:

(1) Spelling is given exactly as in the witness concerned, including the original distribution of *u* and *v*, *i* and *j* (see Simpson 1998: 47).

(2) Capitals are generally reproduced as they appear in the witnesses, but I have departed from Simpson's practice in using long-*I* (i.e. *J*) whenever it appears, whether it represents the letter *I* or *J*. Sometimes it is hard to tell in handwriting whether a capital letter is intended; if this is the case, I have adopted modern conventions. I have also used *ff* whenever it appears for the capital form of *f*, not replacing it with *F*. However, I do not make a distinction between long- and short-*s*, since long-*s* can easily be confused with other letters.

(3) The lineation of the original texts is reproduced as far as possible.

(4) If words – or forms that modern readers might consider separate words – are written conjoined, either accidentally or deliberately, they appear in the transcriptions in that form, e.g. *shalbe* for 'shall be'.

(5) An attempt has been made to reproduce the punctuation of the original witnesses insofar as that is typographically possible. For the *punctus interrogativus* in manuscripts, a question-mark <?> is used, while the *punctus elevatus* is reproduced as <⹎>. The *virgula suspensiva* (virgule) appears as </>; the simple *punctus*, even when it appears in mid-line position, appears as <.>.

(6) Engrossed forms are flagged in bold (and noted) where relevant to the discussion. Large decorated, historiated or illuminated letters cannot be easily reproduced, for typographical reasons. In such cases, I have adopted a convention – rather clumsy, I fear – whereby the form in question is emboldened and a gap is left to indicate the space it occupies, e.g.

> **W**　　han that Aprill with hise shoures soote
> 　　The droghte of March hath perced to the roote
> 　　And bathed euery veyne in swich licour
> 　　Of which v*er*tu/ engendred is the flour
> 　　Whan zephirus eek/ w^{t} his swete breeth
> Inspired hath in euery holt and heeth
> The tendre croppes/ and the yonge sonne
> Hath in the Ram/ his half cours yronne

or, when the space left is smaller, as follows:

> **F** ram þa*m* halʒan easterlican dæʒe: synd ʒetealde
> fiftiʒ daʒa to þisu*m* dæʒe.

(7) In accordance with usual practice, I have used italics in transcriptions to indicate contractions where what is intended by the scribe or printer is clear. However, there are some exceptions in printed texts where italic font was sometimes employed for (e.g.) aesthetic or emphatic reasons, and I wish to retain that distinction. I have, however, generally not expanded 'function' words such as *y*^{t}, *w*^{t}, *&* (i.e. *that*, *with*, *and*) etc., where the context makes the meaning clear, but where possible alternative expansions (e.g. *þet*, *wyth*, *ant*) are attested in Middle English. In some Old and Early Middle English texts a 'crossed thorn', signifying *þæt* etc., appears, e.g. *ꝥ*, and it is reproduced as such. 'Otiose strokes' or flourishes, common in late medieval English and Older Scots, present special problems for the interpretation of handwriting, and I deal with them on a case-by-case basis, since they seem often to be simply decorative (see further Houwen 1990: 22 and references there cited). I use <ß> for the 'flourished *s*' that is a feature of some kinds of Scottish handwriting.

(8) The form <y> is used for both the letter *y* and the letter *þ* ('thorn') when the two letters are not distinguished in the handwriting of the texts; in texts where the two letters are kept distinct <y> appears for the letter *y* and <þ> appears for thorn. Distinguishing, or failing to distinguish, thorn from *y* has a philological implication in Middle

English and Older Scots, and should therefore be marked in editions such as those provided here (see Benskin 1982, to be supplemented by the discursive note in Laing and Williamson 1994: 115–16).

(9) Omitted or damaged letters are generally omitted, and marked by rows of dots, e.g. [. . .]. Very occasionally conjectural emendations are offered, and these are also placed in square brackets.

(10) Yogh can appear as either *ȝ* or *z*; I have kept the distinction between the two, since the history of both letters has some interest for philologists (see the OED entries for the letters, and also Smith 2000a and references there cited). I have also used *ȝ* when it appears as a marker of plurality, e.g. *seruauntȝ* 'servants'. The Anglo-Saxon form for <w>, namely *ƿ* ('wynn'), is used when appropriate, both in Old English texts and to represent the 'counterfeit' versions of Old English script developed from the sixteenth century onwards (see Chapter 2 below). For typographical reasons I have also used *ȝ* to reflect the Anglo-Saxon 'insular *g*'; the appearance of this form, in both manuscript and 'counterfeit' versions, may be seen in Plates II, V and VI.

(11) When ornaments are used, an attempt is made to reproduce them. The pilcrow or paraph-mark is quite common, i.e. ¶, as is – especially in early printed books – the hedera or ivy-leaf, i.e. ❧, and the manicule, i.e. ☞.

(12) Interlineations and additions by the scribe are shown thus: └cowart┘ (cf. Simpson 1998: 48); glosses are offered if the addition is marginal rather than interlinear. Deletions in the text are marked as struck through, e.g. ~~*rewme*~~.

(13) Changes of folio are marked, e.g. *folio 6v* for 'folio 6 verso (i.e. left-hand side of the opening)', *folio 7r* for 'folio 7 recto (i.e. right-hand side of the opening)'. Page-breaks, where used, are flagged similarly. In some early printed books, no pagination or foliation is given; in these cases, signatures are treated as folios, with final *v* and *r* flagging verso and recto respectively, e.g. *sig. K.iij r*, *sig. a.2r*.

(14) In manuscripts, various coloured inks are often deployed for pragmatic reasons, as are engrossed forms, while in some printed books there is variation between fonts (i.e. italic versus roman, or roman versus blackletter), and there are differing practices of justification. I have approached these issues on a case-by-case basis, flagging in discussion the local transcription-conventions I have adopted.

Introduction
Snatched from the Fire: The Case of Thomas Percy

In 1867, John Hales (1836–1914) and Frederick J. Furnivall (1825–1910), two distinguished Victorian men of letters and enthusiasts for earlier literature (Gregory 2006), produced a new edition of a very famous poetic miscellany: the seventeenth-century Percy Folio manuscript. This volume, now London, British Library, MS Additional 27879, is a collection of ballads and romances, many originating (it seems) in the late Middle Ages, albeit heavily revised by a seventeenth-century learned (and, probably, royalist) antiquarian (Donatelli 1993). The new edition superseded that of the manuscript's eponymous first editor, Bishop Thomas Percy (1729–1811), who a century earlier had included much of its contents in his *Reliques of Ancient English Poetry* (1765).

The story of how Percy discovered the manuscript that now bears his name has often been told as a fine example of Romantic recuperation. While a young parson, on a visit to his native county of Shropshire, at the house of his friend Humphrey Pitt of Shifnal, probably in 1753, Percy famously retrieved a tattered ledger-like book 'lying dirty on the floor, under a bureau in the parlour . . . being used by the maids to light the fire' (Hales and Furnivall 1867–8: vol. I, lxiv). Percy reported Pitt's belief that the copyist of the manuscript was Thomas Blount (1618–79), the Worcestershire antiquary and lexicographer, from whose library the book was purchased, but this ascription has been challenged as circumstantial (Donatelli 1993, though see Gregory 2006). Whoever copied it, the manuscript was to become the basis – although with much extra matter – of the collection Percy published a decade later: the *Reliques*.

Percy's *Reliques*, which first appeared under the well-known Dodsley imprint, was one of the most influential publications of its day, rapidly becoming an eighteenth-century bestseller and 'a seminal work of English Romanticism' (*Oxford Dictionary of National Biography*, henceforth ODNB). It was much praised by William Wordsworth in 1815 and survived at least in selection format until late in the nineteenth century; a 'Boy's

Percy', for instance, appeared after Hales and Furnivall's edition, preferring to draw directly on the *Reliques* (Lanier 1883). A first print run of some 1,500 copies of the *Reliques* was almost sold out within six months of publication, responding to the taste for vernacular antiquarianism that contemporaries had also recently acclaimed in James Macpherson's 'Ossianic' *Fingal* (1762) (the latter albeit with a slightly distinct 'Celtic' – as opposed to Percy's 'Gothic' – flavour).[1]

Percy had by the time of the *Reliques*' publication already achieved a degree of recognition in literary circles. He had produced editions-cum-translations of fashionable chinoiserie, alongside some original poetry and a version of the *Song of Songs*; and, in 1763, he had demonstrated his antiquarian interests in the ancient North with the publication of *Five Pieces of Runic Poetry*, in which he had been assisted by the distinguished philologist Edward Lye (1694–1767).[2] Percy had also networked furiously, attracting the patronage of the duke of Northumberland – whose chaplain and secretary he became in 1765, and with whom he liked (they shared the same surname) to claim kinship, albeit distant – and becoming friendly with such figures as the poet William Shenstone (who advised him on the contents of the *Reliques*), Samuel Johnson, and the philosopher and historian David Hume. But the *Reliques* were and remained Percy's

[1] The relationship of Percy's *Reliques* to Macpherson's *Fingal* demands more space than is available here; for a discussion, see Dane and Djananova 2005: 80–2 and references there cited. The title pages and frontispieces for both books were designed by the same man, the well-known book-engraver and founding member of the Royal Academy, Samuel Wale (?1721–86). Although there are similarities – *putti*, 'signifying whatever it is putti signify' (Dane and Djananova 2005: 82), appear in both – there are some subtle distinctions, emphasised inter alia by the illustrative material. The frontispiece for *Fingal* sets the poem within classical antiquity, with a suitably robed and 'Homerically blind bard' (Dane and Djananova 2005: 80). By contrast, that for the *Reliques*, in vol. III, is distinguished by a gothic spire and a galloping horseman in the distance, and in the foreground a group of figures in quasi-medieval dress, including two knights in armour, listening appreciatively to a harpist in a cloak. Not too much perhaps should be made of the distinction between these two images (Dane and Djananova carefully qualify their argument), but the contrast seems nevertheless worth noting. Wale was well-known for his illustrations of historical themes, including *Robert Kett, under the Oak of Reformation at his Great Camp on Mousehold Heath, Norwich, receives the Earl of Warwick's Herald* (c. 1746). This oil painting, now in the Museum of Norwich at the Bridewell, is one of the most famous representations of Kett's rebellion of 1549 (see Chapter 4 below). The painting represents the rebellion as an example of chaotic misrule. A portly Kett, pictured wearing a feathered head-dress, sits on a makeshift podium surrounded by his troops and a soberly dressed adviser, while a youth, deploying a traditional Tudor insult, bares his bottom to a herald in a tabard. In an echo of the *Reliques* illustration, Norwich Cathedral looms in the background. The image of a world turned upside down is vaguely comic, in line with other sceptical eighteenth-century interpretations of the rebellion that viewed it through the lens of the seventeenth-century civil wars. Modern scholarship is clear that Kett's rebellion was a revolt of a desperate populace against oppressive elites (see e.g. Wood 2007).

[2] 'Runic' – sometimes 'runick' – was at the time a broadly cultural reference to anything Germanic rather than to a particular writing-system.

best-known work, even though he continued to publish other works into the 1770s. His literary activity only slackened off when he started to achieve significant ecclesiastical preferment, first as dean of Carlisle (1778) and finally as bishop of Dromore in Ireland (1782). These church appointments eventually distracted him from literary pursuits, and caused him to focus on his increasingly demanding pastoral duties.

The cultural impact of the *Reliques* was profound, but the collection was not received uncritically. The most trenchant near-contemporary attack on 'the right reverend editor of that admired and celebrated work' (Ritson 1783: x) came from another, younger antiquary, Joseph Ritson (1752–1803). Ritson, whose concerns with accuracy and authenticity made him a member of a much tougher school of textual criticism (to which we will return at the end of this book), summed up his view of the *Reliques* in an excoriating footnote:

> That the above work [i.e. the *Reliques*] is beautiful, elegant, and ingenious, it would be ridiculous to deny; but they who look into it to be acquainted with the state of ancient poetry, will be miserably disappointed or fatally misled. Forgery and imposition of every kind, ought to be universally execrated, and never more than when they are employed by persons high in rank or character, and those very circumstances are made use of to sanctify the deceit. (Ritson 1783: x)

Although Ritson's views, because expressed (as was his custom) so intemperately, were generally considered out of order by contemporaries, it is hard not to agree with his verdict that Percy took a strongly interventionist approach to his sources in a way that informed editors of the period – such as the great Richard Bentley, whom we will also encounter in the last chapter of this book – would undoubtedly have regarded as 'polluted with ... monstrous Faults' (Bentley 1732: sig. a.2r). And Hales and Furnivall, a century later, largely agreed with the substance of Ritson's views, while more generously acknowledging Percy's achievement as a significant Romantic precursor: 'He led the van of the army that Wordsworth afterwards commanded, and which has won us back to nature and truth' (1867–8: xx).[3]

[3] Ritson was in addition profoundly suspicious of Percy's account of how the latter found the manuscript, 'roaring away' his views on its being a fake until the end of his life (see Donatelli 1993: 114 and references there cited). For Ritson's turbulent career, which culminated in confinement to an asylum for the insane in Hoxton, see in the first instance ODNB; see also, for an insightful if brief discussion of his impact on Langland studies in particular, Warner 2014: 6–11, who identifies a characteristic *mal d'archive* that – disconcertingly – has regularly afflicted textual critics. The only contemporary willing publicly to defend Ritson seems, entirely unsurprisingly, to have been the

But it is important to recall two points. First, there is good evidence that Percy was quite aware of those other, more 'correct' trends in editorial practice. This awareness is demonstrated rather well by his personal response to the work of his friend Sir David Dalrymple, Lord Hailes, whose *Ancient Scottish Poetry*, which presented an avowedly up-to-date version of the well-known sixteenth-century Bannatyne manuscript (now Edinburgh, National Library of Scotland, MS Advocates' 1.1.6), appeared in 1770. Percy had reason to be grateful to Hailes, who had helped him in the preparation of the *Reliques* (Groom 1999: 208), and of course – given that Percy, unlike Ritson, subscribed to contemporary notions of decorum – nothing critical would be said in public; nor did Percy reproach Hailes personally concerning what he referred to, in a letter to Hailes dated 23 August 1772, as his 'valuable Collection' (Falconer 1954: 121). Hailes indeed made some definite claims about the accuracy of his work in its preface: 'The reader will find the language, versification, and spelling, in the same state as they were in 1568' (Hailes 1770: xx) (see further Chapter 6 below).

However, Percy's own copy of Hailes's *Ancient Scottish Poetry*, with annotations by Percy himself undertaken with direct reference to the manuscript sources, survives in Edinburgh's National Library of Scotland (Ry.IV.f.4), and suggests that his real views were rather different. Percy managed himself to borrow the Bannatyne manuscript for a full two years for his projected comprehensive collection, *Ancient English and Scottish Poems*. This work he never completed (Ogburn 1936), presumably because of the pressure of his ecclesiastical duties, but he did use his access to the manuscript to thorough effect for a critical analysis of Hailes's work. Percy's extensive collations, covering pretty well the entire text of Hailes's volume, demonstrate that Hailes had difficulties throughout with his understanding of Older Scots, replacing *brycht* with *bright*, *yit* with *yet* and so on (see further Falconer 1954: 161–8). It is clear from his collations that Percy had a definite view about correctness in editing. Hailes thought the same; it was just that he seems not to have been very good at what, in his introduction, he says he had set out to do.[4]

genial Walter Scott, despite Ritson's having behaved in such a personally offensive way to Scott's wife that she threatened to have him thrown out of a window.

4 See further Chapter 6, notably for Walter Scott's views on Hailes's work. Percy's notes in his copy of Hailes's edition are pretty comprehensive, and systematically laid out. On the inside front cover he notes that certain abbreviations are 'universally neglected by the Editor of this book'; he observes, as Walter Scott was later to do, Hailes's mistaken reference to 'Ballantine' as the scribe, with the marginal note on p. v reading 'Banatyne [*sic*] MS ubique'; and later on the same page he underlines 'fairly' (in 'fairly copied') and in the margin writes 'See the proofs in the follow[g] Pages'. Percy is known to have borrowed the Bannatyne manuscript between June 1773 and July 1775, having added

Secondly, Nick Groom has pointed out that, in the published form of the *Reliques*, Percy had been 'pulled in opposite directions: towards scholarly precision by his antiquarian associates, and towards polite, elegant revision (and marketability)' by other poets such as Shenstone, and by his publishers, the Dodsleys (Groom 1999: 9). Although the seriousness with which he engaged with the Percy Folio manuscript cannot be in doubt – Percy's numerous annotations of the manuscript, offering interpretative glosses and small factual notes, attest to his thorough approach even if they might nowadays be regarded as vandalism – it seems from the evidence of his behaviour in the published *Reliques* that 'polite, elegant revision' was the stronger impulse when Percy moved to publication.

To exemplify Percy's approach, we might compare the manuscript version of the rather gory ballad *Old Robin of Portingale* with the version that appears in the *Reliques*:

Text (P.1): London, British Library, MS Additional 27879 (Percy Folio), p. 90

[The emboldened **God** signifies an engrossed word in the original.]

God let neuer soe old a man
Marry soe yonge a wiffe
as did old Robin of portingale
he may rue all the dayes of his liffe
ffor the Maiors daughter of Lin god wott
he chose her to his wife
& thought to haue liued in quiettnesse
wth her all the dayes of his liffe
they had not in their wed bed laid
scarcly were both in sleepe
but vpp shee rose & forth shee goes
to Sr Gyles & fast can weepe
saies sleepe yo^{u} wake yo^{u} faire Sr Gyles

to that volume a characteristic emendation, on p. 58 of the so-called 'Draft MS' section. It has also been suggested that he added a title at the top of folio 1r in the 'Main MS' section, reading 'Ane most Godlie, mirrie and lustie rapsodie maide be sundrie learned Scots poets and written be George Bannatyne in the tyme of his youth', although the handwriting – if his – seems to me to be much more elaborate in appearance than his customary usage (but see Fox and Ringler 1980: xvi–xvii). He also consulted another major sixteenth-century Older Scots poetic miscellany, the Maitland Folio manuscript (Cambridge, Magdalene College, MS Pepys 2553), supplying from the latter numerous variant readings – often written in red ink – and sometimes complete stanzas. Percy's activity as a reader can be seen in many of the books that survive from his extensive library, much of which is now housed in the library of Queen's University Belfast; Percy's copy of *Piers Plowman*, in the Queen's collection, will be discussed in Chapter 4 below.

or be not yo^{u} wthin
but I am waking sweete he said
Lady what is yo^{ur} will
I haue vnbethought me of a wile
how my wed Lord we shall spill
24 knights she sayes
y^{t} dwells about this towne
eene 24 of my Next Coȝens
will helpe to dinge him downe

Text (P.2): Percy, *Reliques* (1765: vol. III, 48–9)

LET neuer again soe old a man
Marrye soe yonge a wife,
As did old 'sir' Robin of Portingale;
Who may rue all the dayes of his life.

For the mayors daughter of Lin, god wott,
He chose her to his wife,
And thought with her to have lived in love,
But they fell to hate and strife.

They scarce were in their wed-bed laid,
And scarce was he asleepe,
But upp she rose, and forth shee goes;
To the steward, and gan to weepe.

Sleepe you, wake you, faire sir Gyles?
Or be you not withinn?
Sleepe you, wake you, faire sir Gyles?
Arise and let me inn.

O, I am waking, sweete, he said,
Sweete ladye, what is your wille?
I have bethought me of a wyle
my wed-lord weell spille.

Twenty-four good knights, she sayes,
That dwell about this towne,
Even twenty-four of my near cozèns,
Shall helpe to ding him downe.

It is clear from this comparison that – although obviously in a less extreme form than his contemporary, Macpherson, who is generally accepted to have crossed the boundary from literary engagement with past texts to outright forgery – Percy seems to have seen his role in the *Reliques* as primarily to provide a creative response to the past rather than act as its humble conduit.

Thus, in addition to adding numerous additional poems to those he had inherited from the Folio manuscript, Percy emended freely those texts he had found there. We might compare the opening lines of Texts (P.1) and (P.2):

(P.1):

God let neuer soe old a man
Marry soe yonge a wiffe
as did old Robin of portingale
he may rue all the dayes of his liffe

(P.2):

L ET neuer again soe old a man
Marrye soe yonge a wife,
As did old 'sir' Robin of Portingale;
Who may rue all the dayes of his life.

The engrossed ***God*** in (P.1) has disappeared in (P.2), replaced by an inserted (and delayed) *again*, and Percy has rethought the structure of the last line as a relative clause, loosely linked to those preceding in his exemplar and flagged by an imposed initial *Who*.

An even more radical revision takes place later in the passage, where (P.1) reads as follows:

they had not in their wed bed laid
scarcly were both in sleepe
but vpp shee rose & forth shee goes
to Sr Gyles & fast can weepe
saies sleepe yo^{u} wake yo^{u} faire Sr Gyles
or be not yo^{u} wthin
but I am waking sweete he said
Lady what is yo^{ur} will
I haue vnbethought me of a wile
how my wed Lord we shall spill

We might compare (P.2):

They scarce were in their wed-bed laid,
And scarce was he asleepe,
But upp she rose, and forth shee goes;
To the steward, and gan to weepe.

Sleepe you, wake you, faire sir Gyles?
Or be you not withinn?
Sleepe you, wake you, faire sir Gyles?
Arise and let me inn.

O, I am waking, sweete, he said,
  Sweete ladye, what is your wille?
I have bethought me of a wyle
  How my wed-lord weell spille.

Comparison of these passages shows that Percy has made numerous revisions to tidy up perceived infelicities in his original, making the poem in his own terms more forceful and logical. Emphasising and clarifying the social transgressiveness of the narrative, he replaces in line 12 the first reference to *Sr Gyles* with *the steward*. The structure *fast can weepe* in the original, with the verb phrase preceded by the adverb *fast*, is replaced by the poetically weaker (but more conventionally ballad-like) syntax of the phrase *gan to weepe*, introducing the Middle English auxiliary *gan* that is so common in medieval verse-romances, such as those in the well-known Auchinleck manuscript (now Edinburgh, National Library of Scotland, MS Advocates' 19.2.1). Percy clearly regards the cohesive verb *saies* in line 13 as unnecessary, but then introduces, to remedy a perceived lack of continuity in the action, an invented pair of lines (15–16): a species of parallelism that he clearly likes (we might note also the repetition of *scarce* in lines 9–10). The repetition of *Sweete* in line 18 is perhaps a vague echo of a common Chaucerian usage – Thopas is described as *sweete as is the brembul flour* (Benson 1987: 213, line 746) – while *vnbethought* is replaced by the less striking *bethought*; according to the *Oxford English Dictionary* (henceforth OED), the former verb, while fairly common in Middle English, was restricted to non-standard dialects by Percy's time, as opposed to the much more commonplace latter form.[5] And *we shall spill* in the manuscript is replaced by the less euphonious *weell spille*, replacing *shall* – the auxiliary 'of obligation', as Percy would have perceived it – with volitional *[wi]ll*; the replacement emphasises the status of the wife and steward as (bad) moral actors, fully responsible for their lustful behaviour.

Not only does the anthology demonstrate how texts can be reordered in terms of contents ('substantively') to reflect changes in taste, but it also shows how even the smallest modifications in the text as presented – those features traditionally dismissed by textual editors as 'accidentals' – are vectors of meaning, indicating shifts in socio-cultural function. Percy's text, for instance, deploys the enhanced roman typeface of its day rather than the blackletter still favoured by several contemporaries for the reproduction of medieval vernacular writing; his usage therefore insists on the

[5] The OED has a useful citation, for instance, of a 'provincial' expression, roughly contemporary with Percy, recorded in William Marshall's *Rural Economy of Yorkshire* (1788): I *unbethought myself on't*.

contemporary cultural currency of his verse. It is a noticeable feature of Hales and Furnivall's much more 'professional' edition a century later that blackletter reappeared on their title page, a practice sustained well past the Victorian period, as an antiquarian claim of authenticity.[6] Moreover, throughout the *Reliques* – whether Percy's own responsibility or that of his printer – diacritics (*cozèns*) and marks of punctuation have been introduced, not only to assist readers in their appreciation of the text's structure but also to provide a set of rhetorical guidelines, with differentiated pauses, for those who might wish to perform the text aloud, as part of contemporary 'sociable reading'.

I have chosen Thomas Percy's *Reliques* as my starting-point for a number of reasons, not least because we have so much evidence for Percy's own – as well as his printer's – engagement with his exemplars. But the key reason for choosing him is that the *Reliques* exemplifies so many of the themes of this book.

What forms do medieval English and Scots texts take when they are received in later discourses? How far does such textual reworking reflect cultural and social changes? As just illustrated from Thomas Percy's *Reliques*, this book argues that every aspect of a given physical manifestation of a text is a vector of meaning. Such features of 'expressive form' (Bell 2002: 632) as spelling, script and font, and punctuation – often neglected in critical engagement with past texts – relate closely, it is argued, to dynamic, shifting socio-cultural processes, imperatives and functions as those texts are transmitted across time and space. Drawing on Gérard Genette's now well-known insight that a text 'is rarely presented in an unadorned state' (1997: 1), the book's framing argument is that such delicate textual traces are responses to dynamically shifting socio-cultural functions. All such 'written-language' features can be said, in Mark Sebba's helpful formulation, to 'function as markers of difference and belonging, and be involved in the creation of identities at different levels of social

[6] We might compare J. R. R. Tolkien's EETS diplomatic edition (1962) of *Ancrene Wisse*, where the title in archaistic blackletter is deployed prominently both on the title page and on the front cover: a relic of EETS's origins in the middle of the nineteenth century – origins in which Furnivall had of course played a key role. By contrast, Eric Dobson's sister-edition of *Ancrene Riwle* (1972), also for EETS and from exactly a decade later, presents the title of the work in a modern roman typeface: a discreet acknowledgment of socio-cultural progress during the intervening years. Blackletter typefaces are generally referred to by modern printers as 'gothic'; this term, however, has been avoided in this book since in the eighteenth century 'gothic' – or more correctly 'Gothick' or 'Gothish' – referred to fonts used for printing early Germanic languages, as was the case in Ruddiman's Glossary to his edition of Douglas's *Eneados* (see Chapter 5 below). See further Echard 2008: 25 and 59; see also Dane and Djananova 2005: 90 and references there cited.

organisation' (2009: 36); books are, after all, 'ineluctably, social products' (McKenzie 2002: 553). Examination of how such 'adornments' evolve, whether gradually or in saltatory fashion in relation to moments of greater or lesser social rupture, is the aim of this study. It also addresses an important challenge presented by John Hines and others: 'we should ... not innocently regard the historical document as merely a window through which we gain an image of past reality, but rather as part of that reality itself' (Hines 2004: 32 and references there cited).

The book contributes to the history of textual functions – and, by extension, of that discipline variously known as textual criticism or textual editing – during crucial periods of British cultural formation, e.g. Anglo-Saxon and later medieval England, the reformation and the renaissance, the civil wars, Jacobitism, the enlightenment, Romanticism: simple labels that disguise, as is well known, huge complexity. The texts examined, ranging from *Beowulf* through the *Canterbury Tales* to Gavin Douglas's translation of the *Æneid* and the sixteenth-century Bannatyne miscellany, all have significant afterlives, being chosen for their multiple recuperations and their cultural impact. Several of these recuperations have been explored individually in earlier research, but this book brings such discussions together within an overall frame that goes beyond traditional approaches to 'medievalism'. It does so using the approach known as *historical pragmatics*. It is to that approach that we will now turn.

CHAPTER I

On Historical Pragmatics

1.1 On Form and Function

Historical pragmatics is a mode of analysis that is not only descriptive but also explanatory. Hitherto, most – very valuable – work in historical pragmatics has focused on corpus-analysis, especially of grammatical or lexical features; a 'typical' piece of research from this orientation deploys quantitative analysis to map (e.g.) the linguistic expression of 'polite' discourse (see e.g. the essays in Bax and Kádár 2011). More recently, however, as flagged earlier by Andreas Jucker and Irma Taavitsainen, and developed further by such scholars as Claudia Claridge, Merja Kytö, Matti Peikola, Carla Suhr and Jukka Tyrkkö, the domain has become more capacious and qualitative in orientation, including as additional objects of enquiry features that have traditionally been seen as non-linguistic. Such features include what have been called 'textual traces' or 'graphic cues', e.g. punctuation, word division, capitalisation and script-/font-choice, and also broader codicological/bibliographical matters such as page/folio organisation, annotation and paratextual features generally. Questions of production, provenance and ownership also come into play: all areas that have also been the concern of other burgeoning subdisciplines, such as book history. Tim Machan, in an important theoretical book on textual criticism, has explicitly argued that 'the pragmatics through which a work was articulated included highly expressive features of layout and design that manuscript producers could consciously manipulate' (1994: 165). Machan's early reference to 'pragmatics' is in this context significant, something he was to develop in later work on the correlation between linguistic code-switching and the deployment of distinct scripts and coloured inks (see Machan 2011).[1]

[1] An authoritative introduction to historical pragmatics by two leading practitioners, with special reference to English, is Jucker and Taavitsainen 2013; see also papers in Kopaczyk and Jucker 2013. Important papers on what has become called *pragmaphilology* (see further below) appear in Culpeper

This change aligns with what has been called 'the material turn in philology' (Drout and Kleinman 2010: section 8, cited in Kytö and Peikola 2014: 1):

> a paradigm shift that highlights the importance of the material context of the book for historical linguistics and textual scholarship . . . philologists are now increasingly seen to include non-textual or supra-textual features of the physical book (artefact) as contextual variables in their analyses . . . In doing so, they are informed by research in codicology and palaeography to scrutinize the physical structure, handwriting, layout, decoration and provenance of manuscripts.

And, as Bo Andersson has gone on to argue, 'materiality is an essential semiotic dimension of all texts; it plays an essential role for the reader's reception of the text' (2014: 11). After all, a spoken or written text at any given point in time is a communicative event, the interface between speaking/writing and listening/reading. And unlike most forms of speaking before the period of speech-recordings, writing has communicative functions over space and time, with all the constraints – and openness to change – those functions imply.

The present book is envisaged as an attempt to bring back together approaches – linguistic, paleographical/codicological/bibliographical, socio-cultural – that have until quite recently tended to be deployed apart from each other, occupying parallel strands in scholarly engagement with texts. It is an exercise in the recuperation – or *reimagining* – of a broader notion of *philology*, linking what may be termed book history to linguistic study in ways that would perhaps have been more familiar to eighteenth- and early nineteenth-century scholars than to those of more recent vintage.

and Kytö 2010, and in work by the Turku research group led by Matti Peikola, e.g. Carroll et al. 2013, Peikola 2011, 2015, and Peikola et al. 2017; the latter collection includes not only an insightful introduction by the team (Varila et al.), but important papers by, among others, Samuli Kaislanemi, Yin Liu, Francesca Mackay, Imogen Marcus, Colette Moore, Maura Ratia and Carla Suhr, and Jukka Tyrrkö, all of which include bibliographies to date. Relevant issues are prefigured in O'Keeffe 1990, who devised the term 'graphic cues' in relation to literacy conditions with special reference to Old English texts (for which see further Chapter 2 below). The standard work on punctuation, to be discussed further below, remains Parkes 1992; see also Sherman 2013 and Smith 2017a, and references there cited. There are numerous insights – particularly from a book-history perspective – to be found in Kelly and Thompson 2005, and in Renevey and Caie 2008; in the latter collection, Caie 2008 and Peikola 2008 are especially relevant. Important large-scale case studies include Moore 2014 (on the quotation of speech in Middle English texts), Sherman 2008 (on the annotation of printed books), and Suhr 2011 (on witchcraft pamphlets). A recent collection of significant relevant papers is Kytö et al. 2017.

If this book provokes further cross-disciplinary conversations, therefore, then it will have succeeded. In addition, it is hoped that the approaches deployed in this book for the study of textual transformations from script to print (and different kinds of print) might provide valuable insights for present-day societies at a time of similarly transformational technological change. Thus computer-mediated communication, which, like speech, is evanescent even while deploying a writing-system, raises questions about what it means to be literate that echo those arising from earlier culturally driven technological innovations.[2]

1.2 Speech and Writing

Practices of literacy have changed over the centuries. Developments in the presentation of texts (the shift from scroll to codex, the rise of libraries, the evolution of cursive handwriting, the success of technological and entrepreneurial innovations such as printing, the emergence of visual cues such as title pages, page and folio numbers, and punctuation) all relate to – in Richard Hoggart's famous formulation (1957) – the 'uses of literacy'. Was writing used to record a communicative transaction which was in performative terms achieved orally, or was the writing process itself the means by which that transaction was communicated and implemented? Were texts an *aide-mémoire*, a back-up to memory? Were written texts created for reading aloud to an audience, or for private contemplation? Were texts for display, having a performative function related to their appearance, or were they more workaday? In sum, how does writing map onto speech, and vice versa? It will be clear that such questions engage with some very profound issues about the practices and functions of literacy, and how literacy relates to other ways of organising and transmitting knowledge.

We might, for instance, consider the role of memory in ancient, medieval and early modern cultures. It is clear that many people in the past were capable of what, for most modern Westerners, would seem prodigious feats of memory (see e.g. Carruthers 1990). However, even in

[2] It is an engaging – and perhaps relevant – irony that the term *scroll*, once commonly used only as a noun referring to papyrus or parchment rolls, is now also a verb referring to movement around a computer-mounted document. For an amusing comment on such technological changes, we might recall the now well-known *Medieval Helpdesk* sketch, first presented on the Norwegian TV comedy-series *Øystein og meg* (1997–2001) and now widely circulated on YouTube, e.g. www.youtube.com/watch?v=Hbp0506CcPM, last consulted on 25 May 2019. This sketch has itself developed an intriguing afterlife, inspiring 'an ongoing art, writing and exhibition project' by the writer Lara Eggleton and artist David Steans. See www.doggerland.info/artistled/project/medieval-helpdesk, last consulted on 25 May 2019.

societies that encouraged the development of – by present-day Western standards – remarkable abilities in memorization, there are ultimately limits in the range of texts that can be thus retained: textual engagement in such circumstances may be presumed to have been intensive in comparison with present-day conditions, i.e. a setting whereby individuals frequently encountered a comparatively restricted range of texts. However, the limitations of memory in relation to the emergence of more extensive reading practices – whereby individuals came to encounter an increasingly wide set of texts – probably encouraged an earlier technological breakthrough: the replacement of the scroll with the more convenient codex. Codices can house more text more conveniently than can a scroll, of course, but they have other useful characteristics. Scrolls are acceptable as *aides-mémoire*, but users cannot find their way about them easily, marking a place is not easily done and the codex is clearly a more convenient object for those persons needing to consult many books. The codex therefore is a symptom of a change in the uses of literacy.[3]

However, the shift from scroll to codex is a macro-level change, but not the end of the matter, especially as codices became larger and navigational aids became desirable. In a modern book – such as indeed the present one – paratextual features abound: a title page, a contents page, a dedication, an index, conventions of organisation on the page, including running heads, page numbers, chapter headings and subheadings, footnotes, cross-references and, in certain kinds of text, line-numbers. More local features, such as paragraphing and punctuation, are also relevant, as indeed is hierarchy of font, including the deployment of capital letters. And all of these phenomena derive from conventions that have emerged over several centuries. The purpose of this book is, as already flagged, to demonstrate that formal phenomena traditionally considered to be 'accidental' – spelling, script or font, punctuation – may be related intimately to the socio-cultural functions performed by the texts in which they appear. Malcolm Parkes has already alerted us to this feature, with special reference to the last at least:

[3] Intensive literacy still, of course, exists, and some have preferred to use the term 'varied literacy' as its antonym, in place of 'extensive literacy'; see, for instance, Brewer 1997. Indeed, the expression 'varied literacy' would seem to encapsulate not only the reading of new things but also the repeated *re-reading* of texts which characterized, for instance, renaissance literacy practice. See, for example, Sharpe 2000: 181. The issue seems to be not one of replacement of intensive by extensive literacy but of complementarity, and the boundary is not a precise one. It is important, also, to recognise that modern Western notions of the value of what is sometimes called 'brute memory' can be challenged; in Islamic culture, for instance, the ability to memorise the Qur'an has long been applauded as an important skill.

> Punctuation is not a matter of 'accidentals' but a form of hermeneutics . . . part of the pragmatics of written language, in that it exacts from readers a contribution from their own ranges of experience to assess the broader significances of various kinds of literary, linguistic and semantic structures embodied in the text. (Parkes 1999: 338)

Such a statement challenges the distinction traditionally made in textual criticism between such 'accidental' features as spelling, word division and script/font, as well as punctuation, and 'substantive' changes in grammar and lexicon.[4] All such features are forms, constrained by the socio-cultural functions for which the texts have been created. And, as texts move through time, as they are recuperated, copied, edited, and read and re-read, the changing forms in which they appear track parallel shifts – albeit in complex ways – in those socio-cultural functions.

We might take, for example, one of the questions just raised, to do with the relationship between the spoken and written modes. Should encounters with texts be a matter of listening to a performance, with writing as the script, or should it be a private matter, apprehended silently? In modern literate societies, reading silently is seen as in some sense more 'advanced' than reading aloud. Yet it is fairly clear that this state of affairs was not always the case.

Silent reading was certainly well known in antiquity. Elspeth Jajdelska, in her important *Silent Reading and the Birth of the Narrator* (2007), relates St Augustine's famous anecdote about St Ambrose (*Confessions* VI.iii), dating from the fourth century CE: 'when he was reading, his eyes would scan over the pages and his heart would scrutinize their meaning – but his voice and tongue remained silent' (Hammond 2014: 243). Augustine went on to speculate, in a somewhat puzzled fashion, as to what was going on (it is an interesting commentary on their relationship that Augustine did not ask Ambrose directly):

> Perhaps he was also avoiding having to explain to an engrossed and attentive listener anything that the author he was reading had put in terms unclear, or to give commentary on some other complex subjects. Given all the time he spent on such duties, he read fewer books than he wanted to, though in fact the aim of saving his voice, which all too easily became strained, could be a better justification for reading silently. Whatever his reason for doing so, a man like him was certainly doing it for the best. (Hammond 2014: 243)

Augustine clearly perceived one of Ambrose's goals as 'wanting' to read a large number of books; Ambrose was therefore, it may be presumed, at least

[4] For the 'accidental'–'substantive' distinction, see most famously Greg 1950/1, who considered it central to the discipline of textual criticism as traditionally defined.

in aspiration an early extensive (or varied) reader. However, Augustine is also clear that Ambrose was somewhat unusual: most readers in Augustine's day obviously read aloud, or encountered texts aurally. It seems that, since Augustine's time, there has been some sort of 'turning-point ... when the balance of emphasis moved from reading aloud to reading silently' (Jajdelska 2007: 5; for Augustine see also Stock 2001).

When this turning-point took place is a matter of considerable dispute, and it seems likely that clarity is not to be had. The Augustinian evidence can itself be qualified; in a later passage in the *Confessions* Augustine refers to his own silent reading (*in silentio*) of St Paul's *Letter to the Romans* at a moment of spiritual crisis (VIII: xii.29). Moreover, Malcolm Parkes (1997a: 9) has argued that Ambrose's behaviour was actually not unusual in antiquity: texts were read in private and indeed in silence, even if primarily as preparation for oral delivery. He goes on to cite evidence from the sixth century onwards for the virtues of the practice:

> In the *Regula sancti Benedicti* we find references to private reading, and the need to read to oneself so as not to disturb others ... Isidore [of Seville] preferred silent reading, which ensured better comprehension of the text, since (he said) the understanding of the reader is instructed more fully when the voice is silent. In this way one could read without physical effort, and by reflecting upon those things which one had read, they escaped from the memory less easily. (Parkes 1997a: 9–10 and references there cited)

The *Rule of St Benedict* indeed discusses private reading in Chapter 48, 'On the Daily Manual Labour':

> post sextam autem surgentes a mensa pausent in lecta sua cum omni silentio, aut forte qui voluerit legere sibi sic legat ut alium non inquietet. ['After the sixth hour, having left the table, let them rest on their beds in perfect silence; or if anyone may perhaps want to read, let him read to himself in such a way as not to disturb anyone else.'][5]

Chapter 48 also refers to how monks in Lent were each allotted a book to read through as part of their penitential exercises.

However, that Isidore recommended the practice suggested that it needed to be recommended and was not seen as a completely ordinary activity. And of course when the *Rule* refers to reading 'in such a way as not to disturb anyone else', the injunction may not be to silent reading as

[5] The text of the *Rule* given above is cited from the Hildemar Project, for which see http://hildemar.org/index.php?option=com_content&view=article&id=99&catid=15&Itemid=102, last consulted on 25 May 2019.

modern readers might understand it, but rather quietly vocalised reading, perhaps in an intermediate way comparable with that sometimes used in Qur'anic recitation.[6] In his comprehensive study of silence in Christian history, Diarmaid MacCulloch has commented on how 'there was a fairly regular danger of hearing the hum of a reader in a monastic library and of not being able to do anything about it' (2013: 93). That the *Rule* was concerned about disturbing others could be taken to suggest that potential disturbance was envisaged.[7]

Four points may be relevant here. First, we are, as the reference to the Benedictine Rule suggests, clearly dealing with a particular monastic milieu demanding what Parkes elsewhere referred to as 'professional literacy' (1991: 275), the literacy of scholars, as opposed to other forms which Parkes saw as emerging generally from the twelfth century onwards: 'cultivated' literacy, the literacy of recreation, and 'pragmatic' literacy, harnessed 'in the course of transacting any kind of business'. Secondly, the relationship between these different kinds of literacy is clinal, and the distinctions are therefore fuzzy: an important point that has been emphasised by more recent research into present-day literacy (see e.g. Barton 2007: 93–4 and *passim*). Thirdly, it is almost certain that when the Benedictine Rule or Isidore – or indeed Augustine, who before his conversion had been a professional teacher of rhetoric – refer to such practices they are referring to the reading of Latin; it seems likely that matters worked differently with regard to vernacular texts. Finally, it is worth noting that even in a monastic setting much – perhaps even most – reading was social, either as part of the divine office or to accompany meals. The expression 'private reading' disguises a great variety of encounters with texts, extending from solitary perusal in silence to more sociable, perhaps familial or household events, prefiguring the 'social reading' characteristic of much later periods (see e.g. Williams 2017). Learning to read – especially in the vernacular – seems for most of the period under review in this book to have been a household matter rather than derived from formal education: 'a consequence of the enduring but much less easily detectable presence of mothers teaching their children basic reading skills within

[6] See for instance Al-Qur'an 17: 110: 'And do not recite [too] loudly in your prayer or [too] quietly but seek between that an [intermediate] way' (translation at https://quran.com/17/110, last consulted on 23 June 2019).

[7] For Isidore of Seville (c. 560–636), see Henderson 2007, and for silent reading in antiquity, see Gavrilov 1997, supplemented by Burnyeat 1997. See also Saenger 1997, whose comprehensive study correlates the development of silent reading with the move away from *scriptio continua*, i.e. the writing of texts without spaces between words.

the home' (Fox 2000: 13). In sum, the evolution of reading practices from antiquity through the early modern period and beyond is not straightforward but complex, and not a simple march from one kind of reading (public, oral) to another (private, silent).[8]

As the discussion so far has suggested, it seems likely that many medieval texts existed in a world where writing was much closer to speech than is now common: 'writing is a representation of voice', as Catherine Karkov has put it (2012). Paul Saenger has referred to 'the elitist literate mentality of the ancient world' in which 'much of the labor of reading and writing [was delegated] to skilled slaves, who acted as professional readers and scribes' (1997: 11); such individuals were clearly 'professionally literate' in the Parkesian sense. Rosamund McKitterick detects after c. 1000 CE in western Europe not 'a sudden enlightenment' but rather 'an increase, extension and diversification of literate skills, the next stage in a continuous pattern from late antiquity to the early Germanic kingdoms' (1989: 1). McKitterick's important discussion emphasises the 'pragmatic literacy' of the nobility at least some time before Parkes suggests, and also their interest in epic verse. Such considerations suggest that the transition to which Jajdelska refers varied fairly widely depending on a range of socio-cultural factors, and that it is probably unwise to seek a clear pattern or sequence of evolution.

There is evidence that, in Anglo-Saxon England, something like professional literacy was found outside monasteries from the activity of the magnate Æthelweard (*occidentalium provinciarum dux*, d. 998), who was the dedicatee of some of the Anglo-Saxon homilist Ælfric's sermons and, along with Sigeric, archbishop of Canterbury, a supporter of Ælfric's whole programme. Prefaces addressing Æthelweard survive in both Latin and English in several late Anglo-Saxon manuscripts, e.g. London, British Library, MS Cotton Julius E.vii, dating from the eleventh century, the only manuscript that contains Ælfric's *Lives of Saints* as 'a unified collection' (Magennis 2005). Æthelweard himself was apparently a cultured man, the author of a rather odd work now known as *Æthelweard's Chronicle*, a Latin translation in 'hermeneutic style' of the *Anglo-Saxon*

[8] See further Salter 2015 for some very apposite comments. Abigail Williams has recently argued (2017: *passim*) that practices of communal reading – as part of the culture of sociability referred to in the Introduction – account for the huge commercial success in their own time of Scott's or Byron's verses, something frankly inexplicable to many twenty-first-century readers. Echoes of such practices remain in the custom of performing Robert Burns's *Tam O'Shanter* at Burns Suppers. Williams's discussion complements well Adam Fox's account of the early modern 'literate environment' (2000), and Michael Clanchy's classic discussion of the transition from orality to literacy during the period 1066–1307 (1993).

Chronicle, originally composed as a gift for Abbess Matilda of Essen, herself a descendant of Alfred the Great (see Campbell 1962; see also the ODNB entry for Æthelweard). However, although there is some evidence that advanced literacy was a little more widespread amongst the higher echelons of Germanic societies than Parkes allowed (see e.g. McKitterick 1989), Æthelweard's would seem to be a rather unusual case.[9]

Also relevant, although admittedly from a century earlier, are the series of descriptions of King Alfred's behaviour as described by his near-contemporary biographer, Asser. The king, Asser tells us, spent much time 'reading aloud from books in English and above all learning English poems by heart' (chapter 76; Keynes and Lapidge 1983: 91). Alfred's engagement with texts seems to have been fostered by his mother, in the

[9] It may be noted in this context that the letter to Æthelweard in Julius E.vii precedes Ælfric's *Lives of the Saints*, composed in Ælfric's mature 'rhythmical prose' and characterised by the regular (though not consistent) deployment of alliteration, rather in the manner of contemporary verse: such features are of course primarily apprehended by the ear, and there are features of the appearance of the texts in the Julius manuscript that suggest that they were conceived of as prompts for spoken delivery. Here is a short passage from the Julius manuscript, from the well-known *Life of St Edmund*, in which the humble punctus or point-symbol is deployed to mark pauses when the work was spoken, either aloud or in the 'aural imagination' of readers. For the modern reader's convenience, a translation and an edition in modern format, with conventional present-day punctuation and modernised word division, follows immediately afterwards.

Text (1.1):London, British Library, MS Cotton Julius E.vii, folio 203r

E ADMUND SE EADIGA EASTENGLA CYNINCG
ƿæs snotor ⁊ƿurðful . ⁊ƿurðode symble
mid æþelum þeaƿum þone ælmihtiʒan ʒod.
He ƿæs eadmod. ⁊ʒeþunʒen. ⁊sƿa anræde þurh
ƿunode ꝥ henolde abuʒan to bysmorfullu*m*
leahtrum . neonnaþre healfe he ne ahylde his
þeaƿas . ac ƿæs symble ʒemyndiʒ þære soþan
lare . þu eart to heafod men ʒe set . neahefe
þuðe . ac beo betƿux mannu*m* sƿasƿa anman
ofhim .

[Translation: *The blessed Edmund, king of the East Angles, was wise and honourable, and honoured continually, with noble customs, the Almighty God. He was humble and devoted, and was so directed to righteous behaviour that he did not wish to turn to shameful vices, nor did he in any way abandon his virtues, but was continually mindful of the true teaching: if you are raised up as a chieftain, do not raise yourself up, but be amongst men just like one man amongst them.*

Edition: Eadmund se eadiga, Eastengla cynincg, wæs snotor and wurðful, and wurðode symble, mid æþelum þeawum, þone ælmihtigan god. He wæs eadmod and geþungen, & swa anræde þurhwunode *þæt* he nolde abugan to bysmorfullu*m* leahtrum, ne on naþre healfe he ne ahylde his þeawas, ac wæs symble gemyndig þære soþan lare: þu eart to heafod men geset, ne ahefe þu ðe, ac beo betwux mannu*m* swa swa an man of him.]

same way that noblewomen fostered literacy in the Germanic courts on the continent of Europe (see McKitterick 1989: 223–5, Wormald 1977).

Clearly the issue is a complex one, and here some further insights are useful. First, the notion of 'speech-like' texts, originally formulated by Jonathan Culpeper and Merja Kytö (2010), reminds us that the dividing-line between the written and spoken modes is a fuzzy one, and this notion aligns with Brian Stock's argument (1983) that the simple oral–literate distinction is too clumsy to deal with cultures where engagement with written texts is frequently mediated, and not dependent on the ability to read. Work on present-day literacy suggests that this complexity persists. David Barton, for instance, has noted that, although

> listening is aural and reading visual, they get mixed around: 'I don't see what this book is saying', or . . . where I write ' . . . say in writing the things we discussed on the phone' . . . One researcher even reports the anecdote of the child who thought herself deaf because she could not hear the letters whispering to her – she could not hear what the letters said. (Barton 2007: 17)

Also useful in this context is the typology developed by Joyce Coleman, who has insightfully identified a complex framework of possibilities in relation to textual culture. Coleman distinguishes not only orality from literacy, but also *perorality* (defined as a group experience: no book, but one narrator addressing an audience), *aurality* (a narrator reading aloud from a book to an audience) and *dividuality* (a private, solitary experience, in which a single reader interprets a book for him- or herself). Within dividuality, Coleman distinguishes *voiced* from *silent* private reading (1996: 42).[10]

Building on such insights, Elspeth Jajdelska, drawing upon modern psychological as well as historical research, further breaks down the voiced–silent distinction. She argues that modern 'silent reading' is not simply grammatical interpretation: silent reading, she suggests, entails the 'silent hearing' of an 'imagined writer's words' (2007: *passim*). This insight challenges the traditional notion of silent reading as opposed to speech: silent reading may be considered to be interiorised speech.

[10] For a useful discussion placing Stock's work in context, see Briggs 2000. Coleman 1996 further subdivides orality into *recreative* ('re-creative') and *rote* memory, relating the former in particular to 'oral formulaic' performance. Aurality would require only one person who would be literate in the present-day sense, producing what Adam Fox has helpfully referred to, with reference to early modern England, as a 'literate environment' (2007: 37).

All these observations have implications for how a text is presented. Joyce Coleman's discussion is in this context particularly apposite, and relevant not only to the late medieval and courtly verse with which she was primarily concerned but also to other cultural circles, including those well before and after in date:

> The evidence ... assembled strongly supports the contention that public reading survived well past the announced date of its obsolescence. The strong influences of rising literacy and improving book-technologies, including printing, were countermanded for a considerable period by a simple, persistent preference among elite audiences for the social experience of literature. Such group-listening was synonymous neither with rowdy boorishness nor with paralyzed docility – two extremes frequently mooted by modern scholars. The data suggest, rather, that those who listened to the late medieval texts surveyed here were literate, sophisticated people who participated actively both with their attention and their response. While we can never recover the full experience of such sessions, it behooves us to recognize that they took place. (Coleman 1996: xiii–xiv)

Such an 'emergent' account would also engage with another of Jajdelska's arguments, namely that the turning-point was in the seventeenth century, on the eve of what is traditionally known as the 'reading revolution' that drove the print explosion of the eighteenth century. It might, however, be better, in the light of the discussion so far, to see the development Jajdelska flags as the moment that 'cultivated literacy' in the vernacular, in its Parkesian sense, became extended to a wider social group; the success of printing technology seems, initially at least, to have been a consequence more than a cause of demand for written material. Jajdelska links this turning-point in Anglophone culture to the appearance in the seventeenth and eighteenth centuries of diaries (spiritual, but also secular, as in the well-known case of Samuel Pepys), of newspapers and of the novel, but it is perhaps better seen – as we will see in later chapters – as a phenomenon with a much less precise start-date, gradually emerging amongst readers of English from the Anglo-Saxon period onwards.

Such developments in textual function align well with the evolution of textual forms, even with 'professional' texts. For instance, Cambridge, Corpus Christi College MS 286 is a sixth-century copy of the Vulgate Latin Gospels probably given to St Augustine of Canterbury (d. c. 604 CE) by Pope Gregory the Great (c. 540 – c. 604 CE); it is thus known as the *Gospels of St Augustine*. The text is laid out *per cola et commata*, i.e. set out in rhetorical units to assist oral delivery and aural perception. The terms *colon* (plural *cola*) and *comma* (plural *commata*) used to refer to rhetorical units rather than marks of punctuation, 'meaning something like "by clauses and pauses" ... Each unit is probably what a person would read and speak aloud in a single breath' (de Hamel 2016: 20).[11]

A text where public reading was explicitly recommended shows how this approach persisted much later into the medieval period, even (again) in the context of 'professional' reading. Oxford, Bodleian Library, MS Bodley 277 is an enormous display pandect of the Middle English Wycliffite Bible, copied between c. 1415 and 1430 and owned by a Carthusian monastery. It contains – along with a comprehensive collection of navigational aids, including little tabs of parchment attached to the edges of leaves to mark books of scripture – such cues as *in refectorio* ('in the refectory'), 'sometimes followed with the number of folios to be read' (Wakelin 2018: 90).[12] Given this function, it is no surprise to find that cola and commata are similarly distinguished in Bodley 277 with considerable care, albeit this time by means of sophisticated deployment of special marks: the *positurae*, as they were called in the medieval period.

The positurae – from which modern punctuation ultimately derives – themselves related closely to the spoken mode. This relationship is unsurprising: the term *punctuation* itself derives from 'pointing',[13] the marks made in church service-books which guided the celebrating priest when speaking or intoning a text, but which were subsequently deployed in non-liturgical texts. The positurae were used widely in the Middle Ages to mark pauses of greater or lesser length – the cola and commata respectively, already identified – within a larger syntactic unit such as the *periodus* ('period'), the structure which expressed a *sententia* ('sentence') or complete idea: 'an utterance or complete rhetorical structure which expresses a single idea or *sententia* ' (Parkes 1992: 306). The sentence was a 'thought or opinion; especially the substance or significance expressed by the words of ... a rhetorical "period"' (1992: 306). The positurae therefore are correlative with a primarily rhetorical conception of linguistic structure

[11] Christopher de Hamel has drawn a suggestive modern parallel: 'Winston Churchill typed his great speeches like this, so that they could be read at a glance and his famous oratorical pauses were graphically preordained in the layout of his script' (2016: 22). For further discussion of the *per cola et commata* format, with many illustrations, see de Hamel 2016: 20–2; for the origins of the notions, see Habinek 1985, especially chapter 1 (I owe this reference to Sabina Nedelius). Habinek shows that the terminology was confused in antiquity, but that the most common view was that the colon was a constituent of a sentence, whereas the comma – originally overlapping in meaning with the colon – came to be regarded as a subdivision of the colon, itself a rhetorical–rhythmical unit 'whose boundaries happen to coincide with the boundaries between certain grammatical units' (1985: 11).

[12] Wakelin supplies a fine illustration of the manuscript (2018: 88–9).

[13] The term 'pointing' will recur in later chapters; it was widely used in the eighteenth century, for instance. See for instance the discussion of Thomas Ruddiman's practice in Chapter 5.

that differs from that which underpins the present-day 'well-formed' sentence, which correlates written form with grammatical function; as Bruce Mitchell has stated, 'modern punctuation produces modern sentences' (2005: 154), a point to which we will return.

The positurae flag their own oral, liturgical origins through being based on *neums*, early forms of musical notation that were 'developed from rhetorical acute and grave accents, perhaps in the sixth century, to serve as mnemonic guides to the contours of a melody already known' (Clemoes 1952: 3). Since the positurae originated in the liturgy, it is therefore not at all surprising that their deployment reflects the way in which a text was to be delivered in speech. These marks corresponded with rhetorical units, distinguishing the period, the colon and the comma. Every unit became distinguished from each other by the distinct qualities of intonation or pausing when the text was delivered through speech. Such texts as the Corpus manuscript of the *Gospels of St Augustine* or the Bodley manuscript of the Wycliffite Bible therefore exist as scripts for oral delivery and aural encounter, and the manuscripts' formal features relate intimately to their socio-cultural working at the time of their creation: a working which we might call 'speech-like reading'.

However, it is clearly over-simplistic to conceive of the Corpus and Bodley manuscripts as simply *aides-mémoire* or scripts for oral delivery. Both volumes clearly have a display function as well, designed to inculcate in those encountering them a sense of religious awe, and indeed in the case of the Corpus manuscript the book's performative functions continue: Christopher de Hamel has described vividly the manuscript's current function – albeit only since 1945 – in the ceremonial enthronement of Archbishops of Canterbury (2016: 48–53). As the existence of the humble, modern 'coffee-table book' demonstrates, books have always been objects of admiration and for display, as well as secondary prompts for oral delivery.

1.3 From the New Philology to Pragmaphilology

The rise of pragmatics – the study of how language works in interactive situations – has changed the focus of linguistic enquiry to such an extent that it is possible to refer to a realignment of the discipline away – or even back – from formal towards functional approaches. Pragmatic research typically deals with how language works in particular interactional situations, i.e. in conversations, in speeches, in letters, in computer-mediated communication etc., and typically its practice overlaps with other linguistic subdisciplines, such as sociolinguistics. In all such approaches language is seen in relation to wider social practice: *homo loquens* is also *homo socialis*. As Andreas Jucker and Irma Taavitsainen, two major leaders in this realignment, have modestly put it, 'a shift seems to be taking place in linguistics towards pragmatic approaches . . . with context playing a more prominent role than before' (2013: 43).

Scholars are still, obviously, interested in the formal properties of language, and the notions of 'rules' or 'parameters' are still helpful as *descriptive* tools; but such phenomena are now much more frequently seen in relation to functional approaches, which allow – more ambitiously – for the *explanation* of linguistic behaviour in relation to social patterns and trends. As Geoffrey Leech once summarised the matter, 'formalists study language as an autonomous system, whereas functionalists study it in relation to its social function' (1983: 46). It is now widely – if not generally – accepted that there is, outside the realm of science fiction, neither an 'ideal speaker-listener' nor indeed a 'perfectly homogeneous speech-community'.[14] There may be – there almost certainly is – a distinct language faculty in the brain, but it seems likely to be part of a distributed and general cognitive network that is the outcome of complex and dynamic processes of interaction (see e.g. Kretzschmar 2009). And, as the so-called 'uniformitarian hypothesis' (Heine and Kuteva 2007 and references there cited) suggests, folk in the past may be presumed to be like the author and readers of this book, namely, human, and we can safely assume that their language, like ours, reflected social structure and social interaction (see further Bergs 2012). In sum, natural language is – and always has been – a shared social tool, continually negotiated between its users over space and time, and functional linguistics looks to those connexions in order to account for the phenomena under consideration. Given its explanatory focus, the functional turn in linguistics has brought about a resurgence of interest in the historical study of language, from both sociolinguistic and pragmatic viewpoints, drawing on the insights gained through the study of contemporary usage.

[14] The claim that linguistic theory 'is concerned primarily with an ideal speaker-listener, in a perfectly homogeneous speech-community' is of course Noam Chomsky's (1965: 3). To be fair, this statement is frequently quoted out of context. Chomsky was seeking abstraction in order to produce generalisations about language that he deemed to be of universal significance: his primary concern, in line with a tradition of enquiry that dates from at least the seventeenth century. However, the claim may be taken as the basis for one highly formal approach to the discipline, which emphasises how language works according to a set of abstract rules and/or parameters, i.e. the 'competence' of speakers; typically, such formalists intuit their own examples to illustrate their arguments rather than engage with real-world data. Indeed, for a long time this idealised approach seemed to many scholars to be the only way in which serious linguistics should be pursued.

However, there is one very significant difference between past and present: in historical research, direct access to speech is not possible, and informants are not available for interrogation. Until the end of the nineteenth century, language came down to us through the written mode only. Moreover, that written material survives not through a process of careful selection to represent distinct social groups but as the result of the vagaries of time and chance. Texts from the past are thus never simply repositories of raw data, but all have their own peculiar characteristics: every text has its own history. Diachronic language study therefore demands close attention not just to the vocabulary, grammar and phonology/writing-systems of the text but also to the 'textual setting', i.e. the manuscript or print medium – the document or vector – in which the text survives.

This combination of language study with engagement with textual setting aligns, of course, with a much older disciplinary paradigm: *philology*. This well-established term has historically had a wide range of meanings, and – as ably described by Haruko Momma (2013) – been constantly open to reinvention since it was first deployed in antiquity. The OED in its current edition offers three definitions:

1 Love of learning and literature; the branch of knowledge that deals with the historical, linguistic, interpretative, and critical aspects of literature; literary or classical scholarship. Now chiefly *U.S.*

†2 Chiefly *depreciative*. Love of talk or argument. *Obs.*

3 The branch of knowledge that deals with the structure, historical development, and relationships of languages or language families; the historical study of the phonology and morphology of languages; historical linguistics.

The third of these meanings first emerged in the eighteenth century – the earliest OED citation is from 1716 – and was sometimes referred to by contemporaries as the 'new philology' (the first definition is the 'old' version, with OED citations beginning in 1522). The proper birth of the new philology, arguably the nearest thing to a real (as opposed to a claimed) paradigm shift that has ever happened in linguistics, is traditionally dated to a single event from later in the century: Sir William Jones's *Third Anniversary Discourse to the Asiatic Society of Bengal*, delivered in 1786 (see further Momma 2013: chapter 2). Sir William's speech on that occasion included the following famous passage:

> The *Sanscrit* language, whatever may be its antiquity, is of a wonderful structure; more perfect than the *Greek*, more copious than the *Latin*, and

> more exquisitely refined than either, yet bearing to both of them a stronger affinity, both in the roots of verbs and in the forms of grammar, than could possibly have been produced by accident; so strong indeed that no philologer could examine all three, without believing them to have sprung from some common source, which perhaps no longer exists; there is a similar reason, though not quite so forcible, for supposing that both the *Gothick* and the *Celtick*, though blended with a very different idiom, had the same origin with the *Sanscrit*; and the old *Persian* might be added to the same family, if this were the place for discussing any question concerning the antiquities of Persia. (Jones 1807: 34–5)

Although its novelty has been questioned (see Smith 2012b: 1301–2 and references there cited, especially Campbell 2006), Jones's statement remains – once we look past its specialised eighteenth-century terminology (e.g. *copious*, i.e. 'elaborated', employable across a range of linguistic registers) – a concise outline of the comparative method in historical linguistics, whereby languages were compared in order to reconstruct the nature of their common ancestor. This paradigm, profoundly influential on later thinkers (Momma 2013: chapter 2), was the 'new philology'.

The new philology expressed itself more comprehensively through the hierarchical relationships posited by Jacob Grimm (1785–1863), enunciator of the eponymous Law. In order to reconstruct the archetypal language of common ancestor-languages, Grimm analysed extant *cognates*, i.e. forms that are clearly related to each other and that are, in Jones's words, 'sprung from some common source'.[15] But the new philology also expressed itself in the study of textual relationships, something hinted at by Jones's reference to 'antiquities'. This concern takes us back to the areas covered by the first OED definition: 'the branch of knowledge that deals with the historical, linguistic, interpretative, and critical aspects of literature' (if a broad conception of 'literature' is adopted, meaning written text in general).

Grimm and Jones underpin pretty well all the philological enterprises of the nineteenth and twentieth centuries, from the great Neogrammarians of the 1870s, such as the Danish scholar Karl Verner (1846–96), to what became the OED. Their work also underpinned something we will be returning to in the final chapter of this book: the rise of 'scientific' textual criticism, as practised by Karl Lachmann and others. Philological 'rigour' made subjects new to nineteenth-century universities – such as the discipline that later became 'English studies' – respectable. The philological tradition continued, and never lost the range of concerns that Jones

[15] The term *cognate* is itself a metaphor drawn from family relationships: *co+ gnātus*, 'born together'.

enunciated: a combination of pattern-seeking beside an intense empirical focus on texts.

But, by the second half of the twentieth century, philology seemed as a discipline to have run its course and was ripe for rethinking, not least as scholars began to examine some of the arguably (and sometimes unarguably) dubious nationalist agendas with which it had on occasion become aligned. Philology's prominence in linguistic enquiry had been overtaken in many circles by the rise of linguistics as a discipline distinct from textual study; generative linguistics, the dominant model in the United States particularly, was in its focus on formalism much more akin to philosophy or mathematics. And as an approach to textual study, philology seemed under-theorised in comparison with, say, postmodernism.[16]

However, as its various OED definitions suggest, philology has always been prone to rethinking, and towards the end of the twentieth century the term began to be recuperated. Perhaps most relevant for this book was the appearance of something named by its practitioners – rather confusingly – as the 'new philology'. The influential 'new philologists'[17] who contributed to Stephen Nichols's special number of the journal *Speculum* in 1990 drew on a kind of critical approach that found its most prominent expression, for medievalists at least, in the writings of Derek Pearsall and others from the late 1970s onwards (see e.g. Pearsall 1977). Inspired by current theoretical trends in the humanities, the 'new philologists' wanted a more theoretically sensitive approach to textual study which took on board postmodern, destabilising thinking, triggering what might be described as 'the crisis of the critical edition', whereby the traditional goal of philological enquiry – the reconstruction of authorial intentions – was displaced.[18] They undertook this task by reversing the telescope, as it were, setting aside the focus on archetypes and concentrating on variance – Bernard Cerquiglini famously wrote 'in praise of the variant' (1999) – and what Paul Zumthor had in 1972 called *mouvance*: the ways in which texts were re-presented through their manuscript witnesses, in an act of what Cerquiglini called *réécriture* ('rewriting'). 'Bad texts' had, to echo Kate Harris's influential formulation, 'virtues' (Harris 1983), and Allen Frantzen

16 Momma's excellent discussion of the history of philology (2013), specifically in relation to English studies but with much wider implications, has already been flagged. Another seminal work in this area remains Frantzen 1990, which interestingly engages directly with postmodernist thinking with specific reference to the history of Anglo-Saxon studies.

17 Really, it might be argued, the 'new philologists' were the '"new" new philologists', given that Grimm and Jones were (once) 'new'. See Aarsleff 1967 and references there cited.

18 See, for instance, the essays in Minnis and Brewer 1992.

shortly afterwards called for 'a historicism that attempts to understand earlier editors and readers and to establish a sympathetic perspective in which their work is valued rather than dismissed' (1990: 176). With reference to the Old English epic poem *Beowulf*, Frantzen went on to draw attention to how

> The manuscript history is an archive of the development of Anglo-Saxon studies. The oldest layer of that archive, the manuscript, already comprises several layers of data: corrections, erasures, a palimpsest, damaged and rebound pages. Surrounding this text is a long and contentious history of transcripts, translation, editions, and critical analysis or literary interpretation . . . Placed at the center of our understanding of the poem, the manuscript shows us not how *Beowulf* was created, but how we have created it, making and remaking not just its literary meaning but its language. (Frantzen 1990: 176)

New philology (as for simplicity we will now refer to it), therefore, refocused attention in literary study from attempts to retrieve authorial intention towards observable negotiations of the relationship between a text – or perhaps more correctly the manifestations of a text – and its various audiences across cultural and chronological divides. Tim William Machan's call for 'greater historical sensibility' in textual engagement made explicit the link between textual editing – or 'textual criticism', to use the older, still useful formulation – and the new philology (1994: 193): something to be pursued further in the final chapter of this book.[19]

New philological work typically engaged with manuscripts and early printed books, and (more recently) paratextual features found in both media, such as front matter and annotation. It aimed to reconstruct the shifting reception, media of reproduction and socio-cultural functions of texts rather than presumed original authorial intentions, as in traditional textual criticism. New philology in practice, however, tended not to incorporate the more explicitly linguistic approaches that had been the central focus for its nineteenth- and early twentieth-century predecessors. In recent years, however, new philology has, in some circles at least, mutated into something else, which picks up the discussion with which this chapter began: *historical pragmatics*. Historical pragmatics, which emerged during the 1990s, is the application of pragmatic approaches to the written materials surviving from the past, offering contextually

[19] For a very helpful reassessment of the issues, see Kerby-Fulton 2014; Derek Pearsall's key role in formulating this mode of research is illuminatingly discussed by John Thompson in the same volume (Thompson 2014a). Stephen Morrison 2013 offers a valuable case study of such 'rewriting'.

informed explanations for the linguistic features of the texts under analysis, ranging from lexical and grammatical choices to features of writing-systems, including not only spelling but also those traditionally considered the domain of paleography and codicology, such as punctuation, script and typeface.

The term sometimes used for language study that 'takes into consideration the contextual aspects of historical texts in which past states of the language are preserved' (Carroll et al. 2003: 2) is rather an ugly one: *pragmaphilology*. Pragmaphilology – which at the end of this book I will refer to as 'recuperated' or 'reimagined philology' – is often seen as a synchronic activity, i.e. the study of a text (or a group of texts) at a particular point in time; increasingly, however, the techniques developed are being deployed with a diachronic and comparative orientation. Pragmaphilological research is shedding new light on the emergence and development of societies undergoing shifts from orality to literacy, or from script to print, resulting in insights with profound implications for present-day societies at a time of similarly revolutionary technological change.

The principal argument of this book builds on these recent trends in research, using the methodologies and approaches evolved to trace the development of texts as they move through time, thus breaking down traditional period-boundaries and allowing different versions of texts to be used as mutual controls. Its focus is on texts in English and Scots, but it is hoped that those working in other languages and cultures will find points for connexions and comparisons. The book argues that correlations between textual form and textual function are of very considerable interest not only to scholars working within the paradigm of historical pragmatics but also, more generally, to literary scholars, would-be editors, book historians and indeed those interested in issues of cultural change more generally. It argues that what textual critics used to disparage as 'accidentals' – minutiae within the textual witnesses themselves traditionally seen as not worthy of attention – are in fact vectors of meaning, opening up our understanding of the complex interactions that took place between texts, their copyists and the readers for whom those texts were reproduced. In addition, the book argues that such study should always be aligned with the study of socio-cultural developments – notably, changing uses of literacy. Texts thus do not exist in isolation but are the product of a communal endeavour, i.e. they result from the activities of *communities of practice*, and they are interpreted by *discourse communities*. And, as we will see, in practice these communities overlap.

1.4 Communities of Practice and Discourse Communities

The notion of communities of practice has received a great deal of attention in recent research into historical pragmatics. The notion, first identified in Lave and Wenger-Trayner (1991), began in anthropological and educational studies but rapidly spread into other fields, including linguistics. Penelope Eckert and Sally McConnell-Ginet have defined the notion as follows:

> A community of practice is an aggregate of people who come together in mutual engagement in an endeavor. Ways of doing things, ways of talking, beliefs, power relations – in short practices – emerge in the course of this mutual endeavor. As a social construct, a community of practice is different from the traditional community, primarily because it is defined simultaneously by its membership and by the practice in which that membership engages. (Eckert and McConnell-Ginet 1992: 464)

Communities of practice are to be distinguished from, although overlap with, two other notions in widespread use in pragmatic studies: *social networks* and *discourse communities*. In social network research, which is widely practised in several disciplines (e.g. history, sociology and anthropology, politics and economics), links between groups and individuals may be mapped in terms of close or weak social ties. Perhaps even more relevant for the current project, however, is the notion of discourse communities, i.e. communicative networks that engage with a common world-view and express their ideologies – however conflicting – in mutually comprehensible ways. However, communities of practice differ from discourse communities in that, while the latter share a common language, they do not share a mutual endeavour.[20]

It is an argument of this book that an individual text as reproduced at any given point in time is a site of such a mutual endeavour and thus can be discussed in terms of a specific community of practice; it is also possible to see clusters of texts in the same way. Book historians have recently emphasised how, after production, texts 'enter into perpetual cycles of circulation' (Verweij 2016: 2). Thus authors, copyists (scribes, printers), editors and even readers all participate in the construction of that text's meanings in the widest sense, expressed through a set of signs, some obviously linguistic (lexicon, grammar), and others which are sometimes marginalised by

[20] On discourse communities, see most importantly Swales 1990. For communities of practice as distinct from discourse communities, see the important collection of papers edited by Joanna Kopaczyk and Andreas Jucker (2013).

linguists or even excluded from their consideration altogether: writing-systems in the widest sense, including not only spelling but also script or font, what is called mise-en-page (which might include annotation by readers), and punctuation.

Such communities of practice exist within a wider discourse community, in which the textual conventions deployed are understood both by those who use and by those who encounter them, rather like a common currency. After all, a coin or a banknote in itself means nothing other than the meaning you and I (and others) agree to assign it. Similarly, the lexicon and grammar of a language are arbitrary systems of signs that only work as communication if the speaker–writer and hearer–reader can map them onto a set of shared conceptual understandings. The word *banana* or the sentence *John ate the banana* are only meaningful signifiers if you and I have a shared understanding of what concepts *banana* or *John* or *ate* or *the* – and their ordering – signify, whether presented in spoken or written modes. In order to understand each other, speakers–hearers and writers–readers need to have a shared linguistic practice: they need to be part of the same discourse community, in which the denotations and connotations of signifiers are understood.

The signifier–signified distinction is of course well-established in the scholarly literature on semiotics, most famously in the writings of Ferdinand de Saussure (Bally and Sechehaye 1916). However, it is rarely applied to the study of 'accidental' textual phenomena such as spelling, script or font, and punctuation, probably because the study of writing-systems remains something of a poor relation in linguistic research. Nevertheless, a little thought demonstrates the usefulness of the notion for understanding how written language works, both in relation to discourse communities and communities of practice.

We might begin with spelling. Broadly speaking, written languages are either *phonographic*, where there is a mapping (however conventional) between grapheme and phoneme (or cluster of phonemes), or *logographic*, where there is a mapping between a conventional symbol and a word or morpheme. The relationship between these different systems is of course clinal, and many languages which are essentially phonographic often frequently deploy logographs, e.g. symbols such as '8' or '&' in English texts, corresponding to phonographic 'eight' and 'and' in English but 'huit' and 'et' in French. The discourse community of educated writers and readers of standard written English have mutually agreed that the signifiers 'eight' and '8' map onto a signified numerical concept (see further Smith 2008 and references there cited).

That community has of course evolved. Before standard English spelling emerged, during the transition from Middle to early modern English, there were smaller discourse communities with spelling-systems that were more locally or generically focused. Notoriously, Middle English was the 'age of written dialects', where an item like THROUGH is recorded in 500 different spellings, ranging from broadly recognisable (from a present-day perspective) *thurgh* and *thorow* through *þoro*, *þruȝ* to such exotic-seeming forms as *ȝurx*, *dorȝ* etc. From a modern perspective, such variety seems chaotic, but in medieval terms the variety of usages is comprehensible; if you and I have agreed, within our discourse community, that a form such as <ȝurx> is our spelling for the item THROUGH, then there is no difficulty, and only becomes problematic if we wish to use the spelling in communicating with other discourse communities with different practices. In Middle English conditions, there was a widespread (and prestigious) alternative to using written English to communicate over time and space: use Latin. Only towards the end of the medieval period did written English start to take over some national rather than local or restricted functions, and that change underpins the rise of more commonplace spellings and the disappearance of forms with more restricted currency. In later chapters we will be returning to the rise of spelling-systems – *scriptae* – with comparatively wide circulation, such as the 'antiquarian', archaistic Old English used in the twelfth and thirteenth centuries (see Chapter 2), the so-called 'Central Midlands Standard' frequently used in the production of copies of the Wycliffite Bible (see Chapter 3), or the usage associated with the Ellesmere manuscript of *The Canterbury Tales* (see Chapter 4). Some of these spelling-systems can be accounted for as the outcome of collective mutual endeavours, namely, the production of a particular text or set of texts, and thus are discussed in terms of communities of practice, as well as in the context of wider discourse communities.

'Central Midlands Standard' was a label first used by Michael Samuels in his seminal 'Some applications of Middle English dialectology' (1963), where he identified a series of what he called 'incipient standards'. In Samuels's typology, Central Midlands Standard, a usage which (as its name suggests) was based on that commonly found in Middle English dialects of the Central Midlands, was alternatively called by him 'Type I'; Types II, III and IV, the remaining 'incipient standards' he identified, represented varieties of English found in discrete clusters of texts whose language was localised or localisable in the London area. Type I, according to Samuels, appeared in the latter half of the fourteenth century and persisted in use until the middle of the fifteenth, while Types II though

IV represented a chronological sequence over the same period, reflecting what he interpreted as patterns of immigration into the capital.

Samuels's four 'Types' have received a lot of commentary and criticism since they were first described in 1963, some of it misconceived; the term 'incipient standard' – back in the early 1960s many notions that are now commonplace in sociolinguistic enquiry had not emerged – in particular has caused difficulties. It is important to realise that the Types represent focused – not fixed – usage within the cline 'that is the total range of [Middle English] dialectal variation' (Sandved 1981: 39); they are not in any way 'standards' comparable with present-day 'educated' written English, i.e. a usage that has undergone all the stages of standardisation usually identified – selection, elaboration, codification and acceptance (for which see, classically, Haugen 1966).

Since Samuels's discussion, further research – not least the rise of historical sociolinguistics as a distinctive and relevant discipline – has taken matters forward without, I would argue, occluding the basic typology. Type I (so-called 'Central Midlands Standard'), which Samuels associated inter alia with Wycliffite texts, is now better seen as a broad lingua franca or *scripta* adopted widely to promulgate university learning into the vernacular. The remaining usages, Types II through IV, Samuels saw as varieties characteristic of or originating in London. Type II forms are found in such manuscripts as Cambridge, Magdalene College, MS Pepys 2498 and Edinburgh, National Library of Scotland, Advocates' MS 19.2.1 (the Auchinleck manuscript), from the middle to the end of the fourteenth century; the manuscripts that Samuels chose as Type II, many of which share contents and some of which were copied by the same scribe, will be discussed further in Chapters 3 and 6 respectively. Type III forms appear in key literary manuscripts of Chaucer and Langland dating from around 1400, e.g. the well-known Ellesmere manuscript of the *Canterbury Tales* (San Marino, Huntington Library, MS EL 26 C.9), and also in some London documents. Type IV forms are commonly found in certain government documents after about 1430. Type IV, which Samuels in 1963 rather unfortunately labelled 'Chancery Standard', has been especially controversial because of attempts made to associate the usage with a supposed 'language policy'. All four Types can perhaps best be seen, if not as outputs from particular communities of practice, as the usage of identifiable discourse communities engaging with distinct genres.[21]

[21] For an extended outline of the four Types, see Smith 1996: 68–73; the sequencing of the Types is perhaps not as clear-cut as a casual reading of Samuels 1963 might suggest. It is worth noting that,

The same goes for other aspects of writing-systems. Almost all present-day English educated cursive handwriting is modelled ultimately on the clerks' script of the eighteenth and nineteenth centuries, the famous *round hand* celebrated in (e.g.) Gilbert and Sullivan's *HMS Pinafore*. A *script*, or 'ideal' usage, is and was realised in the handwriting (i.e. the *hands*) of individuals, and thus the manifestations of modern handwriting are very varied. However, all hands aim, more or less successfully in terms of communicative effectiveness, at a particular script-model.

Before the emergence of the 'round hand' script, other handwritten scripts existed. The most notable in English texts were: *italic*, used in the sixteenth and seventeenth centuries as a humanistic script; *secretary*, the common cursive script from the fifteenth through the seventeenth centuries, commonly deployed in documents; *anglicana*, the cursive book-script used in the production of literary manuscripts from the fourteenth century onwards; and *textura*, a non-cursive script used for the reproduction of high-status texts where the speed possible with cursive scripts such as anglicana or secretary was not a requirement. Type I, for instance, was commonly expressed (even in quite humble manuscripts) through non-cursive textura script, adopted presumably to flag the status of the religious works – notably the Wycliffite Bible – in which Type I forms were prototypically deployed. And, at the beginning of the fifteenth century, scribes who deployed Type III forms – many of whom, it has been claimed, worked together as part of a distinctive 'Guildhall group' (Mooney and Stubbs 2013) – prototypically also used the fairly distinctive script known as *anglicana formata* for the professional production of high-status texts (see Chapter 4); whether or not the views of Mooney and Stubbs are accepted,[22] it seems likely that such scribes

given the dynamic growth of London in the late Middle Ages, the city would have been a linguistic melting pot. See further Chapter 4 below; see also Smith 2004 and 2019, and references there cited. For some further thoughts on Type II, see also Hanna 2005. For an authoritative discussion of 'Chancery Standard', including a critique of views on its status, see Benskin 2004 and references there cited. Many insightful comments on the complexities of standardisation of spelling in the late medieval period were pursued further by Samuels in a later article of 1981. The identification of the Types with particular genres/text-types was to my knowledge first suggested in a conference paper by the late Matti Rissanen, but I owe the recuperation and repurposing of the term *scripta* – derived from the practice of French philologists – to Wendy Scase. For the term, see e.g. von Wartburg 1946, and more recently Cerquiglini 1991. It is possible that scholars – including, I should confess, myself in earlier publications – have focused overly, and arguably anachronistically, on 'standard language' during the late medieval period, and should instead see these various scriptae as distinct kinds of linguistic practice rooted in societies where vernaculars had roles rather different from their present-day functions. Arguably the only real standard language in England, in the late medieval period, was Latin.

[22] See Warner 2018 for a different view. A response in this lively controversy is forthcoming from Simon Horobin; see further Chapter 4 below, note 14.

nevertheless formed a distinct community of practice, writing for a particular set of discourse communities who would have become increasingly accustomed – and might have come to expect – to encounter such written-language features. And although it is perhaps pushing the notion of communities of practice too far to describe 'humanism' as a mutual endeavour, the humanists who in the sixteenth century adopted italic script as a marker of 'new learning' seem to be reflecting a comparable impulse. Certainly, humanists formed a distinctive discourse community (see Chapters 2, 3, 4 and 5).

The 'meaningfulness' of particular script-types may be illustrated by some copies of the Wycliffite Bible. Bodley 277 has already been discussed as a 'display' pandect, and it is therefore unsurprising that it is copied in a version of high-status textura. However, it is worth noting that textura could also appear in humbler copies of the same text. For instance, Glasgow, University Library, MS Hunter 176 (T.8.8) is an early fifteenth-century copy of the Wycliffite Bible, measuring 15.9 x 10.8 cm: a small object, with – by comparison with Bodley 277 – modest decoration. Yet it too is copied in a version of the textura script, a sign of the esteem in which the text was held. Another manuscript of the Wycliffite translation of the Pauline epistles, Edinburgh, National Library of Scotland, MS 6127, is even smaller – 12 x 8 cm – but is similarly presented in a calligraphic textura script accompanied by a complex system of rubrication, including internal glossing of words apparently deemed obscure by means of a binomial underlined in red, e.g. *we moun conforte hem þ^t ben in al pressure or ouerleijnge by þe exortacion or monestinge*. Other copies of the Wycliffite Bible, e.g. the important 'earlier version' in Oxford, Bodleian Library, MS Bodley 959 (Lindberg 1959–73), were in addition – as already flagged – copied in Type I. In all these examples, it could be argued that spelling and script were complementary vectors of social meaning.

Something comparable could be said about the emergence of distinct typefaces, such as the *roman* font first developed by the great Venetian printers in the fifteenth century as a humanist attempt to recuperate in print the appearance of high-status handwriting from antiquity. In Britain the roman font became usual for editions of Latin texts in the sixteenth century, competing with antiquarian 'Gothic' *blackletter*, in Britain sometimes referred to as *pica English* and modelled on the scribal textura, which was used for the printing of texts inherited from the medieval vernacular tradition. Roman font was later extended to 'modern' vernacular texts as opposed to 'medieval' ones (thus, for instance, roman was used in the printing of the First Folio of the works of William Shakespeare, dating from 1623). Both roman and blackletter fonts thus flagged for their readers, within the same discourse communities, that they were encountering a particular kind of text with distinctive cultural connotations (Ambrose and Harris 2011). And the community of practice known as the 'Saxonists' adopted a special script, and then font, reflecting distinctive letters used by Anglo-Saxon scribes for copying Old English, for copying and printing works which could be reinterpreted with particular evangelical or (later) nonjuring associations (see Chapter 2).

Such connotations are also a feature of yet another textual element traditionally ignored by linguists: punctuation, which may be taken to include not simply such marks as full stops/periods, commas, semicolons, brackets and so forth but also capitalisation, word division and spacing, including paragraphing. Such phenomena are often taken for granted by readers, but a little thought flags their importance. In what remains the standard work on the subject, Malcolm Parkes stated that the primary purpose of punctuation 'is to resolve structural uncertainties in a text, and to signal nuances of semantic significance which might otherwise not be conveyed at all, or would at best be much more difficult for a reader to figure out' (1992: 1).

Structural uncertainties in a text can be resolved in various ways. Present-day 'correct' English punctuation is essentially *grammatical*, based on the analysis of grammatical structure and designed to help readers. It is commonly conceived of, therefore, as a kind of parsing. We use commas to mark lists, parenthetical statements and apposed qualifiers, and to separate subordinate from main clauses. We use semicolons as an alternative to coordinating conjunctions, to link main clauses, and we use colons (rather sparingly) to introduce lists. Capital letters begin sentences (and in English particular categories of noun); gaps flag distinct words.

However, there is a parallel *rhetorical* use of punctuation that still exists. Rhetorical punctuation relates written text to spoken performance or interpretation. Throughout its history, punctuation has always had this rhetorical function, correlating with the elocutionary needs of those reading aloud. The term *punctuation* derives, as we have seen, from 'pointing', the marks used to guide a priest in oral delivery. We still retain vestiges of this usage in early teaching: a comma is inserted 'when you breathe'; and modern psychological research has demonstrated that even practised modern 'silent' readers are, in Elspeth Jajdelska's handy phrase, listening to 'imagined speakers' in their heads (see Jajdelska 2007: *passim*). In this sense, punctuation-marks are still 'graphic cues' (O'Keeffe 1990: *passim*) reflecting the spoken mode.

Shifting approaches to punctuation again relate to changes in the discourse communities – and indeed the communities of practice – in which they were deployed. In antiquity, for instance, the practice of *scriptio continua*, whereby no spaces were marked between words, emerged.[23] A slave or freedman would be responsible for the production of such an unmarked and thus neutral text, leaving readers (usually the master) – if they so wished – to annotate the resulting text with markings in accordance with their own personal preferences, resulting in the phenomenon known as the *codex distinctus* (see Parkes 1992: 262–3 for an example). *Scriptio continua* offered a text that was a prompt to memory-based performance and did not force readers who used the text into a particular interpretation: performers were prompted by *scriptio continua*, sometimes even marking manuscripts up for their own purposes, as *codices distincti*. In such a production, the resulting text would indeed be the result of a mutual endeavour, and thus within a fairly intimate community of practice; it is no coincidence that even in modern legal documents, produced by a circle of adepts for a very close-knit discourse community (i.e. by lawyers for lawyers), punctuation has traditionally remained very sparing.[24] By contrast, the complex usages associated with the elocutionist movement of the eighteenth century offer a comprehensive repertoire of punctuation, related to particular kinds of formal declamation valued by the Augustans as a reflexion of their admired classical models (see especially Chapters 4 and 5). In a manuscript world – and perhaps, as we will see,

[23] The standard discussion of spacing between words remains Saenger 1997. The traditional view is that the use of *scriptio continua* related to oral presentation – after all, in speech 'spaces' are not perceptible – but there is good evidence that the deployment of the usage in manuscripts in later antiquity was a choice made for the reasons flagged above: it offered a 'neutral' text. It is noticeable that first-century CE Latin texts, including election posters surviving at Pompeii, habitually mark word divisions by dots or interpuncts in accordance with practice inherited from the Etruscans; see Parkes 1992: 10 and references there cited, and his plate 57. However, Parkes goes on to note that 'the practice of writing with interpuncts seems to have died out by the end of the first century, and thereafter Roman scribes imitated Greek ones by copying texts in *scriptio continua*' (1992: 10). The usage could be sustained in inscriptions, as famously on the pediment of the Pantheon in Rome, rebuilt under the Antonine emperors in the second century CE (although the best-known and most visible inscription M·AGRIPPA·L·F·COS·TERTIVM·FECIT is an archaistic retention from a hundred years earlier).

[24] The traditional argument against punctuation in legal documents is that it can easily be added to change the meaning of a text, and that therefore it is the task of the skilled lawyer to phrase matters in such a way, using appropriate discourse markers, that no ambiguity can arise even if punctuation is omitted. It should be noted, however, that there is a movement current amongst legal professionals to adopt punctuation practices more in line with those used in other registers, with a view to improving transparency. See, for instance, www.lawsociety.org.uk/news/blog/5-writing-habits-every-lawyer-needs/, last consulted on 25 May 2019; see also Butt and Castle (2001: 139–40). For punctuation practices in antiquity, which were designed to distinguish both rhetorical and grammatical units, see not only Parkes 1992 but also Habinek 1985: 42–88.

even in the world of the early printed book, the dividing line between discourse community and community of practice is necessarily fuzzy.

In order to illustrate the arguments and notions flagged above – many of which were prefigured in the Introduction – most of the chapters that follow consist of a series of case studies, roughly chronological in sequence, in order to allow for references back to earlier practices to be made, but also focused on particular broad genre-groupings in order to draw parallels and contrasts. Chapter 2 traces the evolution and reception in the later medieval, early modern, enlightenment and Romantic periods of vernacular texts from Anglo-Saxon England. Chapter 3 deals with Middle English prose texts that might be regarded as more formally religious, including guides and sermons; such texts are now rather marginalised in university courses on medieval English literature, but the evidence of their circulation, both diachronically and diatopically, indicates that they were in their own time much more socially salient. Chapter 4 deals by contrast with what are now (and have almost always been) the great canonical authors – Chaucer, Langland and Gower – of the Middle English period, and traces their textual evolution as far as the nineteenth century. Chapter 5 links to those preceding texts with a close study of a series of Scottish and 'border' works: John Barbour's *Bruce* and 'Blind Hary's' *Wallace*, the latter being the first work of verse to be printed in Belfast, and the 'reinventions' of Older Scots verse by key figures in eighteenth-century Scottish culture, Allan Ramsay and Thomas Ruddiman. A final chapter, connecting with the Introduction by beginning with Bishop Percy's spiritual successor, Sir Walter Scott, places more explicitly the recuperations described within the larger context of the history of textual criticism, and suggests some further ways forward for pragmaphilological research: *reimagined philology*.

CHAPTER 2

Inventing the Anglo-Saxons

2.1 The Emergence of *Beowulf*

In the previous chapter, it was claimed that a text's formal features reflect contemporary ideologies, and that as a work is copied and recopied these formal features change to reflect shifting socio-cultural imperatives; texts are not only invented in the ancient rhetorical sense (i.e. *inventio* 'finding'), but in the modern sense as well. This claim is well demonstrated by the transmission history of a work now canonical in Anglo-Saxon studies: the Old English epic poem *Beowulf*, surviving in London, British Library, MS Cotton Vitellius A.xv (part II). In addition to *Beowulf* the codex also contains a poem on the Biblical story of *Judith*, and three prose works: *The Life of St Christopher*, *The Marvels of the East* and *The Letter of Alexander to Aristotle*. The manuscript was copied by two scribes. The first scribe, A, copied the three prose items and the first part of *Beowulf*; Scribe B completed *Beowulf* and copied *Judith*.

Text (2.1) is a transcription of the opening of the poem, keeping the lineation of folio 132r of the manuscript; in accordance with Anglo-Saxon custom, no special lineation is used to distinguish verse from prose. An asterisk in the transcription flags a presumed missing letter caused by damage; the manuscript was singed in the notorious fire at Ashburnham House in 1731 that destroyed or damaged a substantial proportion of the Cotton collection, and the edges of the leaves have as a consequence since then been liable to crumbling.[1] The text is followed by a modern edition of the same lines, and by a present-day English translation.

[1] For the Ashburnham fire which ravaged the collection of Sir Robert Cotton (1570/1–1631), see the relevant number of *The Gentleman's Magazine* (October, 1731: 451):

> A Fire broke out in the House of Mr *Bently*, adjoining to the King's School near *Westminster Abbey*, which burnt down that part of the House that contained the King's and Cottonian Libraries: almost all the printed Books were consumed and part of the Manuscripts. Amongst

Text (2.1): London, British Library, MS Cotton Vitellius A.xv (II), folio 132r

HƿÆT ƿE GARDE
na. inȝear daȝum. þeod cyninȝa
þrym ȝefrunon huða æþelinȝas elle*
fremedon. oft scyld scefinȝ sceaþe**
þreatum moneȝu*m* mæȝðum meodo setla
ofteah eȝsode eorl syððan ærest ƿearð
fea sceaft funden. he þæs frofre ȝeba*
ƿeox under ƿolcnum ƿeorð myndum þah.
oð ꝥ him æȝhƿyle þara ymb sittendra
ofer hron rade hyran scolde ȝomban
ȝyldan ꝥ ƿæs ȝod cyninȝ. ðæm eafera ƿæs
æfter cenned ȝeonȝ inȝeardum þone ȝod
sende folce tofrofre. fyren ðearfe on
ȝeat ꝥ hie ær druȝon aldor * * * ase. lanȝe
hƿile him þæs lif frea ƿuldres ƿealdend
ƿorold are for ȝeaf. beoƿulf ƿæs breme
blæd ƿide spranȝ scyldes eafera scede
landum in.

Modern edited text (after Klaeber et al. 2014: 3):

Hwæt, wē Gār-Dena   in geārdagum
þēodcyninga   þrym gefrūnon,
hū ðā æþelingas   ellen fremedon.
Oft Scyld Scēfing   sceaþena þrēatum,
monegum mǣgðum   meodosetla oftēah,
egsode eorl[as],   syððan ǣrest wearð
fēasceaft funden.   Hē þæs frōfre gebād:
wēox under wolcnum,   weorðmyndum þāh,
oð þæt him ǣghwylc   þāra ymbsittendra
ofer hronrāde   hȳran scolde,
gomban gyldan.   Þæt wæs gōd cyning.
Ðǣm eafera wæs   æfter cenned
geong in geardum,   þone God sende
folce tō frōfre;   fyrenðearfe ongeat –
þæt hīe ǣr drugon   aldor(l)ēase
lange hwīle.   Him þæs līffrēa,

> the latter, those which Dr *Bentley* had been collecting for his *Greek Testament*, for these last ten Years, valued at 2000 *l.*

'Dr Bentley' was Richard Bentley (1662–1742), one of the most significant classical scholars of his time. For Bentley, referred to already in the Introduction, see also Chapter 6 below.

wuldres wealdend   woroldāre forgeaf:
Bēo*w* wæs breme   – blǣd wīde sprang –
Scyldes eafera   Scedelandum in.

[Translation: *Listen, we have heard of the glory of the people's-kings, of the Spear-Danes, in ancient days, how the princes accomplished valour. Often Scyld Scefing deprived many tribes, crowds of enemies, of mead-seats. He terrified nobles after first of all being found destitute. He had comfort for this, he prospered beneath the clouds, he throve with glories, until each of those neighbouring peoples over the ocean had to pay tribute; that was a good king. To that one afterwards was born a young offspring in the dwellings, whom God sent as a comfort for the people. He perceived the grievous distress that they suffered formerly, lacking a lord for a long while. For that reason, the Life-Lord, Ruler of glory, granted fame to him. Beow [for MS* beoꝑulf*], offspring of Scyld, was renowned; his fame sprang wide through Scandinavia.*[2]]

Punctuation throughout the *Beowulf* manuscript – and in the handwriting of both scribes – is minimal, being limited to the simple point or punctus and to word division, although it will be noted that usage can differ from that adopted in present-day editions, e.g. *huða, for ʒeaf* for *hū ðā* 'how then', *forgeaf* 'forgave'. The two scribes also use capitals to flag the beginning of section divisions or *fitts*,[3] and fairly frequently – though not consistently, and not in Text (2.1) – of new sententiae when preceded by a punctus. However, capitals, though used to mark the opening of the poem (as in the passage cited) and new sections, are not used for personal names, thus *scyld, beoꝑulf*. O'Keeffe (1990) has noted that this simplicity in the deployment of what she helpfully calls 'visual cues' – i.e. pragmatic guidelines for the Anglo-Saxon reader – marks the Nowell Codex off from the other three surviving major Old English poetic codices, and she goes on to argue that the usage is therefore an indication that the system witnessed by the *Beowulf* manuscript is comparatively early.

[2] For a less literal translation, see Bradley 1982. For a facsimile of the complete Vitellius manuscript, see now http://ebeowulf.uky.edu, last consulted on 23 June 2019.

[3] The term *fitt* for section division became widely adopted by antiquarian writers in the eighteenth and nineteenth centuries; Byron used the term in *Childe Harold* (1810). The earliest reference to *fitt* with this sense seems to be in the Latin preface to the ninth-century Old Saxon poem *Heliand*, which describes how the author *omne opus per vitteas distinxit, quas nos lectiones vel sententias possumus appellare* 'divide the whole work into fitts [*vitteas*], which we can call "readings" or "passages"' (cited in Klaeber et al. 2014: xxxiii). The OED tentatively suggests a connexion with Old High German *fiza* 'list of cloth', modern German *fitze* 'skein of yarn'; the meaning 'canto' would therefore presumably be a metaphorical extension. See further Chapter 6, note 15 below, and references there cited, especially Hardman 1992.

Scribe A also uses, on three occasions, a rune ᛟ as a brevigraph for *ēþel* 'homeland'; we will be returning to this interesting usage and its implications towards the end of this chapter.

Analysis of the deployment of punctuation in *Beowulf* reveals that the punctus following (e.g.) after *fremedon*, *funden*, *þah* and *cyning* is used generally to mark cola and above all periods, cola being units roughly equivalent to the clause and periods expressing the complete meaning of the utterance (i.e. the sententia; see Chapter 1 above and references there cited). An exception is the prepositional phrase *inȝear daȝum* 'in ancient days' (usually appearing in editions as *in ȝear-daȝum*), which seems to be marked off especially by a preceding and a following punctus. Analysis of the rest of the poem as it survives in the manuscript reveals that such constructions elsewhere are not similarly punctuated; the two punctus-forms in this instance, therefore, seem to be special visual cues. It may be that the reason for the phrase *in ȝeardaȝum* being marked out in this way is thematically driven, given that a major theme in the poem is how the past offers an opportunity for elegiac meditation.

The provenance of the *Beowulf* manuscript is uncertain before the sixteenth century, when the antiquary Laurence Nowell (1530–c. 1570) acquired it. The first full printed edition of the poem *Beowulf* – extracted from its manuscript context – did not appear until 1815, when the Icelandic–Danish scholar Grimur Jonsson Thorkelin (1752–1829), who had visited Britain and Ireland in search of Danish antiquities in 1786–7, published what is the *editio princeps* of the work, with a facing-page Latin translation. In that same year Walter Scott issued *Guy Mannering*, the second of his *Waverley* novels; Jane Austen's *Emma* appeared (to be reviewed by Scott); and Alexander von Humboldt produced the first volume of his *Personal Narrative of Travels to the Equinoctial Regions of the New Continent*. *Beowulf*'s first edition may, therefore, have been an Anglo-Saxon epic, but it is also in some sense a Romantic poem because of when its first full printing appeared; its reception in the nineteenth century, where it became inter alia a symbol of pan-Germanic nationalism, is thus explicable. It is no surprise that a copy of the 1815 edition, with, on the end-papers, an inscribed dedication in Latin from Thorkelin to Scott – 'Vero illustri et generoso Walthero Scott Baronetto Poëtarum Principi et praesidio' – survives from the Abbotsford collection, as Edinburgh, National Library of Scotland, T.387.d.

The basis of Thorkelin's edition consisted of two transcriptions of the poem, now known as Thorkelin A and Thorkelin B; both transcriptions are now in the Royal Danish Library in Copenhagen, as MSS Ny kgl. Saml. 513 4° and Ny kgl. Saml. 512 4° respectively. Thorkelin A was transcribed in an imitation Anglo-Saxon script by a professional copyist, probably James Matthews, in 1787. Matthews – if indeed it was he – carried out his task fairly skilfully, although there are some regular confusions, e.g. a crossed thorn <ꝥ> was sometimes deployed in error rather than a plain one (thus potentially producing curiosities when expanded in accordance with modern conventions, e.g. **þæ*tah*, **þæ*tara*, **þæ*tone*): possibly out of misplaced antiquarian enthusiasm for a form that could be seen as unusually decorative. Moreover, until quite late in the copying process the copyist regularly confused thorn and wynn (thus the meaningless *þeox under þolenum* for *ƿeox under ƿolcnum* 'prospered beneath the clouds'). The second transcription (B), a hybrid edition–transcription, was Thorkelin's own, written in his eighteenth-century 'round hand', although incorporating the special letters thorn, eth and wynn.[4] Texts (2.2) and (2.3), taken from the transcripts, supply the same lines as appear in Text (2.1), namely, the opening of the poem.

Text (2.2): Thorkelin A, page 1

HǷÆt ǷEGARDE_
na inȝear daȝum þeod cyninȝa þrym ȝefrunon hu/ða
æþelinȝas ellen fremedon. oft scyld scefinȝ sceaþen þreatum
moneȝu*m* mæȝþum meodo setla of teah eȝsode eorl syððan
ærest ƿearð fea sceaft funden he þæs frofre ȝebad
þeox under þolenum þeorð myndum ꝥah
oð ꝥ him æȝhƿyle ꝥara ymb sittendra
ofer hron rade hyran scolde ȝoban
ȝyldan, ꝥ þæs ȝod cyninȝ. ðæm eafera ƿæs
æfter cenned ȝeong inȝeardum,
ꝥone ȝod send folce tofrofre, fyren ðearfe on=
ȝeat ꝥhie ærdruȝ=on aldor * * * * * ase. lanȝe
hƿile him þæs lif frea ƿuldres ealdend
ƿorold are forȝeaf. beoƿulf ƿæs breme
blæd ƿide spranȝ scyldes eafera scede
landum in.

Text (2.3): Thorkelin B, folio 129r

Hƿæt Ƿe=gar De-
na ingear dagum þeod cyninga

[4] For a discussion of the background to these two transcriptions, see most authoritatively Kiernan 1986a; for a discussion of the reliability of the transcriptions, see Kiernan 1986b.

þrym gefrunon huða æþelingas ellen
fremedon. Oft Scyld Scefing sceaþen
þreatum monegum mægþum meodo setla
of teah. egsode eorl syððan ærest ƿeard.
fea sceaft funden, he þæs frofre gebad.
Ƿeox under ƿolcnum ƿeorð myndum þah.
Oð þe him æghƿylc þara ymb sittendra
ofer hron rade hyran scolde gomban
gyldan. þæt ƿæs god cyning. Ðæm eafera wæs
æfter cenned geong in geardum þone god
sende folce tofrofre fyren ðearfe on
geat þe hie ær drugon aldor * * * tise. lange
hƿile him þæs lif frea ƿuldres ƿealdend
ƿorold are for geaf. Beoƿulf ƿæs breme
blæd ƿide sprang scyldes eafera sceðe
landum in.

After various vicissitudes, not least the alleged destruction of his notes – but not, perhaps suspiciously, the transcripts – by Lord Nelson's fleet during the bombardment of Copenhagen in 1807, Thorkelin's edition appeared in 1815, with the grandiloquent title *De Danorum Rebus Gestis Secul. III & IV. Poema Danicum Dialecto Anglosaxonica.* The edition was presented in a handsome roman font, retaining thorn for both eth and thorn in the exemplar, but replacing wynn with <w>. The edition was also distinguished by a parallel Latin translation, a title page embellished with an emblem composed of laurel leaves, a lyre and a sword, and a rather grand dedication to Johann von Bülow (1751–1828), a previous Lord Chamberlain in the Danish court and a generous patron of both arts and sciences. Text (2.4) presents the opening lines from the poem as they appear in Thorkelin's own edition.

Text (2.4): Thorkelin (1815: 3–4); line-numbering added

Hwæt wegar Dena
In gear dagum
Þeod cyninga
Þrym gefrunon
Hu þa æþelingas
Ellen fremedon.
Oft Scyld Scefing
Sceaþen þreatum
Monegum mægþum
Meodo setla ofteah
Egsode. Eorl

Syþþan ærest wearþ
Feasceaft funden
He þæs freofre gebad.
Weox under weolcnum
Weorþmyndum þeah
Oþ þæt him æghwylc
Þara ymbsittendra
Ofer hronrade
Hyran scolde
Goban gyldan
Þæt wæs god cyning.
Þæm eafera wæs
Æfter cenned
Geong in geardum
Þonne God sende
Folce to frofre
Fyren þearfe ongeat
Þæt hie ær drugon
Aldor . . . . .
Longe hwile
Him wæs lif frea
Wuldres wealdend
Worold are forgeaf.
Beowulf wæs breme
Blæd wide sprang
Scyldes eafara
Scede landum in.

Magnus Fjalldall (2008) has suggested that Thorkelin's delay in producing his edition was not actually caused by Nelson's bombardments but rather by a lack of confidence in his own editorial abilities; and it seems, unhappily, that this lack of confidence was justified. Reviews of the work can most generously be described as 'mixed'. The antiquarian Sharon Turner, author of a *History of the Anglo-Saxons* (1799–1805) that influenced Scott's *Ivanhoe*, exemplifies the general opinion. The review begins in a kindly fashion: 'As a first translation of a very difficult composition, I ascribe great merit to Dr. Thorkelin' (1799–1805: vol. III, 288), but Turner then goes on to state almost immediately that, 'on collating the Doctor's printed text with the MS., I have commonly found an inaccuracy of copying in every page'. Another reviewer, the legendary Danish polymath Nikolaj F. S. Grundtvig, was more brutally dismissive of Thorkelin's scholarship, to such an extent that a friend of Thorkelin, the Danish translator Frederik Schaldemose, was moved to respond in similar vein. Grundtvig was, wrote Schaldemose,

> a young student who has since distinguished himself right into his old age by vulgar coarseness in his many literary quarrels, [who] with his usual energetic mode of expression threw mud like a street urchin and loaded the old man with filth, without taking account of the many sacrifices he had performed in order to bring the old book to light. (Cited in Haarder and Shippey 1998: 15)

Schaldemose was fighting a losing battle, however, and the crushing verdict of John Mitchell Kemble in his edition of 1833 is now generally accepted: 'not five lines of Thorkelin's edition can be found in succession, in which some gross fault either in the transcript or the translation, does not betray the editor's utter ignorance of the Anglo-Saxon language' (cited in Fjalldall 2008: 331). Perhaps the most comprehensive condemnation of the edition was an unpublished initiative: the detailed and devastating collation of the Thorkelin edition with the original manuscript undertaken by John Josias Conybeare (Rawlinson Professor of Anglo-Saxon, Oxford University, 1808–12) and Frederic Madden, later Keeper of Manuscripts at the British Museum (see further Kiernan 1997; for Conybeare, see now Bray 2013).

The authority of Thorkelin's edition is therefore at best dubious, and it is unfortunate that the editor clearly did not understand the opening line of the poem, glossing *Hwæt wegar* by Latin *Quomodo* 'in what way' (Thorkelin conflated *we* 'we' with *gar* 'spear' in *Gar-Dena* 'spear-Danes' to produce a ghost-form *wegar*). The omission in the manuscript of capitals for proper names caused problems for Thorkelin, who was, later in his translation, to mistake inter alia the first element of the form *gifstol* 'gift-throne' for a personal name *Gif* (see Kiernan 1986b).

In part the edition's faults were probably due to Thorkelin's habit, understandable in the conditions of his time, of using the A-transcript rather than the manuscript itself as the basis for the editorial process (Kiernan 1986b), yielding for instance the reading *Goban* in half-line 21; Thorkelin's own B-transcription reads (correctly) *gomban*, but he seems to have been unconfident of his own interpretation of the mark of abbreviation placed above the letter <o>. A lack of confidence perhaps also accounts for Thorkelin's omission in his edition of the final letters in half-line 30; Matthews's *ase* is accurate, whereas Thorkelin's *tise*, in his transcript but omitted in his edition, makes no sense. Modern editors generally reconstruct the half-line as *aldorlease*. Thorkelin did not know what to do with the *ēþel*-runes, namely ᛟ, so they were simply omitted from the printed edition and no expansion to *ēþel* was offered, even though the last two were reproduced in Thorkelin A, and indeed all three runes were correctly reproduced in the B-transcription.

Thorkelin was thus an uncertain editor. However, it appears from his preface that his primary driver was not to do with scholarship per se but was rather ideological, aiming to ingratiate himself (as an Icelandic outsider) with an intended Danish aristocratic discourse community. As Haarder and Shippey suggest,

> [Thorkelin's] lengthy encomia on Hrothgar and Hygelac . . . are statements about the virtues of monarchy – obviously relevant as Europe was trying to settle down once more in the very last year of the Napoleonic wars – and about the unity of Denmark, island Danes and peninsular Jutes combined: Hrothgar's alleged granting of 'citizenship' to the Jutish plebs and senatorial status to their nobles does not come from the poem but from King Frederik VI's contemporaneous attempts to win the loyalty of Schleswig-Holstein and especially of its troublesome *Ritterschaft*. (Haarder and Schippey 1998: 12)

How Thorkelin saw his edition is also clear from the title page, where the poem is announced as not only 'DE DANORUM', but also 'POËMA DANICUM DIALECTO ANGLOSAXONICA'. He conceived of the poem, it seems, as an assertion of pan-Danish identity, and it is clear from other parts of his biography that these ambitions were grandiose. A Latin translation was itself a bold bid for a pan-European hearing: what Siân Echard has insightfully called 'a classicizing gesture that is to be understood as a salvo in the nationalist competition to claim *Beowulf* as a foundational epic, a Scandinavian *Æneid*' (2008: 114).[5]

Thorkelin's edition may be contrasted with the nearest there had been to an edition of the poem before 1815: a passage from the Nowell Codex transcribed by the distinguished paleographer and librarian Humfrey Wanley (1672–1726), in his catalogue of the Cottonian manuscripts. This catalogue was published as the second volume of George Hickes's *Linguarum Vett. Septentrionalium Thesaurus Grammatico-Criticus et Archaeologicus* (Hickes and Wanley 1705), better-known to later scholars simply as Hickes's *Thesaurus*. Hickes (1642–1715) was a leading member of

[5] That the great lexicographer John Jamieson aligned Scots with Norse has been connected to his encounter with Thorkelin during the Scottish part of the latter's research expedition (see further Rennie 2012), with resonances for imaginative twenty-first-century attempts to identify a distinctive and historically situated 'Nordic' Scottish identity. See further Chapter 5 below.

the 'Oxford Saxonists', a group of university-based scholars interested in Anglo-Saxon studies, including as well as Wanley such figures as Elizabeth and William Elstob, Christopher Rawlinson, Ralph Thoresby and Edward Thwaites. Many of these scholars came from counties in north-west England; many were associated with Queen's College, which was to become known as 'a nest of Saxonists' (Barker 2002: 220). These folk thus formed a close-knit community of practice brought together on a common project, namely, the recuperation of Anglo-Saxon culture. Hickes's *Thesaurus*, although initially printed in limited numbers, was circulated widely to the contemporary intellectual elite, including heads of Oxford and Cambridge colleges, magnates such as Prince George of Denmark (who received the first of the presentation copies, as a patron of the edition), antiquarians such as Ralph Thoresby (1658–1725) of Leeds, and prebendaries of cathedral chapters at Durham and Lichfield. Significantly, six copies were sent to Scotland, it seems for members of the nonjuring Scottish Episcopal Church (see Harris 1992: 105–6). Such figures formed the discourse community at which the *Thesaurus* was aimed.

Many of these individuals aligned their Anglo-Saxonism with a particular politico-religious affiliation. Hickes's antiquarianism was closely connected with his royalist Anglicanism, which led him at first to a bishopric but later to controversy. He clashed with the last Stewart king, the roman catholic James VII and II, but then refused to take the oath of allegiance to the protestant joint-monarchs who displaced James through the 'Glorious Revolution' of 1688 – William and Mary. He thereby became a nonjuror, being forced for a period into hiding, although he eventually returned to scholarship. Hickes recruited the young Wanley to his team, and soon recognised his exceptional qualities: 'I have learnt more from you, than ever I did from any other man' (cited in Wright 1960: 104 n).[6]

Wanley described *Beowulf* as *Tractatus nobilissimus Poeticè scriptus*, and provided a transcription of the opening and of a passage from a little later in the poem (Hickes and Wanley 1705: 218–19). These transcriptions have special value since they were undertaken before the Ashburnham fire that had damaged the Nowell Codex. Wanley's transcription shows that he would have been very capable of producing a fine edition of the poem, but

[6] For details of both Hickes and Wanley, see in the first instance their ODNB entries; a more thorough account of the group is Harris 1992. Still relevant is the interesting essay on Wanley by Kenneth Sisam (1953). See also Wright 1960, Gatch 1998, Gneuss 2001 and (for the Hickes circle) Harris 1992.

he was an ambitious and busy man with other things to do. Having completed his work on the Cotton manuscripts, he turned to the task that was to dominate the rest of his life: the development of the Harleian collection for the Harley family, that is, statesman Robert (1661–1724), prime minister and earl of Oxford, and his son Edward, whose death in 1741 seems to have been hastened by a tragic bibliomania that left him destitute. The Harley family consistently supported Anglo-Saxon studies for much of the eighteenth century; the 'Saxon Nymph' Elizabeth Elstob (1683–1756), for instance, who had been left in straitened circumstances after her brother's death, was eventually offered a position as governess in the household of Margaret Harley, duchess of Portland and granddaughter of Robert.[7]

There are significant differences in the appearance of Thorkelin's and Wanley's versions of *Beowulf*, perhaps most obviously in the former's choice of a roman font, which seems to have had a subtle ideological implication. Thorkelin's edition, it has been argued, was – through its deployment of a typeface that (as its name suggests) was originally derived by late fifteenth-century humanist printers from antique models – 'intended to suggest the world of classical epic' (Echard 2008: 53–6). Thorkelin was not the first to do so; the earlier Danish scholar Peter Suhm, for instance, made no attempt, in his 1787 edition of the Old English metrical charm *For Unfruitful Land*, to reproduce the 'Saxon' characters of the original, simply using <th> in place of thorn and eth, and <v> in place of wynn. This choice of roman font as opposed to antiquarian usages (and for that matter omitting the *ēþel*-runes) may of course have been constrained by what was available to his printer, Rangel of Copenhagen, but Thorkelin's edition has a notably 'modern' look in its adoption of thorn (for both thorn and eth) but not wynn, where Thorkelin used <w> as a roman equivalent.

By contrast, Wanley's transcriptions appear in the special 'Anglo-Saxon' quasi-facsimile typeface that was favoured by many British antiquarian editors for the presentation of Old English texts until well into the nineteenth century, and that, as we will see later in this chapter, had been developed when the Anglo-Saxon world was earlier recuperated in the sixteenth century. The usage had become widespread enough to be cited as 'Saxon Letter' in Joseph Moxon's widely circulated and authoritative

[7] For the Harleys, see again in the first instance their ODNB entries. On their collection, see most importantly Wright 1972. Edward Harley's bibliomania would seem to present a distinct variety of *mal d'archive*, to be set alongside that of Ritson cited in the Introduction.

Mechanick Exercises (1683). Although Wanley clearly recognised that the work was a poem (describing the work as *Poeticè*), he followed the Anglo-Saxon practice of having the text presented as prose:

Text (2.5): Wanley's transcription, in Hickes and Wanley (1705: 218)

Hƿæt ƿe ʒarde na. in ʒear daʒum. þeod cyninʒa þrym ʒefrumon hu ða Æþelinʒas ellen fremedon. Oft Scyld Scefinʒ sceaþena ðreatum moneʒum mæʒðum meodo setla ofteah eʒsode eorl syððan ærest ƿearð feasceaft funden. he ƿæs frofre ʒebad ƿeox under ƿolcnum ƿeorðmyndum þah. oð ꝥ him æʒhƿylc þara ymb sittendra ofer hron rade hyran scolde ʒomban ʒyldan ꝥ ƿæs ʒod Cyninʒ. ðæm eafera ƿæs æfter cenned ʒeonʒ in ʒeardum þone Ʒod sende folce to frofre. fyren ðearfe on ʒeat ꝥ hie ær druʒon aldor * * * are. lanʒe hwilc him þæs lif frea ƿuldres ƿealdend ƿorold are forʒeaf. Beowulf ƿæs breme Blæd ƿide spranʒ Scyldes eafera scede landum in.

Comparison with the manuscript original indicates the odd slip – *ð* for *þ*, *þ* for wynn, <c> for <e> in *hwilc* (for *hwile*) – and Wanley imposed his own practice of capitalisation. But in general Wanley's transcription is, as one might expect from such a skilled Anglo-Saxonist, accurate, and the odd slips are understandable, given the astonishing range of academic tasks that Wanley had set himself. As Peter Heyworth puts it in his ODNB entry for Wanley:

> There is no doubt that Wanley's career can be seen as a happy variation of Stubbs's principle that if you put the worst man in the best place you have all the good ones striving to show how much better they are, and so benefiting the world. He had hopes, more or less well founded, of becoming, at different times, Bodley's librarian, a fellow of Worcester College, Oxford, keeper of the Cotton Library, commissioner of Hackney coaches, and historiographer royal. He also had thoughts, not nearly so well founded – though he prosecuted his candidacy no less vigorously for that – of becoming library-keeper to the lord chancellor, and of succeeding Richard Bentley as keeper of the royal libraries, William Petyt as keeper of the records in the Tower, and John Chamberlayne in his post at the state paper office. In all these he failed, and he was obliged to squander his energies on developing the talents that made him the greatest Anglo-Saxonist of his generation, and one of the greatest palaeographers and librarians of his age.

The special *Pica Saxon* used by Wanley had been developed for the seventeenth-century Germanic philologist Franciscus Junius the younger (1589–1677), who bequeathed his books and other materials, including these fonts, to Oxford University, and who had been introduced to Hickes in the late 1660s (see Bremmer 1998, Barker 2002: 216; the modern Junius and Junicode computer fonts refer to Junius). This typeface and its predecessors were vectors of meaning for the contemporary discourse community that encountered them, becoming associated with the construction of 'Anglo-Saxonism' as a distinctive assertion of the specifically English identity that seems to have emerged in the sixteenth, seventeenth and eighteenth centuries (see, for instance, the essays in Frantzen and Niles 1997). Thus the editions produced by such individuals as Christopher Rawlinson, George Hickes, Thomas Hearne and Joseph Strutt were all printed in Junius's font.[8]

But Thorkelin's edition does not express its ideology solely through the paratexts of his title page, preface and Latin parallel text, or even by the edition's typeface. Other presentational choices made by Thorkelin point forward to approaches to textual criticism and editing that were to become dominant, and which Wanley did not adopt. For instance – unlike Wanley in his catalogue – Thorkelin lineated *Beowulf* as verse, and thus flagged the half-line unit as the basic measure for the text. Thorkelin was not the first to adopt this practice: half-lines had first been distinguished through lineation by Christopher Rawlinson (1677–1733), another 'Oxford Saxonist', in his youthful edition of the Old English *Metres of Boethius* (1698). As Danielle Cunliffe Plumer has pointed out (2000: 263), Rawlinson was apparently prompted to adopt this lineation by his using as his base-text Oxford, Bodleian Library, MS Junius 12: a transcription by Franciscus Junius himself of the sole surviving Old English copy of the poem – London, British Library, MS Cotton Otho A.vi.

Junius had himself been the first scholar to notice that *The Metres of Boethius* was a poem. He was led to this conclusion through his study of a tenth-century manuscript of Old English poetry that is now Junius 12's neighbour on the shelf, Oxford, Bodleian Library, MS Junius 11; Junius had acquired the Anglo-Saxon manuscript from Archbishop James Ussher. Junius 11 is sometimes known as the 'Caedmon manuscript' because of the coincidence of its *Genesis*-poem with the creation account in *Caedmon's Hymn*, as cited in Bede's *Ecclesiastical History*. It is unique among the four great codices of Anglo-Saxon poetry in helpfully deploying a punctus to flag half-lines (see Plumer 2000: 256–7, and O'Keeffe 1990: 182–6); Junius transferred the knowledge he acquired through his encounter with this manuscript to his editing of the Boethius translation, imposing

[8] An anonymous pamphlet illustrating typefaces was published by Oxford University ('Printed at the Theater') in 1693: *A Specimen of the Several Sorts of Letter, Given to the University by Dr. John Fell, Late Lord Bishop of Oxford. To which is Added The Letter Given by Mr F. Junius* (anon. 1693).

'Caedmon manuscript'-style pointing onto his transcription of the Otho *Metres*.

Hickes attempted something similar in volume I of his *Thesaurus*, following Rawlinson in excerpting *The Metres of Boethius* and adding selections from other Old English poems, i.e. *Judith*, *Genesis* and *Exodus*; Hickes also included editions of the fragmentary *Finnsburh*, the poem in praise of Durham that seems to have been composed during the transition period between Old and Middle English, and the poems *Brunanburh* and *The Death of Edgar* that were recorded in some copies of the *Anglo-Saxon Chronicle*. All these works were lineated on the half-line, although Hickes remained uncertain about the principles of Old English metre, and as a result the lineation is occasionally faulty by modern standards (Plumer 2000: 265–8). Wanley himself produced a lineated edition of the Northumbrian version of *Caedmon's Hymn*, a practice also followed by the antiquarian and engraver Joseph Strutt in the edition of the *Hymn* printed in his *The Chronicle of England* (1779: 282). Similarly, Anthony Willich in 1798 published in London a translation of Johann Christoph Adelung's *Three Philological Essays* and included beside it texts of *Caedmon's Hymn* (1798: viii) and *Durham* (1798: xxii–xxiii), lineated in half-lines.

However, unlineated versions of Old English verse remained common throughout the eighteenth century, reflecting in print Anglo-Saxon practice in the presentation of vernacular poetry and, perhaps, not recognising that the works were in verse. Thus Thomas Hearne's (1678–1735)[9] edition of *The Battle of Maldon* appeared in unlineated form (1726: vol. II,

[9] Thomas Hearne represents a distinct line in British eighteenth-century Anglo-Saxon studies. He disliked Wanley, clearly envying the patronage he had received, notably from Arthur Charlett, master of University College Oxford, one of Hickes's most important early correspondents, although their friendship was damaged in the fraught political conditions of the period (e.g. Harris 1992: 69–70). Hearne referred to Wanley, cattily, as 'the Master's pimp', though possibly the attack was aimed at Charlett, who had attempted to suppress one of Hearne's publications, and whom Hearne clearly despised as a man of 'sometimes dubious sincerity' (Harris 1992: 454). Hearne was, as this anecdote suggests, an abrasive individual who developed Jacobite sympathies that seriously impeded his career as a librarian. The deputy keeper of the Cottonian library, David Casley (1681/2–1754), who transcribed the copy of *Maldon* that Hearne used for his edition, seems not to have wanted his association with Hearne – like Hickes, 'a dangerous Oxford non-juror' (Rogers 1985: 149) – to have been widely known. (This transcript is now ascribed to Casley rather than – as it was once – to his predecessor, John Elphinston; for the ascription to Casley, see Rogers 1985, who also – 1985: 150 – provides a reproduction of part of the transcription.) These tensions culminated in one of Hearne's rivals having the locks changed so he could no longer enter the Bodleian. For details and sources for this outline, see the ODNB entries for Wanley and Hearne. We will be meeting Hearne again in Chapter 5, in connexion with the Jacobite circle around Thomas Ruddiman.

570–7),[10] and as late as 1787 Peter Suhm's edition of the Old English metrical charm *For Unfruitful Land*, contained in his *Symbolae ad Literaturam Teutonicam Antiqviorem*, appeared unlineated.[11] It is possible that neither editor recognised that their texts were in verse.

Thorkelin's was by far the most ambitious lineated text to date. Moreover, Thorkelin sided with Wanley and (it seems) Hearne, as opposed to Rawlinson, Hickes and later Willich (following Adelung), in the deployment of punctuation. Junius's pointing had, as just flagged, driven later scholars' understanding of Old English metre. Hickes, in volume I of his *Thesaurus*, followed Junius's and Rawlinson's practice of placing a punctus after most half-lines. In Thorkelin's edition, however, a simple punctus is generally (although not always) deployed in the same locations as in the manuscript, thus attempting to align pointing with the periodic structure of the original. Sometimes nonsenses result, such as with the placing of a punctus (not sanctioned by the manuscript) to separate the verb *Egsode* from its object, *Eorl*. However, in the matter of capitalisation, Thorkelin followed Hickes and Willich – and not Wanley and Hearne – in starting each half-line with a capital, somewhat in the manner of contemporary verse, and also in starting proper names with capitals.

Thorkelin's edition represented, therefore, a step-change in a number of ways. It was by far the longest Old English text yet to be edited, and in presentational terms it followed the best current editorial practice in lineation, in punctuation/capitalisation, and in font-choice. In these two features, however driven he may have been by the constraints of his printer and perhaps tormented by worries about his own uncertain scholarship, Thorkelin was publishing something quite new in its ambition.

Comparison of Wanley's partial edition with Thorkelin's, however, throws the faults of the latter into cruel relief. And Thorkelin's failings are even more apparent when compared with the edition produced by John Mitchell Kemble (1807–57), published less than twenty years later.

10 Hearne's edition remained the sole source of the poem for many years after the original, MS Cotton Otho A.xii, was destroyed in the Ashburnham fire of 1731. However, a transcript, now Oxford, Bodleian Library, MS Rawlinson B.203 (pp. 7–12), was identified by N. R. Ker in 1935. Hearne's edition used the Junius 'counterfeit' typeface. Casley's transcription offered an odd compromise between insular script and right-leaning contemporary handwriting.

11 Suhm had previously collaborated with Thorkelin on an edition and Latin translation of the Old Norse *Eyrbyggja saga* (which Sir Walter Scott owned, and used for his own English translation of 1814; see D'Arcy and Wolf 1987). Interestingly, the Suhm/Thorkelin edition of *Eyrbyggja saga* presents the skaldic verse contained within the prose in verse-form. However, this usage was probably based on the editors' source: the late seventeenth-century paper manuscript, now Copenhagen, MS Ny kgl. Saml. AM 448 4°, copied by the Icelandic scribe Asgeir Jonsson. See http://skaldic.abdn.ac.uk/db.php?id=2913&if=default&table=images, last consulted on 23 June 2019.

Kemble's edition, as we have seen from his comments, was a direct response to the perceived flaws of Thorkelin's. Kemble was a man of remarkable energy, a leading figure in the newly formed Cambridge Apostles and a radical in politics who had (for instance) in 1830 joined an ill-fated expedition to Spain to assist in the deposition of Ferdinand VII: a prefiguration of the International Brigades of the Spanish Civil War a century later.[12] Unsurprisingly, therefore, Kemble's edition of *Beowulf* represents a similarly radical departure from eighteenth-century practice, by an extremely accomplished philologist; the dedication of the work to 'James [sic] Grimm' alone is indicative of Kemble's immersion in up-to-date Germanic linguistic scholarship. The opening lines of Kemble's *Beowulf* appear as follows:

Text (2.6): Kemble (1833: 1)

Hwæt! We Gár-Dena
in gear-dagum,
þéod-cyninga
þrym ge-frunon;
hú ða æþelingas
ellen fremedon.
Oft Scyld Scéfing
sceaþen[a] þreátum
monegū mægþum,
meodo-setla ofteáh
egsode eorl
syððan ǽrest wearð
feá-sceaft funden:
he þæs frófre ge-bá[d];
weox under wolcnum,
weorð-myndum þáh,
oð ꝥ him ǽg-hwylc
þara ymb-sittendra
ofer hron-ráde
hýran scolde,
gomban gyldan:
ꝥ wæs gód cyning.

[12] The Spanish expedition seems to have been especially attractive to budding philologists. One of Kemble's companions was Richard Chevenix Trench (1807–86), later the very respectable – if at times controversial – dean of Westminster and archbishop of Dublin, but probably now better-known for his paper 'On Some Deficiencies in our English Dictionaries', read to the Philological Society in 1857 and generally considered to be the trigger-event for what was to become the OED.

Kemble's ODNB entry describes his edition of *Beowulf* as 'somewhat premature' – he was still in his mid 20s – but such a verdict is rather unfair, for a comparison with Thorkelin's version shows that Kemble had achieved a remarkable advance in scholarship. Lineation remains in half-lines, in accordance with Thorkelin's practice rather than (as in modern editions) in paired half-lines, but Kemble's transcription is much more accurate than that of his Danish predecessor, and he clearly understands thoroughly the grammatical structure of the poem. He thus marks compound words (as he conceives them) with hyphens, e.g. *meodo-setla* or *ge-frunon*, and deploys punctuation that – in line with much more recent editions – juggles rhetorical and grammatical structures, with e.g. a 'rhetorical' semicolon after the clause ending *ge-frunon* and a full stop after the apposed clause ending *fremedon*. Colon-marks are used cleverly to mark upcoming summative statements, such as *ꝥ wæs gód cyning*. Capital letters are adopted for the beginning of sententiae and for proper names. Conjectural emendation is adopted, as is commonly the case in present-day editions of the poem, for *sceaþen[a]*, with the genitive plural inflexion in *–a* added, and for *ge-bá[d]*, where the final letter in the line has crumbled away in the manuscript. Kemble uses an acute accent – not always located in line with present-day scholarship, but generally impressively accurate nevertheless – to flag reconstructed long vowels. A roman typeface is used throughout, with roman forms of ash, thorn and eth deployed in line with the appearance of the letters in the manuscript (contrasting with Thorkelin's replacement of eth with thorn throughout); and, again in line with present-day practice, to avoid easy confusion with <p>, the letter wynn <ƿ> is not reproduced but is replaced by <w>. Kemble also – again in line with present-day practice – replaces insular <ʒ> with Caroline <g>. Abbreviated forms, however, such as 'crossed thorn' <ꝥ> (for *þæt*) and the macron to indicate a nasal, e.g. *monegū* for *monegum*, are left unexpanded.[13]

This short survey of the various versions of *Beowulf* from Wanley to Kemble demonstrates rather well – in line with the general theme of this book – the changing functional, pragmatic imperatives under which each editor laboured, and how these imperatives manifested themselves in the formal features of each text. Wanley's mini-edition was obviously that of a cataloguer, and thus there was no incentive to produce a more comprehensive edition; however, the use of *Pica Saxon* was an assertion of

[13] The disappearance of *–d* in *gebad* might of course have taken place, because of the fragile state of the folio edges, since Thorkelin had encountered the manuscript; the appearance of *–d* without annotation in both Thorkelin A and B transcripts suggests that it was still present when these transcriptions were made.

Wanley's credentials as an antiquarian, communicating, like others in his community of practice, with the (nonjuring) antiquarians who formed his discourse community. For all its faults, Thorkelin's edition was designed to open up the work for a distinct Romantic-nationalist discourse community, comparable with contemporary audiences for Walter Scott's poetry and novels. Finally, Kemble's edition prefigures what might be called the 'academicisation' of English studies in general, the discourse community within which Old English texts now generally exist (cf. some apposite remarks in Matthews 1999: 186, and 187–97). In sum, the editorial practices and related formal features of these various printed versions of the poem may be related to the emergence of distinct discourse communities, and are pragmatic indices of how each of these texts functioned in the socio-cultural circumstances of their times.

2.2 *A testimonie of antiquitie* (1566) and Its Ancestors

Franciscus Junius and the Oxford Saxonists were not of course the first to recuperate Old English texts; the earliest 'modern' attempt at a comparable endeavour dated from the previous century. In late 1566, the London printer John Day (1521/2–84) published an edition of a prose homily by the Anglo-Saxon monastic writer Ælfric of Eynsham (c. 950–c. 1010): *A testimonie of antiquitie, shewing the auncient faith in the Church of England touching the sacrament of the body and bloude of the Lord here publikely preached, and also receaued in the Saxons tyme, aboue 600. yeares agoe.*

Day was a committed evangelical who had suffered persecution in the days of Queen Mary Tudor. Since the accession of Elizabeth I in 1558, however, he had established a reputation as the leading printer of his time, patronised by magnates such as the queen's favourite, Robert Dudley, later earl of Leicester. He produced a series of widely circulated texts, including the *English Metrical Psalter* of Thomas Sternhold and John Hopkins, while a career highlight was John Foxe's *Acts and Monuments*, better-known as the *Book of Martyrs*, with editions appearing in 1563, 1570 and 1576. The first edition of the *Acts and Monuments* was an astonishing virtuoso achievement for the period, consisting of some 1,800 pages presented in a mixture of typefaces and complex paratextual devices, and including some dramatic woodcuts.[14] Such works manifest the complex links

[14] Perhaps the best-known examples of Day's woodcuts are those depicting the martyrdom of Thomas Cranmer. For a convenient image and discussion, see MacCulloch 1996: 602–3. For an assessment of the volume in context, see Collinson et al. 2002: 36–7.

between print, politics and religion – the latter two fields not clearly distinguished – that characterise the early modern period (Barnard 2002: 2). They were aimed at a burgeoning community of readers for whom engagement with religious controversy was clearly worth very considerable investment: a copy of the *Book of Martyrs* was obviously a major purchase (see Collinson et al. 2002: 65–6, Raven 2002).

Day was thus a highly skilled entrepreneur, 'one of the London booktrade's most innovative and adept members' (ODNB), and the obvious choice to produce any high-profile work, such as *A testimonie*, a small (10 x 15 cm) but neatly printed octavo, seems to have been. The text was prepared for publication by John Joscelyn (1529–1603), Latin secretary to Matthew Parker, archbishop of Canterbury; it formed part of a programme of activity developed by Parker and his bishops in support of the 'Elizabethan settlement', which was to be justified by appeal to historical, and specifically English, precedents. One of these precedents was supplied by *A testimonie*, which included the first-ever printed rendering of any Anglo-Saxon work, accompanied by a facing-page translation: an edition of an Old English Easter homily *In die Sancto pasce*, one of Ælfric's *Catholic Homilies* originally composed at the end of the tenth century. The edition drew upon a manuscript – Cambridge, Corpus Christi College, MS 198 – that was collected in the frenzy of ideological antiquarianism that resulted in what is now the college's Parker Library, arguably the finest single collection of its kind in the world. Joscelyn, no doubt overseen by Parker, seems to have written the introduction to the work, which makes explicit the reason for its publication:

> Great contention hath nowe been of longe tyme about the moste comfortable sacrament of the body & bloud of Christ our Sauiour: in the inquisition and determinatio*n* wherof many be charged and condemned of heresye, and reproued as bringers vp of new doctrine ... But that though mayest knowe (good Christian reader) how this is aduouched more boldly then truly, in especiall of some certayne men which be more ready to maintaine their old iudgement, the*n* of humilitie to submitte them selues vnto a truth: here is set forth vnto thee a testimonye of verye auncient tyme, wherin is plainly shewed what was the iudgment of the learned men in this matter, in the dayes of the Saxons before the conquest. (1566: sig. A.ii r–v)

A testimonie was, according to the Preface, concerned with a crucial difference between traditional and reformed religion, the belief in the 'real presence' in the eucharist (i.e. transubstantiation) which the newly formed Church of England considered 'repugnant to the plain words of Scripture', to cite article XXVIII of the Church's Thirty-Nine Articles; these articles were being formulated by Parker and his team at the date of *A testimonie*'s publication, and were to be finalised in 1571. Denial of transubstantiation had been the last point made by Parker's predecessor, Thomas Cranmer, in the final, devastating sermon he delivered before his martyrdom in 1554 (MacCulloch 1996: 603).[15]

Ælfric said nothing about transubstantiation, presumably because he saw nothing to argue about. The issue was not really to become controversial until later in the Middle Ages; the doctrine of transubstantiation was actually not fully articulated until the Lateran Council of 1215, and even then controversy and debate continued (see Macy 1994). However, Parker and Joscelyn conceived it as their task, as the Preface goes on to say, to assert that Ælfric shared the protestant view, that 'the bodily presence' was 'denied', and that any implication to the contrary in the text was the result of 'the farcing afterward of these epistles by byshops' (1566: sig. B.viii r–v). The publication was thus part of a pamphlet war addressed to a discourse community engaged in religious controversy, possibly – as suggested by the early modern title – as a response to the catholic exile Robert Poyntz's *Testimonies for the Real Presence of Christes Body and Blood in the Blessed Sacrament*, which was printed in Louvain earlier in the same year (Kelemen 2006: 374, *pace* Bromwich 1962; see also Butler 2014).

A testimonie continued to be printed during the seventeenth century. A 1623 text (described as 'a second Edition'), printed in London by John Haviland for Henrie Seile 'at the signe of the Tygers head', was included in William L'Isle's edition of Old English 'treatises on the Old and New Testaments'. These 'treatises' were ascribed on the title page to 'Ælfricus Abbas, thought to be the same that was afterward Archbishop of CANTERBVRIE'. They were actually an edition of the Old English versions of the Lord's Prayer, Creed and ten commandments, with an interlinear translation, accompanied by Ælfric's letter to Sigeweard. This last was derived, according to the title page of the edition, from 'The Originall remaining still to be seene in Sr ROBERT COTTONS Librarie, at the end of his lesser Copie of the SAXON PENTATEVCH'. Appended, but not recorded on the title page, are 'the words of ELFRIKE Abbot of *S. Albons*, and also of *Malmesbury*, taken out of his Epistle written to WVLFINE Bishop of

[15] On the ideological underpinning of Parker's collection, see, for instance, Murphy 1969. An interesting approach to *A testimonie* from a discourse perspective, relating the work to the Anglican textual community for which it was devised, is Mele-Marrero 2012. For Joscelyn's wider activities as a lexicographer of Old English, see Graham 2000; other early lexicographers are investigated, in the same collection, in important papers by Kathryn Lowe (on William Somner) and Kees Dekker (on Franciscus Junius).

Scyrburne', found in 'a Canon Booke of the Church of EXETER' (sig. S.1r). The next London edition, which appeared in 1638 ('Printed by E. G. for Francis Eglesfield, and are to be sold at the signe of the Marigold in S Pauls Church-yard'), was re-set as *A Testimony of Antiquity*, with additional expository marginal notes.[16]

The translation of *A testimonie*, in a roman font, was repurposed for a Scottish presbyterian readership in Aberdeen in 1624, incorporated into a collection of other sermons on the eucharist:

> *THREE Rare Monuments of Antiquitie, Or, Bertram, Priest, A French-man, Of the Bodie and Blood of Christ, (written 800 years agoe) with the late Romish purging thereof: Ælfricvs, an English-man, Arch-bishop of Canterburie, His Sermon on the Sacrament, (preached 627 years agoe) And Mavrvs, Abbot, a Scots-man, His discourse of the same (820 years agoe:) All stronglie convincing that grosse Errour of Transvbstantiation. Translated and compacted By M. VVilliam Guild, Minister at King-Edward. Printed at Aberdene, by Edward Raban, For David Melvill, 1624.*[17]

As flagged in his ODNB entry, William Guild was a leading Church of Scotland minister who belonged to the kirk's 'moderate' party, willing to contemplate the retention of bishops; indeed, in his preface he goes out of his way to commend 'that great & glorious Martyr, Bishop *Hooper*, at his going to the fyre' (1624: 18). However, as the title flags, Guild had no time for the 'grosse Errour' of transubstantiation, clearly deemed 'Romish', and *A testimonie* was one text he could deploy, along with two other works: translations of texts by the Frankish monk Ratramnus of Corbie ('Bertram', d. c. 870; see Otten 2000) and by Hrabanus Maurus (c. 780–856), another Frank and author of the famous hymn *Veni Creator*

16 L'Isle's 1623 text of *A testimonie*, with marginal notes, appears on sig. O.2v–T.1r of the edition with the title 'A SERMON on the Paschall Lamb ...... WRITTEN IN THE old Saxon tongue before the Conquest, and appointed in the reigne of the SAXONS to be spoken vnto the people at EASTER before they should receiue the COMMUNION'. The book was dedicated to Charles, Prince of Wales, and the dedicatory copy in its original red velvet binding survives as London, British Library, C.65.l.1. The copy in Edinburgh's National Library of Scotland (DNS/A.5) also includes Franciscus Junius's edition (1655) of the Old English poem *Genesis*, there ascribed to Caedmon ('CÆDMONIS Paraphrasis poetica, Genesios ac præcipuarum sacræ paginæ historiarum', sig. A.1r). Junius's *Genesis* is unglossed, though accompanied by a short Latin index; it is followed by a penitential whose exemplar was London, British Library, MS Cotton Julius A.ii. This latter material is not recorded in the NLS catalogue entry for the volume. For a history of the *Letter to Sigeweard*, see Swain 2011.

17 Edward Raban, Guild's printer and Aberdeen's first, had a track record of religious publication for godly audiences. His later publications included such titles as *The Psalms of David, in prose and metre: with the whole Forme of discipline, and prayers, according to the Church of Scotland* (1633), an edition of the kirk's *Book of Common Order* originally developed by John Knox; David Dickson's *A short explanation, of the epistle of Paul to the Hebrewes* (1635); and *Canons and constitutions ecclesiasticall gathered and put in forme, for the Government of the Church of Scotland* (1636).

Spiritus, who eventually became archbishop of Mainz. Ratramnus had famously influenced Thomas Cranmer (see MacCulloch 1996: 181 and *passim*), while Hrabanus – patriotically claimed by Guild as 'a Scotsman', but who as far as is known never even visited Scotland – was one of the most prominent theologians and poets of the Carolingian court (see e.g. Haarländer 2006). The translation of the sermon, with Ælfric yet again erroneously promoted to archbishop, appears on pp. 117–41 of Guild's collection. Guild's miscellany shows a continuing interest and engagement with the Anglo-Saxon past, but always in the service of contemporary ideological priorities.

All three texts were presented by Guild in translation, without their sources. The Old English version was not printed, and in subsequent seventeenth-century editions of the work the same practice is followed; clearly the presence of the Old English version no longer had cultural traction for the evangelical and reformed discourse communities who engaged with it. Three further editions of the translation appeared in 1675, 1677 and 1687 respectively. The printings of 1675 and 1677 were no doubt responses to the rise of anti-catholic feeling after Charles II's Royal Declaration of Indulgence (1672), which suspended penal sanctions against catholics and dissenters and culminated in the fictitious 'Popish Plot' (1678–81), while the 1687 version was printed on the eve of the 'Glorious Revolution' of 1688, which saw the expulsion of James VII and II, the last roman catholic monarch. The argument was the heart of the matter, and the text in Old English had had, back in 1566, a performative function which seems no longer to have been considered necessary. Perhaps by then 'learned Saxonism' had other agendas, as suggested by the careers of the nonjurors Hickes and Wanley. Elements of the Old English text – printed in *Pica Saxon* – only reappeared in the notes to an edition of the translation from 1736, where it was prefaced by a life of Parker supplied by the antiquarian John Strype. There was then a publishing hiatus until a Victorian edition in 1877.

As already flagged, the exemplar for the 1566 edition of *A testimonie* appears on folios 218r–226r in what is now Corpus 198. At a later stage, the resulting edition was also checked against a second manuscript, in the Cotton collection: London, British Library, MS Cotton Faustina A.ix. The homily appears there on folios 131r–139r. Joscelyn himself annotated both the Corpus and Faustina versions of the homily, inserting variant readings and marking in the manuscripts, where appropriate, the equivalent leaf numbers in *A testimonie* (Ker 1957: 192). Given that no catalogue or finding-list of Anglo-Saxon manuscripts existed in his time, Joscelyn's identification of two copies of the relevant text in quite distinct collections shows a remarkable knowledge of the range of surviving Old English material. This knowledge was clearly the result of immense effort, 'reverse-engineered' through the study of surviving glosses and another of Ælfric's works, his *Grammar* of Latin, which the Anglo-Saxon author had thoughtfully mediated through Old English. Judging by the presence of their characteristic annotations, Parker's team had engaged with at least two eleventh-century copies of the *Grammar*: MSS Cambridge, Corpus Christi College 449, and London, British Library, Royal 15 B.xxii. Joscelyn's editorial activity also implies a sustained dedication to the cultivation of scholarly networks, within a dynamic community of practice.[18]

A testimonie was, as we have seen, an important work in sixteenth-century theological politics, but it is also interesting as a technical tour de force. Day deployed not only roman and italic typefaces, and a variety of ornaments, but the edition was also the first attempt to reflect Anglo-Saxon script in typographical form. Anglo-Saxon scribes generally used two slightly distinct scripts, depending on the language they were copying: Caroline minuscule for Latin and a derived form for copying Old English, namely, Anglo-Saxon square minuscule, a subvariety of the 'insular script' found in Britain and Ireland. The two scripts differed in their forms for the letters *a*, *d*, *e*, *f*, *g*, *h*, *r* and *s*, and of course writing in Old English also required three extra letters: *þ* 'thorn', *ƿ* 'wynn', and *ð* 'eth' (the traditional (Icelandic) name; the Anglo-Saxons knew the letter *ð* as *ðæt*). (For the names of the letters and discussion, see Lucas 1997: 189–90 and references there cited.) There was also the form of thorn with a cross-bar over the ascender, *ꝥ*, used as an abbreviation for *þæt*. Thorn and eth were interchangeable in Anglo-Saxon texts in Old English; in the Faustina manuscript, for instance, the forms *syþþan* 'afterwards' and *syððan* appear within a few lines of each other. When Day printed the work, those letters common to the Caroline and Anglo-Saxon scripts were reproduced in roman fonts, but special letters were cut, probably by the Huguenot typecaster Pierre Haultin (Lucas 1997: 165–6), to reflect the distinctive forms used for copying Old English. The development of such a typeface, as with Junius's *Pica Saxon*, was, in Malcolm Parkes's phrase, 'emblematic of the past' (1997a: 123), and its use in the reproduction of an Old English vernacular homily was designed to evoke an authority derived from a particularly English and 'auncient' identity. Parker and his team were asserting their connexion with writers such as Ælfric, incorporating him

[18] For a discussion of Joscelyn's – and others' – methods in learning Old English, see Lucas 2016.

into a perceived – indeed invented – community of practice extending through time: a 'renewing of the memory' of Anglo-Saxon England (Butler 2014: 154 and *passim*). Day provided a list of these special 'Saxon Caracters' [sic] at the end of the book as a handy point of reference.[19]

The edition represented an extension into print and thus the wider public sphere of a skill that was clearly prized in Parker's circle, that is, the ability to reproduce Anglo-Saxon script by hand. Several examples of such behaviour survive. Perhaps the best-known individual active in this enterprise is Parker's chaplain, Stephen Batman, whose substantial programme of annotation in some thirty medieval manuscripts has attracted a good deal of attention (see further discussion in Chapter 3 below). The term Parker used for such activity was 'counterfeited', but it seems no deception was intended.[20] Parker was completely open concerning what he was about, and even boasted to William Cecil, Elizabeth's chief minister, that he had assembled a substantial body of craftsmen 'within my house' of 'drawers and cutters, painters, limners, writers and bookbinders', all tasked with working intensively on his manuscript collection (Parkes 1997a: 123 and references there cited): a fine example of a substantial community of practice in action. Rather, Parker's aim seems to have been one of conservation as conceived of at the time, and when his scribes undertook their archaizing their 'emphasis was upon recognizable rather than exact reproductions of insular letter-shapes' (Parkes 1997a: 124), designed to 'complement the achievements of medieval craftsmen according to the criteria of sixteenth-century antiquarian tastes and judgement' (Parkes 1997a: 127).

Such a goal – complementation, not counterfeiting in the modern sense – accounts for the changes undertaken in the transfer of the text from manuscript to print, and in order to explore what happened it is necessary to analyse the likely exemplar that *A testimonie* 'counterfeited'. Text (2.7) below is a transcription of the opening of the homily in Corpus 198.

19 The distribution of thorn and eth differs in the Corpus and Faustina manuscripts, one of the means by which it is possible to determine that Corpus, and not Faustina, was Joscelyn's source for the homily. The Faustina scribe also used Caroline rather than insular forms of <g> and <a> in copying the Old English text, exemplifying the 'leaking' between the two writing-systems that later became more and more frequent in the transition from Old to Middle English. For other typographical experiments during the period, see e.g. Dickins 1949.

20 The word *counterfeit* seems to have had a connotation of fraudulence since its first recorded appearance in the English language at the end of the thirteenth century, but relevant other, non-pejorative meanings 'to imitate, copy' and 'to represent/reproduce' seem to have been current from the 1360s to the middle of the seventeenth century. See OED *counterfeit*, v., meanings 8 and 9, and *counterfeit*, adj. and n., meanings A.4, A.9, B.3. Batman's activity, especially in Cambridge, Magdalene College, MS Pepys 2498, will be discussed further in Chapter 3 below.

Text (2.7) requires some extra contextualisation. We know something of the manuscript's earlier provenance. The bulk of the codex, including the stint in which this homily appears, was copied in the first half of the eleventh century, almost certainly in south-west England. It is known to have been in the library of Worcester Priory in the thirteenth century because it was glossed, in Latin, by the famous annotator known to posterity from the shakiness of his writing as the 'Tremulous Hand'. The Tremulous Hand's activity can be detected in numerous Anglo-Saxon manuscripts (Franzen 1991); a Worcester provenance for its origins therefore seems very likely. As Christine Franzen has outlined in detail, the Hand, seeing something of value in these texts from the Anglo-Saxon past, was attempting – like Joscelyn 300 years later – to learn Old English (we will be returning to these 'early antiquarians' in section 2.3 below). The Tremulous Hand also seems to be responsible for inserting small oblique lines to distinguish words; the original scribe of the homily (Scribe 5 of the manuscript, according to Ker 1957: 79) had, in contrast to other scribes involved in the book's production, a tendency to write words so closely to each other that quite often gaps are hard to identify. Conventions of word division were still developing when the manuscript was originally copied; these conventions had become much more embedded by the time the Tremulous Hand intervened (Parkes 1992: 41; see also Saenger 1997: *passim* for a discussion of word-spacing and its implications).

In the transcription from Corpus 198 given below as Text (2.7), the additions made by the Tremulous Hand have not been recorded, but in accordance with the conventions flagged in the Preface, abbreviations (other than *ꝥ*) have been expanded and flagged with italics. Word divisions were not settled in the tenth century, and quite often it is hard to tell where one word stops and another begins; as a result, modern conventions of word division have been adopted. The original Anglo-Saxon lineation has been retained, as has the punctuation, and the engrossed initial 'M' in the first line is flagged in the transcription by being emboldened. To assist the reader, Text (2.8), a transcription of the equivalent passage in the 1566 edition, appears after Text (2.7), followed by the 1566 translation. (A modern edition of the passage, following Godden 1979: 150, but with modernised punctation, appears in the accompanying note.)[21]

[21] Modern edition (after Godden 1979: 150, but with modernised punctuation inserted):

> MEn þa leofostan, gelome eow is gesæd ymbe ures hælendes æriste, hu he on ðisum andwerdan dæge æfter his ðrowunge mihtiglice of deaðe aras. Nu wille we eow geopenian þurh Godes gife be ðam halgan husle ðe ge nu to gan sceolon, and gewissian eower andgit

Text (2.7): Cambridge, Corpus Christi College MS 198, folio 218r

M En ða leofostan ʒelome eoƿ is ʒesæd ymbe ures
hælendes æriste. hu he on ðisum and ƿear
dan dæʒe æft*er* his ðroƿunge. mihtiʒlice of deaþe
aras.· nu ƿille ƿe eoƿ geopenian ðurh ʒodes ʒife be ða*m*
halʒan husle ðe ʒe nu toʒan sceolon. ⁊ geƿissian eoƿer
and ʒyt ymbe ðære ʒerynu æʒþer ʒe æfter þære
ealdan ʒecyþnysse. ʒe æfter þære niƿan:· ðy læs ðe
æniʒ tƿeonung eoƿ derian mæʒe. be ða*n* liflicum
ʒereorde; Se ælmihtiʒa ʒod bebead moysen ðam
heretoʒan on eʒiptalande.· ꝥ he sceolde bebeodan
israhela folce. ꝥ hi namon æt ælcum heorðe anes
ʒeares lamb. on ðære nihte ðe hi ferdon of ðam lande.
to ðam behate nan earde. ⁊ sceoldon ꝥ lamb ʒode ʒe=
offrian. ⁊ syððan sniðan. ⁊ ƿyrcan rode tacn on heora
ʒedyrum. ⁊ ofersleʒum mid ðæs lambes blode etan
syððan ðæs lambes flæsc ʒebræd. ⁊ deorfe hlafas*
mid feldlicre lactucan; God cƿæð to moysen. ne
ete ʒe of ðam lambe nan ðinʒ hreaƿ. ne on ƿætere
ʒesoðen. ac ʒebræd to fyre; Etað ꝥ heafod. ⁊ ða fæt.
⁊ ꝥ inneƿerde. ne his nan ðinʒ ne belife oð meriʒen;
ʒif ðær hƿæt to lafe sy. forbærneð ꝥ. ðicʒað hit on

[folio 218 v]

ðas ƿisan;

**corrected, by the original Anglo-Saxon scribe, from* hlafes

Text (2.8) is a transcription of the equivalent passage in *A testimonie*, sig. C.iij r (after London, British Library, 695.a.31):

M En ða leofostan.
ʒelome eoƿ is ʒe-
sæd ymbe ures hæ-
lendes æriste. hu he on ði-

ymbe þære gerynu, ægðer ge æfter ðære ealdan gecyðnysse, ge æfter ðære niwan, þy læs ðe ænig twynung eow derian mæge, be ðam liflicum gereorde.

Se ælmihtiga God bebead Moysen ðam heretogan on Egypta lande þæt he sceolde bebeodan Israhela folce, þæt hi namon æt ælcum heorðe anes geares lamb, on ðære nihte ðe hi ferdon of ðam lande to ðam behatenan earde; and sceoldon þæt lamb Gode geoffrian, and siððan sniðan, and wyrcan rodetacn on heora gedyrum, and oferslegum mid ðæs lambes blode, etan siððan ðæs lambes flæsc gebræd, and ðeorfe hlafas mid feldlicre lactucan. God cwæð to Moysen, ‘Ne ete ge of ðam lambe nan ðing hreaw, ne on wætere gesoðen, ac gebræd to fyre. Etað þæt heafod and ða fet, and þæt innewearde, ne his nan ðing ne belife oð merigen. Gif ðær hwæt to lafe sy, forbærneð þæt. Ðicgað hit on ðas wisan.’

sum andƿeardan dæʒe æf-
ter his ðroƿunʒe mihtiʒ-
lice of deaþe aras; Nu
ƿille ƿe eoƿ ʒeopenian ðurh
Godes ʒife be ðam halʒan
husle ðe ʒe nu toʒan sce-
olon. ⁊ ʒeƿissian eoƿer and-
ʒyt ymbe ðære ʒerynu.
æʒþer ʒe æfter þære ealdan
ʒecyþnysse. ʒe æfter þære
niƿan. ðy læs ðe æniʒ tƿeo=
nunʒe eow derian mæʒe be
þam liflicu*m* ʒereorde; Se ælmihtiʒa God bebead Moyses
ðam

[sig. C.iiij v]

ðam heretoʒan on eʒypta
lande. ꝥ he sceolde bebeodan
Israhela folce. ꝥ hi namon
æt ælcu*m* heorþe anes ʒeares
lamb on ðære nihte ðe hi
ferdon of þam lande to þam
behatenan earde. ⁊ sceoldon
ꝥ lamb Gode ʒeoffrian. and
syþþan sniþan. ⁊ ƿyrcan
rode tacn on heora ʒedy-
rum. ⁊ oferslеʒum mid þæs
lambes blode. etan syþþan
ðæs lambes flæsc ʒebræd. ⁊
deorfe hlafas mid feldlicre
lactucan; God cƿæð to Moysen. ne ete ʒe of ðam lambe
nan þinʒ hreaƿ. ne on ƿætere
ʒesoðen. ac ʒebræd to fyre;
Etaþ

[sig. C.v v]

Etaþ ꝥ heafod. and þa fæt. ⁊
ꝥ inneƿearde. ne his nan þinʒ
ne belife oþ meriʒen; ʒif þær
hƿæt tolafe sy. forbærneþ
ꝥ. ðicʒaþ hit on þis ƿisan;

Here is the translation offered in *A testimonie* (sig. C.iiij r–C.vi r):

> Men beloued, it hath bene often sayd vnto you aboute our Sauiours resurrection, how he on this present day after hys suffering, mightily rose from death. Now will we open vnto you through Gods grace, of the holy housel, which ye should nowe goe vnto, and instructe your vnderstandyng aboute thys mysterie, both after the olde couenaunte, and also after the newe, that no doubting may trouble you about thys liuely foode. The almyghtie God bade Moyses his captaine in ye land of Ægypt, to commaunde ye people of Israell to take for euery familye a lambe of one yeare old, the night they departed out of ye country to ye land of promise, & to offer y[t] lambe to God, & after to kill it, & to make the signe of ye crosse, with ye la*m*bes bloud vpon the side postes, & the vpper poste of their dore, & afterward to eate y[e] lambes flesh rosted, & vnleauened bread w[t] wilde lettise. God sayth vnto Moyses. Eate of y[e] la*m*be nothing raw, nor sodde*n* in water, but rosted w[t] fire. Eate y[e] head, y[e] feete, and the inwardes, & let nothing of it be left vntill ye morning: if any thing therof remaine, y[t] shall you burne w[t] fire. Eate it in this wyse.[22]

Comparison of Texts (2.7) and (2.8) with the modern edition shows how far presentational practices have changed. Perhaps the most obvious difference is in practices of punctuation, where in the edition modern grammar-based pointing has been deployed. By contrast, punctuation in Corpus 198 (Text (2.7)) is used to indicate rhetorical pauses; as with the *Beowulf* manuscript, the scribe has supplied the 'visual cues' designed to guide speech-like reading. However, a comparison of Corpus 198 with the *Beowulf* manuscript indicates that the former was considerably more sophisticated in its pointing, not least in its deployment of a wider repertoire of positurae.

The positurae, as already outlined in Chapter 1, were originally developed in monasteries to assist in the declamation of the Latin liturgy (Parkes 1992: 34–5) and were widely adopted for sophisticated vernacular prose in late Anglo-Saxon England (Clemoes 1952). In Corpus 198, three positurae are deployed: the punctus (.), the punctus elevatus (⁛) and the punctus versus (;). The last of these marks, in form rather like the modern semicolon, was used here to mark the completion of the *periodus* – the grammatical unit – which expressed the sententia or 'complete meaning' of the utterance; in liturgical use, the punctus versus 'signified the lowering of the voice at the end of the period' (Clemoes 1952: 13; see also Harlow 1959). In this passage the deployment of the punctus versus is generally – if not invariably – reinforced through being followed by a capital letter, and

[22] *housel* = the consecrated elements of the eucharist; *aboute thys mysterie* for 'concerning that mystery'; *thys liuely foode* = for 'that bodily sustenance'; *Moyses his captaine* for 'Moses the chieftain'; *sodden* = boiled; *inwards* = innards, entrails.

indeed in later manuscripts the punctus versus disappeared, as the regular deployment of capitals at the beginning of the periodus made it redundant (Parkes 1992: 39). The punctus elevatus in origin denoted 'an elevation [of the voice]' (Clemoes (1952: 13) at the end of a colon and was transferred to vernacular texts from Latin at the end of the tenth century (Ker 1957: xxxiv). In this passage it is used to indicate a major medial pause within the periodus, preceding a subordinating conjunction such as *ðy læs ðe*, or an adverb such as *nu* which is functioning as a cohesive link. The simple punctus, an older form that actually predated the development of the positurae, is used in the passage to indicate a minor pause, often preceding a coordinating conjunction such as *&* or *ac*.

Comparison between Texts (2.7), (2.8) and the early modern English translation reveals some further interesting similarities and differences. The early modern English translation, for instance, represents a radical reworking in presentational terms. Thus, for instance, the opening two sentences deploy the comma-mark (rather than the punctus) to mark cola and commata, and replace the semicolon used to represent the original's punctus versus with a full stop, flagging the end of the period:

> Men beloued, it hath bene often sayd vnto you aboute our Sauiours resurrection, how he on this present day after hys suffering, mightily rose from death. Now will we open vnto you through Gods grace, of the holy housel, which ye should nowe goe vnto, and instructe your vnderstandyng aboute thys mysterie, both after the olde couenaunte, and also after the newe, that no doubting may trouble you about thys liuely foode.

We might compare the two sentences above with their equivalent in the 1566 edition (for ease of comparison, in this extract the lineation of the original has not been retained):

> **M**En ðа leofostan. ʒelome eoƿ is ʒesæd ymbe ures hælendes æriste. hu he on ðisum andƿeardan dæʒe æfter his ðroƿunʒe mihtiʒlice of deaþe aras; Nu ƿille ƿe eoƿ ʒeopenian ðurh Godes ʒife be ðam halʒan husle ðe ʒe nu toʒan sceolon. ⁊ ʒeƿissian eoƿer andʒyt ymbe ðære ʒerynu. æʒþer ʒe æfter þære ealdan ʒecyþnysse. ʒe æfter þære niƿan. ðy læs ðe æniʒ tƿeonunʒe eoƿ derian mæʒe be þam liflicu*m* ʒereorde;

The translation is a very good one, and not that distant from present-day English, although there are some features that may strike modern readers as archaic, e.g. the retention of a 'verb second' auxiliary after *Now* in *Now will we open*, and the postposed modifier in *Men beloued.* However, some elements of punctuation in the early modern English translation are very different from present-day practice; we might note for instance the use of the comma-marks preceding the object clause beginning *how he* . . . and the adverbial clause beginning *after hys suffering*. Such 'loose' punctuation is 'rhetorical' in comparison with the modern edition, although it has the advantage of capturing the 'speech-like' qualities of the Old English original.

By contrast – in addition to the obvious difference that Text (2.8), the 1566 edition, is a necessarily anachronistic printed version – there is a clear correlation between the punctuation practices in Corpus 198 and the early modern edition of the Old English homily, with marks being deployed in the same positions in the text. Although the punctus elevatus has been replaced by a simple punctus, the punctus versus has been retained, presumably because of the availability of the similarly configured semicolon, itself a mark which had been reintroduced with a distinct 'humanist' function at the end of the fifteenth century. The early modern edition has also retained the Old English deployment of capitals. However, comparison with the Anglo-Saxon exemplar shows that the uncertain word division of the original has been resolved by Joscelyn in favour of a usage that would seem familiar to a modern editor, and that was presumably preferred by the discourse communities to which the edition was addressed. In this task he was clearly guided by the markings made by the Tremulous Hand. The 1566 edition therefore represents a compromise; although by no means a facsimile, in that at least some editorial decisions have been made in the 1566 print about the nature of the Old English lexicon, nevertheless there has been a Parkerian 'counterfeit' antiquarian engagement with regard to letter forms and marks of punctuation, all pragmatic markers of sociocultural significance.

The antiquarian punctuation flags again that the Old English text in general was primarily decorative and evocative. And something of this decorative impulse was sustained in a more ambitious publication that John Day printed in 1571 for the martyrologist John Foxe: a quarto edition of the Old English Gospels, dedicated to Queen Elizabeth and splendidly entitled *The Gospels of the Fower Euangelistes, Translated in the Old Saxon Tyme out of Latin into the Vulgare Toung of the Saxons, Newly Collected out of Auncient Monuments of the Sayd Saxons and Now Published for Testimonie of the Same.*[23] The word *Testimonie* in the title echoes that of the earlier sermon-edition which Foxe also referred to in his Preface, and Haultin's font was once again deployed, this time with a marginal (rather than

[23] A copy of these Gospels, now London, British Library, 675.f.16, has a near-contemporary inscription on the title page: 'This was the Dedication Book presented to the Queenes owne hands by Mr Fox.'

facing-page) early modern English gloss, printed in a blackletter 'gothic' font to further underline the work's antiquity. Old English punctuation practices were again sustained with punctus and punctus versus, although verse-numbering was added as a pragmatic marker to assist sixteenth-century readers wishing to map the Old English text onto the accompanying glosses.

All such works had attractions for later antiquarians. The courtier and Cambridge scholar William L'Isle (?1569–1637), for instance, seems to have used both *The Gospels of the Fower Euangelistes* and *A testimonie*, amongst other works, as cribs for learning Old English (see Pulsiano 2000); we have already noted L'Isle's inclusion of *A testimonie* alongside his 1623 edition of Ælfric's *Letter to Sigeweard*. However, it is worth noting, as we have seen, that the afterlife of *A testimonie* is largely focused on the early modern English translation, easily repurposed as ammunition for other seventeenth-century religious conflicts. Joscelyn's edition was a fine piece of scholarship, but ideology seems, in the printing history of *A testimonie*, to have trumped antiquarianism, and the early evocation of the antique past expressed through the public deployment of a scholarly edition with 'counterfeit' letter forms and punctuation does not seem to have been sustained; its recuperation had to wait for the efforts of Junius and his successors, the Oxford Saxonists, whose antiquarianism seems to have distinct ideological underpinnings. The discourse community of scholarly Anglo-Saxonists in the early seventeenth century was much smaller than that of those who needed explicit affirmation of the historical basis for reformed religion.

2.3 Antiquarian Sentiments

Although *A testimonie* was the first printing of an Anglo-Saxon work, it was not the earliest recuperation of Anglo-Saxon culture. For at least two centuries after the Norman Conquest, writings composed in Anglo-Saxon England continued to be copied and reworked. It is a remarkable fact that, of the forty-two surviving medieval manuscripts recorded in Neil Ker's *Catalogue of Manuscripts Containing Anglo-Saxon* as containing copies of Ælfric's homilies, no fewer than twenty have been dated to the late eleventh, twelfth and indeed thirteenth centuries (see Ker 1957: 511); at least one other copy likely to have been post-Conquest was destroyed in the Ashburnham House fire of 1731 (MS Cotton Otho A.xii, for which see Ker 1957: 22, item 173).

Such 'late' copies were until comparatively recently somewhat neglected as 'unauthoritative'. However, important recent research undertaken by

Elaine Treharne and others has changed scholarly opinion concerning these materials (see especially Treharne 2012, Swan 2010, and the essays contained in Swan and Treharne 2000). Important thirteenth-century manuscripts containing Ælfrician material, such as the homilies found in London, Lambeth Palace, MS 487, are now being reassessed as major recastings for new discourse communities. Mary Swan has for instance suggested that the Lambeth collection, like the earliest copies of the *Ancrene Riwle* (to be discussed further in Chapter 3), may have been devised for the private devotions of a female audience (2007: 42), although she accepts that there is an alternative hypothesis, that the works were reshaped for wider public preaching. And, following some of Treharne's suggestions, Bella Millett has noted that the Lambeth Homilies were produced 'within a period of radical change in preaching and pastoral care' (2007: 45), associated with the rise of scholasticism and the reforming Third and Fourth Lateran Councils of 1179 and 1215. She and Treharne have demonstrated how these homilies show, at least in part, 'an active response to the requirements of a changed theological and pastoral context ... their use of earlier (particularly Ælfrician) material might reflect not nostalgia for the Anglo-Saxon past but a sense of its continuing "authority and applicability"' (Millett 2007: 44).

Some of these developments were inevitable responses to changes in the status and use of the English language during the period, driven by the need to increase the texts' communicative power. Sound-systems changed, and writing-systems were now adjusted to reflect these changes. Inflexional loss and lexical input from languages like Norse – occluded during the Anglo-Saxon period – and French started to be reflected in written texts. With the general exception of input from French, these changes were of course already under way during the late Old English period. However, they became more widely reflected in vernacular writing, as the late West Saxon *Schriftsprache* lost its status as a medium for national communication across space and time, and as usages with only local currency emerged. Ultimately, as a result of such social changes and the emergence of new discourse communities, dialectal divergence became increasingly reflected in English texts as the writing-systems inherited from the Anglo-Saxon period were changed to align more closely with more local varieties of speech.

A comparison of the opening of Ælfric's homily on Pentecost as it survives both in Corpus 198, discussed in the previous section, and in Lambeth 487, illustrates how the Lambeth reviser mixes linguistic conservatism with innovation.

Text (2.9): Corpus 198, folio 253v

F ram þa*m* halȝan easterlican dæȝe: synd ȝetealde
fiftiȝ daȝa to þisu*m* dæȝe. ⁊ ðes dæȝ is ȝe haten pente
costen: ꝥ is se fifteoȝoða dæȝ þære easterlican tide;
þes dæȝ þæs on ðære ealdan æ. ȝeset ⁊ ȝehalȝod; God
be bead moyse on eȝypta lande [...] ꝥ he ⁊ eall is
rahela folc sceoldan offrian æt æl cu*m* hiþisceȝode
an lamb anesȝeares. ⁊ mearcian into þa*m* blode rode
tacn on heora ȝedyru*m*. ⁊ ofersleȝu*m*; þa on ðære nihte

[folio 254r]

ferde godes ænȝel ⁊ acþealde on ælcu*m* huse þæs eȝyp
tiscan folces. ꝥ fru*m* cennede cild. ⁊ ꝥ leofeste;

[...] = *erasure*

Text (2.10): Lambeth 487, folio 30v

[F] ram þan halie hester dei: boð italde. fifti.
daȝa to þilke deie ⁊ þes dei is ihaten pe*n*tecoste
ꝥ is þe fiftuða dei fram þan ester tid. þes dei
þes on þere alde laȝe iset ⁊ ihalden. God het
Moyses on egipte londe ꝥ he ⁊ al ꝥ israelis
ce folk ꝥ he þider iled hefde: ꝥ heo sculden
offrien of elchan hiþscipe gode an lomb of
ane ȝeres ⁊ merki mid þan blode hore
duren. ⁊ hore ouersleaht. þa on þere ilke
niht: iþende godes engel to ⁊ acþalde on
elche huse of þam egiptissen folche: *
**inserted in margin*: þ*us* fru*m*kenede childe ⁊ ꝥ lefeste:

[Translation: *From the holy Easter day fifty days are counted to this day, and this day is called Pentecost, that is the fiftieth day within the Easter period. This day was in the old law established and hallowed. God commanded Moses in the land of the Egyptians that he and all the folk of Israel should offer from every household a lamb once a year, and mark using its blood a sign of the cross on their doors and lintels. Then in the night God's angel passed and killed in every house of the Egyptian people the first-born and most beloved child; . . .*]

In grammar, Lambeth 487 is generally innovative. Although the text has retained elements of inflexion that have subsequently disappeared, such as an inflected determiner-system (*þan*, *þere*, *þam*), adjectives do not always agree with the nouns they modify (*þan halie hester dei*, beside Corpus *haligan*), simply adopting *–e* to flag their location after determiners in a manner that, for example, Chaucer would find familiar two centuries later. Nouns do not consistently inflect either, cf. Lambeth *þan ester tid* beside Corpus *þam halȝan easterlican dæȝe* (although we might note Lambeth's genitive plural *daȝa*). The characteristic Old English *ge*-prefix has been reduced to *i*- in Lambeth.

And in writing-systems Lambeth also points forward to future developments. Very noticeably Caroline <g>, generally restricted to deployment in Latin in Anglo-Saxon times, is in Lambeth now used alongside insular <ȝ> in a vernacular text, with a distinct function, to reflect a plosive in *egiptissen*, beside Corpus's *eȝyptiscan*; <ȝ> is retained, but as the figural equivalent of the approximant /j/, as in *laȝe*. The old Anglo-Saxon distinctions between alphabets used for Old English and Latin, already disappearing in the Faustina manuscript of Ælfric's homilies (see note 19 above), have here broken down entirely.

However, cutting across such modernising tendencies were those scribes who practised what Eric Stanley (1969) once famously called 'antiquarian sentiments'. Corpus 198 was glossed, at some point in the first half of the thirteenth century, by an anonymous scribe we have already met: the Tremulous Hand of Worcester (Franzen 1991: 2). The Tremulous Hand attempted to recuperate past texts, attempting to teach himself Old English. In addition to glossing a set of pre-Conquest texts, the Tremulous Hand also undertook more ambitious activities, notably what may be his own compositions: the earliest English version of the Nicene Creed in Oxford, Bodleian Library, MS Junius 121, and texts in Worcester, Cathedral Library, MS F.174, which contains a copy of Ælfric's *Grammar and Glossary*, followed by two short fragments: parts of a poem on the *Soul's Address to the Body*, and – significantly – a poem on the disuse of the English language, sometimes known after the opening reference as *St Bede's Lament*. Clearly, for the Tremulous Hand the past continued to have considerable cultural traction.

St Bede's Lament in Worcester F.174, usually described as 'a short poem . . . written in what is evidently a development of the [Old English] alliterative line' (Dickins and Wilson 1951: 1), is worth some analysis. Text (2.11) is a transcription from Worcester F.174, folio 68r. The text has been trimmed on the right-hand side and damaged at the foot. A gap has been left at the top of the text for a decorated or even illuminated large initial 'S'. A translation with suggested words for the missing elements follows.

Text (2.11): Worcester F.174, folio 68r

[S] *anctus* beda ƿas iboren her on breotene mid us 7 he wisliche
aƿende ꝥ þeo englise leoden þurh ƿeren ilerde. 7 he þeo cn . . .
ten unƿreih. þe questiuns hoteþ. þa derne diȝelnesse. þe de . . .

ƿurþe is. ælfric abbod þe ƿe alquin hoteþ he was bocare . 7 þe . . .
bec ƿende. Genesis. Exodus. Vtronomius. Numerus. Leuiticus. þu..
þeos ƿeren ilærde ure leoden. on englisc. þet ƿeren þeos biscop . . . . .
bodeden cristendom. ƿilfrid of sipum. Iohan of beoforlai. cuþb . . .
of dunholme. Osƿold of ƿireceastre. Egƿin of heoueshame. æld . . .
of malmesburi. Sƿiþþun. æþelƿold. aidan. Biern of ƿincæstre. . . .
lin of rofecæstre. *sanct* Dunston. 7 *sanct* ælfeih of cantoreburi. þeos læ . . . .
ure leodan on englisc. næs deorc heore liht. ac hit fæire glod . . . .
þeo leore forleten. 7 þet folc is forloren. nu beoþ oþre leoden. þeo læ . . .
ure folc. 7 feole of þen lorþeines losiæþ. 7 ꝥ folc forþ mid. Nu sæiþ . . .
drihten þus. Sicut aq*ui*la p*ro*uocat pullos suos. ad uolandu*m*. 7 sup*er* eo . . .
.. . . . . This beoþ godes ƿord to ƿorlde asende ꝥ ƿe sceolen fæier feþ . . .

[Translation: *Saint Bede was born here in Britain with us and he wisely translated [books] so that the English people were taught and he unravelled the knots [*MS cn..ten, *for* cnotten*], and he unravelled the problems, which are called the 'questions' (i.e. questiones), that obscure puzzle which is precious [*MS de.. ƿurþe *for* deorƿurþe*]. Abbot Ælfric, whom we call Alcuin, he was a writer and translated the [five] books: Genesis, Exodus, Leviticus, Numbers, Deuteronomy. Through these our people were taught in English. There were these bishops [who] preached Christendom: Wilfrid of Ripon [*MS sipum*],*[24] *John of Beverley, Cuthb[ert] of Durham, Oswald of Worcester, Egwin of Evesham, Ald[helm] of Malmesbury, Swithun, Ethelwold, Aidan, Birinus of Winchester, [Paul]inus of Rochester, St Dunstan and St Alphege of Canterbury. These taught [*MS læ . . . *for* lærden*] our people in English. Their light was not dim, but it shone brightly. [Now is] that teaching forsaken, and the folk are abandoned. Now there is another people which teaches [*MS læ . . . *for* læreþ*] our folk, and many of those teachers are damned, and our folk with them. Now [our] Lord speaks thus,* As an eagle stirs up her young to fly, and [hovers] over them.* *These are God's words, sent to the world so that we must [fix upon him] a beautiful faith.*

*Deuteronomy 32: 11, King James version: As an eagle stirreth up her nest, fluttereth over her young, spreadeth abroad her wings, taketh them, beareth them on her wings.]

The contents of the poem have been paralleled with William of Malmesbury's twelfth-century complaints about England having 'become the dwelling-place of foreigners and the property of strangers' (Dickins and Wilson 1951: 1), suggesting a dating later than the Anglo-Saxon period.

[24] The misreading *sipum* for 'Ripon' has been taken to suggest that the scribe – or the hand of his exemplar – was copying from an original in Anglo-Saxon insular script, in which a 'long' <r> was similar to a 'long' <s>, and thus easily confused (Hall 1920: 224). It is also worth noting that 'long' <r> is found in manuscripts copied late in the previous century (see, for instance, the activity of the first scribe in Oxford, Bodleian Library, MS Bodley 343, reported in Irvine 1993: xviii).

Punctuation is considerably less elaborate in comparison with the Corpus and Lambeth texts, with a simple punctus used. The text is nevertheless in broad terms linguistically conservative, although there are some features that mark it off as Middle rather than Old English; thus the French-derived form *questiuns* is found here for the first time in an English text. In nouns, the inherited endingless neuter plural *word* 'words' may be noted, while forms such as *cnotten* 'knots', *leoden* 'people' retain or have taken on the Old English weak plural ending. The dative plural determiner *þen* 'the/those' is marked for inflexion, cf. Old English *þǣm*. The Old English *ge*-prefix, commonly found in past participles, is reflected in *i-* in *iboren*, while *–þ* endings are used for both third person singular and plural present tense verbs, e.g. *sæiþ*, *hoteþ*, even though the distinction between singular and plural in unstressed syllables, typically yielding *bint/bindeþ* (singular) beside *bindaþ* (plural) in late Old English morphology, is not retained. The form *losiæþ*, however, derived from the Old English weak class II verb *losian*, retains the *-i-* found in the plural but not the singular form (cf. West Saxon *losiaþ* beside singular *losaþ*).

For our purposes, however, the letter forms adopted in this text are of greater interest. Some of the Hand's usages are inherited, notably his use of thorn and wynn, but these forms lasted into the Middle English periods; he does not use eth in the *Lament*, although he was aware of the letter and used it in his copying of Ælfric's *Glossary*. Another form that disappeared comparatively early in the Middle English period, ash, is also retained, but in this case – interestingly – its distribution is not entirely in line with inherited practice. It is usually found as the reflex of West Saxon *æ*, e.g. *næs*, *fæire*, although <a> is used in *þas* (West Saxon *wæs*) and <e> in *þet* (West Saxon *þæt*). Also unexpected is the ash in *losiæþ*, already cited (West Saxon *losiaþ*). Such unhistorical reflexes are 'back spellings', indicating the loss in the equivalent spoken mode of a distinction between Old English *a*, *æ*. Such oddities are found elsewhere in the text, e.g. *leore* 'teaching' (Old English *lār*), beside the scribe's more usual <o> as the reflex of Old English *ā* in *glod* 'shone'; <eo> is a common digraph in Old English usage, but became increasingly restricted in use to western dialects in Middle English. It is tempting, given the Hand's evident antiquarian interests, to see such usages as 'archaistic' attempts to retain – while being a little uncertain of their distribution – features characteristic of the Anglo-Saxon past, as pragmatic markers for the appreciation of fellow-antiquarian readers.[25]

[25] Other examples of such archaisticism could be adduced from the Early Middle English record, most notably the distinct versions of Lawman's *Brut*. See especially Stanley 1969 for a classic discussion of Lawman; the title of this section is, as already flagged, a small homage to the late Eric Stanley's work.

2.4 The Runes in *Beowulf*

But archaisticism was by no means new in the Early Middle English period. For a final example of an evocation of the Germanic past – curiously resonating with that of the sixteenth-century antiquarians – we might return to the Nowell Codex containing *Beowulf*. The Anglo-Saxons were, as we will see, themselves quite capable of evoking the past through delicate textual detail; and the following example – the runes in *Beowulf* – demonstrates that Old English texts were, like those from later centuries, as much about visual appearance as aural apprehension.

Although related at least tangentially to the segmental writing-systems that developed across the Mediterranean world, runes took a distinct path, being commonly deployed across the Germanic world in the first millennium CE, generally for inscriptions on stone, wood and metal. They lasted longest in the areas speaking North Germanic languages, i.e. Old Norse and its varieties (Swedish, Norwegian, Danish, Icelandic, Faroese), but they also appeared elsewhere, including the British Isles. However, by the time of the Nowell Codex, dated to around 1000 CE, runes were archaic in England at least.

There has for a long time been a curious problem with the runes: how did they function? Were they 'simply' a writing-system, or were they something more, i.e. with magical significance? This tension between the 'practical' and the 'magical' has bedevilled runic studies since the runes were 'recuperated' in the seventeenth and eighteenth centuries, and persists until the present day. The runic writing-system has therefore had a special, often dubious, twentieth- and twenty-first-century afterlife: an esoteric afterlife that many scholars have valiantly (and understandably) striven to discredit, but which the uses of the term *rūn* in Old English writings nevertheless somewhat – it must be admitted – encourage. We might briefly contemplate the range of meanings covered by the following citations, with present-day English glosses, from the Old English epic poem *Beowulf*:

beadu-rūn 'battle-counsel, hostile speech' (501)
hel-rūnan 'those skilled in the mysteries of hell', i.e. 'demons' (163)
rūn '(secret) consultation' (172)
rūn-stafas 'runic letters' (1695)
rūn-wita 'confidant, trusted adviser' (1325)

The semantic fields covered by these lexemes strongly suggest that the word *rūn* was associated with a special skill, mystery or puzzle, and there is persistent evidence – albeit disputed by many scholars – that in Germanic times the runes were considered to have arcane properties. A somewhat cryptic stanza in the Old Norse eddic poem *Hávamál*, for instance, surviving in the Codex Regius (now Reykjavík, Arni Magnusson Institute MS GKS 2365 4°), has been taken to indicate that the god Odin, having been hanged on the world-ash tree Yggdrasil for nine days, was then able to interpret the runes (see further, however, Bremmer 1991). Such narratives have led many folk since the eighteenth century at least to consider runes as somehow magical, an association that has been stubbornly retained in present-day popular culture, encouraged by (e.g.) the fantasy writings of J. R. R. Tolkien.

One use of the runes that has caused some puzzlement is their sporadic appearance, alongside Latin-derived writing-systems, in late Anglo-Saxon manuscripts, apparently as a piece of Anglo-Saxon antiquarianism: and one such survival is found in the sole surviving manuscript containing the Old English epic poem *Beowulf*, Cotton Vitellius MS A.xv (part II), where, as already flagged, Scribe A sporadically deploys a manuscript rune as a logograph, using the rune ᛟ to signify the Old English word *ēþel* 'homeland'. It seems unlikely that the form is used simply in order to save space (i.e. as a brevigraph), given that Scribe A is somewhat sparing in the deployment of abbreviations for such purposes. Scribe B seems by contrast to have been keen to use abbreviations, and, if runic equivalents were available, it is actually somewhat surprising that they were not used in the portion of the manuscript copied by the latter.[26]

Inmaculada Senra Silva (1998) has argued that the use of these runes was a carry-over from the scribal exemplar, since they are not found elsewhere in the section for which Scribe A was responsible. However, even if such an interpretation is accepted, it is worth asking why they were deployed at all, whoever was responsible at whatever stage in the poem's transmission. Daniel Fleming (2004) and Brian Cook (2017) have both suggested that the three occurrences of these runes had a special thematic function: 'the runes mark passages in which Beowulf's character is reinterpreted in light of an imagined Germanic past' (Cook 2017: 351). The first use, at line 520b

[26] For the 'names of the runes', see especially the curious Anglo-Saxon *Rune Poem*, a set of ninth-century verses that were recorded in MS Cotton Otho B.x. Otho B.x was lost in the fire of 1731 that destroyed or damaged much of the Cotton collection, and thus never reached the British Museum (and subsequently the British Library) with other surviving Cottonian manuscripts, but it had already been copied by the antiquary Humfrey Wanley in his contribution to Hickes's *Thesaurus* (1705: 135).

during the 'flyting' between Unferth and Beowulf, coincides with a cluster of tribal names, which Fleming thinks are there 'used as evocations . . . the rune serves as an exclamation point to further the emphasis for the reader' (2004: 183). The second occurrence at line 913a seems, according to Cook, similarly evocative of the past: it takes place when Beowulf's killing of Grendel is being celebrated by Hrothgar's minstrel or *scop*, who contrasts him with an ancient Danish ruler, Heremod. And the final use of the *ēþel*-rune (line 1702a) seems to echo the appearance of *rūnstafas* 'runic letters' carved on the sword-hilt that Beowulf has brought back from his encounter with Grendel's mother: 'the remains of the most ancient heirloom to appear in the poem' (Fleming 2004: 184). Hrothgar then proceeds to expound the significance of the object, including a short sequence of 'hypermetric' lines, longer than usual, that seem to be deployed in Old English verse at moments of special solemnity. Fleming argues that such usage 'is an evocation of all things glorious and Germanic and ancient' (2004: 185), although also, it might be added, elegiac, in line with the Christian themes that dominate the poem and that are highly characteristic of the 'wisdom' element in Old English poetry.

Runes are found sporadically in other Anglo-Saxon manuscripts, often in connexion with personal names, and the suggestion has been made that something similar is happening in the Nowell Codex.[27] The poet Cynewulf's name, for instance, appears as a puzzle-acrostic in four works in two of the remaining extant poetic codices: *Elene* and *The Fates of the Apostles* in the Vercelli Book (now Vercelli, Biblioteca Capitolare, MS CXVII), and *Juliana* and *Christ II* in the Exeter Book (now Exeter, Cathedral Library, MS 3501). Other examples include that of Farman, the scribe responsible for the Old English glosses in the Rushworth

[27] The argument that the *ēþel*-rune is a name-element, in the manner of Farman, has been made by Fleming, who suggests that it could be a punning reference to the scribe or even the author of the poem; however, that interpretation seems to me not to exclude the possibility that a reference is being made to the Germanic past as well, even if not necessarily 'glorious'. See www.inthemedievalmiddle.com/2017/11/damian-fleming-on-rethinking-ones-own.html, last accessed on 7 December 2017. I agree wholeheartedly with Fleming's later, more nuanced view, as expressed in his blog, that the poem is 'deeply melancholic, explicitly Christian, and critical of the pre-Christian culture it presents'. Sinisterly – and in this context perhaps ironically – the rune has developed, since the middle of the twentieth century, extreme nationalist associations. The Nazis deployed a large number of runic or rune-like symbols as part of their perverted fake-antiquarian aesthetic; the *ēþel*-rune, generally referred to by its 'elder futhark' name *ōdal*, seems to have been unlucky enough to be particularly favoured. The rune has also, as an alternative to the often-banned swastika and some other symbols, since been adopted as the emblem of Italian, German and American neo-fascists/Nazis, and by white supremacist terrorist groups in South Africa. See for instance www.huffingtonpost.co.uk/entry/nazis-white-supremacists-fear-in-middle-tennessee_us_59f3f2f5e4b07fdc5fbe585c, last accessed on 7 December 2017.

Gospels (Oxford, Bodleian Library, MS Auct. D.2.19), who presents his name as *far* ᛗ, using the rune ᛗ 'man' for the second syllable of his name.

However, the *ēþel*-rune does appear in other manuscripts when it is hard to perceive a correlation with a particular name. It is used again, once each, in the fragments surviving of the Old English epic poem *Waldere* in Copenhagen, MS Ny kgl. Saml. 167b, and in the Old English translation of Orosius's *History against the Pagans*, in London, British Library, MS Additional 47967 (the Tollemache Orosius): in both cases, as a brevigraph for *ēþel* where it is hard to argue for the form being part of a name. Tom Birkett has suggested that 'the use of runic abbreviations often seems to coincide with a particular literary impulse: moments when the idea of unlocking or releasing is raised in the passage in which they are embedded' (2014: 95), thus relating to the riddle element that is such a significant feature of Old English verse and that seems to be a common feature of Germanic poetry (e.g. in Old Icelandic skaldic verse).[28]

Such an encounter has of course subsequently become obscured by print editors. Thorkelin's *editio princeps* of 1815, as we have seen, simply omitted the rune altogether, even though it does appear in the preparatory transcriptions for his edition; the rune did not fit with the classicising aesthetic that Thorkelin wished to propound. And the rune is consigned to footnotes in modern editions, as in the authoritative Klaeber text, e.g.:

'Þæt, lā, mæg secgan   sē þe sōð ond riht
fremeð on folce,   feor eal gemon,
eald ēþelweard,   þæt ðes eorl wǣre
geboren betera.   Blǣd is ārǣred
geond wīdwegas,   wine mīn Bēowulf'

(Klaeber et al. 2014: 57, lines 1700–4; cf. *Beowulf* manuscript, folio 170r)[29]

[28] The *ēþel*-rune in the *Waldere* fragment is worth a short note. It appears on folio 1b, line 31; a facsimile is provided by Arne Zettersten (1979: 16–17). The rune was written over the letter *e* in the manuscript, and Zettersten suggests that the *e* 'was probably written first. The loop of this letter [is] visible inside the rune' (1979: 17). It seems therefore that the scribe started to write the word out in full but then changed his mind. As in the *Beowulf* manuscript, the *Waldere* rune is preceded and followed by a punctus. It is perhaps significant that the word is preceded by the modifying accusative adjective *ealdne* 'old': a common collocation that suggests that here too the presence of the rune is thematically driven. The *ēþel*-rune in the Tollemache Orosius appears on p. 103 (Ker 1957: 165, item 133). Ker dates the *Waldere* fragments to 's.x/xi(?), and the Orosius to the first half of the tenth century. For further runes in the Tollemache Orosius, added around 1000, see www.bl.uk/onlinegallery/onlineex/illmanus/other/largeimage74598.html, last consulted on 25 May 2019.

[29] The manuscript has recently been refoliated; the folio containing the rune is now 170r, rather than 167r as cited in Klaeber et al. (2014).

[Translation: *'He who practises truth and right among his people, remembers all from far back, an old defender of the homeland, can well say that this man was born superior. Your glory is upraised, my friend Beowulf, through wide ways'*; translation after Fulk 2010: 199.]

The deployment of runic symbols in Old English verse is something of a challenge to conventional – i.e. oral/aural – views about how the Anglo-Saxons engaged with vernacular literature. Since the runes are visual symbols that map onto a single word, a listener would not have been aware of their presence in any oral performance. Their presence must flag, therefore, that the manuscript – however it mapped onto real or imagined speech – was originally encountered, in pragmatic terms, as an artefact viewed by eye rather than – or as well as – apprehended by ear. They represent a puzzle or riddle, to be interpreted by folk who have some special, indeed arcane knowledge.

Such a 'riddling' interpretation would align with some recent interpretations of the much more substantial programme of runes found on that most famous of Anglo-Saxon Christian monuments, the Ruthwell Cross in Dumfries-shire. The runes carved on this object present a 'speaking-cross' poem related, it is generally held, to *The Dream of the Rood* in another great Anglo-Saxon poetic codex already referred to: the Vercelli Book of religious texts in verse and prose.

Although the Cross itself seems to date from the eighth century, the runes have been interpreted by Patrick Connor (2008) as a later imposition on the decorative framework, just possibly dating from roughly the same time as the Nowell Codex. Connor's arguments would seem to account for readers familiar with both Latin and runic script; he argues that the Ruthwell monument received its runes 'modishly' (2008: 51), relating to the Easter worship associated with the *Adoratio Crucis*, in a form that 'we cannot document in England before the late tenth century' (2008: 50). If Connor's argument is accepted, then the Ruthwell runic text could be part of the same late Anglo-Saxon 'antiquarian' impulse as the occurrence of the *ēþel*-runes in *Beowulf*; the runes may have been added as icon-like aids to meditation and prayer, in line with late tenth-century practices of worship.

Whatever the date of their imposition, however, the layout of runes on the Cross, in clusters of three letters, is hardly conducive to ease of interpretation; they are, in Ray Page's words, 'maddeningly hard to read'

(1999: 147). Elizabeth Okasha's arguments, discussed by Connor (2008: 28–9), remain relevant, even though she retains the original dating of the runic text:

> I am, however, of the opinion, that it is highly unlikely that anyone in eighth-century England could stand in front of the Ruthwell cross, read its texts and understand them. Firstly, there is the physical problem of reading letters some five centimetres in height located up to four meters above one's head. Secondly, it would be necessary to be literate both in Old English and in Latin. Thirdly, one would have to be able to read both roman and runic script. Fourthly, the texts are not well organised for easy reading. The Latin texts are set partly horizontally and partly sideways to the reader; the Old English texts in runes read horizontally but are placed in such narrow bands that each line of text contains a maximum of four letters and one word can therefore be spread over up to three lines. It may be that in rural Northumbria in the eighth century there were people capable of reading the Ruthwell cross texts in spite of all these difficulties, but it does not seem very likely. To me it seems clear that the commissioner of the cross and the drafter of the texts had other motives in mind than the conveying of information to a reading public. (Okasha 1992: 87–8)

The Ruthwell runes – and indeed those in the Nowell Codex – may be most explicable as a decorative evocation of the past, a usage motivated 'not by a desire to *maximise* readability but by a desire to *obstruct* readability' (Liu 2017: 139 – my italics): legible only to an adept elite, *rūnwitan* skilled in the mystery of *rūnstafas*. They are part of the visual pragmatics of the text in question. Both manuscript and Cross, therefore, are artefacts that work as 'performing' objects as much as textual conduits. And – in accordance with the insights of historical pragmatics – their formal characteristics reflect their contemporary socio-cultural functions.

CHAPTER 3

'Witnesses Preordained by God': The Reception of Middle English Religious Prose

3.1 The Uses of *Ancrene Riwle*

Towards the end of the fourteenth century, someone, somewhere (probably) in the English West Midlands, decided to make a substantial investment: the production of a vast manuscript miscellany of religious texts in the vernacular. This book, Oxford, Bodleian Library, MS Eng. poet. A.1, is better known nowadays as the Vernon manuscript, after Edward Vernon, its seventeenth-century owner who gifted it to the Bodleian in 1677. Such miscellanies seem to have been fashionable at the time of its making; for instance, John Northwood's collection in London, British Library, MS Additional 37787, associated with Bordesley Abbey in North Worcestershire, where Northwood entered as a novice in 1386, contains some twenty English works of vernacular devotion, several in common with Vernon. Thorlac Turville-Petre (1990) has in addition drawn attention to shared material in Vernon and in the 'Clopton manuscript', which was split into three sections when sold by the recusant Giffard family in 1937 (now MSS Washington DC, Folger Shakespeare Library, V.b.236; Princeton, University Library, Taylor 11; and London, University Library, V.17; see further Perry 2007). And Wendy Scase has described many other analogues, albeit less massive; for instance, Cambridge, University Library, MS Gg 1.1, a multilingual collection which dates from c. 1330, is an early instance of what Scase calls 'the collective vernacular tradition' (2013a: 256; see also Scase 2013a: 254–5 for further examples). The similarities between these books suggest that they catered for comparable discourse communities. But the Vernon manuscript was on a different scale of magnitude, although not unparalleled: a sister volume of comparable scope, the Simeon manuscript (now London, British Library, Additional MS 22283), also survives, albeit in mutilated form.[1]

[1] See further the important essays in Connolly and Radulescu 2015.

The statistics associated with the compilation of the Vernon manuscript are staggering. It has, now, over 350 leaves, although it seems that originally there were a hundred or so more; it measures about 54 x 39 cm; it weighs some 22 kg; and it is estimated that in order to produce its parchment some 211 calfskins would have been required, with all the infrastructure of preparation that such a figure implies: what Ralph Hanna has aptly called 'the agricultural underpinning of medieval literary production', necessarily 'predicated on extreme social exploitation' (2005: 158). It now contains some 370 religious texts; others, on the missing pages, have been lost.

There are also numerous accomplished decorations. For instance, the 'Paternoster' page (folio 231v) *in a table ypeynted* offers a sophisticated grid-like diagram, as a meditative aid, that aligns Latin texts of the seven petitions of the Paternoster, the seven gifts of the Spirit, the seven virtues and the seven vices, with Middle English expanded glosses and commentary: 'The harmony of its various elements is not easy to describe: though it is at once apparent to the surveying eye, words can only distort the effect by giving temporal precedence to one or other element' (Henry 1990: 90). Its physical appearance – rather like that of the Ruthwell Cross, discussed at the end of the previous chapter, is clearly an important part of how the book 'works'. Compendia such as the Vernon and Simeon manuscripts, and to a lesser extent the Clopton manuscript (see Perry 2007), and Cambridge, Magdalene College, MS Pepys 2498, to be discussed later in this chapter, can be seen as assertions or celebrations of spiritual presence, rather in the same way that a great church building can. As Ryan Perry has put it in a particularly perceptive study, 'a magnificent . . . book [such as Vernon] might be comparable to a crucifix, relic, or a rosary; a book might become a potent and recognizable spiritual emblem' (Perry 2007: 158).

Although a great deal of work has been carried out in recent years on the Vernon manuscript, most notably by Derek Pearsall and Wendy Scase (e.g. Pearsall 1990, Scase 2013b), there is still a degree of uncertainty about where, for whom, and even why this monstrous book was produced. The texts were copied by two scribes whose language has been localised to Worcestershire, and there are several large religious houses in that area which might – just – have been able to support the substantial community of practice required for such an ambitious enterprise. Alternatively, the book may have been commissioned for a wealthy aristocratic patron; one name that has been flagged by Scase is that of Sir William Beauchamp, a member of the powerful family that also included the earls of Warwick and part of a circle of courtiers that also included Geoffrey Chaucer. Beauchamp had originally been intended for the Church, and it has been suggested that he had sympathies with Lollardy, the reformist movement associated with John Wycliffe at the end of the fourteenth century (ODNB; see also Scase 2013c: 269–93).

However, the contents of the Vernon manuscript itself – if it was indeed for Beauchamp – are not conclusive in this regard. The major texts included in the Vernon manuscript are for the most part those comparatively orthodox works that were circulating widely in the late fourteenth century, e.g. *The South English Legendary*, the writings of Richard Rolle, *The Northern Homily Cycle*, *The Prick of Conscience*, numerous devotional lyrics, and – admittedly a rather more worrying composition – Langland's *Piers Plowman*. There are no distinctively Lollard pieces in the book, and interestingly Ryan Perry has suggested – with necessary qualifications – that such items as *Septem miracula de corpore Christi*, interpolated in the texts of the *Northern Homily Cycle* in both the Vernon and Simeon manuscripts, 'had very obvious anti-heretical connotations' (2013a: 95), responding to contemporary anxieties about the nature of the eucharist. Perry illuminatingly cites Nigel Saul's comments on monumental brasses: '[I]t is a truism of cultural history that the commissioning of prestige works can be indicative of anxiety. At one level, the raising of great monuments can attest confidence, pride and ambition; at the other it can betray insecurity and fear' (Saul 2001: 238, cited in Perry 2013a: 71). Indeed, Perry has even suggested that the whole enterprise of producing the Vernon manuscript reveals 'the perception of some sort of threat' (2013a: 70). Nevertheless, Vernon's contents do articulate with the wider shift to 'vernacular theology' that characterises religious expression in the late fourteenth and fifteenth centuries and of which Lollard texts in English were part (see e.g. Watson 1995, Gillespie 2007). The Vernon manuscript may be an egregious example of the form, but it is still a product designed for a broadly identifiable discourse community concerned with *sowlehele* 'soul-health', as flagged on the opening page of the volume, followed by a contents list (folio i r): 'Here bygynnen þe tytles off þe book þat is cald in latyn tonge salus anime. and in englyhs tonge sowlehele.'

One Vernon text, however, is somewhat unusual for the period (although not unparalleled, as we will see): a copy of the anonymous prose treatise *Ancrene Riwle*, which survives for the most part in a clutch of manuscripts dating from at least a hundred years before the Vernon manuscript, at around the time that the Lambeth Homilies, discussed at the end of the previous chapter, were copied.[2] The list of contents in the Vernon manuscript refers to this text as *Þe rule of reclouse*; it appears towards the end of the manuscript (folios 371v–392r), preceded by *A Talking of the Love of God* and *The pains of sin and the joys of heaven*.[3]

Ancrene Riwle was originally composed in the late twelfth/early thirteenth century, either by a Dominican friar or an Augustinian canon, as a guide to the anchoritic life for three female religious, but it was subsequently more widely circulated as the community grew, surviving not only in Middle English but also in Latin and French translations. Bella Millett has argued that the *Ancrene Riwle* is a 'dynamic' text whose 'continuing functionality was sometimes seen as more important than its textual integrity' (Millett 2005: xlv). This emphasis on the text's *mouvance* has been extensively pursued by Cate Gunn: 'it is not a product of religious context and literary construction belonging to a static point in time, but rather a work in process over the centuries' (Gunn 2008: 208).

A comparison of the Vernon *Ancrene Riwle* with earlier versions demonstrates that the later scribe did indeed make significant efforts to turn this by then archaic text into something more readable for his contemporaries. The Vernon text is most closely related in stemmatic terms to the copy of *Riwle* in London, British Library, MS Cotton Nero A.xiv, which dates from the middle of the thirteenth century; both texts seem to derive from a common lost ancestor (ζ) in the *stemma codicum* first suggested by Eric Dobson (1975), now slightly modified by Bella Millett (2005: xxix). There is also some evidence that the text as it survives in the Vernon manuscript has been influenced in some way by the most authoritative thirteenth-century witness for the work, Cambridge, Corpus Christi College, MS 402, i.e. there has been contamination of the Vernon/Nero tradition from the Corpus tradition, not only in substantive terms (as pointed out by Dobson) but even in terms of layout.

Whether this revision was the work of the Vernon scribe himself or of some reviser intermediate between Dobson's putative ζ and the Vernon

[2] As is well known, the *Ancrene Riwle* is often referred to as the *Ancrene Wisse* after the title given to it in one of its most important earlier witnesses, Cambridge, Corpus Christi College, MS 402, dating from the thirteenth century (see Tolkien 1962). To avoid confusion, and following usual practice, I will be referring to the work as *Ancrene Riwle* throughout, rather than using the name assigned it in the Corpus manuscript, or indeed the title *The Recluse*, by which the late versions are sometimes known. The following section builds on a preliminary study, that of Smith 2013a.

[3] *The pains of sin and the joys of heaven* also appears in Oxford, Bodleian Library, MS Bodley 938, and (interestingly) in Pepys 2498, discussed further below.

scribe is of course impossible to determine with certainty, unless some new manuscript of the work, a missing link between Vernon and Nero, were to emerge. However, whoever was responsible for them, the practices of revision as evidenced by the Vernon text are of considerable interest as examples of scribal updating. To demonstrate these changes, we might compare the beginning of Book 5 of *Ancrene Riwle* in two versions: Nero and Vernon. Texts (3.1) and (3.2) below offer transcriptions of short parallel passages; a translation appears beneath Text (3.2).

Text (3.1): London, British Library, Cotton Nero MS A.xiv, folio 80v

M onie kunnes fondunge beoð ine þisse uorme
dole. and misliche urouren. & moniuolde saluen.
vre lou*er*d ȝiue ou grace ðet heo moten ou helpen.
of alle þeo oðre. þeonne is schrift. ðe biheueste.
of hire schal beon þe vifte dole ase ich bihet þeruppe.
and nimeð ȝeme hu euerich dole; ualleð into oðer.
ase ich er seide. her biginneð ðe uifte dole of schrifte.
O f two þinges nimeð ȝeme of schrifte; iðe bigin
nunge. þet forme þing. of hƿuche mihte hit beo.
þet oðer þing. hƿuch hit schulle beon. þis beoð nu.
ase tƿo limes. and eiðer is to dealed. þe uorme; o
six stucchenes. ðe oðer; o sixtene. nu is þis of ðe uorme.
S chrift haueð monie mihtes. auh nullich of
alle; siggen buten sixe. þreo aȝean ðe deouel.
& þreo onont us suluen. schrift schent þene deouel.
& hackeð of his heaued. & todreaueð his ferde. schrift

[folio 81r]

ƿascheð us of alle ure fulðen. & ȝet us alle ure luren.
& makeð us* godes children. and eiðer haueð his þreo. **inserted above line*
preoue ƿe nu alle. þe ereste þreo beoð alle i scheaƿed
ine iudittes deden. Iudit ðet is schrift ase ƿas ȝeare iseid;
slouh oloferne. ðet is ðe ueond of helle. turn ðer uppe
ase ƿe speken of fuƿelene cunde. ðet beoð i efned
to ancre. heo hackede of his heaued. & seoððen co*m* and
scheaƿede hit to ðe buruh preostes. þeonne is ðe ueond
i schend. hƿonne me scheaƿeð i ne schrifte. alle his
cƿeadschipes.

Text (3.2): Oxford, Bodleian Library, Eng. poet. MS A.1 ('Vernon'), folio 385v, column 2

M ony cun*ne* fondynges. is I. þis feorþe Bok. Moni diu*er*se
su*nnus*. & moni maner saluen. Vr lord ȝiue ou grace

[folio 386r, column 1]

þat heo ow mote*n* helpen. Of alle þe oþ*ur*e þe*n*ne: is schrift þe
beste. Of hire schal ben þe fyfþe Bok. as ich bi heet þ*er*vppe.
And nymeþ ȝeme how vch a Bok. falleþ into oþ*ur*: as ich er seide.
Her beginneþ þe fyfþe Book.
T Wo þinges nymeþ ȝeme. of schrift. I.þe biginnynge.
þe ffurste: of whuch miht hit beo. ¶ þat oþur:
whuch hit schule ben. ¶ þeos beoþ. as two limen.
And eiþer is to delet ¶ þe ffurste. on sixe. ¶ þat
oþ*ur*: on sixtene parties ¶ Nou is þis: of þe furste.
S chrift haþ mony mihtes. Ac I.nulle of alle: sigge bote
sixe. ¶ þreo a ȝeyn þe deuel: and þreo on vs seluen.
chrift schent þe deuel. hakkeþ of his heued. And al to
dreueþ his strengþe. ¶ Schrift wasscheþ us: of alle vr fulþe*n*.
¶ ȝeldeþ us. alle ur leoren. ¶ Makeþ vs. Goddes children.
Eiþer haueþ his þreo. Preoue we nou alle. ¶ þe ffurste
þreo: beoþ alle I.schewede. in Iudith deeden. ¶ Iudith: þ[t]
is schrift. as was ȝare iseid. slouȝ Oloferne. þat is þe fend
of helle. Torn þ*er* vppe þer we speken of foulene kuynde.
þat beoþ I.liknet to Ancre. He hakked of his hed. And seþþ[e]
co*m* & schewede hit. to þe Borwh preostes. ¶ þe*n*ne is þe feond
I.schent: whon me scheweþ in schrift. al his quedschupus.

[Translation, with minor modifications to reflect Vernon text, after White 1993: 138–40:

There are many kinds of temptation in this fourth part, many diverse sins, and many sorts of remedies. May our Lord give you grace that they may help you. Of all the others then, confession is the most beneficial. The fifth Book will be about it, as I promised above. And take note how each Book flows into the next, as I said before.

Here begins the fifth Book.

Take note of two things about confession at the beginning. The first, what its power is; the second, what it must be like. These are like two limbs, and each is divided, the first into six, the second into sixteen parts. This now is about the first.

Confession has many powers, but I do not want to speak of them all, only six: three against the devil and three concerning ourselves. Confession puts the devil to shame, hacks off his head and routs his strength. Confession washes us of all our filthinesses, gives us back all our losses, makes us God's children. Each has its three parts: let us now demonstrate them all. The first three are all shown in Judith's deeds. Judith – that is, confession, as was said already – killed Holofernes – that is, the fiend of hell. Turn back to where we spoke of the nature of birds which are compared with anchoresses. She hacked off his head and afterwards came and showed it to the city priests. The fiend is then put to shame when all his wickednesses are shown in confession.]

Some of the linguistic differences between Nero and Vernon represent fairly straightforward updatings. The spelling of the Vernon *Riwle* is in line with that of the rest of the manuscript, and several of the usages differentiating Vernon from Nero represent a simple shift to a more current, if still fairly conservative, South-West Midlands orthographic usage. Thus, for instance, the obsolete letters eth <ð> and wynn <ƿ> have been replaced by thorn <þ> and <w> respectively, while the inherited Old English consonantal clusters <hƿ, cƿ> have been replaced by <wh, qu> respectively, e.g. Nero *hƿuche, cƿeadschipes* are reflected by *whuch, quedschupus* in Vernon. Nero's characteristic <ea> spellings are no longer used in Vernon, cf. Nero's *deadlich, aȝean, scheaped* as opposed to Vernon's *dedlich, aȝeyn, schewede.* Medial <u> for a presumed bilabial fricative in Nero's *louerd, heaued* disappears in Vernon's *lord, hed* (beside, however, *heued*). Initial and medial <u> in Nero is replaced by <f>, cf. Vernon's *biforen, fe(o)nd(es), fallep* for Nero's *biuoren, ueond(es), ualleð* etc. The <eo> spellings characteristic of South-West Midlands Middle English are restricted to rather fewer items in the later copy, e.g. *beoþ, þreo* (beside *þre*), *preoue, feond* (beside *fend*) alongside *þenne, seþþe, deuel* in Vernon, cf. in Nero *beoð, þeonne, deouel, ueond, seoððen.* However, forms highly diagnostic of the South-West Midlands, e.g. the medial <o> in *hƿon(ne)* (Nero), *whon* (Vernon) reflecting a rounding of an earlier /a/ in the environment of a following nasal, represent dialectal continuity. Certain morphological features are similarly common to both Nero and Vernon, e.g. *heo* for 'they', the weak plural nominal inflexions in *–en* in *honden, sunnen*, and the retention of the reflex of Old English *ge-* in *i-*, e.g. *I.schent* beside Nero's *i schend*; the deployment of the 'detached' morpheme *i-* found in both texts might be noted as another inherited feature.

Beside these comparatively modest differences in spelling, however, the Vernon text offers more radical differences from Nero in substantive readings, i.e. changes in vocabulary and syntax. Thus the word *ferde* 'army' (cf. Old English *fyrd*) is at one point replaced by the less metaphorical, but also less archaic, form *strengþe*, and at another point by *host* (although *feerde* is also retained half-way through the passage). Archaic *dole* is replaced by *Book*; archaic *onont* has been replaced by more commonplace *on; ȝet* is replaced by *ȝeldeþ; ereste* has been replaced by *ffurste; i efned* has been replaced by *I.likne, licamliche* by *bodiliche.* Vernon omits some archaic expressions altogether, e.g. Nero's *alle ðe uorrideles.* The native form *foes* is at one point replaced by *enemyes* – though *fo* is later retained – and *bitechen* is replaced by *bi taken.* More subtly, *nullich* is replaced by *I. nulle, so sone so* by *assone as, ðe hwule ðet* by *while*, and *uorto* by *to.*

Perhaps even more noticeably to the eye, however, the Vernon text is supplied with much more thoroughgoing punctuation than the early texts of *Ancrene Riwle* are. The pilcrow or paraph-mark, ¶, is used frequently throughout, varying with punctus, punctus elevatus and punctus interrogativus. The punctus and punctus elevatus are generally used to indicate commata and cola respectively, while the paraph-mark, often accompanied by a capital letter, is regularly deployed to signal the completion of a periodus. The punctus interrogativus, or question-mark, is occasionally deployed with 'rhetorical' questions, e.g. *Ho stod a ȝeyn him?* Capital letters are much more commonly found in Vernon than in Nero, and the beginning of the fifth book is marked by an inset title, not marked in Nero. As Roger Dahood pointed out in a pioneering article on the developing layouts of the *Ancrene Riwle* tradition, the Vernon scribe 'seems to have been especially concerned to make Part Five accessible for reference' (Dahood 1988: 96). The comprehensive scheme of punctuation provided by the Vernon scribe, much more extensive and substantial than in Nero, is clearly designed to help readers make sense of the text more easily.[4]

The presentation of the *Riwle* in the Vernon manuscript, therefore, both in the updating of spelling and morphology and in the more comprehensive system of punctuation, indicates a considerable degree of concern for making the text legible for the local or regional discourse community for which it was intended. The Vernon *Ancrene Riwle* has not been treated as a curiosity for antiquarians, but as a living work, with conventions for the work's presentation that differ from those deployed a century before. Whatever function the Vernon manuscript may have had, and however successful or unsuccessful it may have been in fulfilling that function, its revised version of the *Ancrene Riwle* suggests that it was conceived of as a repository of living, not dying, texts.

[4] It is interesting that Vernon's punctuation for verse differs from that for prose. Ian Doyle discussed the usage as follows:

> The punctuation of verse lines by the plain punctus and prose by punctus, punctus elevatus and punctus versus is so very consistent in the texts copied by the scribes A and B of both [Vernon and Simeon] . . . that it must have been either habitual to them or inserted beforehand in those of their exemplars which did not have it . . . Scribe A of [Simeon] is distinguished by his propensity for a punctus at the end of most of his verse lines, but employed with respect to sense. The customary repeated oblique thin pen stroke (//) in the left margin of lineated verse and in continuous verse or prose, with or without a punctus, is regularly used by each scribe for more pronounced pauses where a coloured paraph-sign ¶ was to be inserted in the course of decoration. (Doyle 1987: 5)

A second surviving late version of *Ancrene Riwle* appears in another important large miscellany: Cambridge, Magdalene College, MS Pepys 2498, part of the collection bequeathed to the college by the seventeenth-century diarist. The authoritative library catalogue (Beadle and McKitterick 1992) records nine substantial medieval items in this book. Of these items, several are translated from Anglo-Norman: an English version of the *Miroir* of Robert de Greetham; an exposition on the ten commandments preceded by an account of the pains of hell and the joys of heaven (a version of the latter also appears in the Vernon manuscript); an annotated Apocalypse; a prose *Complaint of Our Lady*; and a translation of the *Gospel of Nicodemus*. A Latin Psalter with an interlinear Middle English gloss is also included; the English text seems to be a translation not directly of the Latin but rather of a French original (see Black and St-Jacques 2012: lxvi–lxvii). Other texts are English in origin: a Gospel harmony, unique to the manuscript, which seems to have been used to introduce the translation of the *Miroir*; a clutch of short prayers at the end of the volume; and, placed between the glossed Psalter and the *Complaint*, the *Ancrene Riwle* in a modified form. Like the Vernon text, this version of the *Riwle* is given a title: *Þis good book Recluse*. The volume is a substantial one, albeit not as large as the Vernon manuscript. There are indications, though, that it was originally going to be even more impressive than it is: although the rubrication in the Psalter is complete, gaps have been left, marked by just small red guide letters, for what seem to have been planned as a series of elaborate historiated initials, flagged by an unfinished outline of an elaborated version of the 'B' in 'Beatus' (p. 263b), in the shape of a fish or sea-monster.

Pepys 2498 has received a great deal of attention in recent years, most notably in important discussions by Ralph Hanna (2005), who sees the book as a useful comparator for the contemporary Auchinleck manuscript of Middle English romances, now Edinburgh, National Library of Scotland, MS Advocates' 19.2.1: a book perhaps devised for a rather similar discourse community, albeit less piously inclined. Unlike Auchinleck, Pepys 2498 contains only devotional writings in prose. However, like Auchinleck, the Pepys manuscript seems to have been put together in London in the second half of the fourteenth century, drawing in many instances – again like Auchinleck – from materials that originated in the West Midlands. Moreover, the Pepys scribe is known to have copied at least two other manuscripts, now MSS London, British Library, Harley 874, and Oxford, Bodleian

Library Laud Misc. 622. The main text in Harley 874[5] is the annotated Apocalypse found in Pepys 2498, although set out in a rather simpler fashion; the Harley manuscript is carefully written, but decoration was restricted to the unshowy deployment of red initials, many of which were never inserted. In this context it is especially interesting that the Laud manuscript brings together the religious concerns of Pepys with the romance concerns of Auchinleck. The main text in Laud 622 is the romance of *Kyng Alisaunder* (folios 27v–64r), followed by a note of remarkable things and places to be seen by pilgrims to the Holy Land (folios 64r–64v), but other texts include *The Siege of Jerusalem* – possibly the most widely circulated alliterative poem apart from *Piers Plowman* – and *The Vision of St Alexius*, and four short works: Adam Davy's *Five Dreams about Edward II*, an incomplete *Temporale*, *Fifteen Tokens before the Day of Judgement* and *Lines on the Birth of Christ*. It may be noted that *Kyng Alisaunder* also appears in the Auchinleck manuscript, and indeed in appearance and layout Laud Misc 622 is very similar to Auchinleck. All four manuscripts are almost certainly 'products of the same London book-trade' (as Ralph Hanna has put it), and quite possibly the same community of practice. They are certainly aimed at similar discourse communities. Hanna considers that both Pepys 2498 and Auchinleck 'were produced for similar London audiences. In both ... the same activities of literary appropriation occur, for both are imitative products which present English texts derived from aristocratic Anglo-Norman environments' (Hanna 2005: 154). And of course all four manuscripts were identified by Michael Samuels back in 1963 as witnesses for Type II language. It seems fairly probable that further research into texts classified as Type II would lead to new insights into the development of what we might call a special scripta (see Chapter 1 above, section 1.3).

The text of the Pepys *Riwle* differs radically from that in other versions, and as a result its textual relationships are hard to establish; there are similarities to the Nero text, but also to another early version, the curious thirteenth-century London, British Library, MS Cotton Titus D.xviii, which underwent partial and somewhat clumsy revision for a male

[5] Images of Harley 874 are available from the British Library website: www.bl.uk/manuscripts/FullDisplay.aspx?ref=Harley_MS_874&index=164, last consulted on 23 June 2019.
The manuscript is now incomplete, ending with the beginning of 'St Michael III' from the *South English Legendary*; as the library catalogue flags, a catchword at the bottom of folio 31v indicates that at least one quire is missing. For the Auchinleck manuscript, see further Chapter 6 below.

audience (see Mack 1963: xv–xvii). However, there are also in Pepys 2498 unique deletions and some fairly substantial additions.

The major differences between the Pepys *Riwle* and the other versions were set out first by Eric Colledge in 1939. Traditionally, these changes have been seen as Lollard interventions, but Anne Hudson has pointed out that the additions include an exhortation on the need to observe the canonical hours, and tables on saints and church fathers – neither elements likely to be favoured by Lollards – and she also notes that the anchoritic way of life was something that Lollards specifically disfavoured. Hudson argues that

> it seems likely that this version of *Ancrene Riwle* has been through at least two stages of modification, the first by an orthodox reviser who added material reinforcing the intentions of the original author, the second by a perfunctory and unorthodox redactor who endeavoured rather sporadically to convert the text to a secular purpose. This does not explain the second reviser's perverse choice of text, but it does help towards resolving the apparent contradictions within the revision. (Hudson 1988: 28)

Of course, composition, possession and reading of vernacular texts could always attract suspicion, especially when indulged in by 'lesser' folk; it is no coincidence that the Earthquake Council of 1382 that condemned Wycliffe was of the view that heretical vernacular writings were involved in the Peasants' Revolt of the previous year (including famously a reference to *peres the plowman*, quite possibly to Langland's worryingly obscure poem; see further Hudson 1994, and also Chapter 4 below). Suspicion of vernacular religion reached its height in the period following the 1407–9 *Constitutions* of Archbishop Thomas Arundel,[6] which required the licensing of vernacular renditions of the Bible, including works of such impeccable orthodoxy as Nicholas Love's Gospel harmony *The Mirror of the Blessed Life of Jesus Christ* (a translation of the pseudo-Bonaventuran *Meditationes Vitae Christi*) (we will be returning to Love later in this chapter). Even Bishop Reginald Pecock (c. 1392–c. 1459), who undertook a programme of vernacular composition explicitly to 'counter the spread of heterodox ideas in Lollard books' (ODNB), could attract condemnation; in 1457, Pecock was forced to make a recantation of notions deemed heretical, and to take part in a public burning of his own writings.

[6] For the impact of Arundel's *Constitutions*, see most notably the essays collected in Gillespie and Ghosh 2011. The Earthquake Council was so called because its deliberations were indeed interrupted by an earthquake, taken by participants as a sign of God's displeasure. For the reception of *Piers Plowman*, see Chapter 4 below.

Vernacular devotion may be related to the efflorescence of personal piety that Eamon Duffy has identified as a positive characteristic of late medieval English religion (see Duffy 2005, especially 78–9); but, *pace* Duffy, such developments were as often challenged by the authorities as encouraged.

The most thoroughgoing recent interpretation of the Pepys *Riwle*, that by Ralph Hanna (2005), expands on these insights and addresses the question implicit in Hudson's statement. Hanna's study of the interpolated materials shows that whoever revised the work reshaped it in line with the rest of the contents of the manuscript as 'a prose biblical translation with commentary' (2005: 203). Thus, for instance, Hanna describes how the concluding section on 'the outer rule', appropriate for anchorites and found in the thirteenth-century versions, is replaced by apocalyptic material on the New Jerusalem, while – more radically – the role of *lewed folk* in 'salvific' (although not sacramental) activity is emphasised by interpolations in the fourth section of the work (on Temptations) (see Hanna 2005: 203–4, 207). It seems that, as with the Vernon manuscript, the Pepys texts represent another manifestation of vernacular theology, developing in parallel with Wycliffite writings and part of the same much wider discourse community, rather than within a specifically Lollard community of practice. Helen Spencer's comments on the Vernon text are relevant here: she argues that Vernon 'belongs to the period when there were still many ways, even apparently conflicting, of being orthodox' (in Zettersten and Diensberg 2000: xxii), and the same could be said of the Pepys *Riwle*.

Hanna describes how the 'Pepys scribe adjusts the original *Riwle* to bring the *mise-en-page* into accord with that of other manuscript contents, the prose Apocalypse and the Psalter' (2005: 203), but despite this attempt at textual homogenisation some rough edges remain. Arne Zettersten, in his edition of the Pepys *Ancrene Riwle*, notes that the text 'contains numerous errors due to the scribe's carelessness ... sometimes mistakes have been corrected by expunction, transposition marks, erasures etc. ... Although some of the errors must have been inherited from intervening manuscripts, the scribe must have been himself responsible for most of the mistakes' (Zettersten 1976: xx–xxi). It is noticeable that such mistakes are much more frequent in the scribe's copying of *Ancrene Riwle* than in other materials copied by the same hand. Geoffrey Smithers, for instance, who edited *Kyng Alisaunder* from the Laud manuscript, commented not only that '[c]orruption in [the Laud text of *Kyng Alisaunder*] is neither serious nor extensive' but that the copy 'and its antecedents are the work of scribes who were intelligent and who scrupulously refrained from rewriting difficult passages' (1957: 9). Moreover, elsewhere within the Pepys manuscript signs of correction are much less frequent; it seems that the copyist struggled with what must have been an archaic text. Text (3.3) is the passage in Pepys whose beginning is equivalent to that in Nero and Vernon (see Texts (3.1, 3.2) above). The substantive omissions and revisions are those in the original; the manuscript is paginated rather than foliated.

Text (3.3): Cambridge, Magdalene College, MS Pepys 2498, p. 425a

N Ow we schull telle of schrift two þinges
nymeþ ȝeme of schrift. þe first of which
miȝth it is. þat oþ*er* what it schulde be. Now
ichille dele þis on sextene p*ar*tyes as men
breken bred to childer þat bot ȝif þe bred wer*e*
broken to he*m* hij miȝtten dyen for hunger.
Schrift haþ many miȝttes. Ac ichil tellen bot
of sex þre to þe fende & þre to oure seluen
schrift schendeþ þe fende & toheweþ of his
heued & to dreueþ al his feerd. And our*e* seluen it wassheþ of al oure filþe. & ȝeldeþ vs
þat we hadde lorne & makeþ vs goddes
childer. Iudyf is schrift on oure tunge þ^t

[p. 425b]

is þe fende whan Men schewen her sy*n*nes to þe
p*re*est & ben sori þ*er*fore þan schenden hij þe fende
whan a Man is in wille to done his synnes
nomore þat raþer he wolde dyen & draweþ out
al þe rote þe likyng þan is his heued of.

Comparisons between the Pepys and Vernon texts show a general shared tendency to replace seemingly rare or archaic vocabulary. Like Vernon, Pepys replaces *dole* 'part' with *book(e)* throughout. Although Pepys retains *feerd* 'army' beside *ferde* (cf. Vernon *strengþe*), the rare form *gunfaneur* 'standard-bearer', evidenced in other early *Riwle* texts, is replaced by more commonplace – and still current – *baneoure* (cf. *gunfanuner* in Corpus 402, *Gunfaneur* in Titus and *gumfainuner* in London, British Library, MS Cotton Cleopatra C.6, another early *Riwle* manuscript); the older form is retained in Vernon as *Gonfanounner.*[7] The form *Iudyf/Iudif* for 'Judith' is a notable peculiarity in Pepys, not found in other versions. The form *nullich* in Nero is

[7] Interestingly, the only fourteenth-century citation of *baneoure* in the OED is from *Piers Plowman*, drawing attention to a connexion between Langland's poem and the Pepys manuscript.

reflected in Pepys not by *I.nulle* as in Vernon, but through a rephrasing: *Ac ichil tellen bot of sex*.

In linguistic accidentals, the spelling and morphology of the Pepys text represent a mid to late fourteenth-century London scripta of the kind first identified by Michael Samuels in 1963, and already referred to in Chapter 1 above: unsurprisingly so, since – as already briefly flagged – Samuels used the three manuscripts copied by the Pepys scribe, alongside the usage of the Auchinleck manuscript, as representatives of the focused linguistic variety which he referred to as 'Type II', and which we might now refer to, more loosely, as an emerging late fourteenth-century London literary scripta (see further Machan 2003 and references there cited). In Text (3.3) above, one of the forms especially flagged by Samuels as characteristic of Type II appears, namely, *hij* 'they'. Given the orthographic variation in a focused – as opposed to a fixed 'standard' – usage such as Type II, other forms that might be accommodated in this set are *nouȝth* 'not' and *aȝein* 'again' (cf. the forms *nouȝt*, *aȝen* similarly flagged by Samuels). Elsewhere in the text, other forms characteristic of Type II appear, e.g. *þat ilch* 'the same', *werlde* 'world', *þeiȝ* 'though', *stondende/stoondande* 'standing' (present participle), *noiþer* 'neither', *schuld(en)* 'should', *wil* 'will'. There are no <eo> spellings in Pepys – by the fourteenth century such forms are restricted to the West Midlands – but reflexes of Old English *y* in <u>, though generally seen as a western feature, continued to appear in London fairly frequently, e.g. in *ȝutt* 'yet'. The Midlands character of Type II is indicated by the *–eþ* (singular)/*–en* paradigms of the present tense verb, e.g. *schendeþ*, *bereþ* beside *schewen*, *schenden*. The plural inflexion of the noun in *–en* is reflected in Pepys by *–es* in *handes*, *synnes*, in line with present-day English, but the form of 'children' as *childer* (from Old English *cildru*) is more archaic. On the whole, however, the linguistic forms in Pepys seem to represent an updating in the direction of usages that were to become more commonplace later in the history of English. Just as the language of the Vernon text was being updated for a discourse community used to South-West Midlands usage, so the Pepys text was being modified for a burgeoning metropolitan readership.

At first sight, the system of punctuation in the Pepys *Ancrene Riwle* seems rather less developed than the Vernon usage, but closer inspection indicates that it is deployed according to a different, but still logical, system. We might first examine the decorated and engrossed letters occupying two lines that appear in the Pepys text, as at the beginning of Text (3.3):

> **N** Ow we schull telle of schrift two þinges
> nymeþ ȝeme of schrift. þe first of which

There are almost 500 such letters in the Pepys *Riwle*. Of these, some 420 are deployed at the beginning of the Latin quotations from the Bible, while the remainder are used for English, which confirms Hanna's view that the work has been reshaped as a prose translation/commentary on Latin texts positioned in prime place. The Latin engrossed letters appear pretty well throughout the text, while the English equivalent tend to appear in clusters: in the apocalyptic discussion added towards the end of the work, for instance, or for the list of sins, personified by animals, that appears in part 4 'On temptations', e.g. ***Þ****e Lyoun of pride* (p. 408a), ***Þ****e vnicorne of wraþþe* (p. 409b) etc. The paraph is often – although not always – used after the Latin quotations to introduce their corresponding English translations and 'commentaries'. Lesser capitals are deployed fairly consistently to mark clauses, often in conjunctions such as *Ac* or *And*, and less consistently in names, e.g. *Oloferne*. The only mark of punctuation deployed, fairly freely, in the Pepys *Riwle* is a punctus, sometimes alongside capitals, to mark medial or main pauses, i.e. cola and commata. The punctuation practice in the *Riwle* text is comparable with that found elsewhere in the manuscript,[8] suggesting that it was the scribe's own, and formed part of a homogenisation in textual presentation that underpins the book's design, as discussed by Hanna (2005). A further parallel is with the practice in English Wycliffite sermons of distinguishing meticulously between lections from scripture and other quotations: 'The care with which the lection's words are marked off obviously reflects Lollard concern for the precise words of scripture, and for the education of the laity and clergy in the discernment of authority' (Hudson and Gradon 1983: 135). Latin citations from scripture are presented in red ink, with the discussion set apart in black. Given the possible Lollard associations, the parallel is perhaps significant: ideas about layout may have been borrowed even if the scribe did not want to engage with potentially unorthodox ideas about theology.

The Pepys manuscript was annotated in the sixteenth century by Stephen Batman, chaplain to Archbishop Parker, and so had the afterlife in the Parker circle described in Chapter 2 above. Batman was part of John

[8] There is one exception in the Pepys manuscript: in the prose Psalter text, the paraph-mark/pilcrow, punctus elevatus and a mark rather like a modern comma are used, and the punctus is not found. However, the Psalter is unusual in the manuscript because of the distinctive and complex alternation between rubricated Latin and a plain text in English, which would present challenges to the scribe as he undertook the stint, and distinct practices of punctuation would seem there to make sense.

Joscelyn's team and claimed in that capacity to have collected some 6,700 books for Parker (see Summit 2008: 109). He was also a significant antiquarian in his own right, whose annotations have been identified so far in some thirty medieval manuscripts (Parkes 1997b, Edwards and Horobin 2010, Horobin and Nafde 2015, Kraebel 2015); Tony Edwards and Simon Horobin have flagged 'the breadth of [Batman's] denominational and geographical reach' (2010: 231), which included access to the libraries of a variety of religious houses ranging from Yorkshire to Somerset. The markings in the surviving Batman manuscripts, as we might expect from someone in Parker's circle, offer a protestant commentary on the past, comparable with that to be found in Joscelyn's preface to *A testimonie of antiquitie*. Batman's *The Doome Warning All Men to Iudgement* (1581) is especially valuable as an explicit insight to the mindset of Parker's circle, who saw 'the past as supplying not only precedents but portents' (Parkes 1997b: 129).

Batman's annotations in Pepys 2498 have been discussed most thoroughly by Kate McLoughlin (1994), to whose important article further reference should be made. Most of Batman's markings in the manuscript appear alongside *The Mirror*, but some in the text of the *Riwle*. Above the opening of the latter, for instance, he writes 'The Canticle vpon the Masse, worth the keping, to Answer therr wilfull blindnes. &c. svmwhat strainge'; in this example, *therr* clearly refers to roman catholics. Other additions are in a similar vein, including the italic annotation *you fayle* next to an explicit discussion of transubstantiation (p. 377a). Most substantially, he wrote a twenty-line poem on a blank page immediately after the translation of Greetham's *Mirror* and preceding the *Riwle* (p. 370b), which includes the following stanza:

The first part is veri good
thowghe a worde or two doo varie
The second is not sound
smaule truthe dooth carie
Yet as the one. without the other thow cannot bee
Else falshod with trwthe mixed thow cannot see.

Intriguingly, Batman uses a variety of scripts, ranging from an italic hand in his annotations to imitations of Anglo-Saxon script based on that devised in Parker's circle – as we saw in Chapter 2 – for the 'counterfeiting' of Old English texts. Thus the word *first* in the stanza quoted above appears with the distinctive Old English forms of <f>, <r>, <s> and <t>, very similar to the forms adopted in Day's printing of *A testimonie*; such forms do not appear in the medieval script in Pepys 2498, and represent therefore an archaistic and anachronistic telescoping of the past, an evocative visualisation of imagined earlier expression. Other stanzas appear in imitations of the Pepys hand's anglicana script (reproducing Pepys's form of the archaic letter yogh), of the roman font favoured by humanist printers and of a more contemporary secretary script (for an illustration, see McLoughlin 1994: plate 13). This virtuoso evocation of both the past and the modern not only aligns Batman with the distinctive community of practice associated with Parker's network but also encapsulates rather neatly the complexity of reactions to the medieval past current in Elizabethan England.

Batman's response is part of the artefactual afterlife of Pepys 2498, but the *Riwle* text in the manuscript, of course, like the Vernon version of the same work, was already an example of dynamic textual *mouvance*, showing a repurposing of older material for a new function. At this point, therefore, it is worth asking what those functions might have been. Hanna's comment on the Pepys manuscript seems very probably also relevant for Vernon: 'So imposing a volume seems explicable only as a lectionary or as a stationary reference volume, for group use in a household or chapel' (Hanna 2005: 153). Such a setting aligns, moreover, with the suggestion that Vernon was probably 'couched' on a lectern as an accessible spiritual encyclopedia (Robinson 1990: 26 and references there cited).

Such a setting is in some ways rather like that in which the *Riwle* was originally delivered: the intimate, conversational style of the text as it survives in the early manuscripts, with its repeated appeals to *mine leoue sustren*, suggests an oral setting. But the distinctive features of the two fourteenth-century manuscripts suggest some differences as well. First, each book contains a substantial library of diverse texts, representing comparatively extensive programmes of reading. We can expect the thirteenth-century manuscripts of *Ancrene Riwle* to have been continually reread, at the heart of the anchoritic life; the *Riwle* texts in Pepys and Vernon were simply one amongst many possibilities for devotional reading in the pious households – the discourse communities, Hanna's 'groups' – for which they were so carefully prepared, in line with the 'aural' setting described by Joyce Coleman (1996) and discussed in Chapter 1. We know, for instance, that devotional reading at mealtimes was a family activity encouraged in the Beauchamp circle: 'Let the book be brought to the table as readily as the bread. And lest the tongue speak vain or hurtful things, let there be reading, now by one, now by another, and by your children as soon as they can read . . . Expound something in the vernacular which may edify your wife and others' (cited in Perry 2007: 156, and see references there cited; the document in which this passage occurs was probably written for John Throckmorton, head of council for Richard Beauchamp (1382–1489), Earl of Warwick).Such behaviour was clearly possible in humbler households than Throckmorton's or Beauchamp's. When the suspected heretic Joan Baker was quoted, in the early sixteenth century, as saying that 'she cold here a better sermond at home in hur howse than any doctor or prist colde make at Powlis crosse or any other place', she seems to be referring to a communal experience (cited in Hudson 1996: 132). Bishop Reginald Pecock (d. in or after 1459), who undertook a programme of vernacular composition to 'counter the spread of heterodox ideas in Lollard books' (ODNB), saw the reading and rereading of such texts as permitting 'the layman to memorize a fixed set of words which he could then repeat to others without distorting the information' (Spencer 1993: 41); Pecock himself refers – albeit as devotional practices less effective than the contemplation of images – to 'the hearing of other men's reading, or ... hearing of his own reading', thus 'assum[ing] the *speaking* of books' (Aston 1984: 114, and references there cited; see also Swan 2010, cited in Chapter 2 above).

And, secondly, the Vernon and Pepys are much more physically substantial than the thirteenth-century manuscripts of the *Riwle*. Whereas the earlier books are quite small, even pocket-sized, the fourteenth-century codices are designed to impress the onlooker with their appearance. Vernon's opulence was underlined by its lavish programme of illustration; although the programme of decoration was not completed, the Psalter text at least in Pepys was clearly intended to have a similarly elaborate appearance. The Paternoster page in Vernon referred to earlier in this chapter only 'works' visually. Avril Henry's description, already cited, is worth repeating: 'though it is at once apparent to the surveying eye, words can only distort the effect by giving temporal precedence to one or other element' (1990: 90). The splendour of the book, and of its companion the Simeon manuscript, has been described as 'carry[ing] symbolic meaning ... proclaim[ing] something semiotically, as objects which synthesized potent physical form with devotionally efficacious textual contents' (Perry 2013a: 73).

Both differences perhaps account for the change in the practices of punctuation between the Nero *Riwle* on the one hand and the Vernon and Pepys versions on the other. In an intensive reading culture such as that for which Nero seems to have been prepared readers would have become deeply acquainted with the text through repeated perusal and/or utterance. Now, when texts are read repeatedly, they become *aides-*

mémoire rather than opportunities for encounters with new information, and intensive reading cultures typically place less emphasis on punctuation. Thus (it could be argued) such performers were not only part of the audience – the discourse community – for whom the text had been designed, but also of the community of practice participating creatively in the text's delivery.

However, Vernon and Pepys represent distinct approaches to text that reflect new uses and practices of literacy. Vernon is because of its size 'not . . . an easy book for a reader to find his or her way about in' (Robinson 1990: 16), so the more help on hand the better. Pepys's principle of organisation, i.e. as a work focused on Bible commentary, seems to have driven the kind of punctuation practices in the *Riwle* that made distinguishing scriptural citation and commentary comparatively straightforward, including a comprehensive system of rubrication that is naturally visual. Both manuscripts were designed to be looked at as well as listened to. Moreover, the punctuation in both manuscripts reflects, it might be argued, the emergence of a new, more extensive or varied culture of vernacular devotion; both manuscripts contain a substantial – in Vernon's case, very substantial – number of texts. In more extensive reading cultures, where readers regularly encounter new and varied forms of text, more guidance is needed, and, as a result, more comprehensive programmes of punctuation are required. Comparison of the early, somewhat sparsely punctuated texts, such as Nero, with that in later texts of the *Riwle* seems to demonstrate such a step-change. The fuller punctuation of the *Riwle* in Vernon and Pepys would seem to show the repurposing of an old text for a discourse community where literacy was – no doubt uncertainly – becoming more extensive: a response which is both traditional (drawing upon an older text) and innovative (presenting that text in a new way).

3.2 The Afterlife of Thomas Wimbledon's *Sermon*

In Chapter 2 we saw how Ælfric's homily on Easter Day was repurposed in the 1566 edition of *A testimonie of antiquitie* in support of the reformed interpretation of transubstantiation. But this latter publication, though the first early modern work to engage with Anglo-Saxon culture, was by no means the first to look to the past as a 'witness preordained by God, so many years before us, for the confirmation of our doctrine'.[9] Margaret

[9] A quotation from Martin Luther's preface to an edition of the *Commentarius in Apocalypsin* (Wittenberg, 1528), which itself derived from an abbreviated version of a Latin Lollard work (*Opus*

Aston and Anne Hudson have ably described how reworkings of Wycliffite materials in particular were produced throughout the sixteenth century, as perceived precursors of the new style of religion. For instance, *The Examination of Master William Thorpe*, an account of the interrogation of a Lollard by Archbishop Thomas Arundel, survives in Oxford, Bodleian Library, MS Rawlinson C.208 from the early fifteenth century. This text was subsequently printed in Antwerp in 1530, and later incorporated (as chapter 91) into John Foxe's *Acts and Monuments* (1563).

The Vernon and Pepys versions of *Ancrene Riwle* were therefore not the only medieval English attempts to update older material. As Fiona Somerset has aptly pointed out, 'late medieval religious writing in England more generally had magpie tendencies, prompted or facilitated by the circulation of loose leaves and unbound booklets from which material could readily be recopied or excerpted within other books' (Somerset 2013: 74). Examples of such practices abound. For instance, parts II and III of *Ancrene Riwle* were reworked as a treatise on the five senses in London, British Library, MS Royal 8 C.i (for which see Baugh 1956), while echoes of the *Riwle* seem to underlie works printed by Wynkyn de Worde at the end of the fifteenth century: *The Treatise of Love* and *The Chastising of God's Children* (see for instance Blake 1972: 174). Lollard versions of older texts include not only (possibly, as we have seen) the Pepys *Riwle* but also 'farced' versions of Richard Rolle's *English Psalter Commentary* and of John Thoresby's so-called *Lay Folks' Catechism* (see Hudson 1985). Such works represent what Somerset has called 'a textual culture of creative adaptation' (2013: 89). The reworking of the Pepys *Riwle* is thus not alone.

The most radical reworkings of religious material, naturally, took place in iterative relation to broader social developments: 'the enhanced prestige of English, the interests of an increasingly literate laity in more advanced matters of theology than the rudiments of Christian behaviour, and dissatisfaction with the Church, expressed by orthodox and heterodox alike' (Spencer 1993: 14). Numerous examples demonstrating these trends may be identified, such as the appearance of 'common profit' books designed for

Arduum). Luther's words are cited in a foundational study by Anne Hudson (1983: 174, after Aston 1964: 157). See further Aston 1984: 227 and Hudson 1978. Key further reference points for this discussion are Spencer 1993 and Walsham 2007. George Hickes's comments, in a letter from 1714, are in this context relevant: 'I know not any work an antiquary can do more serviceable to the Church than this, which will show the faith and other chief doctrines of the English-Saxon Church to be the same as ours, and perfectly answer that never ending question, "Where was your church before Luther?"' (cited in Barker 2002: 210).

sharing vernacular works of devotion, such as John Colop's collection of mystical and Lollard texts, now Cambridge, University Library, MS Ff.6.31 (see Scase 1992), or the widely circulated, and apparently orthodox, 'vernacular libretto' for the liturgy now known as *The Lay Folks' Mass Book* (for which see Jasper and Smith 2019, and references there cited). Such works as the latter catered for the habit, referred to both in writing and occasionally in manuscript illustration, whereby the laity either followed books during church services – something that has even been related to the growth in the size of windows in fifteenth-century church architecture (Spencer 1993: 39) – or, as preparation for their witnessing of the liturgy, undertook a programme of pious reading and reflexion.[10]

Catering for such practices were books of sermons, such as the reformist Wycliffite Sermon Cycle or the more orthodox *Festial* of John Mirk. Such books were initially designed as reference points for the clergy, either as scripts for direct delivery or as prompts (it seems) for more extempore oral performance. However, such books developed what Helen Spencer has called 'an afterlife as private reading' (Spencer 2004: 152). Elsewhere, Spencer has pointed out that such an 'afterlife bestowed on sermons when they are published befogs the distinction between sermons and treatises, between public preaching and private teaching' (1993: 33). Thus a work such as the English translation of St Edmund of Abingdon's *Speculum Ecclesie* in London, British Library, MS Additional 10053 could be referred to as *þe sermon*, while appearing as *a tretijs* in another, considerably smaller manuscript clearly designed for much more intimate use: Oxford, Bodleian Library, MS Douce 25 (for which latter, see Wakelin 2018: 44–6). 'Private reading' – 'an important complement to hearing Christian doctrine in sermons' (Spencer 1993: 40) – was, as we have seen in Pepys 2498, something undertaken by the pious laity as well as clergy (Duffy 2005: 53–87), either in a small social situation, such as a family at mealtime, or even as an act of solitary perusal. Susan Powell has argued that her two principal textual groupings of manuscripts of John Mirk's *Festial*, Group A and Group B, reflect this contrast between sermon and treatise, i.e. respectively a text devised primarily for preaching and one devised

[10] It should be noted that the manuscripts containing *The Lay Folks' Mass Book* are – with the exception of the 'holster book' that is now Edinburgh, National Library of Scotland, MS Advocates' 19.3.1 – bulky volumes, not easily portable; see further Jasper and Smith 2019. A better candidate for portable use as a 'vernacular libretto' might be Oxford, Bodleian Library, MS Wood empt. 17, a small sixteenth-century book containing 'B. Langforde's' vernacular *Meditatyons for goostly exercyse, in the tyme of the masse*. The *Meditatyons* is the only text in the manuscript (see further Aston 1984: 123). For a discussion of punctuation practices in Mirk's *Festial*, see Smith 2013b.

primarily for private use of the kind just described. Interestingly, the printed editions of Mirk's *Festial* are based on the 'treatise'-like Group B (Powell 2009: l, lv). There are strong associations between the early printers and religious foundations – for example, Wynkyn de Worde, and perhaps William Caxton himself, with the wealthy Bridgettine convent of Syon Abbey (Powell 1997: 48–77, especially 57–8); however, it is clear that printers aimed to maximize their income through 'widening [the] appeal' of such texts for 'a lay as well as religious clientele' (Powell 1997: 58).

Such reworkings could take radical or conservative form, and were clearly given substantial extra impetus by the appearance of print technology during the fifteenth century. Revision of such materials could be very substantial, as when, for instance, Chaucer's *Canterbury Tales* was transformed – it seems – into a 'reformist' text by the addition, a century after the poet's death, of the spurious *Plowman's Tale*. However, subtler changes in format are similarly linked to social trends. In this context, works that span the transition from script to print are especially significant, and it is to such items that we might now turn.

Perhaps the most widely circulated of these repurposed works – although it should not, as we will see, be easily pigeonholed as 'Wycliffite' or 'Lollard' – is Thomas Wimbledon's *Sermon*, first preached at Paul's Cross in 1387–8. This work, usually referred to by its opening Latin text, *Redde rationem villicationis tue* ('Give an account of your stewardship'), begins with the Biblical parable of the vineyard, from Matthew 20, and then goes on to attack contemporary social abuses, notably by the clergy. The *Sermon* was, in Alexandra Walsham's words, 'an uncompromising dissection of the vices of English society and an urgent call to amendment of life' (2007: 630). Paul's Cross was a high-profile location, and – though surprisingly little is known about Thomas Wimbledon – the work is a skilled example of its kind, demonstrating 'new-style' scholastic sermonising carefully structured around key points.

Such an attack on clerical misdemeanours was not unprecedented at the time; indeed, there are clear thematic parallels with Langland's *Piers Plowman*, 'straddl[ing] the porous and unstable boundary between "orthodoxy" and "heterodoxy" that must be seen as a defining feature of this era' (Walsham 2007: 639). Nevertheless, there were tensions throughout the latter half of the fourteenth century that meant Wimbledon's *Sermon* had the potential – as did, as we will see in Chapter 4, *Piers Plowman* – to be an insurgent or socially destabilising text. Six years beforehand, the kind of abuses identified by Wimbledon had fed into the Peasants' Revolt, and – as we have already seen – works such as Wimbledon's, like Langland's, may have been in the minds of the participants of the Earthquake Council of 1382.

However, Archbishop Arundel, in his *Constitutions* of 1407–9, was to forbid priests from criticising clerical faults before lay audiences, which – perversely, from Arundel's point of view – made Wimbledon's *Sermon* attractive to those with reformist ideas; it is no accident that the text appears, for instance, in the pious miscellany that is now Cambridge, Sidney Sussex College, MS 74, alongside a Wycliffite Sermon Cycle and treatises on the Angelus and the Incarnation (see Hudson 1988: 426; see also Somerset 2013). Several of the many fifteenth-century manuscripts of the *Sermon* that survive were annotated by evangelicals, who often added Biblical cross-references, e.g. in Oxford, Bodleian Library, MS Hatton 57. Ione Kemp Knight, who published in 1967 the standard modern critical text of the work, identified fifteen medieval manuscript copies (including two translations into Latin) and eighteen sixteenth- and seventeenth-century individual editions; the work was also incorporated (significantly) into John Foxe's *Acts and Monuments* (1563) and Joseph Morgan's *Phoenix Britannicus* (1732). Judging by the entries in the *Linguistic Atlas of Late Mediaeval English* (LALME), the *Sermon* seems to have had a wide circulation; the language of individual manuscripts has been localised widely across the southern half of England, ranging from Essex to Northamptonshire. Although of course the localisation of a language does not necessarily mean that texts were physically written there (scribes, after all, were mobile), this range of dialectal usages is suggestive of substantial societal reach.[11]

[11] Of the thirteen Middle English copies of the *Sermon*, LALME localises the linguistic profiles of six: Cambridge, Sidney Sussex College, MS 74 (LP705, Northamptonshire); London, British Library, MS Additional 37677 (= LALME LP6170, Essex); London, British Library, MS Harley 2398 (= LP7200, Gloucestershire); London, British Library, MS Royal 18 B.xviii (LP6751, Berkshire); Oxford, Bodleian Library, MS Hatton 57 (= LALME LP6690, Buckinghamshire); San Marino, Huntington Library, MS HM 502 (= LALME LP4675, Warwickshire). Two other manuscripts are flagged in LALME as having localisable language: Cambridge, Trinity College, MS B.14.38 (322) (hand 1: Somerset, hand 2: Lincolnshire), and Oxford, University College, MS 97 (Staffordshire). The language of the remaining manuscripts was not localised for LALME: Cambridge, Corpus Christi College, MS 357; Cambridge, Magdalene College, MS Pepys 2125; London, British Library, MS Royal 18 A.xvii; and two manuscripts once at Helmingham Hall, Suffolk, MSS LJ II.2 and LJ II.9 (now in a private collection and Oxford, Bodleian Library, Eng. th. f.39 respectively, for which see Edwards and Griffiths 2000). Corpus 357 was the basis for Knight's edition. Royal 18 A.xvii was in Wales by the sixteenth century, judging by ownership inscriptions written in Welsh, but my short examination of the opening of the text suggests that the language is East Midlands in character, with nothing diagnostic of a more precise localisation. A brief analysis of Pepys 2125 suggests a possible localisation of the language on the Monmouth–Shropshire border, with *meny* 'many', *shulleþ* 'shall' (plural) and the infinitive *hyry* 'hire' with a retained *–y* ending reflecting an Old English weak class II verb. I have not been able to examine the Helmingham texts.

London, British Library, MS Harley 2398 is a late fourteenth-century collection of devotional writings, including an important treatise on the ten commandments with an anonymous citation from Wycliffe on the problematic character of images (see Aston 1984: 153–5); John Wycliffe's tract 'Of wedded men, and wyves and children also' appears later. Other texts include treatises on the five senses and on visiting the sick. Wimbledon's *Sermon* is the third item in the book. Text (3.4) is a transcription of its opening. The first three lines are written in textura, with red underlining; the remainder of the text is in anglicana, save for the paraph-marks in alternating red and blue. In appearance the book rather resembles Pepys 2498 and Harley 874, although its dimensions are considerably smaller. The language has been localised by LALME to Gloucestershire.

Text (3.4): London, British Library, Harley MS 2398, folio 140r

Sermo mag*istr*i Thome Wymyldou*n* apud crucem in
cimiterio Sancti Pauli londou*n*
R   Edde racionem villicacionis tue. lucas 16mo.
My dere frendes ȝe schulleþ vnderstonde þat
crist Ih*esu* auctor & doctor of treuþe in his boke
of gospel lyknynge þe kyngdome of heuene
to an housholder Seyþ in þis man*ere*. lyke is þe kyngdome
of heuene to an housholdenge man þat wente out first at
þe morwe to hyre workemen into his vyneȝerd. ¶ Al So
aboute þe þrydde / Sexte / nynþe & elleueþe hours he wen=
te oute & fonde men stondynge ydele & Seyde to hem goþ
ȝe in to my vyneȝerd & þat ryȝt is .I. schal ȝyue to ȝow
Whan þe day was a go. he clepede his Styward & hete to
ȝyue eche man a peny. ¶ To Spiritual vnderstondyn=
ge þis housholdere is oure lord ih*esu* crist þat is þe heued
of al þe housholde of holy churche & þus clepeþ men in
dyu*erse* hours of þe day þat is in diu*erse* agys of þe world
as in tyme of lawe of kynde he clepede inspiryng Abel
& Ennok// Noe & Abraham. ¶ In tyme of þe ol=
de lawe// Moyses/ dauyd/ ysaye & Ieremye. & in tyme
of grace apostels martyres confessours & virgynes.//
Also he clepyþ many men in diuerse agys. So*m*me in chil=
dehode as Ioh*an*n Baptiste. So*m*me in state of wexynge/

[folio 140v]

as Joh*a*n þe Eu*a*ngeliste. So*m*me in State of manhede as pe=
tre & Andrewe & Some in olde age as Gamalyel & Ioseph
of Aramathie & þes he clepeþ to trauaille in þis vyne þat
is þe churche & þat on dyuerse man*ere*.

The earliest printed edition of Wimbledon's *Sermon* appeared in 1540–1, at a moment of special tension between evangelicals and conservatives that included Archbishop Cranmer's abortive proposal for a revised set of homilies for use in the newly reformed church (MacCulloch 1996: 293). It is perhaps not surprising therefore that the first edition of Wimbledon's potentially provocative writings should be printed anonymously, even though its title page proudly proclaims it to be produced *CVM privilegio ad imprimendum solum*. This title page offers a blend of 'old' and 'new' in its typography: a mixture of blackletter and roman font, with decorative hederae or ivy leaves. The hedera – the oldest-known punctuation symbol, regularly appearing in inscriptions from antiquity – was deployed by the great Venetian printer Aldus Manutius as his trademark: a sign of humanism, flagging that the work is being repurposed for a discourse community engaged with the 'new learning'. This mixture of old and new is clearly reflected in the text, which the title page flags as authoritative, 'Nether addyng to, neyther demynyshynge fro, Saue tholde and rüde Englysh therof mended here and there'; a diaresis over <u> in *rüde* is presumably an antiquarian archaistic ornament, while the reference to 'mending' the English language recalls the kind of thing William Caxton, a generation before, was calling for in his Preface to the *Eneydos*. The blackletter Preface is explicit:

> Lo christen reader, whyle the worlde not slombred, but routed, & snorted in ye depe, and deed slepe of ignorau*n*cy some lyuely spirites were wakyng, and ceasede not to calle vpon the drousy multitude of men, & to stire them vp from the longe dreames of synfull lyuynge, that ones at the laste they wolde crepe out of darkenes and come forth to the hote shynynge sonne of Gods worde, that bothe ye fylthy mystes of theyr hertes myght be dryuen away, and also theyr heuye and dyinge spirites, recreated, refreshed, and quickened. (sig. A.i.v)

The opening of the *Sermon* in the 1540–1 print appears as Text (3.5). The Latin inscription *Redde rationem uillicationis tue* and marginal annotations are in roman font, but the body of the English text is blackletter, with the opening line of the *Sermon* engrossed. The initial <C> is, as flagged in the transcript, decorated.

Text (3.5) [Wimbledon] (1540–1: sig. A.iii r)

Luc. XVI
Redde rationem uillica=
tionis tue.

C hrist the authoure Mat.xx
and doctour of all tru-
the: in his boke gospell, lyke-
nethe the kyngdome of
heaue*ne*: to a housholder:
seying on this wyse: Lyke is the
kyngdome of heauen, to a housholdynge man, that went forthe first at
in the mornynge, to hyre workeme*n*
into his vyneyard: so dyd he about
the thyrde houre, the syxth, y[e] nynth
and the eleuenth And as he found:
men standynge ydle, he sayd to the*m*:
why stande ye here vnoccupied: Go
ye into my vyneyard and that that
is dewe ye, I shall gyue you. And
when the day was ended, he called
hys stewarde & badde that he shuld
gyue euery man a penye. Spiritually this housholder is our master

[sig. A.iii v]

and Lord Christ the true housholder, and heed of his churche here in
erth: which callethe men in dyuers
houres of the day that is in dyuers
ages of the worlde. As in the tyme
of nature, he called by inspiration,
Abel: Enoch, Noe, Abraham and o-
ther lyke. In tyme of the olde lawe,
he called Moses, Dauid, Esay and
Jeremy, with the prophetes. And
in the tyme of grace he called the a-
postles, martyrs, confessours and
virgyns. He calledde also some in
childehoode, as John Baptyste.
Some in theyr youth, as John the
Euangelyst, some in middleage, as
Peter and Andrew: Some in their
latter dayes, as Gamaliel, and Joseph of Arimathye. And all those be
called to laboure in the Lordes vyneyarde: that is hys churche. Yea
and that sondry wayes.

Although examination of the collations supplied by Knight's edition seems to suggest that the 1540–1 edition was derived from a lost exemplar, the differences between the first edition and the Harley manuscript are suggestive. Some differences – as suggested by the printed edition's title page – seem to be replacements of archaisms, e.g. *called* for the older form *clepede*, and possibly *youth* for *state of wexynge* (although the verb *wax* 'grow' remains well attested in early modern English), but others are simply substitutions for rarer forms that are not necessarily more old-fashioned, e.g. *on this wyse* and *sondry weyes* for *in þis manere* and *dyuerse manere*, or *laboure* for *trauaille*. By contrast, the punctuation displays significant updating; corresponding in the printed edition to the virgule and punctus in Harley is a fairly wide repertoire of usages, including punctus, double punctus, comma-mark and punctus interrogativus, illustrated by the following line: 'he sayd to them: why stande ye here vnoccupied? Go ye into my vyneyard and that that is dewe ye, I shall gyue you.'

Other sixteenth- and seventeenth-century versions of the *Sermon* are all based on the 1540–1 print, beginning with the same introductory discussion, although there are some interesting minor changes in content and format. The version in John Foxe's *Acts and Monuments* (1563), printed – like *A testimonie* – by John Day, was clearly based on the 1540–1 edition, even down to reproducing the heading with the introductory hedera. Foxe was keen in the first edition of the *Acts* to connect his discussion to a higher-profile figure than Wimbledon, and in his new blackletter introduction claimed that the work 'seemeth to be of Wickleffes doing' (1563: 175); however, in later editions he withdrew this claim and reassigned the work to Wimbledon. The text itself that followed was in roman typeface, emphasising its contemporary significance.

A more notable change appears in the title page of John Awdeley's 1575 edition (in contrast with his earlier edition of 1573), where the adjective *GODLY* – a distinctively evangelical–protestant usage – was interposed at the top of the page in roman capitals to describe the *Sermon* and announce its perceived confessional connexion. Archaic-looking blackletter was varied with a more extended use of 'modern' roman font, blending the old and the new, and thus advertising the printer's virtuosity, as was the custom; but Awdelay's seems to have been the first edition to emphasise the text's subversive intention by claiming that it was *found out beyng hyd in a wall*. Awdeley underlined the point by repeating *godly(e)* and the claim of its being *found in a wall* both in the heading of the *Sermon* proper (sig. A.iii r) and as a running head throughout the book. Awdeley, who, according to his ODNB entry, 'apparently drove a thriving trade' that included a mixture of ballads, news sheets and larger works, clearly knew his market. His printing of Wimbledon's *Sermon* also aligns with his interest in situating the Elizabethan settlement within a historical context, otherwise exemplified by his publication of a work composed by himself: *The Wonders of England* (1559), a poem that 'demonstrated Elizabethan concern with English history and its situation within a natural order' (ODNB).

Awdelay's combination of *godly* and *found in a wall* persisted in some early modern copies, although *godly* disappeared from the title page, as the word seems to have become increasingly recognised as a puritan – and thus potentially problematic – signifier. Later printers included John Charlewood, James Roberts and William Jaggard, the last being better known as the printer of the 1623 First Folio of the works of William Shakespeare. These men all formed a distinct social network, with a claim to being a community of practice. Charlewood had inherited much of Awdeley's materials, Roberts married Charlewood's widow and Jaggard was Roberts's partner from around 1604, taking over the business when Roberts retired in 1606; their edition of Wimbledon's *Sermon* appeared in 1617. The 1635 edition of the *Sermon* printed in London by Thomas Cates retained a modified form of Awdeley's phraseology (*found out in a wall*), and although Cates dropped *godly* from the title page he kept it in the running head and in the heading of the *Sermon* proper.

By contrast with members of the Charlewood circle, surprisingly little is known of the historian Joseph Morgan, who included the *Sermon* in his short-lived periodical, *Phoenix Britannicus: being a Miscellaneous Collection of Scarce and Curious Tracts*, which was published for only six numbers in 1731–2. Morgan's ODNB entry is brief, consisting for the most part of a list of his writings, and the only extended study of his career (Thomson 1995) focuses on his sympathetic engagement with Islamic culture, notably in his *Complete History of Algiers* (1731) and *Mahometism Fully Explained* (1723–5); Morgan was clearly a man interested in cross-cultural differences, both diatopic and diachronic. The prefatory dedication to the *Phoenix Britannicus* suggests an extra aspect of his career, however. The collection was dedicated to Charles Duke of Richmond and Lenox, a prominent Whig who served loyally in the 'King's' ministries of the first half of the eighteenth century. Richmond's interests ranged widely, as a patron of the arts and especially as a sportsman, but the connexion Morgan especially flags was Richmond's appointment, in 1724, as master of the Grand Lodge of Freemasons in England; Morgan's preface refers to 'that worthy

Fraternity, whereof I have the Happiness of being a *Member*' (1732: iii). It is clearly for a Masonic discourse community that *Phoenix Britannicus* was presented. Although Freemasons trace their origins to the founding of King Solomon's Temple, they were – and indeed remain – profoundly interested in medieval topics.[12] It is no surprise therefore that Morgan was interested in a medieval text such as Wimbledon's *Sermon*, which appears as the first item in *Phoenix Britannicus*.

The text of the *Sermon* in Morgan's collection included the prefatory material first offered in the edition of 1540–1, claimed to be 'among the earliest Products of the English Printing Press'. Awdeley's references to the *Sermon* being *godly* and *found in a wall* have disappeared, but Morgan is clearly sensitive to the Anglican sensibilities of his intended readers, some of whom, he suggests in a postscript, were troubled by the *Sermon*'s catholic content: 'Bless us! How can this be? . . . how can any of us well take Exceptions at Extracts given us from writings of approved Authors of our own Belief?' Text (3.6) is a transcription from Morgan's edition:

Text (3.6): Morgan, *Phoenix Britannicus* (1732: 2)

Math.ii. **C** Hriste, the authour and doctoure of all truth, in hys gospel, likeneth the
kyngedome of heauen, to a housholder, saieng on this wyse. Lyke
is the kyngedome of heauen to a housholdynge man, that wente forth
fyrste in the morninge, to hyre workemen into his vyneyarde: so dyd
he aboute the thyrde houre, the syxthe, the nynth, and the eleuenth. And as he found
men standing ydle, he sayed to them: why stand ye here vnoccupied? Go ye into my
vyneyarde, and that that is dewtye I shall gyue you. And when the daye was ended,
he called hys stewarde, and bad that he shulde gyue euery man a peanye.

Spiritually, thys householder is our maister and lorde Christ the trew housholder, and

[12] Well-known Masonic medievalists include the royalist antiquarian Elias Ashmole, an enthusiast inter alia for collecting medieval artefacts and manuscripts, who was made a mason in 1646. Central to modern Masonic ritual even now is the Middle English tag *so mote it be*, deemed equivalent to 'amen'; I owe this example to Andrew Prescott.

head of hys churche here in earthe; whiche calleth men in dyuers houres of the daye,
that is in dyuers ages of the worlde; as in the tyme of nature, he called, by inspiration,
Abell, *Enoch*, *Noe*, *Abraham*, and other lyke. In tyme of the olde lawe, he called
Moses, *Dauid*, *Esaye*, and *Jeremy*, wyth the prophetes; and in the tyme of grace,
he called the apostles, martyrs, confessours and virginis. He called also some in chylde-
hode, as *Johan* Baptiste; some in theyr youth, as *Johan* the Euangeliste; some in myddle
age, as *Peter* and *Andrewe*; some in theyr later dayes, as *Gamaliel* and *Joseph* of
Arimathye. And all those he called to laboure in the Lordes vyneyarde, that is his
churche, yea and that sundrye wayes.

The text of the *Sermon* in *Phoenix Britannicus* offers a balance between inherited and contemporary presentational tastes, as demonstrated by comparison with the earlier versions. It is printed in a roman typeface, in line with 'modern' trends, but Morgan insists, in a short preface in italics (with occasional words in emphatic roman), on his authenticity in reproducing the spellings of his exemplar, '*as some might have blamed me for robbing this careful Editor* [i.e. the sixteenth-century printer] *of the Honour of his* Corrections, *as also my Readers of such a Curiosity*'. Comparison with earlier versions suggests that Morgan indeed kept to the orthographic usage of his exemplar, even down to the deployment of <u> for later <v>: an antiquarian practice flagging a concern with authenticity. Nor does Morgan introduce into the text of the *Sermon* deployment of capitals in line with eighteenth-century practice, namely, to distinguish nouns or other 'emphatical' words. However, he does allow changes of '*the puzzling* Abreviations [sic], *erroneous* Pointings, *and some few gross* Literal *Faults, where the Sense was absolutely perverted*' (1732: 1).

This last statement flags that notions of correctness in 'Pointings' (i.e. punctuation) existed, and the *Phoenix Britannicus* deploys a variety of usages, ranging from full stops and semicolons to colons, commas and question-marks. However, it is quickly apparent that there are some usages that, by present-day conventions, would themselves seem '*erroneous*'. Thus, in the following passage, semicolons are used to mark off subordinate constructions (*whiche calleth . . . as in the tyme . . .*) from main clauses, rather than – as in present-day practice – equiparatively:

> Spiritually, thys householder is our maister
> and lorde Christ the trew housholder, and
> head of hys churche here in earthe; whiche
> calleth men in dyuers houres of the daye,
> that is in dyuers ages of the worlde; as in the
> tyme of nature, he called, by inspiration,
> *Abell, Enoch, Noe, Abraham*, and other lyke.

And in the following passage the colon-mark seems to have two functions: to introduce speech ('he sayed to them: why stand ye here vnoccupied?'), which is a known present-day English usage, even though omission of inverted commas might be noted, but also where modern practice would be to deploy a semicolon or even a full stop to pass from one main clause to another ('into his vyneyarde: so dyd he . . . ').

> Lyke is the kyngedome of heauen to a housholdynge man, that wente forth fyrste in the morninge, to hyre workemen into his vyneyarde: so dyd he aboute the thyrde houre, the syxthe, the nynth, and the eleuenth. And as he found men standing ydle, he sayed to them: why stand ye here vnoccupied?

The usage of the *Sermon* in *Phoenix Britannicus*, then, departs from present-day practice, and seems to indicate an alignment not so much with grammar as with degrees of pausing, i.e. there is a markedly rhetorical element in the deployment of punctuation. Such an emphasis on rhetorical rather than grammatical punctuation might seem a throwback to an earlier age, but in fact it was very up to date, albeit influenced by classical models. The approach was recommended to contemporary discourse communities, not only in the very numerous editions of grammar-books and 'letter-writing manuals' that survive from the period but also in the rise of a particular intellectual movement: *elocutionism*, which related to the ongoing social life of the written word, expressed through formal declamation, that is an important element of the 'reading revolution' we associate with the enlightenment, and that seems to have been a crucial element in the forging – and expression – of national identities in the emerging British state. We will be returning to both elocutionism and national identity in subsequent chapters.

3.3 Nicholas Love: From Thomas Arundel to Thomas More

Recuperation of medieval texts by reforming evangelicals was not the only early modern response: as might be expected at a time of religious ferment, conservatives in religion also found something in past texts that met their ideological needs. In or around 1410, Nicholas Love, prior of the

Charterhouse of Mount Grace in Yorkshire, submitted for institutional approval his translation into English of Johannes de Caulibus's *Meditationes Vita Christi*, a meditative rendering of the Gospel accounts of the life of Christ. Love's translation, *The Mirror of the Blessed Life of Jesus Christ*, was already in circulation, but its matter, however orthodox, was as a vernacular version of Biblical matter potentially troubling to the authorities. The Middle English Wycliffite Bible had by the first decade of the fifteenth century emerged as both theologically and politically threatening to the established order; and, as already flagged, Archbishop Thomas Arundel had tightened the institutional Church's grip on vernacular versions of the Bible, by means of his *Constitutions* of 1407–9:

> no one from now on should translate any text of holy scripture on his own authority into the English language or any other, by way of book, pamphlet or tract, nor should anyone read such a book, pamphlet or tract newly composed since the time of John Wyclif, or in the future to be composed, in part or in whole, publicly or privately, under pain of excommunication, until that translation be approved by the local diocesan, or, if need be, by provincial council. (Translated in Sargent 2004: xviii)

The production of other vernacular Bible-based narratives, however hedged about (as was the *Mirror*) by orthodox interpretation, was therefore naturally concerning, and Love wisely sought approval from Arundel. The *Mirror*, as flagged by the so-called 'Memorandum of Approbation' that is found in some of the surviving manuscripts of the text, was to become the authorised vernacular response to the Wycliffite translations of the Bible. It became one of the most circulated texts in late medieval England, surviving in some sixty-one manuscripts and nine early printed editions, including four incunabula.[13] In sum, the *Mirror*, along with other vernacular monuments such as John Mirk's sermon-cycle the *Festial* and Walter Hilton's work of spiritual guidance *The Scale of Perfection*, represents a key text in the flowering of orthodox, late catholic religious expression celebrated so eloquently by Eamon Duffy (2005).[14]

Some twenty years ago the editor of Love's *Mirror*, Michael Sargent, established authoritatively the complex textual relationships between the manuscripts and early editions of the work, identifying three major 'branches' within its 'family tree' of textual descent, its *stemma codicum*:

[13] For the ongoing impact of Arundel on print culture, see especially Powell 2011.

[14] I am especially grateful to Francesca Mackay for discussion of the issues involved with the punctuation of the Love tradition; see further Mackay 2012. Other important studies on punctuation in the medieval Love tradition include Parkes 1997c, and, most recently, Moore 2014. On audience engagement with Love, see Thompson 2013a, Perry 2013b.

an original authorial text, an authorial revision, and a scribal version (see Sargent 1997; see also Sargent 2004, 2005). Sargent flagged that there was remarkably little textual variation in substantive terms between these branches, suggesting that scribes took considerable care in the copying process.

Indeed, the *Mirror* even came to sustain in its copying tradition an interesting retention of Yorkshire dialect forms that may be plausibly presumed to derive from the authorial archetype and developed into a species of scripta, appropriate for this particular text. It seems to have been a work where the 'accidental' features of the text were felt by its intended discourse community to be vectors of textual authority, worthy of reproduction even when the scribes themselves clearly had a distinct dialectal formation. Such features were sustained as the work made the transition from script to print, as meticulously demonstrated by Lotte Hellinga (Hellinga 1997, revised and updated as Hellinga 2014). Hellinga draws attention to such northern features in Caxton's editions of Love as *myke(l)* 'much', by the end of the fifteenth century a recessive form even in Northern England, and she suggests inter alia that such usage possibly represented 'a conscious wish to preserve the character of the author's language, his "voice", which gives such outstanding individuality to Nicholas Love's translation' (2014: 383). It is also possible that this 'northern' dialectal element aligns with Arundel's general favouring of Cambridge-educated northerners, which included as well as Love such other prominent figures as Richard Scrope and Henry Bowet (both later archbishops of York), John Newton (later treasurer of York Minster) and Walter Hilton. All these men, who were employed by Arundel early in his career when bishop of Ely, are known to have engaged with the mystical vernacular writings of perhaps the best-known Yorkshire writer of the later Middle Ages, Richard Rolle (d. 1349).[15]

The development of a distinctive Love scripta was probably a gradual process. Cambridge, University Library, MS Additional 6578, owned by the Charterhouse at Mount Grace from an early date, has been identified by Michael Sargent as the most authoritative witness of the alpha-branch of the text's *stemma codicum*. The manuscript contains a small note to the

[15] Further research on such 'northern-inflected' writing, in particular its relationship to Cambridge- as opposed to Oxford-influenced Lollard usages, could lead to valuable new insights. Wendy Scase suggests to me a possible connexion with the Cambridge students from *a fer north contree* in Chaucer's *Reeve's Tale*. A starting-place might be the exciting work recently undertaken on Cambridge vernacular documents by Geir Bergstrøm (2017). For Arundel's circle, see ODNB and references there cited.

copyist on folio 2v, flagging that certain forms are to be avoided in favour of others: 'caue de istis verbis gude pro gode / Item hir pro heere in plurali' ('The words "gude" [good] and "hir" [their] are not to be used, with the forms "gode" and "heere" instead'). Although the manuscript belonged to Mount Grace Charterhouse itself, the language of the main hand was localised by LALME to Northamptonshire; possibly the scribe had moved to Yorkshire and took his usage with him, although it seems unlikely that a Yorkshire reader would have found spellings such as *gude* objectionable in the first quarter of the fifteenth century, before the impact of southern-based tendencies to orthographic standardisation. It may be noted that *hir* is not in any way an especially northern form, so 'northernness' per se does not seem to have been problematic for the fussy annotator on folio 2v; something like *þair* or *yair*, the latter with <y> for thorn, would be much more characteristic of northern usage. Later scribes do not seem to have paid attention to this advice, and such northernisms were regularly deployed as part of the Love tradition.[16]

Such a usage would have contrasted with the spelling-system that has been identified as characteristic of the textual tradition with which Love's *Mirror* was explicitly designed to compete, namely, the Wycliffite Bible and associated texts, which are commonly transmitted in the focused variety known – a little misleadingly – as 'Central Midlands Standard'. As already noted in Chapter 1, Central Midlands Standard was 'Type I' in Michael Samuels's nomenclature, first distinguished in 1963, of 'incipient standards', distinguished from London-based Types II through IV by its Central Midlands basis. Type I, in use from the middle of the fourteenth century onwards, is found in the majority of manuscripts attributed to Wycliffe and his followers, although it is not restricted to them; Samuels reported the usage in, for instance, copies of the writings of Reginald Pecock from the middle of the fifteenth century. Characteristic texts in Type I use a mixture of forms common in the Central Midlands counties in Middle English times, e.g. *sich* 'such', *mych* 'much', *ony* 'any', *silf* 'self', *stide* 'stead', *ȝouun* 'given', *siȝ* 'saw'.

However, Hellinga also noted some interesting changes as the printing tradition developed. The English language during the end of the fifteenth and beginning of the sixteenth century was increasingly undergoing dialectal muting in the written mode, being replaced by usages characteristic

[16] The language of Additional 6578 was analysed in LALME as LP9340. The hand of Additional 6578 was also the first hand (A) in another early Love manuscript: Cambridge, University Library, MS Additional 6686. Descriptions of both these manuscripts appear at www.qub.ac.uk/geographies-of-orthodoxy/, last consulted on 23 June 2019.

of the South-East Midlands, specifically London, and the spelling traditions/scriptae associated with particular texts/genres began to be overtaken by a broader concern with communicative accessibility. The 'northern' spellings of the Love tradition were increasingly displaced; the editions published by Wynkyn de Worde and Richard Pynson both replace presumably archetypal *myke(l)* with the much more commonplace *moch(e)*, to a lesser or greater extent (Hellinga 2014: 382). De Worde's first edition is particularly interesting in this regard, showing that whereas *mykel* was sustained in the early part of the print, it wholly disappears later, demonstrating a transition from a faithful reproduction of delicate textual detail in favour of forms, such as *moche*, with wider currency (Hellinga 2014: 381). Such changes demonstrate what Hellinga describes as 'a process of adaptation' (2014: 367), as the older discourse communities for whom 'northernism' was a meaningful vector began to be replaced by wider groupings with other concerns.

It is perhaps worth asking further questions about the social drivers behind this 'process of adaptation', commonly referred to as standardisation. Part of the reason must have been a response to later emerging linguistic norms, themselves reflecting wider cultural attitudes to the vernacular within the discourse community that formed Love's readership. As is increasingly being noted, linguistic standardisation in the written mode is a complex business. The traditional view was that standardisation emerged as a result of the increasing 'top-down' prestige of a particular model usage, i.e. that found in late medieval/early modern London, and such prestige must be part of the story.

But more important, it is now understood, were also 'bottom-up' pressures to do with communicative function: as literacy in English became more widespread, with readers likely to encounter a wider range of new texts, what used to be termed 'grosser provincialisms' such as *mykel* became more communicatively inconvenient and were replaced by forms with wider currency at the time when the text was being reproduced (see Smith 2000b: 136 and references there cited). Such linguistic choices of less dialectally distinctive forms, departures from what were almost certainly in the printers' exemplars, represent decisions made on pragmatic grounds, aimed at improving the legibility of the text for the intended – presumably wider, and almost certainly lay – pious discourse communities for whom the burgeoning printing trade catered. Muting of dialectal variation, therefore, can be related to shifts in the reception of the text during the transition from script to print.

To this general picture can now be added such cross-cutting phenomena of the kind identified by Hellinga: what we might now call the 'Love scripta', a special writing-system distinguished by a particular congeries of spellings, emerging temporarily, and dominant in a particular textual tradition until replaced by more general dialectal muting. It seems likely – as has been suggested already for Types I and II – that Samuels's Types are of this kind, and in the following chapter we will see – mutatis mutandis – a special usage, comparable to that found in texts of Love's *Mirror*, in copies of Gower's *Confessio Amantis*. It seems that certain texts achieve a kind of authority that offers a model spelling, and that model can even spread to other traditions (as for instance when scribes used to copying Gower move to copying Chaucer; see Smith 1988c and 1988a).[17]

Alongside these shifts in spelling, it is also possible to identify other formal features that evolve in interesting ways in the Love tradition, such as punctuation. The punctuation of Love's *Mirror* has attracted attention ever since Elizabeth Salter's pioneering article from some sixty years ago (Salter 1956), which focused on the usage in the authoritative early manuscript already discussed – Cambridge, University Library, MS Additional 6578. How Love originally intended to present his text is, in the absence of an authorial holograph, impossible to determine with certainty, but as Salter argued the text as presented in Additional 6578 probably gives us a good idea of the starting-point for the tradition. Text (3.7) is a short transcription:

Text (3.7): Cambridge, University Library, MS Additional 6578, folio 84v

And þan seide þe au*n*gele to hi*m*. Beþ þen now of
gude cou*n*forte my lorde & worcheþ manfully. ffor it is seme
ly to hi*m* þat is in hye degree.˙ to do grete þinges & worþi. & to hi*m*
þat is a manful man .˙ to suff*ir* harde þinges. ffor þoo þinges þ*at*
bene harde & peynful shole sone passe. & þoo þinges þat bene
ioyful & gloriose shole come aft*er*. Þe fader*e* seiþ þ*at* he is &
shale be euer*e* w^t^ ȝowe. & þat he sal kepe ȝo*ur* dere modere &
ȝo*ur* disciples. at ȝo*ur* wille. and shale ȝiue hem safe aȝeyne to ȝowe.

17 Once researchers are liberated from the arguably anachronistic search for standard English, it may be possible to distinguish more of these particular text-type focused scriptae. More could be done on the so-called Central Midlands Standard (Type I), for instance (see Stenroos forthcoming, and Peikola 2003); Claire Jones's work (2000) on East Anglian medicas could be pursued further; and my impression is that a survey of copies of Richard Rolle might prove fruitful.

In the above passage, which is typical of the manuscript's general usage, three marks of punctuation are deployed: the punctus, the punctus elevatus and capital letters. Malcolm Parkes, in the most thorough discussion of punctuation practices in the Love tradition to date, offers a careful interpretation of the passage above in line with the marks of punctuation, noting that the text has been 'divided into five sententiae, each of which begins with a littera notabilior [i.e. capital letter]' (1997c: 48), with each sententia representing a stage in the argument. Subdivisions within the sententiae are marked by the punctus and punctus elevatus. Thus, for instance, 'Within the third *sententia* the *punctus elevatus* ... has been applied ... to introduce the two complements of "it is seemly" ("to do grete þinges", and "to suffir harde þinges"), and hence to emphasize the importance of propriety in the moral interpretation' (Parkes 1997c: 49). As Salter points out, the punctuation in this manuscript represents 'an intelligent commentary on the sense, grammatical structure, and rhythm of the prose' (1956: 18).

Something similar may be noted in another early copy of the text whose language is much nearer in character to the northern usage that we might presume to be archetypal in the Love tradition, although not necessarily from Yorkshire: London, British Library, MS Additional 19901. Text (3.8) is a transcription of the same passage as in Additional 6578:[18]

Text (3.8): London, British Library, Additional MS 19901, folio 58r

And ya*n* said
þe au*n*gel to hi*m*. Bese þen now of gude comforth my lord. & worches
manfully ffor it is semely to hi*m* y^t is in hie degre to do gret thinges
& worþi & to hi*m* y^t is a manful man: to suffer hard thinges. ffor yo
thinges y^t bene harde & payneful sal sone passe & yo thinges yat
bene ioyful & glorious sal come aft*er*. ye fader sais y^t he is & sal be
eu*er* w^t ȝow. & yat he sal kepe ȝo*ur* dere moder & ȝo*ur* disciples at ȝo*ur* will.
& sal ȝife yai*m* safe aȝeyne to ȝowe.

The punctuation in Additional 19901, which according to Michael Sargent is the earliest surviving manuscript from the alpha- or most 'authoritative' tradition in the *Mirror's stemma codicum*, is fairly simple, with punctus and

[18] Additional 19901 makes no distinction in form between thorn and <y>, a dialectally distinctive feature in medieval English handwriting, so none is made in Text (3.8). Sargent places the text in Leicestershire/Nottinghamshire on the basis of the combination of forms used, but there are definite distinctive northernisms recorded, not easily accommodated in Leicestershire/Nottinghamshire, that seem to be part of the emerging Love spelling-tradition already discussed, notably *suld* 'should', *gude* 'good', *lufe* 'love', *saule* 'soul'.

capitals used to flag most units, and a punctus elevatus to mark an emphasised complement, e.g. *to suffer hard thinges*.

Parkes went on to show that, although textual variation in the manuscript tradition was – in Sargent's words just cited – 'on the whole remarkably little', by contrast 'punctuation in the surviving witnesses presents a variety of different interpretations of the text' (1997c: 47–8). One such early interpretation, contrasting markedly with that offered in the punctuation of Additional 6578, is in Tokyo, Waseda University Library, MS NE 3691, where punctuation was extremely sparse, and sometimes non-existent. Unfortunately, Waseda 3691 is defective for the passage analysed by Parkes, but here is a passage from later in the manuscript.[19] The underlined words are in red ink; the capital 'E' in the first line immediately after the red section occupies four lines of the text.

Text (3.9): Tokyo, Waseda University Library, MS NE 3691, folio 124v, column a

¶ Than john p*re*ied
hir*e* to stint of suche

[column b]

soriful wordes and to ce
se of wepinge and con
forted hire in the best ma
nere that he myghte ¶ And
thou also be deuote yma-
ginacion as thou were
there bodily p*re*sent confort
our lady and that felaw
ship preiyng hem to ete
somwhat for yit theye
bene fastinge. And after
slepe But that I trowe
was ful litell And so ta
kinge hir*e* blesseng gou*n*
her way as at this tyme
what our lady and oþ*ere*
with her did on the Sat*er*
day Capitulum xlixm ¶ + die sa
E rly on the mo bate
row vppon

[19] For an image, see the frontispiece to Oguro et al. 1997.

the Saterday
stoden in þe
foreside hous the gates
spered Our lady John
and other women be
fore ne*m*pned in gret mo*ur*
nynge and sorowe/ ha
uynge in mynde the gret
tribulacion and Anguissh
of the daye before not
speking but be tyme lo
kinge ou*er* vpon a nother

It will immediately be observed that in the Waseda manuscript hardly any punctuation at all has been deployed other than capitals and paraph-marks, with only sporadic examples of the virgule or punctus. Paraphs and capitals mark sententiae and larger units; the single example of the virgule in the above passage, rare in the manuscript, marks off a non-finite subordinate clause. Parkes offered several reasons for why scribes could omit punctuation, but the most plausible suggestion is that Love regularly deployed 'easily recognizable lexical syntax markers: conjunctions and adverbs' (1997c: 55), and this characteristic is exemplified in the transcription offered, where forms such as *and* and *but* are commonplace. It is noticeable that the rare virgule in the passage above precedes not an adverb or a conjunction but a non-finite verb heading a subordinate clause, *hauynge*.

Such sparing deployment of punctuation seems to have been characteristic of this scribe, whose hand has been detected by Linne Mooney and her research team in some ten manuscripts, including not only two texts of the *Mirror* (Waseda 3691, and Edinburgh, National Library of Scotland, MS Advocates' 18.1.7) but also two early manuscripts of Chaucer's *Canterbury Tales* (Petworth House, Kent, MS 7, and Lichfield, Cathedral Library, MS 29), and an early copy of Gower's *Confessio Amantis* (Cambridge, Pembroke College, MS 307). This scribe was, it is clear, a highly practised copyist who seems, like several of his contemporaries, to have combined the production of literary texts with clerkly service to one of the London guilds, in his case the Skinners' Company (see Mooney and Stubbs 2013: 120–1).[20]

[20] For the identification of the other manuscripts by the Waseda scribe, see the *Late Medieval Scribes* website, www.medievalscribes.com/. All these manuscripts are similarly sparing in the deployment of punctuation. Accessible images of this scribe's copies of Chaucer and Gower, lodged on the *Medieval Scribes* website authored by Mooney's team, include: www.medievalscribes.com/index.php?browse=aspect&id=3&navlocation=Petworth&navlibrary=Petworth House, The National Trust&msid=116&nav=off www.medievalscribes.com/index.php?browse=aspect&id=57&navlocat

It would seem that the scribe of Waseda 3691 felt that 'figuring out' the structure of the text he was copying – a process that punctuation was developed to assist – was something that could be safely left to the reader. Parkes has drawn attention to how such omission of punctuation in devotional texts can be paralleled in French and Latin texts; such 'neutral' presentations, he argues, offered 'devout readers the opportunity to figure out for themselves subjective readings to apply to their own spiritual needs' (1997c: 58–9). Some readers would have been ready to undertake such tasks; as John Thompson (2013b: 133) argues, readers were often expected to move around a text 'in order to keep them intellectually alert for the meditative task in hand': a process whereby the discourse community for which the text was written became involved in its creation, arguably shading into a community of discourse. Communal reading seems to have been regularly practised (Perry 2013b). And as Thompson (2014b) and others have shown, there was a tradition of 'active', engaged reading of manuscripts of Love's text that continued well into the period of the reformation, as witnessed inter alia by marginal annotations undertaken by identifiable pious individuals and families. Such activity raises some interesting questions about the role of readers in textual interpretation: are they part of the community of practice involved in a common hermeneutic enterprise? We may be reminded, when pondering on Waseda 3691, of the argument that *scriptio continua* was adopted in antiquity because of its neutrality (see Chapter 1 above, *passim*).

Such variation in interpretation was potentially, of course, increasingly a risky business at a time when the authorities were keen to distinguish between inappropriate (i.e. Wycliffite) and appropriate uses of the vernacular for religious expression. Oxford, Brasenose College, MS 9, copied by a scribe who was also active in producing other major literary texts, including Gower's *Confessio Amantis* and Trevisa's *Polychronicon* (see inter alia Doyle and Parkes 1978: *passim*), is in this context an interesting example. Originally a witness for the beta-branch of the textual tradition of the *Mirror*, which contained some unauthorised materials, the Brasenose manuscript was very carefully corrected to bring its content into line with that found in the more 'authoritative' alpha-witnesses (Parkes 1997c: 57); along with numerous erasures and removal of leaves, a corrector also carefully went through the punctuation of the text. Parkes argues that the modifications found

ion=Cambridge&navlibrary=Pembroke College&msid=181&nav=off All these sites were last consulted on 24 May 2019. For further discussion of the Petworth scribe, see Chapter 4 below.

in the Brasenose manuscript could be related to the text's emerging authorised status during the first quarter of the fifteenth century; assertive punctuation imposed on what had originally been a more neutral text was one means of controlling the way the work was subsequently received.[21] Such control fits well with what was evidently Love's purpose: that reading the *Mirror* was intended to 'train [his] vernacular readers in how to read meditatively and in imaginative contemplation of Christ's sacrifice' (Thompson 2013b: 131). That Love's writings were conceived of as having some kind of authority would also account for the respectful reproduction of a special Love scripta.

Such diverse ways of engaging with the texts of Love's *Mirror* continued until the end of the fifteenth century, as exemplified by the latest manuscript witness for the alpha-tradition in Sargent's classification, New Haven, Yale University Library, MS Beinecke 535. Text (3.10) is a transcription of the same passage in Beinecke 535 as in 3.7–3.8):

Text (3.10): New Haven, Yale University Library, MS Beinecke 535, folio 68r

¶ Ande yan saide ye angell to hym Bey
yen now off gude confort my lorde & wyrchey ma*n*fully ffor it is semly
to hym yat is in hye degre// To do grete thyng*is* & worthy & to hym
yat is a ma*n*full ma*n* to suffre hard thyng*is*// ffor yo thyng*is* yat ben hard
& peynfull schull sone passe ande yo thynges y[t] bene ioyfull & glorious schull come aft*er* ye fadyr sayith y[t] he is & schall be eu*er* w[t] ȝhow & yat
he schall kepe ȝo*ur* dere moder & ȝour disciples at ȝour wyll and

[folio 68v]

& schall ȝeue hem safe aȝane to ȝhow ¶

Beinecke 535 relates closely in stemmatic terms to the printed tradition, which seems to derive wholly from the alpha-branch of the text. The *editio princeps* of Love's *Mirror* was issued in 1484 by William Caxton (d. 1492) (STC 3259); only two copies of this early edition survive – an imperfect

[21] Wendy Scase reminds me of the 'punctuation poems' that appear in the early sixteenth century, in line with humanistic concerns with punctuation. See Parkes 1992: 210–11, who illustrates an addition, on the fly-leaf of Cambridge, Pembroke College, MS 307, of two versions of the same poem, but with distinct deployments of punctuation leading to different meanings. Intriguingly, the body of this manuscript, in an anglicana formata hand of the early fifteenth century, is by the Waseda scribe, who is, as we have just seen, rather sparing in his deployment of such marks. Could it be that the sixteenth-century scribe ('thoma Smyth') is offering a discreet critique of his medieval predecessor?

copy in Cambridge University Library and a fragment in the library of Lambeth Palace (see Hellinga 2014: 366 n. 1, and references there cited). This edition, in textual terms, underpins all subsequent printed versions. Clearly the publication met a demand, since Caxton printed the work again in 1490 (STC 3261). Here is the test passage transcribed from the 1484 edition:

Text (3.11): Caxton (1484: cap xl, folio 92r)

And thenne said the Aungel to hym. Be thenne now of good
comforte my lord/ and wyrcheth manfully/ For it is semely
to hym that is in hyhe degree. to doo grete thynges and worthy
and to hym that is a manful man to suffer harde thynges/
For thos thynges that ben hard and peyneful shall soone passe
and tho thynges that ben ioyeful and glorious shall come af=
ter the fader saith/ that he is and shalle be euer with you. and
that he shall kepe youre dere moder and youre discyples at yo=
ur wille and shall yelde him sauf ageyne to you.

And here is the same text as presented in the 1490 edition (after London, British Library, C.10.b.15):

Text (3.12): Caxton (1490: cap xl, sig. N.vi r)

and thenne sayd the aungel to hym/ Be thenne now of goode
comforde my lorde. and wyrcheth manfully/ For it is semely
to hym that is in hyhe degree. to doo grete thynges and worthy
and to hym that is a manful man to suffer hard thynges.
For tho thynges that ben hard and peyneful shall soone passe
and tho thynges that ben ioyeful and glorious shalle come af=
ter the. fader sayth that he is and shalle be euere wyth you: and
that he shalle kepe your dere moder and your discyples at your
wylle and shalle yelde hem sauf ageyne to you.

Comparison of Beinecke 535 and Caxton's two prints shows interesting differences in the range of usages adopted. The manuscript, for instance, is comparatively selective in its use of marks of punctuation, in this passage using the virgule (//), in a way comparable with the punctus elevatus in Additional 6578, to mark off the complements *To do grete thyngis & worthy* and *& to hym yat is a manfull man to suffre hard thyngis* in order 'to emphasize the importance of propriety in the moral interpretation', but otherwise distinguishing sententiae and other units simply by means of capitals. In that sense, Beinecke 535 manifests an ongoing instability in punctuation practices, whatever the pressures may have been to move to consistency in the presentation of the textual content. By contrast, although the Caxton prints draw upon a more limited repertoire of punctuation-marks, they deploy more of them, demonstrating a closer, more directive engagement with the structure of the text on the part of the printer. And although there is an interesting contrast between the two editions, with the single virgule being reduced in the later text in favour of the punctus (including its erroneous introduction in *the. fader*), the location of the pointing seems to be comparatively stable.

This more insistent and increasingly stabilised pattern of punctuation – presumably related to humanistic concerns with the matter – is found to an even greater extent when we turn to the work of the two later printers of the *Mirror*, Richard Pynson (c. 1449–1529/30) and Wynkyn de Worde (d. 1534/5), both of whose sets of editions derive textually from Caxton, and are thus within the alpha-tradition of the text. Two editions, of 1494 and 1506, have been ascribed to Pynson.[22] Again, there are some interesting distinctions between the two editions, both in the direction of simplifying the repertoire of marks deployed:

Text (3.13): Pynson (1494: cap. xl, sig. m.5v)

/ and than sayde the aungell to him. Be thou
nowe of good comforte mylorde and wurch manfully. For it is seme
ly to him that is in hye degree to do greate thinges/ and worthy/ and to
him that is a manfull man to suffer harde thinges. For tho thynges
that been harde and paynfull shall sone passe. And tho thinges that
been Joyfull and glorious shal come after: the fader saith that he is
and shall be euer with you and that he shall kepe your dere moder &
youre disciples at youre wyll and shall yelde theym sauf ageyne to
you.

22 The ascription to Pynson of the 1494 edition is given in EEBO. Pynson inherited the use of Caxton's mercer's mark, which appears at the end of the book. In the copy that is now London, British Library, IB.55527, the heading for this page – and this page only in the signature – erroneously reads 'Ca. xli' for 'cap. xl'. Interestingly, a printed tip-in at the beginning of IB.55527 offers a window into eighteenth-century antiquarian practice, with facsimiles of Caxton's various fonts headed 'A SPECIMEN of CAXTON'S LETTER'. At the bottom of the tip-in appears the following inscription: 'To Mr Wm CASLON, a good Promoter of this Work, this Plate is Inscribed. By *J. A. J. Ames, del.* and as suitable to the Principal LETTER FOUNDER. *G. Bickham sculp.*' The reference is probably to William Caslon the elder (1692–1766), the prominent type-founder whose fonts were much admired in his day and have remained so ('When in doubt, use Caslon' apparently remains a printer's axiom). His son and successor, William Caslon the younger, seems to have been less interested in typographical innovation. If – as seems probable – the elder Caslon is referred to, then 'G. Bickham' was probably George Bickham (1683/4–1758), the engraver, who was succeeded by his son George in that profession (the persistence of first names in this community is a notable annoyance for subsequent historians). 'J. A. J. Ames' is Joseph Ames (d. 1759), the bibliographer and antiquary, whose history of printing, *Typographical Antiquities*, appeared in 1749. Accounts can be found in ODNB of all these men, who clearly formed a distinct discourse community of enthusiasts for printing history.

Text (3.14): Pynson (1506: sig. M.iii r)

and thanne sayde the aungelle vnto hym. Be tha*n*ne
nowe of gode conforte my lorde and worke manfully. For it is semely

[sig. M.iii v]

to hym that is in hye degree to doo greate thynges and worthy: and to
hym that is a manfulle man to suffer harde thynges. For tho thynges
that ben harde and peynfulle shal sone passe. And tho thynges that be
Joyful and gloryous shal come after: the fader sayth that he is & shall
be euer wyth you and that he shalle kepe your dere moder and youre
Dyscyples at your wylle and shalle yelde theym saufe ageyne to you

Pynson's two prints deploy punctuation rather differently, with a reduced use of the virgule in the later edition (virgules are found elsewhere in the 1506 edition, but certainly less commonly than in the 1494 version), and the sporadic use of the double punctus (:), an innovation in the fifteenth and sixteenth centuries, but it is noticeable that the pointing is even more insistent than in Caxton's prints.

Wynkyn de Worde was the most prolific and sustained publisher of editions of Love, with no fewer than five editions surviving, culminating in one from 1530. The last of these versions was 'almost certainly' recommended by no less a figure than Thomas More as a means of rebuttal of the heretical publications of Tyndale and others (see Thompson 2014b). Again, all the passages come from the 'Friday section' in the work, but the usages exemplified here are typical of the text as a whole. Here are transcriptions of de Worde's 1517 and 1525 editions (taken from London, British Library C.37.d.4 and C.37.d.5 respectively):

Text (3.15): Wynkyn de Worde (1517: folio 116r (foliation supplied by library))

And then sayd the aun
gell to hym/ be then now of good comfort my lorde/ and
werche ma*n*fully. For it is semely to hym that is in hygh
degree/ to do grete thy*n*ges and worthy and to hym that
is a manfull man to suffre harde thynges. For tho thyn=
ges that ben harde and paynfull shall soone passe/ & tho
thynges that ben Joyefull and gloryous shall come af=
ter/ the fader sayth that he is and shall be with you/ and
that he shal kepe your dere moder & youre dyscyples at
your wyll. And shall yelde them sauf agayn to you/

Text (3.16): Wynkyn de Worde (1525: sig. U.vi r)

> And than sayd the aungell to hym/ be than now
> of good conforte my lorde/ and werke manfully. For it
> is semely to hym that is in hygh degree/ to do grete
> thynges and worthy/ and to hym that is a manfull
> man to suffer harde thynges. For those thynges that
> ben harde and paynfull shall soone passe/ and those
> thynges that ben Joyfull and gloryous shall come af=
> ter/ the father sayth that he is and shall be euer with
> you/ and that he shal kepe your dere mother and your
> dyscyples at your wyll/ & shall yelde them safe agayne
> to you.

Wynkyn de Worde, in contrast with Pynson, retains throughout his printing of the *Mirror* a comparatively wide repertoire of marks of punctuation, ranging from virgules and punctus to capitals; it is also particularly noticeable from the presentation of Texts (3.15) and (3.16) presented above that, although the lineation indicates that editions were set up at various times, the punctuation is fairly regular. It seems in sum that a more insistent and settled pattern of punctuation for the Love text – in tandem with a more standardised form of spelling, assisting the communicative reach of the work – was emerging as printing became established as the primary medium for the text in the first decades of the sixteenth century.

Such textual stability would have pleased Sir Thomas More, who specifically recommended the *Mirror* (*Bonauenture of the lyfe of Cryste*) to *the people unlerned*:

> For surely the very best waye were neyther to rede thys not theirs but rather the people unlerned to occupy them selfe beside theyr other busynesse in prayour, good medytacyon, and redynge of suche englysshe bookes as moste may norysshe and encrease deuocyon. Of whiche kynde is Bonauenture of the lyfe of Cryste, Gerson of the folowynge of Christ, and the deuoute contemplatyue boke of Scala perfectionis with suche other lyke then in the lernynge what may well be answered vnto heretykes. (Cited in Thompson 2014b: 198)

This recommendation was clearly behind the continuing afterlife of Love's *Mirror*, which saw a series of editions – in English – published by Jesuit- and Franciscan-associated printers in France in the first half of the seventeenth century (see especially the important discussion by Johnson 2015, who offers a detailed and fascinating comparison of the paratextual materials in early copies of Love and the recusant editions published by Charles Boscard of Douai in 1606 and 1622).

More's perspective was clearly, mutatis mutandis, much like that of Arundel over a century before: the suppression of heresy and the encouragement of orthodox reading practices. Textual control, expressed inter alia through stabilised practices of punctuation that offered increasingly clear (and thus directive) interpretative assistance for its intended discourse community, would have been part of this programme of regulation of religious practice along approved lines; punctuation, after all, was a means of guiding interpretation.[23] In a manuscript culture, such control was difficult, as the examples of the very varied practices sketched out above demonstrate. However, the world of print, as exemplified in Wynkyn de Worde's texts, offered new ways to control the dissemination of a particular form of the text even as it also allowed for the wider circulation and consumption of works of (in More's terms) more dubious provenance, such as Wimbledon's *Sermon* would prove to be a few years later. Both conservative–catholic and evangelical–protestant discourse communities, therefore, could engage productively – from their own perspectives – with their inheritance from the past through the new emerging medium. And the pragmatic, editorial shaping of this inheritance in subsequent centuries reflected the varying socio-cultural functions these texts were expected to perform.

[23] See Smith 2017 for a very different example – the punctuation of public documents in sixteenth-century Scotland – but driven by a comparable impulse.

CHAPTER 4

The Great Tradition: Langland, Gower, Chaucer

4.1 Reinventing *Piers Plowman*

William Langland's *Piers Plowman*, one of the greatest English poems of the late fourteenth century, was first printed in 1550. This edition was produced by Robert Crowley (c. 1517–88), who combined his short-lived commercial activities – supported, albeit without acknowledgement, by the king's printer, Richard Grafton – with a longer career as a polemical author and reformed clergyman, active in the evangelical interest and inter alia a major source for the protestant martyrologist John Foxe. He has, perhaps a little over-enthusiastically, been described as 'the most significant poet between Surrey and Gascoigne' (King 1982: 320). *Piers Plowman* was Crowley's most ambitious verse publication in terms of size, and was clearly a success for him. No fewer than three impressions (1550a–1550c) appeared in the same year, in a substantial quarto format; with the exception of an edition of the Psalter, all Crowley's other publications were more modest octavos. But his *Piers Plowman* was more than simply a commercial success, for its evolution during the year his editions appeared illustrates well the themes of this book.

Judging from the *English Short-Title Catalogue* (henceforth ESTC), most of Crowley's publishing activity was concentrated in the years 1548–51: some nineteen works are recorded there, including ten he composed himself. In the same year that his edition of *Piers Plowman* appeared, Crowley printed his own *One and Thyrtye Epigrammes*, a satirical poem on alehouses, beggars and usurers, and *The Way to Wealth*, a prose pamphlet 'wherein is taught a most present remedy for sedicion' which 'suggested how the poor, property owners, and clergy could help to restore social harmony' (ODNB). As these summaries suggest, there is clearly a thematic link between all three works, and it is worth recalling that the widespread Edwardian uprisings of 1549 against such social abuses as enclosure, culminating in the bloody suppression of Robert Kett's East Anglian rebellion late in the year, would have resonated with many of the themes of *Piers Plowman*. There is good reason, on the basis of his publications, to suppose that Crowley was conscious of the grievances underpinning these so-called 'commonwealth' demonstrations, albeit from a nervously 'moderate' position; an early work by Crowley, published by John Day in 1548, was a prose pamphlet with the self-explanatory title *An Informacion and Peticion Agaynst the Oppressours of the Poore*, while his later poem *Philargyrie of Greate Britayne* (1551) was an allegorical attack on human greed. Links between these commonwealth movements and the evangelical party in the Church are fairly well attested: Matthew Parker, himself a Norwich man in origin, although by 1549 a distinguished Cambridge academic, preached in Kett's camp on Mousehold Heath just outside Norwich – albeit unsuccessfully – 'in favour of submission to authorities for the common good' (ODNB); he was lucky to escape with his life. The fact that Parker had tried to find a middle way during this turbulent period at all is interesting. Crowley seems to have had a similar approach: in 1549 he published a pamphlet poem, *The Voyce of the Laste Trumpet*, which, while identifying a series of social ills, called for each estate to accept its lot ('Co*n*tent thiselfe to that degre', 1549: sig. A.iii r).[1]

Philargyrie's metrical form (dimeter) owed something to the model of John Skelton (d. 1529), whose 'dame Philargera' (i.e. 'lady love-of-money') appears in *Why come ye nat to Courte*, printed by Robert Copland, probably in 1545; a second impression of Skelton's poem was printed by Robert's son, William, in – again probably – 1554, the year after William's edition of Douglas's *Eneados* (to be discussed in the following chapter). After a period as an exile in Frankfurt during Mary's reign, Crowley returned to England in 1559 following Elizabeth's accession, becoming well-known as a controversialist with a special distaste for what he considered 'popish' elements of ecclesiastical dress. He remained a prolific author; although he does not seem to have returned to printing in his own right, he seems to have

[1] The complexities of Crowley's engagement with Langland, demonstrating his 'middle way' approach, are revealed through analysis of his paratextual material, notably his prefaces and marginal annotations. See Scanlon 2007, and above all Diane Scott's important study (2015), especially pp. 72–147 and references there cited. For Kett's rebellion, see for instance MacCulloch 1996: 429–39, Wood 2007 and especially Jones 2011, who specifically engages with Crowley's complex response. Wood's comment on Crowley and the other so-called 'commonwealth writers' is especially apposite: 'to categorise the commonwealth writers as "conservative" is both to simplify and to dismiss their message. What makes the commonwealth writers so difficult to pin down is precisely their contradictory, multifaceted nature' (2007: 34).

retained a connexion with the profession, preaching to the Stationers' Company in 1586 and being involved in the licensing of books from 1579 until his death in 1588.[2]

As the contents of his works printed in 1548–51 suggest, there are some clear connexions in topic between Crowley's own writings and Langland's poem; indeed, Crowley modelled the verse form of *One and Thyrtye Epigrammes* on Langland's alliterative long line. Moreover, as was flagged in Chapter 3, there is material in *Piers Plowman* that had considerable potential for evangelical repurposing, clearly an added attraction. In his preface to Langland's poem, Crowley explicitly drew the parallel between *Piers Plowman* and Wycliffe's works, seeing them both as precursors of reformed religion, 'cry[ing] oute agaynste the worckes of darkenesse, as did Iohn wicklefe' (sig. *.ii r); in so doing he was following the view of another well-known reformer, John Bale, who – although he later changed his mind – had at one time ascribed the poem to Wycliffe's authorship (King 1982: 325 and references there cited). John King has argued (1982: 323) that the poem's failure – contrasting with those composed by Langland's courtly contemporaries Chaucer and Gower – to reach the printing press until the reign of Edward VI may have owed something to its potential for subversive reinterpretation. This lacuna is otherwise somewhat puzzling, given *Piers Plowman*'s widespread geographical reach, as suggested by its dialectal manifestations in the Middle English period (see Samuels 1985). However, the numerous post-reformation annotations on medieval copies attest to the poem's continuing impact, as does the appearance of surviving sixteenth-century manuscripts, e.g. New Haven, Yale University Library, MS Takamiya 23 (olim Sion College), a copy of the B-version of the poem roughly contemporary with Crowley's edition; Cambridge, University Library MS Gg 4.31 of the B-text, from the first quarter of the sixteenth century; and Oxford,

[2] For a brief sketch of Crowley's career, see ODNB; a more developed account, with a good bibliography to date, appears in Scott 2015. The year 1550 also saw Crowley's printing of the first edition of William Salesbury's *A briefe and playne introduction, teachyng how to pronounce the letters of the British tong*, a guide to the pronunciation of Welsh (see Dobson 1968: 11–18). Later, in 1567, Salesbury (d. c. 1580) published a second edition of this work, as *A playne and a familiar introduction*, including a reference (sig. C.i r) to 'the booke of the Sermon in the Englyshe Saxons tonge, which the most reuerend father in God D.M.P. Archbishop of Canterbury hath lately set forth in prynt': a clear reference to *A testimonie of antiquitie* (1566), for which see Chapter 2 above. The printer for this 1567 edition was Henry Denham, who in the same year printed Welsh translations of the Book of Common Prayer and the New Testament; Salesbury was responsible for the former and was closely involved – with others – in the production of the latter. Crowley and Salesbury were clearly part of the same discourse community, if not indeed the same community of practice.

Bodleian Library, MS Digby 145, a copy of the A-text.[3] Some of these annotators and copyists may have been adherents of the old religion; Digby 145, for instance, dating from 1534 and once in the library of the recusant Sir Kenelm Digby (1603–65), is in the hand of Sir Adrian Fortescue (d. 1539), later venerated as a catholic martyr for allegedly opposing Henry VIII's royal supremacy. That Fortescue went to the trouble of copying *Piers Plowman* attests to a personal commitment to radical medieval religion, whether conservatively orthodox or evangelical in orientation.[4]

Fortescue's story is actually a complex one, demonstrating that the poem was open to multiple interpretations. It seems likely that Fortescue's execution in 1539 owed more to 'some unguarded words' or unfortunate family connexions rather than to a distaste for Henry's reforms (ODNB); Fortescue was a cousin of Anne Boleyn, who of course favoured reformed religion, and he is known to have used prayers acknowledging Henry's self-proclaimed assertion of the headship of the Church of England. John Thompson (2004) has drawn attention to a copy of Crowley's second edition in Thomas Percy's collection (Belfast, Queen's University Library, Percy 571), where a sixteenth-century annotator, James Lamb, urges readers to 'marke and rede' Crowley's marginal note on the inefficacy of requiem masses. According to a note on the fly-leaf, Lamb bought the book on 6 November 'anno marie primus', and, if the note on masses dates from that year, it was rapidly becoming apparent that Queen Mary was returning England to roman catholicism. By contrast, Charlotte Brewer (1996: 18–19) has commented on interesting annotations on another copy of the second edition (Oxford, Bodleian Library, Douce L.205) owned in 1613 by 'an educated Catholic', Andrew Bostock. Bostock 'was able to detach the editor from the poem – the heretical margin from the text – and come up with a different interpretation' (1996: 19), clearly valuing *Piers Plowman* as a work suitable for catholic pietistic reading. As we saw in Chapter 3, it was possible to be radical

[3] I follow the traditional distinctions in *Piers Plowman* studies between the A, B and C versions of the poem. For a discussion of this division, which also includes the suggestion of a fourth Z-text, see Brewer 1996 and references there cited. An edition of Takamiya 23 is in preparation by Ian Cornelius (I owe this information to Tim Machan).

[4] Crowley was not alone in attempting an imitation of Langland; we might also note the soldier and poet Thomas Churchyard (?1523–1604), whose *Davy Dycars Dreme*, 'brought vp in Pierces scole', appeared around 1552. The *Dreme* is a fairly conventional social satire. See further Scase 2007b.

in religion in many different ways throughout the Middle Ages, and indeed beyond.[5]

Although they are often treated as a single unit by commentators, Crowley's three 1550 editions (ESTC 19906, 19906a, 19907) were not simple reprints: Kane and Donaldson (1988: 6–7 and *passim*) have shown that Crowley modified his text as new manuscripts became available to him. He was clearly a conscientious man who went out of his way to 'not onely gather togyther suche aunciente copies as I could come by but also consult such me*n* as I knew to be more exercised in the studie of antiquities, then I my selfe haue ben' (ESTC 19906, sig. *.ii r). As Thorne and Uhart (1986: 252–3) suggest,

> Crowley felt a strong obligation to reproduce a text faithful to the MS tradition which he came into contact with, or at least to the one that he regarded as best. The extent of his Protestant bias in his own writings and in the marginal commentary to *Piers Plowman* is quite clear. The faithfulness of his text must be attributed to other, stronger, factors: principally, we suggest, the breadth of readership that the poem had already attained in manuscript in the previous two centuries or so. In view of this, and presumably of the printer's wish to secure a large and immediate sale, the question of rewriting was unlikely to have arisen. That the contemporaneous Sion College MS [now Takamiya 23] does demonstrate a rewriting of sorts simply illustrates one of the differences between the potential readership for a printed text and that for a MS: one large, imaginary and with diverse interests, the other small and specialist. Crowley's texts ride on the back of a popularity, or at least a popular notion, of what *Piers Plowman* was like, established in something like two hundred years of manuscript transmission. (Thorne and Uhart 1986: 252–3)[6]

Comparison of the three versions bears out this impression of careful revision, even in accidentals, which indicate that Crowley had the text reset

[5] Annotations in other copies of Crowley's *Piers Plowman* reveal the range of functions this complex – and arguably baffling – text could perform. Thus, for instance, the copy of Crowley's first edition in Glasgow University Library (Sp Coll 1168) was owned at one time by Robert Burton (1577–1640), author of *The Anatomy of Melancholy* (1621), who decided that its fly-leaves were an appropriate repository for improving Socratic aphorisms along the lines of Erasmus's *Adages*: 'Prayse lytle but disprayse lesse', 'Silence ys the aunswere of foolish questions', 'There ys no dyfference betwene a great Seller of tydynges and a lyer', 'Womans counsayle ys weake and a chylds vnperfet', 'Nothing becommeth a wyse man so muche as temperaunce'. Such commonplace reflexions are fairly unspecific, but two others perhaps echo the poem, at least in their deployment of alliteration: 'Repentaunce deserueth pardon', 'P*er*forme whatsoeuer thow promysest'.

[6] It was from some of these men 'exercised in the studie of antiquities' that Crowley learned of the author: 'Roberte Langelande, a Shropshire man borne in Clybirie [i.e. Cleobury], about viiii. myles from Maluerne hilles' (sig. *.ii r). Modern scholarship has modified this view somewhat, but Crowley's interest in the complex and still controversial issue of the poem's authorship is notable.

between ESTC 19906 (Kane and Donaldson's Cr^{1}) and 19906a (Cr^{2}), and carried out further corrections with 19907 (Cr^{3}). Kane and Donaldson's outline of the process (1988: 7) would therefore seem to be confirmed:

> The first impression of Crowley's edition represents the text of a lost manuscript, in places arbitrarily emended by Crowley. The second impression was reset, and appears to offer a conflated text based on a new manuscript (also lost) under constant comparison with the text of the first impression. The text of the third impression may incorporate 'correction' from yet another manuscript.

Kane and Donaldson's focus, as textual critics, was on establishing the genetic relationship of witnesses for a reconstructed archetypal B-text rather than tracing detailed distinctions between Crowley's three texts, so they did not pursue matters further.[7] In order to demonstrate how 'accidental' features were modified as Crowley's edition evolved, we might compare three parallel passages (Texts 4.1–4.3). The lineation added is that of Kane and Donaldson (1988: 363–5), and follows them in not assigning numbers to lines in Latin:

Text (4.1): Crowley 1550a (STC 19906 = Cr^{1}), folio 34v

And y^{t} he weneth wel to haue, I wil it him bereue.
Kynd witte wolde that ech a wight wrought
Or in dikinge or in deluynge, or trauayl in prayers,
Contemplatiue life, or actiue life, Christe would they
The psalter saith in psalms of Beati omnes (wrought
The freke that fedeth him self w^{t} his faithful laboure

[folio 35r]

Be blessed be the boke in bodye and soule.
Labores manuum tuarum. et c.
Yet I pray you qd Pierce praye Charitie & ye canne,
Any leche crafte lere it me my deare
For some of my seruauntes and my selfe bothe
Of al a weke worke not, so our wombeaketh
I wote well qd Hunger, what sikenes you ayleth
Ye haue manged ouer muche, & y^{t} maketh you grone
And I hote the qd Hunger, as thou thy hele wilneste
That thou drinke no day, er thou dyne somewhat
Eate not I hote the, ere Hunger the take,
And send the of hys sauce to sauour wyth thy lyppes

How Pi=
res pray=
eth hu*n*ger
to teche
him a lich
ckraft for
hym and
for hys
seruantes

[7] For Crowley's merits as an editor, see for an authoritative discussion Brewer 1996: 7–19.

And kepe some tyll souper time, and sytte not to long
And rise vp ere appetite haue eaten his fyll
Lette not syr Surfet syt on thy borde
Leue him not for he is lecherours & licorous of tong
And after mani maner of meat his maw is a hu*n*gred
And if thou diet the thus, I dare laye my eares
That phisike shal his furred hodde, for his foode sell
And hys cloke of Calabrye, w^{t} al his knaps of golde,
And be fayne be my fayth his phisike to lette
And lerne to laboure w^{t} hond, for lyuelode is swete,
For murtherers are many leches lorde hem amende.
They do me*n* dye by their drinkis yer destiny it wolde
By .S. Paule qd Pierce these ar profitable wordes
Wend y^{u} honger when y^{u} wylt, y^{t} wel be thou euer

Text (4.2): Crowley 1550b (STC 19906a = Cr^{2}), folio 34v

And y^{t} he weneth well to haue, I wil it him bereue
Kynde wyt woulde, that ech a wyght wrought.
Or in digging or in deluing, or trauaile of prayers,
Conte*m*platiue life, or actiue life, Christ wold thei wro=
The psalter saith in y^{e} psalmes of beati omnes, (ught
The freke y^{t} fedeth him selfe, w^{t} hys faythful laboure

[folio 35r]
He is blessed by the boke in body and in soule.
Labores manuum tuarum, quoniam manducabis Psal. 128.
Yet I pray you qd Pierce pur charitie & ye can
Any leefe leche craft, lere it me my deare
For some of my seruaunts, and mi selfe both
Of al a weke worke not, so our wombe aketh,
I wote well qd hunger, what sikenes the ayleth,
Ye haue manged ouer muche, & y^{t} maketh you grone,
And I hote the qd hunger, as thou thy hele wilneste,
That thou drinke no day, ere thou dine somewhat,
Eate not I hote the, ere hunger the taketh
And send the of hys sauce, to sauour with thy lyppes,
And kepe some tyl souper time, and syt not to longe,
And ryse vp ere appetite haue eaten his fyll,
Let not syr Surfyte syt at thy borde,
Leue him not for he is licherous, & lycorous of tong,
And after mani maner of meat, his maw is a hu*n*gred,
And if thou diet the thus, I dare laye my eares
That phisike shal his furred hode, for his fode sell,
And his cloke of Calabrie, with all y^{e} knaps of golde,
And be fayne be my fayth, his phisike to let

Howe Pi= res pray= eth hu*n*ger to teache him a lich crafte for hym and for hys seruau*n*tes

And learne to laboure w^{t} hond, for lyuelode is swete,
For murtherers are many leches, lorde hem amende,
They do me*n* dye by their drinks, yer destinie it wolde
By .S. Paule qd Pierce, these are profetable wordes
Wend nu honger when thou wylt, y^{t} wel be thou euer,

Text (4.3): Crowley 1550c (STC 19907 = Cr^{3}), folio 34v

And y^{t} he weneth well to haue, I will it him bereue
Kynde wyt woulde, that ech a wyght wrought.
Or in digging or in deluing, or trauaile of prayers
Co*n*te*m*platiue life, or actiue life, Christe wold they wor=
The psalter saith in y^{e} psalmes of beati omnes, (ught
The freke y^{t} fedeth him selfe, w^{t} hys faythful laboure

[folio 35r]

He is blessed by the boke in body and in soule.
Labores manuum tuarum, quoniam manducabis — Psal. 128.
Yet I pray you qd Pierce, pur charitie & ye can
Any leefe leche craft, lere it me my deare
For some of my seruaunts, and mi selfe both
Of al a weke worke not, so our wombe aketh,
I wote well qd hunger, what sikenes the ayleth,
Ye haue manged ouer muche, & y^{t} maketh you grone
And I hote the qd hunger, as thou thy hele wilneste,
That thou drinke no day, ere thou dine somewhat,
Eate not I hote the, ere hunger, the taketh
And send the of hys sauce, to sauour with thy lyppes,
And kepe some tyl souper time, and syt not to longe,
And ryse vp ere appetite, haue eaten his fyll:
Let not syr Surfyte, syt at thy borde,
Leue him not for he is licherous, & lycorous of tong,
And after many maner of meat, his maw is a hu*n*gred,
And if thou diet the thus, I dare laye my eares
That Phisike shal his furred hode, for his fode sell,
And his cloke of Calabrie, wyth all ye knaps of golde,
And be fayne be my fayth, his phisike to let
And learne to labour w^{t} hond, for lyuelode is swete
For murtherers are many leches, lorde hem amende,
They do me*n* dye by their drinks, yer destinie it wold
By .S. Paule qd Pierce, these are profetable wordes
Wend now honger when thou wylt, y^{t} wel be y^{u} euer,

[Margin: Howe Pi= res pray= eth hu*n*ger to teache him a lich crafte for hym and for hys seruau*n*tes]

Examination of Texts (4.1) through (4.3) shows that, although there are nevertheless some differences between them, (4.2) and (4.3) tend to agree against (4.1), both in substantives and in accidentals. For our purposes we might notice in particular the punctuation of the three texts, which is clearly something attended to by the printer with a degree of care, and with reference to some clear principles. In Text (4.1) punctuation is sparing, used only occasionally to mark Langland's half-lines; it is therefore metrically deployed. In Text (4.2), however, not only are half-lines marked much more consistently, but extra punctuation is often used at the end of lines as well, to assist in disambiguation of cola and commata. In Text (4.3) the repertoire of pointing becomes even more regular and indeed sophisticated, with ends of lines tending to be marked more frequently when the first word in the next line flags the beginning of a new colon, e.g.:

> For some of my seruaunts, and mi selfe both 255
> Of al a weke worke not, so our wombe aketh,
> I wote well qd hunger, what sikenes the ayleth,
> Ye haue manged ouer muche, & y^{t} maketh you grone
> And I hote the qd hunger, . . .

There has been an increase in the printer's repertoire of marks, moreover, with a double punctus being deployed to indicate a lengthier pause after a sequence of cola beginning with *And*. There is even a usage that was later to become more common, whereby a thematic subject is followed by a comma, as in *ere hunger, the taketh*:

> Eate not I hote the, ere hunger, the taketh 261
> And send the of hys sauce, to sauour with thy
> lyppes, . . .

How are these changes to be interpreted? Before answering this question, it is worth comparing Crowley's texts with manuscript witnesses for the B-text of the poem. The following seem particularly relevant for our purposes:

(1) Cambridge, University Library, MS Ll 4.14, dating from the first half of the fifteenth century. Thorne and Uhart (1986), pursuing some earlier suggestions by Walter Skeat, were able to show that glosses and annotation in this manuscript corresponded with those found in Crowley's edition: 'A comparison between Crowley's texts and the glossary reveals that Crowley almost invariably uses the word in the same form as they appear in the text of the poem in CUL MS Ll.iv.14' (1986: 248). However, pointing out that the habit of glossing and annotating *Piers Plowman* was fairly widespread in the sixteenth century, they do not feel able to go the extra step and identify the glossator as Crowley, a suggestion made by Skeat: 'there is

insufficient evidence to decide the matter either way' (1986: 251). Whether Crowley drew upon Ll 4.14, therefore, is uncertain, and Kane and Donaldson's collations indicate that it cannot have been one of the 'lost manuscripts' they flag as Crowley's exemplars; it is simply too far away in the genetic relationship of the text. Nevertheless, the manuscript is a fair representative of the B-text tradition in the fifteenth century, and thus offers a point of comparison. Here is a transcription of the parallel passage in Ll 4.14 to that in Texts (4.1)–(4.3).[8]

Text (4.4): Cambridge, University Library, MS Ll 4.14, folio 32v

And that he weneth well to haue I wolle it him bere*n*
kynde witt wolde þ^{t} iche awiȝte wrouȝte
Or in dykinge or in deluyng ⁖ or traueilinge in p*ra*yeris}
Contemplatijf lijf or actijf ⁖ crist wolde þei wrouten}
The sauȝt*er* seiþ in þ^{e} salme ⁖ of beati omnes*
The ffreek þ^{t} ffediþ him self ⁖ w^{t} his ffeiþffull labour*e*
labores manuu*m* tuaru*m* et c.*
he is blessid be þ^{e} book ⁖ in bodi and in soule
Ȝit I p*ra*ie ȝou qd peers* ⁖ p*ur* charite & ȝe ku*n*ne
ony leef of leche crafte ⁖ lere it me my dere leche craft*
ffor su*m*me of my s*er*uants & my self ⁖ ben seke oþ*er* whyle
Of alle þe weke worchen not ⁖ so our*e* wombe akeþ
I woot well qd hung*ur* ⁖ what seeknesse ȝou eiliþ
Ȝe han manged to moche ⁖ and þ^{t} makiþ ȝou to grone
and I hote þe qd hung*ur** ⁖ as þ^{u} þin hele wilneste
{þ^{t} þ^{u} drinke no day ⁖ er þ^{u} dyne sum what
{Ete not I hote þe ⁖ er hunger þe take
and sende þe of his sauce ⁖ to sauere w^{t} þi lipis
and kepe sum to sop*er* tyme ⁖ and sitte not to longe
and rise vp er appetijt ⁖ haue eten his fille
late not Sir Surffayt ⁖ Sitten at þi borde
leue him not ffor he is leccherus ⁖ and lekerous of his tunge
And aft*er* many man*er* metis ⁖ his mawe is afygred
and if þ^{u} diete þe þus ⁖ I dar ley my*n* eres
þ^{t} phesik* shall his ffurrid hood ⁖ ffor his ffode selle
and his cloke of calabre ⁖ w^{t} alle þ^{e} knoppis of golde

[8] In this manuscript, the text appears in black ink throughout; certain lines, phrases and words are underlined as indicated. Most of the underlining is also in black, save for those words marked with an asterisk, where the underlining is in red; the latter practice seems reserved for marginal place markers (as in *leche craft*), Latin quotations or – not always consistently – for characters in the poem, personified or otherwise. The black underlining may be a later imposition on the manuscript, suggested inter alia by its use to mark 'difficult readings'. Curly brackets ({}) in the transcription indicate a brace. The clearly later marginal note *leches ar murderers*, interestingly, seems to be in an archaising hand from the sixteenth century.

and be ffayne be my ffeiþ ∻ his phesik to lete
And lere to laboure w^{t} lond ∻ for lijflode is swete
{ffor murþerers ar many leches ∻ lord hem amende leches ar murderers
{They don me*n* dye þoruȝ her drynkis ∻ er his tyme wolde
By Seynt poul* quod peers ∻ þese arn p*ro*phetable wordis
wende now hung*ur* whan þ^{u} wylte ∻ þ^{t} well be þ^{e} eu*ere*

(2) New Haven, Yale University Library, MS Takamiya 23 (olim Sion College) has already been referred to, as a work dating from roughly the same date as Crowley's editions. It also forms with them, according to Kane and Donaldson (1988: 32–4), a 'persistent genetic group' in textual terms, albeit with some 'contrary indications'; despite these latter, therefore, it offers an interesting contrast with Crowley's printed texts in terms of presentation. Engrossed words are transcribed in bold; the underlining is in black.

Text (4.5): New Haven, Yale University Library, MS Takamiya 23 (olim Sion College), folio 26r

And that he wenith well to haue / I will it him bireue
Kynde wit wold / that eu*ery* man wrought

[folio 26v]

Outher in dyking or deluyng / or trauaile in p*ray*ers
Contemplatiue life or Actiue life / Christ wolde thei wrought
The psalter seith in psalme of **Beati omnes**
The man that fedith himself / w^{t} his feithffull labo*ur*
He is blessed be the book / in bodie and in Soule
Labores manuu*m* tuaru*m* et c.
Yet I p*ray* you qd Piers / for charitie and ye can
Any leaf of lechecrafte / Lerne it me my dere
ffor some of my se*r*uant*is* / and my self also
Of all a wike worke not / So oure wombe aketh
I wot well qd hunger / what disease y^{u} haste
Ye haue eaten ou*er*much /& that make you grone
But I warne the qd hunger / as y^{u} thine helth wilt haue
That y^{u} drink no daie / ere thou eate somewhat
And eate not I warne the / ere hunger the take
And send the of his sauce / to sauo*ur* w^{t} thi lippes
And kepe some to souper / and sitt not to longe
But rise w^{t} an Appetite / & ere he be fillid
Lat not *ser* Surfet / sit at ye boorde
Trust him not he is lecherouse / & likerouse of tong
And after many su*n*drie meat*is* / his mawe is ahungred

and if ye diet you thus / I dare laie myne earis
That Phisike shall his ffurred hoodis / for his food selle
And his Cloke of Calaber / w^{t} all the knappes of gold
And be fayne be my faith / his phisike to leue
And lerne to labo*ur* w^{t} lond / for lifelode is swete
ffor many leches are Murtherers / the lord them amende
They cause me*n* die through their drink*is* / ere their tyme come
By saint Paule qd piers /thise are profitable word*is*
Go now hunger when y^{u} wilt / & well be thou eu*er*

Comparison of these two manuscript versions with each other and with Crowley's editions reveals some interesting distinctions. First, Takamiya 23 is in some ways a more 'modern' text than Crowley's editions. Certain modernisations are common to both: for instance, thorns (except occasionally as <y> in function words) and yoghs are not deployed in either. But in substantive variants Takamiya 23 is markedly more 'up to date' than the other witnesses under examination, with a series of significant differences in vocabulary, all in the direction of forms that have become more widely current. By contrast, in almost all these cases the Crowley editions agree with the more old-fashioned Ll.4.14. 'Modernised' readings in Takamiya 23, compared here with Crowley 1550a (Cr^{I}), are *euery man* (247) beside Cr^{I}'s *a wight, outher . . . or* (248) beside *Or . . . or* (a distinctive Langlandian form, presumably related to Latin *aut . . . aut*), *man* (251) beside *freke, lerne* (254) beside *lere, disease* (257) beside *sikenes, eaten* (258) beside *manged, warne* (259, 261) beside *hote, Trust* (266) beside *leue, sundrie* (267) beside *maner, leue* (271) beside *lette, cause* (274) beside *do, Go* (276) beside *Wend.* Some of these forms, e.g. *man* for *freke,* were adopted despite their disturbance of the alliterative pattern. The only form in this passage where Crowley's editions agree with Takamiya 23 against Ll.4.14 is *ahungred* (267), where the latter manuscript has the odd form *afygred*; the annotator has underlined this form in Ll.4.1.4, along with *manged* on the same folio. The form *afygred* is fairly explicable as simply a matter of a missing abbreviation-mark for <n> over <y>, which would yield *afyngred.* The form *afingred* etc., 'very hungry', according to the OED derived from *ofhungred,* is fairly well attested in Middle English, e.g. *afingret* in *The Fox and the Wolf,* line 110 in Oxford, Bodleian Library, MS Digby 86, but was clearly obscure in the sixteenth century; the OED's last record of the form is in a speech assigned to a Cornishman in a curious miscellany by the sixteenth-century physician and traveller Andrew Boorde: *The fyrst boke of the introduction of knowledge* (1555).[9]

[9] Kane and Donaldson (1988: 364) emend line 267 with the form *alonged,* which seems to be conjectural and without manuscript authority. However, the reading *afyngred,* widely attested in the early witnesses, seems to me to make good sense in context, and is a suitably 'difficult reading'.

Manged, by contrast, though still rare, achieved the status of deployment in Richard Stanyhurst's translation of Virgil (1582), no doubt favoured for its French etymology (cf. OED *maunge* v.), given Stanyhurst's taste for 'linguistic virtuosity' (ODNB).

Secondly, however, and by contrast, the punctuation of Takamiya 23 seems to look backwards, aligning with the usage of Ll.4.14 and the first Crowley edition. Both manuscripts mark half-lines, Ll.4.14 with a punctus elevatus and Takamiya 23 with a virgule, while the first Crowley edition, although (as we have seen) inconsistent, follows a similar pattern; punctuation in these cases is clearly an aid to the apprehension of the poem's metre. By contrast the remaining two Crowley editions, again as we have seen, deploy punctuation in an increasingly more complex way to indicate grammatical structure, and this practice persisted in the remaining sixteenth-century edition, that printed by Owen Rogers in 1561. Rogers's edition has been condemned as an inaccurate reproduction, without any independent authority, of Crowley's third edition (Brewer 1996: 20), but for our purposes it is an interesting confirmation of sixteenth-century punctuation – in print – of a poem in what was by this time an increasingly archaic verse-form.

Text (4.6): Rogers 1561, sig. J.iv v

And that he weneth well to haue, I will it him bereue
Kind wit woulde, that ech a wight wrought.
Or in digginge or in deluynge, or trauaile of praiers
Co*ntem*platiue lyfe, or actyue life, Christe woulde they wroughte,
The psalter saith in the psalmes of beati omnes
The freke that fedeth himself, with hys faithful labor
He is blessed by the boke in body and in soule.
Labores m*anuum* tuaru*m*, quonia*m* manducabis Psalm. 128.
Yet I pray you qd Pierce, pur charitie and ye can
Anye leefe leche craft, lere it me my deare
For some of my seruantes, and my selfe bothe
Of all a weke worke not, so our wombe aketh,
I wote well qd hungre, what sickenes the ayleth,
Ye haue manged ouer muche, and that maketh you grone,
And I hote thee qd hungre, as thou thy hele wilneste,
That thou drinke no day, or thou dine some what,
Eate not I hote thee, ere hungre, thee taketh
and send the of his sauce, to sauour wyth thy lippes,
and kepe some til souper time, and sit not to longe,

and rise vp ere appetite, haue eaten his fyll
Let not syr surfyte, syt at thy borde
Leue him not for he is licherous, & licorous of tonge,
and

[sig. K.i.r]

And after many maner of meat, his maw is ahu*n*gred,
and if thou diet the thus, I dare laye my eares
That phisike shal his furred hode, for his fode sell,
and his cloke of Calabrie, wyth al the knaps of golde
and be faine be my faith, his phisike to let
and learne to labour with hond, for liuelode is swete
For murtherers are many leches, lorde hem amende,
They do men die by their drinks, yer destinie it wold
By Sainte Paule qd pierce, these are profetable
wordes.
Wend now hunger when thou wilt, that wel be thou
euer.

Rogers's practice, however clumsy it may be (we might note the mangled Latin in line 252a), is in accidentals an advance on Crowley's third edition. An attempt has been made to reflect half-lines with comma-marks, but comma-marks and the punctus are also deployed fairly carefully to distinguish grammatical structures. Even more interestingly, there is a degree of variation in the use of capital letters at the beginning of lines: the variation between *And* and *and* on sig. K.i r, for instance, seems to coincide with changes in cola.

How are these differences between more or less contemporary texts such as Takamiya 23 and the Crowley/Rogers editions to be interpreted? It seems that Takamiya 23 – like Sir Adrian Fortescue's Digby manuscript – was developed for personal use; the lexical updatings indicate that the work continued to be regarded as a living text, and glossing could be incorporated into the text rather than being part of the text's paratextual apparatus, banished to the margins by Crowley and (even further) to a separate glossary by Rogers. And Takamiya 23's punctuation, emphasising the work's poetic rather than grammatical form, would fit with a manuscript culture in which reader–audience were envisaged as cooperating with the scribe in the re-creation of the work, arguably as part of a community of practice.

By contrast, Crowley – who approached his task with the kind of seriousness to be seen in the preparation of *A testimonie of antiquitie* a few years later, consulting manuscript sources to re-create the past –

worked more in the manner of a modern critical editor. His punctuation, especially in the second and third editions, shows someone who wished to present the text to a wider contemporary discourse community that needed extra help in engaging with structures (and a verse-form) that would have been perceived as increasingly alien. Crowley, therefore, points forward in his own way to the editing practices we have already seen in later centuries. Such radicalism – as it has regularly done since – has of course attracted critical comment, especially when *Piers Plowman* was re-evaluated by antiquaries in the eighteenth century.[10]

4.2 The Return of John Gower

At the end of the sixteenth century the antiquarian John Stow, in his *Survey of London*, offered the first description of the tomb of the poet John Gower, in what was then the church of St Mary Overy ('over the river') in Southwark:

> *Iohn Gower,* Esquire, a famous Poet, was then an especiall Benefactor to that worke, and was there buried on the North side of the said Church, in the Chappell of Saint *Iohn,* where he founded a Chantry, hee lyeth under a Tombe of Stone, with his Image also of Stone over him. The haire of his head aburne, long to his shoulders, but curling up, and a small forked beard; on his head a Chaplet, like a coronet of foure Roses, an habite of Purple, damasked downe to his feet, a Collar of Esses of gold about his necke, under his feet the likenesse of three Bookes, which hee compiled. The first, named *Speculum Meditantis*, written in French: The second, *Vox Clamantis*, penned in Latine: The third, *Confessio Amantis*, written in English, and this last is printed. (Stow 1598: 450)

Gower's tomb is still *in situ*, in what is now Southwark Cathedral on the south bank of the Thames near London Bridge, near the places of entertainment of Elizabethan and Jacobean London, including such theatres as The Rose, The Swan, The Hope and – most famously – The Globe. It is therefore no surprise that the church was frequented by successful actors and playwrights of the period, including John Fletcher and Philip Massinger, who were both buried there, as was Edmund Shakespeare, William's brother. Although there is no surviving record of his attendance, it seems almost certain that William would have known the church well, and the tomb of Gower, in the church's nave, would have been hard to miss

[10] For further discussion of Crowley's punctuation practices and those of Rogers, showing shifts within as well as between the various editions, see most importantly Scott 2015.

(see Hines et al. 2004: 36–41). And in 1607–8, in the play *Pericles*, Shakespeare (or his possible collaborator) had the older poet return to life not only as the story's source but as the chorus, speaking in the distinctive octosyllabic couplets he had used for the *Confessio Amantis*. For Shakespeare, and indeed for his Southwark audience, Gower would have been a revenant from the nearby church. His presence on the stage made a subtle comment on changing practices of – and beliefs about – posthumous memorialisation, something of a theme in the play (Walsh 2013).

Shakespeare and his contemporaries would have encountered Gower's *Confessio Amantis* probably through one of the editions of Thomas Berthelette (d. 1555),[11] who printed the work in 1532 and 1554; there was no other edition of the *Confessio* until the nineteenth century, and Berthelette's editions remained in fairly wide circulation.[12] As Siân Echard has noted, it was a high-grade production, as was to be expected from the workshop of someone who had been – until the monarch's death in 1547 – Henry VIII's King's Printer, charged with the production inter alia of statutes and proclamations, outputs whose appearance had a performative function. Siân Echard (2004: 117) has drawn attention to the hierarchy of typefaces used in the production of the *Confessio*, possibly adopted to emphasise the poet's role as commentator or compiler:

> a blackletter font for the English text; a smaller blackletter font for the Latin glosses; and yet a third font, a small Roman, for the Latin verses. Thus Berthelette's edition clearly marks out for a reader the different parts (and languages) of the *Confessio*, and in so doing, it emphasises the poem's apparatus.

Berthelette's productions were explicitly designed to displace the only earlier edition, that printed by William Caxton in 1483; Berthelette, in his preface, complains that the earlier printer omitted 'lynes and columnes, ye and sometyme holle padges' (1554: sig.*.iii. r). Yet, in assessing

[11] As was frequently the case, Berthelette's name was spelt in various ways in his own time. I have adopted here the spelling of his name in Echard 2004, but ODNB, from which I have derived biographical information, uses *Berthelet* and *Berthelot*. The printer seems to have been French in origin, possibly related to the bookseller Jacques Berthelot (d. 1541), who was active in Caen and Rennes. It is noticeable that Berthelette's own coat of arms included a fleur-de-lis.

[12] The wide circulation of Berthelette's editions is well attested. The copy of the 1554 edition in Glasgow University Library (Sp Coll Bm5–f.18), for instance, seems to have reached Scotland by the end of the sixteenth century, passing through the hands of at least eight people before the library acquired it. One was James Dougall, deacon of the splendidly named Incorporation of Gardeners in Glasgow (active 1640–61), followed by a 'Captain John Anderson', who sold it to the university along with other volumes in 1693. I am grateful to Bob Maclean for discussing this copy with me.

Berthelette's authority as an editor as well as a printer, it is worth comparing his edition with the text as it appears in the manuscript generally acknowledged to be closest to Gower's own holograph: Oxford, Bodleian Library, MS Fairfax 3, which was used by G. C. Macaulay as the base manuscript for what is still the standard edition of the *Confessio Amantis* (Macaulay 1900).

Fairfax 3 is a rather curious volume in a number of ways. It represents what has become known as the 'third recension' of the poem, in which sections at the beginning and end of the text, which originally contained praise of Richard II, were replaced by passages lamenting the state of England and offering support for the man who eventually displaced Richard: Henry Bolingbroke, the future Henry IV. These passages were added in two hands that – although using a similar script – differ from that which produced the bulk of the manuscript; however, it has long been observed that these other scribes deployed the same distinctive spelling-system as that adopted by the main hand in the volume. This system also appears in another early revised copy of the poem in yet another hand, the 'Stafford' manuscript, now San Marino, Huntington Library, MS EL 26 A.17.[13]

Although it seems likely that both Fairfax 3 and the Stafford manuscript were produced in London ateliers, the spelling-system common to the manuscripts' various scribal stints differs in a number of ways from the usage found in contemporary late fourteenth-century London texts, namely 'Type III' language, prototypically found in e.g. the Ellesmere manuscript of Chaucer's *Canterbury Tales* (now San Marino, Huntington Library, MS EL 26 C.9), or Cambridge, Trinity College MS B.15.17, a copy of Langland's *Piers Plowman*. Type III is the second in the sequence of London-based usages first identified by Michael Samuels in 1963. As already flagged in Chapter 1, Type III represents focused – not fixed – usage within the cline 'that is the total range of [Middle English] dialectal variation' (Sandved 1981: 390) and is not in any way a 'standard' comparable to present-day 'educated' written English, i.e. a usage that has undergone all the stages of standardisation usually identified, such as selection, elaboration, codification and acceptance. Rather, it should be considered another linguistic scripta, deployed in the production of high-status texts circulating in particular in court and government circles, and

[13] For the most recent description of Fairfax 3, see www.wcu.edu/johngower/scholarship/PearsallMS/MSS/Fairfax3.html. For a description of the Stafford manuscript, see http://catalog.huntington.org/search?/tConfessio+Amantis/tconfessio+amantis/1%2C6%2C17%2CB/frameset&FF=tconfessio+amantis+manuscript&1%2C1%2C. Both urls were last consulted on 25 May 2019.

generally presented in the special handwriting variety known as anglicana formata.[14]

Text (4.7) from Fairfax 3 demonstrates some of the distinctive usages that differentiate the language of Fairfax 3 from Type III. The text appears early in Book 3 of the *Confessio*; the lineation is Macaulay's (1900: 227).

Text (4.7): Oxford, Bodleian Library, MS Fairfax 3, folio 47r

M I goode fader tell me þis:
What thing is Ire. Sone it is.
That in oure englissh Wraþe is hote
Which haþ hise wordes ay so hote
That all a ma*nn*es pacience.
Is fyred of þe violence
ffor he wiþ him haþ eu*er*e fyue
Servantȝ þat helpen him to stryue
The ferst of hem Malencolie:
Is cleped which in compaignie
An hundred times in an houre
Wol as an angri beste loure.
And noman wot þe cause why
Mi sone schrif þee now forþi
Hast þou be Malencolien?
Ȝ E fader be seint Julien
Bot I vntrewe wordes vse
I mai me noght þ*er*of excuse
And al makþ loue wel I wot
Of which myn herte is eu*er*e hot

[column b]

So that I brenne as doþ a glede
ffor wraþe that I mai noght spede.
And þus fulofte a day for noght
Saue onlich of myn oghne þoght

[14] The Ellesmere manuscript of the *Canterbury Tales* and the Trinity manuscript of *Piers Plowman* have been ascribed by Linne Mooney and Simon Horobin to the hand of the scribe Adam Pinkhurst (see especially Mooney 2006, Horobin 2010, and especially Mooney and Stubbs 2013). Although this claim has been challenged by Jane Roberts (2011), and more recently by Laurence Warner (2015, 2018), a vigorous defence of the ascription, by Horobin, is forthcoming; as Horobin points out, in all such research the issue is essentially one of plausibility. Mooney and Horobin based their discussion on the seminal identification, by Ian Doyle and Malcolm Parkes, of a distinctive scribal community of practice in the early fifteenth-century engaged in the copying of important manuscripts of Chaucer's *Canterbury Tales* and Gower's *Confessio Amantis*, all presented in anglicana formata (see Doyle and Parkes 1978). The correlation of linguistic behaviour with a distinctive script is one that deserves further investigation.

I am so wiþ miseluen wroþ
That how so þat þe game goþ
With oþre men I am noght glad
Bot I am wel þe more vnglad
ffor þat is oþre mennes game
It torneþ me to pure grame
Thus am I wiþ miself opp*re*ssed
Of þoght þe which I haue imp*re*ssed
That al wakende I dreme and meete.
That I wiþ hire al one meete
And preie hire of som good ansuere
Bot for sche wol noght gladly swere
Sche seiþ me nay wiþouten oþ.

Many of the linguistic features in Text (4.7) will be familiar to any student of Chaucer who will have almost certainly first encountered that poet's writings as transmitted through the spellings and grammar of the Ellesmere manuscript. Grammatical features common to both Ellesmere and Fairfax 3 include, for instance, the inflected form of the vocative adjective in *Mi goode fader*, compared with the uninflected strong form in *som good ansuere*; the inflected plural *hise*;[15] the present plural verb in *–en*, e.g. *helpen*; and the pronoun *hem* 'them' (alongside *þei* 'they' elsewhere). Spellings in Fairfax 3 that align with Type III include *bot* 'but', *schold(e)*, *whan* 'when', *wol* 'will' etc.

Other forms in Fairfax 3 are somewhat distinct from those in Ellesmere, but not uncommon in London texts of the period, as witnessed by (for instance) the documents collected by Chambers and Daunt (1931). Some forms such as *noght* 'not' (cf. prototypical Ellesmere *nat*, though *noght* is a minor variant in that manuscript), *such(e)* (cf. Ellesmere *swiche*), *þese* (cf. Ellesmere *þise*) are not especially regionally distinctive. The spelling *ferst* 'first', though traditionally a south-eastern usage, is fairly common in many texts that can be localised to London at the time.

However, other forms are more uncommon within the Middle English dialect continuum, and certainly atypical of late fourteenth-century London usage. For instance, the present participle inflexion in *–ende*, in *wakende*, and the syncopated third person singular verb in *makþ*, though not unknown in earlier London texts, would undoubtedly have been considered archaic by the Ellesmere scribe – they were certainly recessive in Middle English dialects – while the spelling *oghne* 'own' (adjective)

[15] In the form *hise*, the inflexion *–e*, being an analogical linguistic innovation, is not counted towards the iambic measure of the line.

would have seemed decidedly odd; the online LALME has sporadic records of *oghne* and similar forms (e.g. *oghene*) from the North Midlands, but there is a much more focused cluster in Kent.[16] These non-London usages, when supplemented by forms from elsewhere in Fairfax 3, such as *seluer* 'silver', *soster* 'sister', *þerwhiles þat* 'while', *boþen* 'both', *ȝoue* 'given', *or . . . or* 'either . . . or' and medial *-h-* in *hyhe* 'high', *sihe* 'saw' etc, enabled Michael Samuels and myself many years ago to identify the language of Fairfax 3 – in all scribal stints – as a mixture of Kentish and Suffolk usage (see Samuels and Smith 1981). And since this distinctive usage was also found in other copies of the *Confessio* with a distinct genetic ancestry reaching back to the archetypal ancestor of the text, such as the Stafford manuscript, it seemed to Samuels and myself a reasonable assumption to consider this archetypal language to be that of John Gower; that Gower was associated with land ownership in Kent and Suffolk would seem to offer some support to – albeit of course not absolute proof of – this conclusion.

Whether or not our identification or indeed localisation of the archetypal language of the Gower tradition with Gower's own usage are still accepted, it is nevertheless an intriguing fact that – rather as with the transmission of Love's *Mirror* discussed in Chapter 3 – a number of these linguistic features persisted in the Gower tradition through and beyond the fifteenth century: there was, it seems, a 'Gower scripta'. Of the forty-nine extant manuscripts of the *Confessio*, for instance, no fewer than thirty retain forms of 'own' with medial *-gh-*, either as *oghne*, *oughne* or in a slightly modified form, e.g. *ogne*. Variants of *sihe* 'saw' (cf. Ellesmere *saugh*) are even better attested in the *Confessio*, appearing in forty-three witnesses, including the printed editions by Caxton (1483a) and Berthelette (1532, 1554).

Comparison of Fairfax 3 with the later prints, both Caxton's of 1483 and Berthelette's of 1532 and 1554, nevertheless, does show a general tendency to mute this distinctively Gowerian dialectal usage, in the same way that – as discussed in Chapter 3 – prints of Nicholas Love gradually purge the characteristic northernisms of that tradition and presumably for the same reasons: a response to increasing general pressures towards orthographic standardisation that extended beyond the transmission or particular texts or text-types. But there are also some interesting further distinctions between the prints that show

[16] For the online LALME ('eLALME'), see www.lel.ed.ac.uk/ihd/elalme/elalme.html, last consulted on 25 May 2019.

other processes, notably in the increasingly sophisticated deployment of punctuation.

Fairfax 3, as the transcription in (4.7) above shows, is sparing in its use of punctuation-marks. Punctus and punctus elevatus are used at the start of the passage, to indicate interaction between the characters of Amans and his 'confessor', Father Genius, but with the exception of a stray – and rather inexplicable – punctus elevatus in line 27, the only other marks used in the passage are a punctus interrogativus, and decorated and illuminated initials. Caxton's 1483 print is, if anything, even more sparing, omitting engrossed initials in favour of simple indentation, dropping the punctus interrogativus and deploying a simple punctus in the opening lines of the passage to indicate the shift from one speaker to another:

(Caxton 1483a: folio 52r, column a)

  My good father telle me this
what thynge is Ire. Sone it is
That in our Englysshe wrath is hote

However, Berthelette's two editions show the evolution of the text in rather more interesting ways. Texts (4.8) and (4.9) are transcriptions from the editions of 1532 and 1554 respectively (the foliation is that of the original prints):

Text (4.8): Berthelette (1532: folio 47r, column b)

¶ My good father telle me this
what thynge is Ire? Sonne it is
That in our englysshe wrath is hote
which hath his wordes ay so hote
That all a mannes pacyence
Is fyred of the vyolence
For he with hym hath euer fyue
Seruauntes, that helpen hym to stryue
  The fyrst of hem melancoly
Is cleped, whiche in company
An honderde tymes in an houre
woll as an angry beast loure
And no man wote the cause why
  My sonne shryue the nowe for thy
Hast thou be melancolyen?
¶ My father ye be seynt Julyen
But I vntrewe wordes vse
I maie me not therof excuse
And all maketh loue well I wote

Of whiche myn herte is euer hote
So that I brenne as doth a glede
For wrath, that I may not spede

[folio 47v]

And thus full ofte a day for nought
(Saufe onlyche of myn owne thought)
I am so with my seluen wroth
That howe so that the game goth
with other men I am not gladde
But I am well the more vngladde
For that is other mens game
It tourneth me to pure grame
Thus am I with my selfe oppressed
Of thought, whiche I haue impressed
That all wakynge I dreme and mete
That I alone with her mete
And pray her of some good answere
But for she wolde not gladly swere
She sayth me naye withouten othe

Text (4.9): Berthelette (1554: folio 47r, column b)

¶ My good father telle me this,
What thynge is Ire? Sonne it is,
That in our englisshe wrath is hote,
Which hath his wordes ay so hote,
That all a mans pacience
Is fired of the violence.
For he with him hath euer fiue
Servantes, that helpen him to striue.
  The first of hem melancoly
Is cleped, whiche in company
An honderde tymes in an houre
Woll as an angry beast loure.
And noman wote the cause why.
  My sonne shryue the nowe for thy,
Hast thou be melancolien?
¶ My father ye be sainct Julien:
But I vntrewe wordes vse,
I maie me not therof excuse.
And all maketh loue well I wote,
Of whiche myn herte is euer hote,
So that I brenne as doth a glede
For wrath, that I maie not spede.

[folio 47v]

And thus full ofte a daie for nought
(Saufe onliche of myn owne thought)
I am so with my seluen wroth,
That howe so that the game goth,
With other men I am not glad,
But I am well the more vnglad.
For that is other mens game,
It tourneth me to pure grame.
Thus am I with my selfe oppressed
Of thought, whiche I haue impressed,
That all wakynge I dreme and mete,
That I alone with hir mete,
And pray hir of some good answere.
But for she wolde not gladly swere,
She seith me naye withouten othe.

Comparison of the two editions shows an evolution in the approach to the text comparable with that already noted – in a rather more telescoped time frame – in the Crowley editions of *Piers Plowman*. In the 1532 edition, punctuation is sparing, but nevertheless still deployed in a principled fashion. Some marks relate to interaction between the characters, such as the punctus interrogativus used in lines 20 and 33 and the paraphs in lines 19 and 34. The brackets in line 42 – a humanistic mark, famously referred to by Erasmus as *lunulae* 'little moons' (1530: sig. N.v r)[17] – frame a parenthetical colon, while the comma-marks in lines 40 and 50 seem to be metrical, indicating the end of an enjambment. Otherwise, however, punctuation is lacking, presumably because there is alignment between linguistic structure and verse-line. Thus, in lines 52–5,

That I alone with her mete
And pray her of some good answere
But for she wolde not gladly swere
She sayth me naye withouten othe

it may be observed that each line corresponds with a clause, the first three distinguished by the discourse markers *That*, *And* and *But* respectively; in principle, the structure of the verse does not demand any punctuation at all, since ambiguities do not arise. However, Berthelette, by 1554, clearly felt that something more was needed. The punctuation of the later edition,

[17] The bracket, which first appeared in humanist handwriting at the end of the fourteenth century, famously reflected 'the needs of those who were accustomed to the habit of silent reading' (Parkes 1992: 48–9).

therefore, is much more thoroughgoing, with the punctus and comma-mark deployed consistently at the end of lines:

That I alone with hir mete,
And pray hir of some good answere.
But for she wolde not gladly swere,
She seith me naye withouten othe.

As with Crowley's second and third editions of *Piers Plowman*, this development in punctuation would seem to reflect a more directive approach to the text, guiding readers in pragmatic terms more insistently towards the interpretation of Gower's verse. A new kind of audience for the poem, it would seem, is being envisaged, one for whom more assistance of this kind is clearly perceived as necessary.

4.3 Chaucerian Receptions

Both Langland's and Gower's poems challenged their early modern readers by their antiquity. Although Gower's *Confessio Amantis* retained its authoritative status in the half-century after Berthelette's edition, interestingly no reprint followed. Gower's appearance as a choric character in *Pericles*, and famously as a source of examples in Ben Jonson's posthumously published *Grammar* (1640), may be acknowledgements of his literary canonicity, but he was clearly perceived as old-fashioned; Shakespeare refers to him as 'ancient Gower' come 'from ashes' to 'sing a song that old was sung' (*Pericles*, Act I: Prologue, lines 1–2 = 1609: sig. A.2r), and – as has already been pointed out – it is noticeable how the playwright, deviating from his usual five-measure verse-line, adopts the tetrameter in many of Gower's speeches to capture what must have seemed to contemporaries to be the old-fashioned flavour of the *Confessio*.

The even more archaic verse-form of *Piers Plowman*, too, presented later readers with special difficulties. Extracts from the poem were printed at various times as part of verse anthologies, and interesting and perceptive comments were made on the work by various scholars, including Thomas Percy and Thomas Hearne; Hearne owned two copies of Crowley's edition, as well as a copy of Rogers's, and worked in addition with at least two manuscripts of the poem (Brewer 1996: 21). However, no other 'full' edition of Langland appeared between those of Crowley and Rogers and that of Thomas Whitaker in 1813. Alliterative 'pure-stress' poetry was, it seems, becoming something of a curiosity, dismissed as 'tumbling verse' for use in 'flyting or Inuectiues' by James VI of Scotland in his *Essayis of a Prentise in the Divine Art of Poesie* (1585): a self-confessedly unsophisticated but perhaps therefore comparatively typical statement of literary aesthetics at the end of the sixteenth century.

James was much more keen on what he called '*Ballat Royal*' and '*Troilus* verse', referencing the burgeoning reputation of the one poet who would – and continues to – dominate the medieval English literary canon: Geoffrey Chaucer, described in 'E. K.''s preface to Edmund Spenser's *Shepheardes Calendar* (1579: sig. ¶.ij r) as 'the olde famous Poete Chaucer: whom for his excellencie and wonderfull skil in making, his scholler Lidgate, a worthy scholler of so excellent a maister, calleth the Loadstarre of our Language' – a phraseology that recurred in contemporary editions.

Chaucer's works have a fairly continuous printing history in comparison with that of Langland and Gower. William Caxton's first edition of the *Canterbury Tales* (1477) is one of his earliest productions, clearly flagging that England's first printer – successful because a shrewd businessman – had identified a text for which there was a secure demand. Caxton issued the work again in 1483, as did his successors Richard Pynson (1492, 1526), and Wynkyn de Worde (1498), while other major early editions include those by William Thynne (1532, 1542, ?1550), John Stow (1561), and Thomas Speght (1598, 1602). Speght's edition was the version of Chaucer known to the seventeenth century, the edition of 1687 usually ascribed to John Harefinch being simply a careful reprint of the 1602 edition (Pearsall 1984: 91). 'Modern' editing of the poet emerged in the eighteenth century, with John Urry's posthumous edition of 1721 and Thomas Tyrwhitt's version of 1775. We will be discussing several of these versions shortly.[18]

The current 'standard' edition of Chaucer's works is Oxford University Press's *The Riverside Chaucer*, published in 1987 by a distinguished group of scholars led by Larry Benson. Here are the opening lines of the General Prologue as they appear in the Riverside version:

Text (4.10): Benson (gen. ed.) (1987: 23)

Whan that Aprill with hise shoures soote
The droghte of March hath perced to the roote,
And bathed euery veyne in swich licour
Of which vertu engendred is the flour;
Whan Zephirus eek with his swete breeth
Inspired hath in euery holt and heeth

[18] The standard history of Chaucerian editing remains that edited by Paul Ruggiers (1984), which includes preliminary assessments of Urry and Tyrwhitt by William Alderson and Barry Windeatt respectively.

The tendre croppes, and the yonge sonne
Hath in the Ram his half cours yronne
And smale foweles maken melodye,
That slepen al the nyght with open eye
(So priketh hem nature in hir corages),
Thanne longen folk to goon on pilgrimages,
And palmeres for to seken straunge strondes,
To ferne halwes, kowthe in sondry londes;
And specially from every shires ende
Of Engelond to Caunterbury they wende,
The hooly blissful martir for to seke,
That hem hath holpen whan that they were seeke.

The Riverside editors tell us that 'the texts have . . . been repunctuated in a style more clearly in accord with modern usage' (1987: xliii). Four marks of punctuation are used in Text (4.10): the full stop or period, the semicolon, the comma and the bracket, each being carefully chosen to assist readers in understanding the grammatical structure of this passage. The full stop at the end of line 18 indicates the end of the sentence, while the brackets flag an apposed clause, and commas have been deployed in line with present-day usage, to mark off subordinate from main clauses.

But there are clearly limits to this process of modernisation. The one exception to present-day conventional usage in Text (4.10) is in line 4: the editorial semicolon, used prototypically in present-day written English in place of a conjunction to link two main clauses when an equiparative comparison is sought, is here deployed to mark off the opening, albeit rather long, subordinate clause beginning *Whan that*. The reason for the editors' violation of present-day prescribed usage is clear: for all its extraordinary sophistication of thought, the opening sentence of the *Tales* does not fulfil the canons of formal style that have been developed since the eighteenth century. As the Riverside editors sensibly go on to say, using an approach to which we will return in the last chapter, 'Middle English differs from Modern English in ways that make it impossible to use a completely modern style of punctuation . . . and works intended for oral recitation naturally differ from those intended solely for reading' (1987: xliii). The Riverside choice is arguably purposely alienating for modern readers, gently reminding them of the alterity of the medieval reading experience, in which – as we have regularly seen – those encountering the text shared intimately in its performance.

The extent of this alterity is confirmed when we compare the Riverside version of these lines with those in the earliest manuscript records. Here is the same passage as it appears in the Riverside's copy-text, the Ellesmere manuscript already discussed:

Text (4.11) San Marino, Huntington Library MS EL 26 C.9, folio 1r

W han that Aprill with hise shoures soote
The droghte of March hath perced to the roote
And bathed euery veyne in swich licour
Of which v*er*tu/ engendred is the flour
Whan zephirus eek/ w^{t} his swete breeth
Inspired hath in euery holt and heeth
The tendre croppes/ and the yonge sonne
Hath in the Ram/ his half cours yronne   ¶ .i. sol in Ariete
And smale foweles maken melodye
That slepen al the nyght with open eye
So priketh hem nature/ in hir corages
Thanne longen folk/ to goon on pilgrimages
And Palm*er*es/ for to seken straunge strondes
To ferne halwes/ kowthe in sondry londes
And specially/ fram every shires ende
Of Engelond/ to Caunterbury they wende
The hooly blisful martir for to seke
That hem hath holpen whan þ^{t} they were seeke

The Ellesmere manuscript is not an authorial original. However, it is nevertheless very near to Chaucer in terms of date and milieu, even if some have challenged the hand's identification as that of 'Chaucer's own scribe', Adam Pinkhurst (see section 4.2 above). Yet its presentation is clearly distinct from the 'critical edition' – the reconstructed 'author's original conception', as traditionally defined – of the lines, as presented in the Riverside Chaucer.

In Text (4.11) the Ellesmere scribe has used only a single mark of punctuation: the *virgula suspensiva* or virgule. However, considerable sensitivity to the structure of the verse may be discerned in the virgule's deployment, something underlined by how final *–e* appears in line with the pattern required by Chaucerian prosody, e.g. *the yonge sonne*, *smale foweles*). The Ellesmere scribe thus uses the virgule in interestingly interpretative ways, to mark the caesura (e.g. 'The droghte of March/ hath perced to the roote', 'Thanne longen folk/ to goon on pilgrimages', 'So priketh hem nature/ in hir corages'), but omitting it when the line is followed by a subordinated relative clause (e.g. 'And smale foweles . . . eye' in lines 9–10, and 'The hooly . . . seeke' in lines 17–18). The virgules that frame the subordinated adverbial in lines 15–16 ('fram . . . Engelond') are clearly designed to separate the unit from the main adverbials in the clause ('specially . . . to Caunterbury'). Other deviations from expected syntactic orderings are similarly marked through punctuation; thus the virgule after *The tendre croppes* flags the completion of an enjambment, allowing for a brief breath-pause before the rest of the sentence resumes with a following coordinating conjunction *and*. (It is interesting that *The tendre croppes* regularly attracted a following virgule in later texts, as for instance in Caxton's editions of 1477 and 1483.) Such guides were aids to performance, deployed by the scribe as his contribution to the community of practice that brought the text to its intended discourse community.

An examination of other early copies of the work reveals a wide variety of punctuation patterns. Here, for instance, is part of the same opening passage from the *Tales* transcribed from London, British Library, Harley MS 1758, dating from the middle of the fifteenth century, in which the scribe uses solely a humble punctus:

Text (4.12) London, British Library, MS Harley 1758, folio 1r

[H] Ere begyneth the book. of tales of Caunterburye. compiled by Ger fraie Chaucers. of Bretayne chief poete.//

W han that Aprill. w[t] his schoures swote.
The drought of Marche. hath perced to þe rote.
And bathed euery veyne. in suche licoure.
Of whiche vertue. engendrid ys the floure.
And ȝephirus eke. with his swete breth.
Enspired hath. in euerie holt & heth.
The tendre croppes. & the yong sonne.
In to the Ram. his half cours ronne.
And smale fowles. maken melodye
That slepen all the nyght. with open eye.
So priketh hem nature. in here corages.
Than longen folk. to gou*n* in pilgrymages.
And palmers for to seke. straunge strondes
To ferne halwes. couthe in sondry londes.
And specialy. from euerie schires ende.
Of Englond. to Caunterburye thei wende.
The holy blisfull martyr. for to seke
That hem hath holpen. whan þat þei were seke.

The punctus in the Harley manuscript is regularly (if not consistently) placed at the end of lines and there would seem to be otiose: perhaps a pen-rest, comparable with the usage of (e.g.) the Vernon manuscript.[19]

[19] I owe this insight and example to Wendy Scase.

However, it is also deployed medially, and there it seems to have a metrical function, often coinciding with the metrical caesura. This metrical sensitivity, however, does not extend to adjectival inflexion, yielding *The yong sonne* where the expected final *–e* does not appear; the inflexion was dying out in the early fifteenth century, and the Harley scribe no longer understands the grammatical principle underpinning its original deployment. Despite this issue, however, there would seem to be a system of textual presentation that reflects a distinct conception of verse structure.[20]

Yet other contemporary approaches to the text, however, made greater demands on the interpretative skills of readers or audiences. We might consider, for instance, the practice adopted by the scribe who produced the Petworth manuscript – Petworth House, Kent, MS 7 – of the *Tales*.[21] The Petworth manuscript dates from the first quarter of the fifteenth century:

Text (4.13) Petworth House, Kent, MS 7, folio 1r

W han that aprille with his shoures soote
The drouht of marche hath perced to þe roote
And bathes euery veyne in swich licoure
Of which virtue engendrid is þe floure
Whan ȝephirus ek with his swete breth
Inspired hath in euery holt & heth
The tendre croppes & þe yonge sonne
Hath in the ram his half cours yronne
And smale foules make melodye
That slepen al nyght with open eyghe
So prikeþ hem nature in here corages
Than longen folk to gon on pilgrymages
And palmers for to seke straunge strondes

[20] Interestingly, the scribe of Harley 1758, though retaining the end-of-line punctus, seems to have abandoned the mid-line usage during the course of copying the manuscript, from line 955 of *The Knight's Tale* onwards. Five examples of a mid-line punctus appear in the tale after line 955, but after line 2064 on folio 22r the scribe seems to have abandoned the practice altogether, for reasons we can only guess at. The only variation is in *The Tale of Sir Thopas*, where the end-line of each stanza concludes with a slightly modified punctus combined with a delicate following reverse *-s* flourish, and in prose texts, i.e. *The Tale of Melibee* and *The Parson's Tale*, where the punctus is used to mark commata and cola. The Harley scribe uses only the end-line punctus in the other manuscript where his hand has been detected, i.e. London, Society of Antiquaries, MS 134, a copy of John Gower's *Confessio Amantis* and Thomas Hoccleve's *Regiment of Princes*, preceded and followed by fragmentary copies of John Lydgate's *Life of our Lady* and John Walton's translation of Boethius's *De Consolatione Philosophiae*.

[21] For an image, see https://issuu.com/petworthhousent/docs/reduced_one_pages_pt1, consulted last on 25 May 2019. The Petworth manuscript is sometimes referred to as the Leconfield manuscript, after one of the titles of the Wyndham family, who inherited the Petworth estate in the eighteenth century.

To ferne halowes couthe in sondry londes
And specially fram euery shires ende
Of engelond to Caunterbury they wende
The holy blisseful martir for to seke
That hem hath holpen when that þey were seke

We encountered the Petworth scribe at the end of the previous chapter, as the hand also of Tokyo, Waseda University Library, MS NE 3691, of Nicholas Love's *Mirror*. This scribe was a fairly prolific individual, a professional copyist responsible, according to Linne Mooney and her team, for some ten manuscripts, including not only copies of the *Canterbury Tales* and Gower's *Confessio Amantis* but also another copy of Love's *Mirror* alongside the Waseda manuscript.[22] Although there are some obvious slips, e.g. *bathes* for *bathed*, the Petworth text of the *Tales* is a fairly 'good' one in terms of its relationship to what is presumed by most editors to be the author's original conception of the work, not least in his fairly accurate retention of final *–e* in weak/plural adjectival inflexions, e.g. *yonge*, *smale*. But for our purposes we might observe something very simple: although capital letters are sporadically deployed, e.g. in *Caunterbury*, and of course line-breaks are used to mark verse-lines, the text is otherwise generally innocent of punctuation as modern readers would understand it. And it is noticeable that, as we saw in Chapter 3, the Petworth copyist is similarly sparing in his deployment of punctuation in his copies of Nicholas Love (see Parkes 1997c, Smith 2017b).

In one sense Chaucer himself made it possible for readers to interpret his text by his careful use of conjunctions and sentential adverbs, many of them at the beginning of verse-lines; it is noticeable how many verse-lines begin with forms such as *That*, *And*, *Whan*/*Whan that* etc., which in one sense makes punctuation redundant. Such grammatical cues – some of them emphasised by 'extended' or emphatic subordinating constructions, such as *whan that* for *whan*, or *for to* for *to* – ensure that the overall meaning of the passage is clear. And of course, if the text were to be read aloud, the nearest to punctuation would not be some verbal signal of the presence of punctus or virgule but rather interpretative gestures or intonations: perhaps the embodied manicule that we see Chaucer himself adopting in contemporary or near-contemporary pictorial representations (see Smith 2012b and references there cited).

[22] For the identification of other manuscripts by the Petworth scribe, see Chapter 3 above and references there cited, and also the *Late Medieval Scribes* website, www.medievalscribes.com/, last consulted on 24 May 2019.

Even so, the Petworth practice would seem to present the biggest challenge to any readers seeking the resolution of those 'structural uncertainties which might otherwise not be conveyed at all, or would at best be much more difficult for a reader to figure out' (Parkes 1992: 1). In the case of the Petworth manuscript – and indeed the other texts he copied – it would seem that the scribe felt that such 'figuring out' was something that could be safely left to readers. The (lack of) punctuation in the Petworth Chaucer is thus a reminder of a distinctive hermeneutic approach to text, where the copyist is producing a work not just for a wider discourse community but also as part of community of practice that includes not only the author who created the text, and the scribe who disseminated it, but also the reader(s) who might encounter the manuscript and would be expected to collaborate in its interpretation.

The Riverside editors were – in a discreet, scholarly way – confronting one of the major paradoxes in the production of a critical edition that is something of a theme of this book: is it ever possible to produce an edition that represents the author's original conception of the work when the original readership for that work no longer exists? The same paradox confronts, of course, anyone trying to recreate the experience of a work of art from the past for a modern audience; as any musicians playing a piece of early music on 'original' instruments are always strongly conscious of, their audience brings to the performance such a distinct set of sociocultural experiences and attitudes that the occasion cannot be 'the same' as that experienced by those who encountered the work the first time it was played. And musicians (or indeed any public performer) always acknowledge that audiences matter; even academic lectures are a conversation – an odd one, admittedly – with others in the room.

The parallel between a critical edition and a musical performance on original instruments suggests that the communities of practice we have identified as working in a fairly extreme way in the Petworth manuscript – author, scribe, readers – remained active in the transition to print, although challenged by changes in the English language since Chaucer's time, most notably inflexional loss. To illustrate the point, we will turn to a series of early editions within the great tradition of Chaucer editing: those by William Thynne, Thomas Speght, John Urry and Thomas Tyrwhitt.

William Thynne (d. 1546) was a significant official at the court of Henry VIII, but he is now better known as a literary enthusiast, a patron of the poet John Skelton, and the first individual to approach the task of editing Chaucer in accordance with the 'respectful treatment that humanist scholars had been according to classical Greek and Latin scholars since the fourteenth century' (Blodgett 1984: 36): the comparison is with e.g. the poet Petrarch's editing of Cicero. Such a combination of humanist learning and court activity was commonplace, as illustrated also by the king's secretary, Brian Tuke, who supplied a dedicatory preface to Thynne's Chaucer and who seems to have worked closely with him (see Walker 2005, especially chapters 4 and 5). Thynne assembled, according to his son Francis, 'some fyve and twentye' versions of works ascribed to Chaucer, including not only manuscripts but also William Caxton's edition of the *Boece*, and also the 1526 edition by Richard Pynson. Thynne established the 'Chaucer canon' that was to feed critical interpretation of the poet in later centuries, including works now known not to be by him, such as Thomas Usk's *Testament of Love*, Thomas Hoccleve's *The Letter of Cupid*, John Lydgate's *The Complaint of the Black Knight*, and Robert Henryson's *The Testament of Cresseid*.

We can detect Thynne's approach to his task by comparing his black-letter edition to the Middle English copies he is known to have used. Two survive at Longleat, which is still the Thynne family estate: the copy of Caxton's *Boece*, and Longleat House, Wiltshire MS 258, an anthology of love poetry including *The Parliament of Fowls*, the *Complaints* to *Mars* and to *Pity*, and *Anelida and Arcite*. Perhaps the best-known of Thynne's exemplars, however, is the sole surviving manuscript of the Middle English *Romaunt of the Rose*, now Glasgow, University Library, MS Hunter 409 (V.3.7). The Hunterian *Romaunt* has been marked up regularly with the word *coll* and with numbers, corresponding respectively in Thynne's edition to the beginning of the second column on each page, and to the equivalent signatures of twelve folio pages (i.e. 'sixes'); such practices were commonly deployed by Tudor printers when marking up their copy-texts, the usage in this case probably that of Thomas Godfray, Thynne's printer. Supporting, if not conclusive, evidence for the book being Thynne's exemplar is supplied by the name *Ihon Thin* which appears on folio 60r. The Hunterian *Romaunt* is now defective, having lost several leaves; it seems that decorated and/or illuminated folios were removed by later book-collectors (see further Caie 2011 and references there cited).[23]

A comparison of the Hunterian *Romaunt* with Thynne's version, as exemplified by Texts (4.14) and (4.15) respectively, demonstrates the kinds of modification Thynne and Godfray undertook:

[23] A leaf from another manuscript of the *Romaunt* has been identified in the National Library of Scotland; see Caie 2011: 155–6, and Horobin 2006.

Text (4.14) Glasgow, University Library, MS Hunter 409 (V.3.7), folio 13r

E Ntentif weren forto synge
These briddis that nought vnkunnyng
Were of her craft and apprentys
ffor of song sotil and wys
And certis whan I herde her songe
And sawe the grene place amonge
In herte I wexe so wondir gay
That I was neuer erst er that day

[folio 13v]

So iolyf nor so wel bigoo
Ne merye in herte as I was thoo
And than wist I and sawe ful well
That ydelnesse me serued well
That me putte in sich jolite
Hir freend wel ought I forto be
Sith she the dore of that gardyne
Hadde opened and me leten Inne

Text (4.15): Thynne 1532, folio 131v

E Ntentyfe weren for to synge
These byrdes/ that not vnkonnyng
Were of her crafte/ and aprentyse
But of songe subtyl and wyse
And certes/ whan I herde her songe
And sawe the grene place amonge
In herte I wryt so wonder gay
That I was neuer erst/ er that day
So iolyfe/ nor so wel bygo
Ne mery in herte/ as I was tho
And than wyste I/ and sawe ful wel
That ydilnesse me serued wel
That me put in suche iolyte
Her frende wel ought I for to be
Sythe she the dore of that gardyn
Had opened/ and me lette in.

Thynne and Godfray have made a series of significant changes in relation to their exemplar. Spellings have been slightly modified, including the obvious example of *subtil*, from Anglo-Norman/Old French *sotil*, but remodelled on the basis of Latin *subtīlis*: a 'mock-learned' usage commonly paralleled in other early modern English texts, cf. *debt* for Middle English *dette*, cf. Old French *dette*, Latin *dēbitum*. Other usages raise more complex issues, notably the common introduction of final *–e*, in Chaucer's day an inflexional marker that, with inflexional loss, had not only become available as a flourish in the manner of an ornament, archaistic or otherwise, but also seems sometimes deployed to indicate an optional extra syllable to restore metrical regularity. Thynne's edition also uses forms of slightly wider currency in line with the communicative drivers that prefigured later spellings we now consider standard, e.g. *suche* for Hunterian *sich*. Interventions in punctuation are, however, more thorough. Whereas the Hunterian *Romaunt* deploys a battery of illuminated/decorated initials to mark sententiae but is otherwise innocent of punctuation, Thynne's edition is much more sophisticated. As in the following lines

Sythe she the dore of that gardyn
Had opened/ and me lette in.

virgules are regularly introduced to mark in-line (though not end-line) cola: in this case a punctus is used to mark the completion of the sententia.

A similar pattern may be detected in a text where Thynne's exemplar is uncertain: the opening of his edition of the *Canterbury Tales*. Here is Thynne's version of the opening of the General Prologue:

Text (4.16): Thynne (1532: folio 2r)

W Hanne that Apryll
with his shoures sote
The drought of Marche
had perced the rote
And bathed euery vayne
in suche licoure
Of which vertue/ engen=
dred is the floure
Whan ʒephirus eke with his sote breth
Enspired hath euery holte and heth
The tendre croppes/ and the yonge sonne
Hath in the Ram halfe his course yronne
And smale foules maken melodye
That slepen al nyght with open eye
So prycketh hem nature in her courage
Than longen folke to go on pylgrymage
And palmers to seken straunge strondes
To ferne halowes couthe in sondry londes
And specyally fro euery shyres ende
Of Englonde to Caunterbury they wende

The holy blysful martyr for to seke
That hem hath holpen/ whan they were seke.

Thynne's text of the Prologue is a spare interpretation compared with the Ellesmere version, but as with the latter virgules are deployed when cola divisions are mid-line, as in

The tendre croppes/ and the yonge sonne

and in

That hem hath holpen/ whan they were seke.

where the completion of the sententia is marked by a line-final punctus. However, it is noticeable that Thynne punctuates more insistently in prose works, where line-endings of course do not apply, as in the following passage from his edition of *The Parson's Tale*, where a sophisticated repertoire of punctus, double punctus and virgule is used over quite short passages. The reason for the difference is not hard to find: whereas the verse-line can be reflected typographically and used as an aid to 'figuring out' the meaning of the text, prose presents a greater challenge to contemporary interpreters. Clarity was important to Thynne, especially in such a passage as Text (4.17), with its clear assertion of moral imperatives; as Greg Walker has shown, both Thynne and his collaborator, Tuke, as 'moderate' royal counsellors at a fraught period, sought to present Chaucer as a provider of 'advice literature . . . with a proven track record of success with Henry VIII's royal predecessors' (2005: 84).[24]

Text (4.17) Thynne (1532: folio 107v)

O Ur swete lorde God of heuen/ that
no man wol perissh/ but wol that
we tourne all to the knowlege of
him/ and to the blysful lyfe that is
perdurable/ amonessheth vs by the prophete
Ieremye/ that sayth in this wyse. Stondeth
vpon the wayes and seeth/ and asketh of olde

[24] Greg Walker, in his important study of the terrifying social conditions in which such folk worked, has plausibly argued that several of the non-Chaucerian pieces included in Thynne's edition, including Thomas Hoccleve's 'To the Kynges Most Noble Grace and to the Lordes and Knights of the Garter', are all carefully presented to emphasise the 'advice' aspect of the collection. In Henrician conditions, this argument – a courageous one – had to be couched obliquely. See further Walker 2005: 73–99. Some of the complexities of the period have been more recently and fascinatingly pursued in MacCulloch 2018, where Tuke is referred to as a 'humourlessly acquisitive royal servant' (2018: 170).

> pathes: that is to say/ of olde sentences/ whiche
> is the good waye/ and walketh in that waye/
> and ye shal fynde refresshynge for your sou=
> les, &c.

Thynne's editing, it is clear, is explicable as a principled sixteenth-century response to the medieval original: a reshaping of a past text that has been presented to connect with a carefully targeted discourse community. His collection was advisedly the basis for the next major edition of the poem, that by Thomas Speght (d. 1621), who included Thynne's dedication to Henry VIII within his prefatory material even though he was clearly of the view that Thynne's was a defective work – a view that was contested by Thynne's antiquarian son, Francis, in his *Animadversions* of 1599 (see Furnivall and Kingsley 1865; see also Cook 2012). Speght, a friend of philologists such as the lexicographer John Baret and the orthoepist Alexander Gil, and of the antiquarian John Stow, produced two editions of Chaucer in 1598 and 1602 – the latter with the assistance of Francis Thynne – with the aim of '*doing some reparations on his works, which they iudged to be much decaied by iniurie of time, ignorance of writers, and negligence of Printers*' (1598: sig. *.i v). Speght claimed a series of innovations for his work:

> *For whose sakes thus much was then by me vndertaken, although neuer as yet fully finished: First, His life collected. Secondly, The text by old written Copies corrected. Thirdly, Arguments to euery booke prefixed. Fourthly, Old words explaned. Fiftly, Difficulties opened. Sixtly, Authors by him cited, declared. Seuenthly, Sentences noted. Eightly, Some things of his added which neuer had bene printed.* (Speght 1598: sig. *.i v)

In the preface to the 1602 edition, Speght adds the following passage, more explicitly acknowledging – doubtless with Francis's encouragement – William Thynne's efforts:

> *Now therefore, that both by old written Copies, and by Ma. William Thynns praise-worthy labours, I haue reformed the whole Worke, whereby Chaucer for the most part is restored to his owne Antiquitie.* (Speght 1602: sig. *.ii r)

Texts (4.18) and (4.19) are transcriptions of the 1598 and 1602 editions of the opening lines of the General Prologue. As was becoming customary, Speght's editions retained blackletter for the printing of the Middle English text while elsewhere using a variety of roman and italic fonts, mostly for the paratextual material. The name 'Zephirus' appears in roman font in both editions, marked here by underlining in the transcriptions:

Text (4.18): Speght (1598: sig. A.ii r)

W hen that April with
his shoures sote
The drought of march
hath perced to ye rote,
And bathed euery vain
in such licoure,
Of which vertue, enge*n*-
dred is the floure:
When Zephirus eke with his sote breath
Espired hath in euery holt and heath
The tender crops, and that the yong sonne
Hath in the Ram halfe his course yronne,
And small foules maken melodie
That sleepen all night with open eie
So pricketh hem nature in her courage
Than longen folke to go on pilgrimage
And palmers for to seeken straunge stronds
To ferre halowes couth in sundry londs
And specially fram euery shires end
Of Englond to Canterbury they wend
The holy blisful martir for to seeke
That hem hath holpen, whe*n* they were seke.

Text (4.19): Speght (1602: sig. A.ii r)

W hen that Aprill with his shours
sote
The drought of March had
pierced to the rote,
And bathed euery vaine in suche
licour,
Of which vertue engendred is the flour:
When Zephirus eke with his sote breath,
Espired hath in euery holt and heath
The tender croppes, and that the yong sonne
Hath in the Ram halfe his course yronne,
And small foules maken melodie,
That slepen all night with open eie:
So pricketh hem nature in her courage,
Then longen folke to goe on pilgrimage,
And palmers to seeken straunge strondes,
To ferne hallowes couth in sundry londes:
And specially, fro euery shires end
Of Englond, to Canterburie they wend,

The holy blisfull martir for to seeke,
That hem hath holpen, when they were seke.

Comparison between the 1598 and 1602 editions, and with Thynne's of 1532, shows some significant changes, all – despite Speght's claims of authentically Chaucerian '*Antiquitie*' – in the direction of more modern usage. Spelling accords more closely to present-day usage in some respects, with *breath*, *heath* for Thynne's *breth*, *heth*, and final *–e* is uncertainly deployed: Thynne's version of line 7

The tendre croppes/ and the yonge sonne

is close to the 'authentic' Ellesmere usage, whereas Speght's versions are certainly unChaucerian, attempting to remedy the obvious metrical 'roughness' of *the yong sonne* by adding an extra word, *that.* Both Speght's editions show even greater deployment of punctuation than Thynne's, but the 1602 edition much more so, with increased use of end-line comma and double punctus, and mid-line parenthetical markers for cola and commata in the last four lines of the passage:

And specially, fro euery shires end
Of Englond, to Canterburie they wend,
The holy blisfull martir for to seeke,
That hem hath holpen, when they were seke.

The distinction is even more marked between Speght's 1598 and 1602 editions of the *Romaunt of the Rose*, presented as Texts (4.20) and (4.21):

Text (4.20): Speght (1598: folio 116r = sig. Aa.ii r)

M any menne saine that in
sweuenings
Ther nis but fables and
lesings
But menne may some
sweuen sene
Which hardly that false
ne bene
But afterward ben apparaunt
This may I draw to warraunt
An authour that hight Macrobes
That halt not dremes false ne lees
But vndoth vs the auisioun
That whilom mette king Cipioun
And who so saith, or weneth it be
A iape or els nicete

To wene that dremes after fall
Let who so list a fole me call

Text (4.21): Speght (1602: folio 109r = sig. U.i r)

M Any men sain that in swe=
neueninges,
Ther nis but fables and
lesinges:
But menne may some swe=
uen seene,
Which hardely that false
ne beene,
But afterward ben apparaunt:
This may I draw to warraunt,
An authour that hight Macrobes,
That halt not dreames false ne lees,
But vndoth vs the auisioun,
That whilom mette king Cipioun.
And who so sayth, or weneth it be
A yape, or else nicete
To wene that dreames after fall,
Let who so list a foole me call.

The difference between the limited punctuation in the 1598 version and its comprehensive introduction in the 1602 version is very noticeable. In the 1602 edition, commata are marked by commas, cola by a double punctus, and sententiae by a single punctus followed by an indented verse-paragraph. A clear attempt has been made in 1602 to offer a much more comprehensive repertoire of interpretative aids than in the edition from four years previously.

Speght's edition of 1602 remained dominant for readers of Chaucer for at least a century; indeed, Walter Scott owned a copy, now in the collection of Edinburgh's Faculty of Advocates, that was a gift from a fellow antiquarian, George Henry Gilchrist of Newcastle. It was not really superseded by the next edition, that of John Urry, published in 1721. Urry was a nonjuring member of Thomas Ruddiman's circle (see Chapter 5), of Scottish ancestry, though for much of his life based at Christ Church, Oxford; his edition appeared posthumously. His edition was widely criticised, not least by a later editor, Thomas Tyrwhitt (1775: xx):

> The strange licence, in which Mr. Urry appears to have indulged himself, of lengthening and shortening Chaucer's words according to his own fancy,

> and of even adding words of his own, without giving his readers the least notice, has made the text of Chaucer in his Edition by far the worst ever published.

And Urry's literary executor, Timothy Thomas, while praising him in a preface as 'a Gentleman so remarkable, not only for his Learning and Industry, but more particularly for his great Charity, constant Integrity, and a peculiar Happiness of being most agreeable to his private Friends' (1721: 50), was moved to cite Urry's elegant deprecation of his abilities, describing how he had been 'perswaded to undertake [the edition], though much against his inclination',

> For, though (as he says) his skill in the Northern Language spoken in the Lowlands of Scotland qualified him to read this Poet with more ease and pleasure than one altogether bred be-South [sic] *Trent* could do with more than common Application, yet he assures us, he had not the least thought of publishing his private Diversions. (Urry 1721: 41)

Despite these caveats and careful qualifications, however, Urry's edition achieved a number of firsts: it was the first to supply a description of the manuscripts the editor had consulted, and the first to print two Chaucerian apocrypha, the tales of *Gamelyn* and *Beryn*. It certainly attracted praise from at least one contemporary: Queen Anne's royal licence, inserted into the edition, referred to his study in glowing terms: 'not only all the former Editions of Value, but many rare and ancient manuscripts not hitherto consulted; from the collating of which he hath in a great measure restored and perfected the text, amending many Errors and Corruptions that have crept in, and continued in all the Editions hitherto printed' (Urry 1721: 60).

Urry's engagement with the *Romaunt* illustrates his approach to the text:

Text (4.22): Urry (1721: 220)

ENtentife werin for to sing
These birdis, that not unkonning
Were of ther craft, and a prentise,
But of song subtill and eke wise;
And certis, whan I heard ther song,
And sawe the grenè place emong
In herte I wext so wondir gaie,
That I was nevir er that daie
So jolife, nor so well bigo,
Ne mery' in herte, as I was tho;
And than wist I, and sawe full well,
That idilnesse me servid well,

That me put in soche jolitè,
Her frende well ought I for to be
Sithe she the dore of that gardin
Had opinid, and let me in.

Some obvious quasi-modernisations may be noted in comparison with the Hunterian manuscript, Speght's editions and Thynne's, e.g. *ther* 'their' (687), *let me in* (700) for Hunterian *me leten Inne*, and widespread replacement of <u> for <v> to represent a labio-dental fricative, e.g. *servid* (696) beside *serued* in the other witnesses. Urry agrees with Speght (1598, 1602) with *heard* (689) beside Hunterian/Thynne *herde*, and shares an intrusive <b> in *subtill* (688) with both Thynne and Speght, contrasting with Hunterian *sotil*.[25] However, Urry's is not a straightforward modernisation, but something more complex, flagged by the forms *grenè*, *jolitè* and *mery'*. The grave accents seem to indicate a 'sounded' *–e*, while the apostrophe in *mery'* suggests an elision with following *in*. Urry's usage is uncertain, but he does at least seem to be attempting to reconstruct Chaucerian practice. As Timothy Thomas pointed out in his preface (1721: 42):

> The Final Syllables were for the most part such as might be said rather to be added in the Pronunciation, than by Writing: The chiefest of which, and the most, and the most frequently made use of to help out a Verse otherwise deficient, was the Final *è*, which he always marked with an accent when he judged it necessary to pronounce it; as *swetè*, *halvè*, *smalè*, Prol. 5, 8, 9. for *sweet*, *halve* or *half*, *small*; of which there are many Instances in every page. Whether the assistance of this Final *è* be not here too frequently, and sometimes unnecessarily, called in, is not my business at present to enquire into: But it seems beyond contradiction that it was anciently pronounced; and I have seen a Note of Mr. *Urry's*, wherein he affirms that in some parts of *England* it is still used, and instances in the words *pipè*, *buttonè*, *don't finè*, &c. wherein the Final *è* is pronounced in *Dorsetshire* at this day.

Urry seems to have regarded it as entirely acceptable to modify inflexions conjecturally, based on his own conception of Chaucerian verse-form; even if his approach was flawed by the standards of later editors, the attempt represented a new approach to the presentation of Chaucer. Originally, Thomas tells us (1721: 43),

> I find it acknowledged by him [i.e. Urry], 'That whenever he could by no other way help a Verse to a Foot, which he was perswaded it had when it

[25] *Ententife*, 685, is by contrast a throwback to Speght 1598 and earlier versions, cf. Speght 1602's *Ententiue*.

> came from the Maker's hands, but left by the Ignorance of Transcribers, or Negligence of Printers, he made no scruple to supply it with some Word or Syllable that serv'd for an Expletive': But I find at the same time that he had once a design of enclosing such words in hooks thus [ ] to distinguish them from what he found justified by the authority of MSS. but how it came to pass that so just, useful and necessary a Design was not executed, I cannot satisfy the curious Reader.

Urry was clearly presenting a text for a discourse community of antiquarians, rather than one, like those that read Thynne's or Speght's editions, which focused on Chaucer's presumed moral or aesthetic qualities. Speght himself referred to the former when he drew attention to how 'Prouerbes and Sentences [i.e. moral adages]' were 'marked' in his edition (1602: sig *.i v), while Francis Beaumont, in his prefatory remarks to Speght's 1602 edition, referred to the latter when he identified in Chaucer

> one gift he hath aboue other Authors, and that is, By excellencie of his descriptions, to possesse his Readers with a more forcible imagination of felling that (as it were) done before their eies, which they read, than any other that euer hath written in any tongue. (Speght 1602: sig. *.iv r)

Urry's edition represented therefore, for all its evident flaws, a distinctly scholarly approach to Chaucer that aligned at least in aspiration with that of his friend and fellow nonjuror George Hickes.

Urry's approach continued – albeit carried out with much greater skill – with the final editor under review, whose edition, like that of Speght earlier, set the standard for the presentation of Chaucer for a century following: Thomas Tyrwhitt (1730–86). Tyrwhitt's edition of the *Canterbury Tales* appeared in four volumes in 1775; a fifth volume containing a glossary appeared in 1778. Tyrwhitt's varied career included an Oxford fellowship, a stint as a civil servant, clerk to the House of Commons and curator of the British Museum, and scholarly achievements such as detector of the Chatterton forgeries and editor inter alia of Aesop and Plutarch. His obituary in the *Gentleman's Magazine* observed that he had a knowledge of 'almost every European tongue' and was 'deeply conversant in the learning of Greece and Rome' (ODNB). Unsurprisingly, Tyrwhitt transferred practices for editing the classics to Middle English: something he had in common – as we will see – with Ruddiman's circle. But whereas Urry claimed close engagement with the manuscript tradition, Tyrwhitt 'casts himself as working with the manuscripts rather than imposing himself on them', holding that 'all editorial contributions to the text should be signalled to the reader' (Windeatt 1984: 119).

Tyrwhitt's considerable philological abilities are displayed in his 'Essay on the Language and Versification of Chaucer', including a 'scanned' version of the opening lines of the *Canterbury Tales*:

> I shall conclude this long and (I fear) tedious Essay, with a Grammatical and Metrical Analysis of the first eighteen lines of the Canterbury Tales. This will afford me an opportunity of illustrating at once a considerable part of that Theory, which I have ventured to propose in the preceding pages, with regard to the Language and Versification of Chaucer . . .
>
> I. *Whánne* that Ápril with his *shoúres sóte*
> II. The droúghte of Márch hath *pérced* tó the *róte*,
> III. And *báthed* évery véine in *swíche licoúr*,
> IV. Of whíche *vertúe* engéndred ís the floúr;
> V. Whan Zéphirús eke wíth his *sóte* bréthe
> VI. *Enspíred* háth in évery hólt and héthe
> VII. The téndre *cróppes*, and the *yónge* sónne,
> VIII. Háth in the Rám his *hálfe* coúrs *yrónne*,
> IX. And *smále foúles máken* mélodie,
> X. That *slépen álle* níght with ópen éye,
> XI. So príketh *hém natúre* in hír *coráges*;
> XII. Than *lóngen* fólk to *gón* on pílgrimáges,
> XIII. And *pálmer'es* fór to *séken stránge* strróndes,
> XIV. To *sérve hálwes coúthe* in sóndry lóndes;
> XV. And spécially' from évery *shíres* énde
> XVI. Of *Englelónd* to Cánterbúry *they wénde*,
> XVII. The hóly blísful mártyr fór to séke,
> XVIII. That *hém* hath *hólpen*, whán that théy were *séke*.
>
> (Tyrwhitt 1775: vol. IV, 106–7)

Italicised forms are given notes in Tyrwhitt's commentary, e.g. his notes on *Whanne* and *palmer'es*:

> *Whanne*, Sax. Hpænne, is so seldom used as a *Disyllable* by Chaucer, that for some time I had great doubts about the true reading of this line. I now believe that it is right, as here printed, and that the same word is to be pronounced as a *Disyllable* in ver. 703.
>
> But with these relikes *whanne* that he fond – . . ..
>
> *Palmer'es*, Dis. the *e* of the termination being cut out by Syncope, as it generally is in *Plural Nouns* of *three* Syllables, accented upon the *first*, and in the *Past Tenses* and their *Participles* of *Verbs*, of the same description, ending in *ed*.

Such discussions demonstrate the considerable expertise Tyrwhitt was able to deploy in his editorial practice, including – as here with *Hpænne* – the deployment of *Pica Saxon* as an etymological gloss.

As a reference point for his collation of the various manuscripts to which he had access, Tyrwhitt used John Harefinch's 1687 reprint of Speght's 1602 edition, a choice that was simply a matter of operational convenience. Harefinch's edition was a fairly straightforward reprint with a few minor additions; as Derek Pearsall has pointed out, the claim on its title page that it has 'lately been Compar'd with the best Manuscripts', although gesturing interestingly to contemporary antiquarian claims of authority, is demonstrably false (Pearsall 1984: 91). Nevertheless, a comparison between Tyrwhitt's and the Harefinch edition captures some of the changes the former has made to the latter.

The text of the opening lines of the Harefinch edition of the *Tales*, in blackletter and based in the Speght 1602 edition with a few minor changes in spelling, reads as follows:

Text (4.23): Harefinch (1687: 1)

W hen that Aprill with his shours
sote,
The drought of March had pier=
ced to the rote,
And bathed euery vaine in suche lycour,
Of which vertue engendred is the flour:
When Zephyrus eke with his sote breath,
Espired hath in every holt and heath,
The tender croppes, and that the yong sonne
Hath in the Ram halfe his course yronne,
And small foules maken melody,
That slepen all nyght with open eye:
So priketh hem nature in her courage,
Then longen folke to goe on pilgrimage,
And Palmers to seeken straunge strondes,
To ferne hallowes couth in sundry londes:
And specially, fro every shyres end
Of Englond, to Canterbury they wend,
The holy blissful martyr for to seeke,
That hem hath holpen when they were seeke.

And here for comparison is the opening of Tyrwhitt's edition:

Text (4.28): Tyrwhitt (1775: 1)

WHANNE that April with his shoures sote
The droughte of March hath perced to the rote,
And bathed every veine in swiche licour,
Of whiche vertue engendred is the flour;

Whan Zephirus eke with his sote brethe
Inspired hath in every holt and hethe
The tendre croppes, and the yonge sonne
Hath in the Ram his halfe cours yronne,
And smale foules maken melodie,
That slepen alle night with open eye,
So priketh hem nature in hir corages;
Than longen folk to gon on pilgrimages,
And palmeres for to seken strange strondes,
To serve halwes couthe in sondry londes;
And specially, from every shires ende
Of Engelond, to Canterbury they wende,
The holy blisful martyr for to seke,
That hem hath holpen, what that they were seke.

There are some places where the text seems strange to modern eyes; *serve* in line 14, for instance, appears in place of *ferne* 'distant', the familiar Ellesmere form, presumably the result of a misreading at some point in transmission of 'long-s' and the minims for <n>. But overall Tyrhwitt's is a highly intelligent edition, demonstrating his firm grasp of Chaucerian grammar, most notably in his choice of *the yonge sonne* and *smale foules*, compared with Harefinch's (and Speght's) *the yong sonne*, *small foules*; Tyrwhitt understands, unlike his predecessors and (frankly) many of his successors, the principle of *–e* in relation to weak singular and plural adjectives respectively, something of a breakthrough in Chaucerian studies. But perhaps for our purposes the key element to note in Tyrwhitt's editing practice is that the comma and semicolon are deployed in line with patterns of pausing, and it is therefore not surprising that the semicolon appears, as it does in the Riverside edition, at the end of line 4.

The connexion with speech might seem to be a throwback to an earlier conception of textual function; after all, the eighteenth century has traditionally been seen as the period of the 'reading revolution'. But the emphasis on writing–speech relationships was favoured by contemporary *elocutionist* thinking, of the kind briefly discussed in Chapter 3. Elocutionists, deriving their inspiration from admired classical models, emphasised the superiority of speech over writing; they also emphasised the role of formal performance in education. Elocutionist ideas underpin the common eighteenth-century interest in formalising language through prescriptive grammars, dictionaries and works on pronunciation, and it is no coincidence that many of those who wrote and published such works came from the peripheries of the new British state (Scotland, Ireland, the colonies).[26] 'Forging the nation' – to use Linda Colley's term (1992), to which we will return at least in part in the next chapter – required the 'methodization' of language.

Elocutionist ideas had a philosophical basis which looked back to Descartes's *Les passions de l'âme* (1649). According to Jerry Mohrmann,

> tones, looks and gestures were external signs of internal emotions . . . The increasing concern with mind–body problems encouraged inquiries into the nature and function of the natural language in all areas relating directly to man's emotions and its expression. The topics were as various as religion and physiognomy, but discussions of the natural language construct centered upon human communication, particularly in the arts . . . In sum, it was almost universally accepted that the creative artist was to observe and record the natural language of the passions . . . [the artist] was to perceive and delineate the 'operations, affections, and energies, of the mind itself . . . manifested and communicated in speech'. (Mohrmann 1969: v–vi)

As Malcolm Parkes pointed out, 'The effect of such ideas on the use of punctuation was to encourage attempts to reflect the phenomena of spoken discourse' (1992: 91), and these notions informed the conventions adopted by contemporary printers, where the distinctions between plays, novels and poetry were blurred, a blurring reflected in typographical practice. Such blurring was encouraged by the focus on social reading, well-attested in the eighteenth century (see references in Chapter 1, especially Williams 2017). Tyrwhitt's edition of Chaucer, therefore, was punctuated in accordance with eighteenth-century 'elocutionist' notions, whereby the text was presented in a form ready for oral declamation by its intended discourse community, which in performance would develop its own community of practice. It is a fascinating reflexion on the ongoing complexities of the

[26] A good example of such an 'outsider' figure is a famous graduate of Trinity College Dublin: Thomas Sheridan. Sheridan is perhaps better known today as the father of Richard Brinsley Sheridan, the MP and playwright, and as the biographer of another famous (if somewhat reluctant) Dubliner, Jonathan Swift, but in his own time he was an important cultural figure, gaining notoriety as an actor-manager and more influential fame as a lecturer on linguistic matters. In 1759, Sheridan's *A Discourse . . . Being Introductory to His Course of Lectures on Elocution and the English Language* was issued by Andrew Millar, the distinguished Scottish publisher; the *Discourse* had been originally delivered (according to the title page) in the (Sheldonian) Theatre at Oxford, the 'Senate-House' in Cambridge, and the 'Spring-Garden' in London. When Sheridan's lectures were delivered in Edinburgh in 1761, a London newspaper of that date, *The St James's Chronicle*, reported on his 'very extraordinary' success: 'You may soon therefore expect to find Scotland the standard of elocution and of the English tongue: And while Britain is to be the Greece of Europe, Scotland is to be the Athens of Britain.' This statement was reprinted (with due acknowledgement) by the *Edinburgh Evening Courant* later in the same year (see Sher 2006: 67). On actors and elocution, see Goring 2004. See further Smith 2013c, which includes some material linked to the present discussion.

writing–speech relationship that such ideas were inherited by the Riverside editors some 200 years later, complicating their own attempts to present an older text in modern guise. Changes in formal features, once more, reflect pragmatically changing socio-cultural functions, while also reminding us of the challenges faced by textual critics as their discipline mutated over time.

CHAPTER 5

Forging the Nation: Reworking Older Scottish Literature

5.1 Barbour's *Bruce* and Hary's *Wallace*

In 1489, John Ramsay, a 'notary public' in Fife, copied a manuscript for the use of Symon Lochmalony, vicar of Auchtermoonzie in the same county. This book, now Edinburgh, National Library of Scotland, MS Advocates' 19.2.2, contains the two principal epic-romances of Older Scots literature: John Barbour's *Bruce*, a poem originally presented to Robert II, King of Scots, in 1375, and 'Blind' Hary's *Wallace*, which dates from a century later. Ramsay had already completed a copy of *The Bruce* two years before, although this earlier manuscript, now Cambridge, St John's College, MS G.23, seems to be drawn from a different exemplar; the Cambridge manuscript is moreover much damaged, the first three books of the poem being missing. The Edinburgh manuscript is the sole surviving medieval witness for Hary's poem.

We know something about John Barbour (c. 1330–95), from 1356 archdeacon of St Machar's Cathedral in Aberdeen. Barbour's reward for his poem was a pension, which passed to his legatees on his death; he was buried in St Machar's, where his tomb can still be seen. In addition to be being a churchman, he was also – as was commonplace during the period – a royal servant who acted as an auditor of the royal exchequer at least twice in the 1370s. He is known to have studied in England and France.

By contrast, we know very little of Hary. *Blind(e) Hary* – *Hary* may be a surname – is recorded as receiving the king's bounty on five occasions between 1473–4 and 1492, such events all taking place at Linlithgow Palace and presumably relating to the presentation of his poem, although – as with *The Bruce* – no royal copy survives. He was therefore a contemporary of Ramsay and Lochmalony, although there is no evidence for any personal engagement on his part with the Edinburgh manuscript; the volume seems to derive from a distinctive Fife culture focused on the university of St

Andrews and involving lesser nobility and clergy (see Brown 2015). Hary's blindness, although suspiciously Homeric, seems to be well attested; along with Barbour, he is commemorated in William Dunbar's *Lament for the Makaris*, dated from internal references to after July 1505 (Bawcutt 1998: 333, 337), where he is referred to as 'blind Hary' (Bawcutt 1998: 96, line 69). The historian John Mair in 1518 records Hary's authorship of *integrum librum Guillelmi Wallacei*, naming him *Henricus a nativitate luminibus captus* 'Henry [who] was blind from birth'.

Hary's *Wallace*, although a century later in composition, makes a fitting companion-piece to *The Bruce*, given the latter's persistent references to *fredome* and *richt*, and its central concern with personal chivalric behaviour and the assertion of a distinctive Scottish polity in the face of near-contemporary English claims of insular hegemony (Duncan 1997: 13). Both *The Bruce* and *The Wallace* were composed as moral epic-romances which emphasise not fantasy but *suthfastnes*, drawing upon historical materials, in the manner of *Beowulf*, to present particular exemplary patterns of moral behaviour. Fascinatingly, this exemplary role seems to have continued, as both poems continued to be printed and read throughout the sixteenth, seventeenth and eighteenth centuries. In both cases, however, the changes they underwent in transmission through print reflected the shifting socio-cultural contexts in which they were produced.

The printing history of the two poems is complex. Printing itself began in Scotland in 1508, when Walter Chepman and Andro Myllar founded their press in Edinburgh. Although there is no extant direct evidence that Chepman and Myllar printed *The Bruce*, some leaves survive from their edition of *The Wallace*, dating from about 1509. These leaves, in folio format, are currently split between Cambridge University Library and the Mitchell Library in Glasgow (Syn.3.50.3 and S.R.341201 respectively).

Chepman and Myllar's enterprise was short-lived, ceasing to operate by 1510. It seems that the contemporary Scottish demand for luxury items such as printed books was simply not sufficient to sustain their enterprise; books in the Scots language, presumably aimed at a Scots-speaking market, were for many years often printed abroad. Examples include William Copland's editions of Gavin Douglas's *Palice of Honoure* and translation of Virgil's *Æneid*, both printed in London in 1553, or John Gau's *The Richt Vay to the Kingdom of Heuine*, which more exotically appeared in Malmö in 1533. This last text was produced in Sweden because its Lutheran author had earlier been exiled to Scandinavia, and his work would have been deemed heretical by contemporary Scottish authorities.

The earliest surviving full editions of the two poems, printed sixty years after the closure of Chepman and Myllar's enterprise, are those produced by Robert Lekpreuik, the first really successful Scottish printer. Lekpreuik produced editions of *The Wallace* and *The Bruce* in 1570 and 1571 respectively. Only single copies of these editions survive: one imperfect copy of *The Bruce*, lacking a title page and part of a prose preface, survives from the collection of the nineteenth-century antiquarian David Laing, and is now in the Pierpont Morgan Library in New York (PML 15586), while the only surviving copy of *The Wallace* is now in the British Library (C.39.d.24). This latter is 'said to have belonged to Queen Elizabeth' (Dickson and Edmond 1890: 240, repeated by Geddie 1912: 134), although there are no surviving annotations in the copy to confirm this claim. Lekpreuik's edition states that he printed the work 'at the Expensis of Henrie Charteris, & [they] ar to be sauld in [Charteris's] Buith, on the North syde of ye gait abone the Throne', i.e. the Tron in Edinburgh's High Street, so-called because it was the location of the public weighing-machine. Henry Charteris printed *The Wallace* on his own account in 1594, and Charteris's son, Robert, to whom Henry had passed his business, produced an edition in 1601; the inventory in Henry Charteris's will records *fyue scoir tua Wallaces* (cited in Brunsden 1999: 76), suggesting a substantial stock had been produced for an anticipated large readership.

Interestingly, given the relative prominence of the two poems in modern Scottish literary histories,[1] there were many more pre-nineteenth-century editions and versions of *The Wallace* – with a wider geographical spread and by a wider range of printers – than of *The Bruce*, which difference offers an interesting perspective on early modern taste.[2] Some editions of *The Wallace* were printed alongside *The Bruce*, but in such instances the

[1] E.g. Kurt Wittig's still often-referenced account of 1958.

[2] Wittig's survey devotes a whole chapter to Barbour's *Bruce* but dismisses Hary's *Wallace* (while praising it) in two pages (1958: 104–5). While selections from *The Bruce* are still common in standard student readers, *The Wallace* is rarely included. It does not, for instance, appear in Ronnie Jack and Pat Rozendaal's excellent anthology (Jack and Rozendaal 1997), even though Jack's opening essay in this anthology, 'Where Stands Scottish Literature Now?', offers a useful assessment of Wittig's powerful influence as a Leavisite evaluator of Scottish literary values (1997: ix–xi); Jack argues that Wittig's overall approach is limited by its emphasis on a particular kind of 'Scottishness'. However, there is some more recent evidence that *The Wallace* is undergoing a 'revaluation'. Felicity Riddy (2007), for instance, not only offers a fine reading of Hary but also argues that his reception in subsequent centuries underpins the evolution in Scottish discourse of 'a mythical geography of nationhood, a Scotland of the mind' (Riddy 2007: 115). Colin Kidd underlines the complexities of the cult of Wallace – as a 'Unionist–nationalist' figure, inter alia – in the same collection (Kidd 2007). An important, more recent discussion is Murray 2009, which not only places *The Wallace* within the context of dream-vision poetry but also offers a comprehensive bibliography of the poem to date. For the northern Irish version, see Smith 2016.

title of the former text appeared in prime position on the title page with *The Bruce* referred to as an addendum. However, Andro Hart of Edinburgh, who succeeded Lekpreuik as the most successful Scottish printer of his time, produced editions of *The Bruce* at least twice (1616 and 1620), and there were further copies printed by Gedeon Lithgow (Edinburgh, 1648a), Andrew (Andro) Anderson (Edinburgh, 1670) and Robert Sanders (Glasgow, 1672). In the eighteenth century, editions were issued by Alexander Carmichael and Alexander Miller (Glasgow, 1737) and by Robert Freebairn ('1715'/'1758'a based on Hart's edition of 1620 and combined with Hary's *Wallace*). John Pinkerton's edition of 1790 (printed by H. Hughs for G. Nicol) was based on Ramsay's manuscript, but was transcribed 'by another [unspecified]' (Geddie 1912: 65). Pinkerton was aware of the limitations of his edition, and it was at his (and others') urging that John Jamieson, the great lexicographer, published his major critical edition in 1820 (Jamieson 1820a), alongside his edition of *The Wallace* (1820b). Jamieson's edition remained the standard text until those of the Early English (Skeat 1870–89) and Scottish Text Societies (McDiarmid and Stevenson 1980–5).

Andro Hart printed *The Wallace* in 1611, 1618 and 1620, and in 1633 he published a distinct and interesting Latin poem on the legend (*De Gestis Illustrissimi GULIELMI VALLÆ*): the *Valliados* by Patrick Panter, a seventeenth-century professor of theology at St Andrews (see further Smith 2016 and references there cited). Copies of Hary's Scots poem were printed by Edward Raban (Aberdeen's first printer) in 1630, by James Bryson in Edinburgh in 1640 and 1645, by Gideon Lithgow in Edinburgh in 1648b and 1661, by an anonymous Society of Stationers in Edinburgh in 1661, and by Andrew Anderson in Edinburgh in 1666 and 1673. The 1717 inventory of the estate of Anderson's widow, Agnes, a leading printer in her own right, records that she possessed *662 Wallaces* (see Brunsden 1999: 76). The Glasgow firm of Robert Sanders (elder and younger) seems to have made a speciality of *The Wallace*, printing the poem in 1665, 1684, 1685, 1690, 1699 and 1713. In the eighteenth century, editions of *The Wallace* continue to outnumber those of *The Bruce*, with Edinburgh prints of the former dating from 1701, 1711 and 1758. This last edition, which also included *The Bruce*, was by the Jacobite printer Robert Freebairn,[3] and Freebairn (with Andrew Symson and Henry Knox) also printed Panter's *Valliados*. The appearance of a Belfast

[3] The 1758 edition was actually printed in around 1730; see further below, and also McDiarmid 1968: xii and references there cited.

edition of Hary's poem by James Blow in 1728 relates to the significant role of Scottish culture in northern Ireland. And in 1722, William Hamilton of Gilbertfield produced a modernised poem for a contemporary readership, and Hamilton's version, 'read across the eighteenth-century Scottish nation' (Crawford 2009: 48), swiftly dominated publishers' lists until the middle of the nineteenth century, with no fewer than twenty-three editions appearing by 1870.[4]

We might begin our analysis of formal features with Ramsay's 1489 copies of *The Bruce* and *The Wallace*. Text (5.1) is a transcription from the Edinburgh manuscript of the opening lines of *The Bruce*. In this diplomatic transcription, expanded contractions are italicised; the letter 'thorn' generally appears in Older Scots texts in a form indistinguishable from <y>, and is so reproduced here; and final flourishes, which seem to be otiose strokes, are not recorded (thus the final <s> in *Storys* appears in the manuscript as <ß>. The punctuation of the original, restricted to the punctus <.>, the virgula suspensiva </> and capital letters, has been retained. The manuscript is throughout written in a distinctively Scottish variety of secretary script.

Text (5.1) Edinburgh, National Library of Scotland, MS Advocates' 19.2.2, folio 1r

Storys. to rede ar delitabill
Suppos y*at* yai be no*ch*t bot fabill/
yan suld storys y*at* suthfast wer
And yai war said on gud maner
Hawe doubill plesance in heryng
ye fyrst plesance is ye carpyng
And ye toy*ir* ye suthfastn*es*
Y*at* schawys ye thing ry*ch*t as it wes
And suth thyng*is* y*at* ar likand
Tyll ma*n*nys heryng ar plesand
Yarfor I wald fayne set my will
Giff my wyt my*ch*t suffice y*ar*till
To put in wryt A suthfast story
That it lest ay furth in memory

[Translation (after Duncan 1997: 46): *Stories are enjoyable to read, even if they are only fables, so stories that are true, if spoken well, should give double pleasure in the hearing. The first pleasure is in the reciting, and the second in the*

[4] William Hamilton of Gilbertfield's version is 'little known today' (Crawford 2009: 48), although a new edition appeared fairly recently (King 1998). Hamilton's version was the basis for Mel Gibson's controversial 1995 film, *Braveheart*. See Riddy 2007: 111.

truthfulness that reveals things just as they were, [for] truthful events that are pleasing are entertaining to the hearer. Therefore, I am firmly resolved, if my wits are up to it, to put in writing a true story so that it will be remembered for ever in [people's] memories.]

It will be observed that Ramsay hardly uses any punctuation at all; from the point of view of distinguishing periods, where lines are aligned with cola and commata, punctuation is unnecessary. Most lines in this opening passage begin with discourse markers which distinguish the periodic structure pretty adequately: conjunctions (coordinating or subordinating, e.g. *And*, *Giff*, *Yat*), sentential adverbs (*yan*, *Yarfor*), and prepositions (*To*, *Tyll*). The single punctus after *Storys* seems to flag an emphatic pause after an opening trochee (for the metrically expected iamb), while the virgule after *fabill* corresponds to a break in the sense of the verse after the opening.

Ramsay's copy of *The Wallace*, illustrated here as Text (5.2), is similarly presented:

Text (5.2) Edinburgh, National Library of Scotland, Advocates' MS 19.2.2, folio 71r

Our antecessowris yat we suld of reide
And hald in mynde yar nobille worthi deid
We lat ourslide throw werray sleuthfulnes
And cast*is* ws eu*er* till vthir besynes
Till honour Ennymy*is* is our haile entent
It has beyne sene in yir tymys bywent
Our ald Ennemys cu*m*myn of saxonys blud
That neuyr ȝeit to scotland wald do gud
Bot eu*er* on fors and contrar haile *yer* will
Quhow gret kyndnes yar has beyne kyth yai*m* till
It is weyle knawyne on mony diuers syde
How yai haff wrocht in to yar mychty pryde
To hald scotlande at wndyr euirmar
Bot god abuff has maid yar my*ch*t to par
Ȝhit we suld thynk one our bear*is* befor
Of yar p*ar*ablys as now I say no mor
We reide of ane ry*ch*t famous of renown
Of worthi blude *yat* ryng*is* in yis regioun
And hensfurth I will my proces hald
Of Wilȝham Wallas ȝhe haue hard beyne tald

[Translation: *Through real slothfulness, we have allowed our ancestors – whom we ought to read about and [whose] noble worthy deeds [we ought to] hold in mind – to be forgotten, and [we] apply ourselves always to other activity. It has been seen in these past times that our entire intention is to honour enemies – our ancient enemies come from Saxon blood – who wished never yet to do good to Scotland; always their whole desire [is] in force and enmity, although great kindness has been shown to them. It is well known on many [and] various sides how they have wrought in their powerful pride to place Scotland beneath them for ever, even though God above has caused their power to fade. Still we ought to think on our forebears. Concerning their tales, I say no more for the time being; we read of a very famous [person] of renown, of worthy blood, whose [reputation] resounds in this region, and henceforth I will keep to my narrative. You have heard tell of William Wallace* ...]

Although the lines in Text (5.2), being composed in a five-stress rather than four-stress measure, are longer than in *The Bruce*, and the grammatical structure of the text is at times looser (even bordering on incoherent according to present-day canons of taste), its formal presentation is very similar to that in the older poem. No punctuation appears in this passage from *The Wallace*; discourse markers such as *That*, *Bot*, *Quhow* etc. at the beginning of each line flag the text's structure. Capitals are deployed sparingly outside line-beginnings, other than appearing – perhaps significantly – for the name of the hero, *Wilȝham Wallas*, and for the English opposition, flagged twice as *Ennemys* (for a discussion of the political situation at Hary's time, see McDiarmid 1968: xiv–xxvi).

Such simple presentation contrasts with the apparently more sophisticated usage adopted by Robert Lekpreuik. Text (5.3) is a transcription from Lekpreuik's edition of *The Bruce* (1571):

Text (5.3) Lekpreuik (1571: sig. A.i r)

HIstoryis to heir ar Delectabill,
Suppois yat nocht co*n*tenit, bot fa-
Tha*n* suld Historyis y*at* suithfast wer, (bill*
Gif thay be spokin in gude maner,
Haue dowbill plesour in heiring.
The first is: thair plesand carping:
The vther is, the suithfastnes,
That schawis the thing richt as it wes.
And suith thingis that ar lykand,
To mennis heiring ar plesand.
Thairfoir I wald fane set my will,
Gif my wit micht suffice thairtill,
To put in writ ane suithfast Historie,
That it may lest in Memorie.

* as in the print; the form *fabill* has been split over two lines.

In comparison with Ramsay's text, punctuation in Lekpreuik's edition is much more thoroughgoing, and at first sight resembles modern usage: comma-marks (which replaced the virgule), a double punctus like the modern colon, and the punctus. But closer examination shows that punctuation in Lekpreuik's text is actually deployed in ways that depart from those expected by a modern reader. We might examine, for instance, the following lines:

> The first is: thair plesand carping:
> The vther is, the suithfastnes,
> That schawis the thing richt as it wes.

We might note the parallelism between *thair plesand carping* and *the suithfastnes* but also the distinct punctuation deployed. Both are noun phrases, but the first is framed by colons and the second by commas. Various explanations for the difference are possible, but the most plausible is that the second unit, *the suithfastnes*, which is grammatically a complement, is itself modified by the qualifying period of which the following line is comprised (and which is concluded with a punctus); a less emphatic linking mark is therefore needed.

Lekpreuik sustains a fairly comprehensive repertory of Scots linguistic features, at least comparable in extent with those in Ramsay's text: we might note such forms as *nocht*, the inflexion in *–it*, *suld*, *suithfast*, *Gif*, *gude* etc., though *Tyll* is replaced by *To*. But he does print an opening line which differs rather markedly from Ramsay's: *HIstoryis to heir* as opposed to *Storys. to rede*. Where this distinct phraseology comes from is uncertain, but a critical interpretation is possible, aligning with Lekpreuik's choice of emphatic capitals in these opening lines. Three words are thus marked: *Delectabill*, *HIstoryis* and *Historyis*, and *Memorie*. Ramsay's *rede* is replaced by Lekpreuik's *heir*, and it could plausibly be suggested that the emphasis Lekpreuik is thus placing on the pleasures of orally transmitted memory relates to a particular reading of Barbour, as a repository of an older tradition.

Lekpreuik's 1570 edition of *The Wallace* adopts similar presentational strategies, as illustrated in Text (5.4):

Text (5.4) Lekpreuik (1570: sig. A.i r)

OUR Antecessouris, that we suld of reid,
And hald in mynd yair nobill douchtie deid
We let ouir slyde throw verray sleuthfulnes
And castis vs euer to vther besynes.

On vane gamming is set our haill Intent,
Quhilk hes bene sene in till thir tymis by went.
Our nixt nichtbouris cu*m*min of Brutus blude,
That oftentymis to Scottis willit lyttil gude.
Thocht now of lait God turnit yair mynd & will,
That greit kyndnes yai haue schawin vs till.
The hartis of pepill the Lord hes in his hand,
He may yame rewle and gyde at his command.
And thocht all Leidis wald haue yis la*n*d in thrall,
Oppone his power, God can aganis thame all.
As we haue sene in our foirbearis afoir,
Bot of thir Parabillis, as now I speik no moir.
¶We reid of ane, richt famous of Renoun,
Of worthy blude that Regnit in this Regioun.
And hyne furth now, I will my purpois hald,
Of William Wallace, as ȝe haue hard heir tald.

There has of course been a major substantive change in the text: *the ald Ennemys* in Ramsay's text have been replaced by a much more measured – indeed friendly – account of the English, now characterised thus:

Our nixt nichtbouris cu*m*min of Brutus blude,
That oftentymis to Scottis willit lyttil gude.
Thocht now of lait God turnit yair mynd & will,
That greit kyndnes yai haue schawin vs till.

[Translation: *our nearest neighbours come from the blood of Brutus, who once wished little good to Scots. Though now recently God turned their mind and desire, so that they have shown to us great kindness.*]

The English are no longer alien *saxonys* but native to the island of Britain, *of Brutus blude*, and *God* has *turnit yair mynd & will.* Brutus, the eponymous founder of the British nations, was alleged to have assigned Scotland to his son Albanectus, and he thus figured in 'the traditionary claims of English kings to be overlords of Scotland' (McDiarmid 1968: 124–5). The reference to religion is significant: Lekpreuik's text reflects his own connexion with the protestant (and pro-English) party in Scottish politics of the 1560s and 1570s, a connexion reflected in (e.g.) the warm personal correspondence between prominent Scottish reformers, such as George Buchanan and John Knox, and English magnates and politicians, such as Sir William Cecil (Lord Burghley), Sir Robert Dudley (Earl of Leicester) and Sir Thomas Randolph (son-in-law of Elizabeth I's spymaster, Sir Francis

Walsingham, and principal ambassador from the English to the Scottish court) (see Smith 2010 and references there cited).

Such a connexion is confirmed by another feature of Lekpreuik's text of *The Wallace*: an annotation which appears towards the end of the poem. Lekpreuik's edition was printed *at the Expensis of Henrie Charteris* (folio 184r), and Charteris's sponsorship seems to have encouraged the appearance of one such annotation. On folio 179r, a manicule, i.e. <☞>, appears next to the following line:

> All Charteris landis ye gude king to him gaif

However, the marginal note relating to Charteris's property, which appears in some later editions, is omitted. Much more significant is an extended passage which appears before the introduction of new character, a *monk of bery* (i.e. Bury St Edmunds), who has a vision of Wallace's salvation. On folio 180v of Lekpreuik's edition appears the following passage, in a smaller version of the blackletter type used for the body of the text:

> ¶Becaus that the mair part of thir thingis followand, ar
> altogidder superstitious and not agreeabill to ye treuth
> of Goddis word, we haue thocht it expedient to admo=
> nische the (gude Reidar) that albeit we haue Insert yame
> efter the forme of our Copie, ȝit notwithstanding we do
> na thing les than allow or approue thame for ony treuth,
> bot rather on the ane part we haue retenit thame still to
> schaw the blyndnes and errour of that tyme, quhairin me*n*
> wer (as it wer) enforcit to beleif sic vaniteis and leis: yat
> now that may be steirit vp to gif thankis to the Eternall
> our God that hes oppinnit thair eyis and deliuerit yame
> from Ignorance, yat yai may cleirly discerne betuix licht
> and mirknes, richt and wrang. On the vther part to sa=
> tisfie the appetytis of mony that culd nocht esely permit
> ony thing to be tane away or alterit in this wark, quhair
> in we haue borne with thame, alterand almaist na thing
> heirin, lest thay suld Iudge vs rasche or haistie in doing
> thairof, at our libertie and pleasure.

This inserted prose passage emphasises the authority of the text presented, while at the same time acknowledging the tastes and views of the protestant readership for whom Lekpreuik catered.

As in his printing of *The Bruce*, punctuation has been added to Lekpreuik's text of *The Wallace*. There is some evidence that Lekpreuik's exemplar was related to the Chepman and Myllar edition of 1509, judging from a comparison of substantive readings (from books 6, 10 and 11) in the fragments and parallel passages in the 1570 text, but Chepman and Myllar do not deploy punctuation, and capitals are there restricted to the beginning of lines.

As already flagged, Lekpreuik printed both texts throughout in a blackletter font, which seems to have been his common practice in printing verse and 'public' prints, such as broadsides (for details, see Dickson and Edmond 1890: 207–72, and, for a discussion of his broadsides, Smith 2017a); he seems to have kept roman typefaces for prose works, especially the devotional writings which seem to have formed a large proportion of his output. Later printers, throughout the remainder of the sixteenth and into the seventeenth centuries, continued to employ blackletter for *The Wallace*, sometimes using roman type for supplementary purposes, e.g. to flag personal names. That this choice was not always an easy one to make is proven by the example of Henry Charteris himself, whose own edition of 1594 survives in one imperfect copy, in Edinburgh's National Library of Scotland (Ry.III.e.8). Charteris attempts to print the work throughout in blackletter, but occasionally he – or his compositor – runs short of type and has to insert roman letters, sporadically, into the text. He also sometimes introduces mistaken letters to which he is clearly unused, e.g. substituting <p> for <y>, which look to the untutored eye rather similar in blackletter type; the implication is that the printer is more accustomed to roman fonts. Such errors are interesting: they flag that Charteris and his team were keen to sustain blackletter as a vector of antiquarian sentiment, even though they struggled to fulfil this intention.

Blackletter was also deployed in later editions of *The Bruce* and *The Wallace*, but sometimes more subtly. Andro Hart's editions of *The Bruce*, for instance, demonstrate an interesting blending of fonts: the introductory material and the names of persons within the text are all printed in roman typeface, but the body of the text is in blackletter. Hart's choice of blackletter for his editions of *The Bruce* and *The Wallace* was very definitely a conscious choice, since he commonly used roman in verse, as in (for instance) his edition of the poems of his contemporary, William Drummond of Hawthornden, printed in the same year (1616) as his first edition of Barbour's poem. A hint as to why Hart made this choice lies in part of the frequently applied phraseology of the title pages to his editions of *The Bruce*: *Newly corrected and conferred with the best and most ancient Manuscripts*. The claim is not just to authority (*corrected . . . the best*) but also to antiquity (*most ancient*), and also to the handwritten format

(*Manuscript*) which, still, represented authorial authenticity: an authenticity emphasised by Hart's use of a capital letter.

However, the claims of authenticity and antiquity need some qualification. The opening lines of Hart's 1616 edition of *The Bruce* (Text (5.3)) appear as follows:

Text (5.3) Hart (1616: 1)

STories to read are delectable, (ble
Suppose they nought containe but fa-
Then sould Stories *yat* soothfast were,
If they be spoken in good maner:
Haue double pleasure in hearing:
The first is their pleasant carping,
The other is, their soothfastnesse,
That shewes the thing right as it wes.
And soothfast things that are likand,
To mens hearing are pleasand:
Therefore I would faine set my will,
If my wit might suffice theretill.
To put in write a soothfast Storie, **[folio 1v]**
That it may last in memorie:

For Hart, *The Bruce* is above all a *Storie*, the only word attracting a capital letter in this opening. He deploys comma, colon and full stop, but (except in *The other is,*) always at the end of lines, and sometimes in a rather puzzling fashion, as in *If my wit might suffice theretill.*, where a modern editor would naturally impose a comma to mark the ending of a parenthetical subordinate clause. It sometimes seems in Hart's edition that there is an uneasy tension between 'old' typography, associated with antiquity, and 'new' punctuation, imposed because it is what contemporary readers expect in a book. And it is of course notable that, again despite his claims of authenticity, Hart's text generally omits linguistic forms distinctive of Scots, the distinct language variety, descended from Old English, that emerged in Lowland Scotland during the later medieval period. In the above passage, for instance, *sould* is retained, as is *likand*, although in the latter case it is possible that a constraining factor is its rhyme with Scots *pleasand* 'pleasing', possibly confused with English *pleasant*.[5] The Scots form *theretill* (cf. prototypically English *thereto*) is retained, in rhyme with *will*. However, many Scots forms found in

[5] We might note *pleasant* a few lines earlier, in mid-line position, cf. Lekpreuik's *plesand* at the same point.

Ramsay's or Lekpreuik's texts are in Hart's edition replaced by forms current in contemporary early modern English: *nought*, *soothfast(nesse)*, *good* etc.

Hart's editions of *The Wallace*, which like Lekpreuik's include the 'Brutus' introduction and the inserted attack on superstition, are similarly presented. All of Hart's editions are generally in blackletter, but, as with his editions of *The Bruce*, they harness roman type for the title page, for introductory materials and for names in the text. Text (5.4) below comes from his edition of 1620, the same year in which he also published a second printing of *The Bruce*. Underlined names are in roman typeface in the original.

Text (5.4) Hart (1620b: 1)

OUr Antecessours whome wee should
of reade,
And holde in minde their fame and wor-
thie deede:
Wee let ouerslide through very sloath-
fulnesse,
And castes vs euer to vther businesse:
On vaine gaming is set our whole intent,
Quhilk hes beene seene into these times by went.
Our next neighbours that came of Brutus blood,
They often times to Scots wisht little good.
Though now of late God turnd their mind & will,
That great kindnesse they haue showne vs vntill.

[p. 2]

The hearts of people the Lord hath in his hand:
He may them rule, and guide at his command.
And though all leids would haue this Land in thrall,
Oppone his power God can against them all.
As wee haue seene in our forebeares before,
But of these Parables as now I speake no more.
Wee reade of one right famous of renowne,
Of worthie Blood that reigned in this Region:
And hencefoorth now I will my purpose hold,
Of William Wallace, as yee haue heard told:
. . .

As in Hart's editions of *The Bruce*, punctuation is largely restricted to the ends of lines, and movement of the language away from Scots in the direction of early modern English is further advanced. Thus, where Lekpreuik's edition has the Scots forms *suld*, *reid*, *hald*, *haill Intent*, *intill*, *thir*, *blude* rhyming with *gude*, *Thocht*, *turnit* and *hes* (for instance), Hart's edition has anglicised *should*, *reade*, *holde*, *whole intent*, *into*, *these*, *blood* rhyming with *good*, *Though*, *turnd* and *hath*. Hart keeps, however, *Quhilk*. There are also weaker readings, which may indicate that Hart did not understand some of the vocabulary presented in his exemplar, cf. *yair nobill douchtie deid* in Lekpreuik's edition beside Hart's *their fame and worthie deede*.

Hart's editions seem to have circulated widely during the first half of the seventeenth century, and collations indicate that they were the basis for many subsequent editions, although as the century proceeded presentational conventions underwent a change. Although printing of *The Bruce* is more restricted, blackletter disappears from the much better-attested *Wallace* tradition in the early eighteenth century, in the editions produced by the younger Robert Sanders and in James Blow's Belfast edition of 1728. It seems that the discourse community for which these texts were produced no longer demanded this visual 'testimony of antiquity'.

However, blackletter made a return in the rather curious eighteenth-century folio editions of the two poems, produced by Robert Freebairn. In the early years of the eighteenth century Freebairn was at the forefront of a group of printers attempting to depose the notorious Agnes Campbell (Mrs Anderson) from her 'reign of terror' as royal printer in Scotland, a struggle in which he was successful, being appointed to the post himself in 1711 (SPAT 1990: 7) despite personal flaws allegedly including 'advancement "in the school of Bacchus"' (Duncan 1965: 43); at that time he was already employing Thomas and Walter Ruddiman, later to become prominent figures in the history of publishing in their own right, demonstrating his ambition in developing his enterprise (McDougall 2012; see also section 5.2 below). However, Freebairn's success was short-lived. In 1715 he took over the press of an Aberdeen rival, James Nicoll. The date is significant: Freebairn was a Jacobite, a supporter of the Old Pretender. Nicoll's equipment was transported to Perth, whither Freebairn had fled after taking part in a failed assault on Edinburgh Castle. There it was used by him for the printing of Jacobite proclamations, e.g. *Scotland's Lament, Confabulation and Prayer* (1715), *The Miserable State of Scotland since the Union, briefly represented* (1716), and also an account of the Battle of Sheriffmuir (SPAT 1996: 15). With the collapse of the rebellion, Freebairn fled abroad, only returning 'surreptitiously' (SPAT 1990: 8) to reclaim his post as royal printer, which he seems to have pursued with some success. He died in 1747.

Freebairn's editions of *The Bruce* and *The Wallace* seem to have been printed – or perhaps set up in type – as long ago as 1714–15, the date usually assigned to them in recent discussions (e.g. MacDonald 2012: 556). However, their 'issue was delayed by the Rebellion in which [Freebairn] took part' (Geddie 1912: 144), and the title pages record them as 'Printed in the Year MDCCLVIII'. Freebairn's name is not mentioned, possibly because the texts were circulated posthumously. I have not yet been able to find any account of who was responsible for the edition's circulation: presumably an executor or inheritor of the printer's estate, although Freebairn's will does not seem to have survived.[6]

The opening lines of Freebairn's edition of *The Bruce* read as follows:

Text (5.5) Freebairn ('1715'/'1758'a: 1)

STORIES to read are delectable,
Suppose they be nought but fable:
Then should stories that soothfast were,
If they were said in good manner,
Have double pleasance in hearing.
The first pleasance is the carping,
And the other the soothfastness,
That shews the thing right as it was.
And soothfast things that are likand,
To mens hearing are most pleasand;
Therefore I would fain set my will,
If my wit might suffice theretil,

[6] London, British Library, G.18516, a copy of Freebairn's *Wallace*, was bequeathed to the British Museum by Thomas Grenville (1755–1846), who was not only a major politician (a friend and associate of Charles James Fox) but also a significant book collector. A note on the fly-leaf of this copy reads as follows:

> Pinkerton in his List of Scottish Poets discredits this edition
> which had been printed by Freebairn in 1714, but it's
> publication, stopped by the rebellion, was suspended till
> 1758. Dr Jameson, a much more able & candid critick,
> in his edition of Bruce & Wallace 4°. 1820 p.ix says
> 'I am under the necessity of differing from Mr Pinkerton; to me
> the editions printed by Freebairn appear more correct than
> any of the preceding, & his Wallace even preferable to
> the Perth edition of 1790'

Further down on the same fly-leaf appears the following:

> Blind Harry is mentioned by John Major, the
> Scotch Historian, who was born about 1470,
> to have been living in his time.
> vide Warton's Hist: of Eng: Poetry
> vol.1 p.321
> vol.2 p.334

[p. 2]

To put in writ a soothfast story,
That it last ay forth in memory,
. . .

Although the title page and other apparatus of Freebairn's text is in roman type, as are – following Hart's practice – the names within the text, the body of the poem is set in the archaic blackletter format: a throwback to Hart's usage, which by this time is a clear archaism, prefiguring that to be adopted in the antiquarian practices of the following century. However, archaic font is blended with significant linguistic changes: examination of the language and punctuation of the passage cited quickly reveals that the editor has interpreted 'careful correction' from Hart's 1620 edition very liberally. Thus, in the lines cited above, the rhymes *likand: pleasand* and *theretil: wil* are retained, but otherwise Scotticisms are generally expunged. And although in the eighteenth century many writers habitually capitalised 'emphatical' words (usually nouns, as in present-day German typography), this system was in decline. By the middle of the eighteenth century, the modern English practice, whereby capitals are employed to flag the beginning of (grammatical) sentences and to mark names, was generally recommended in mid eighteenth-century printers' manuals. Freebairn employs capitals in the modern fashion; his text is therefore an interesting blend of the archaic (or even archaistic) and the new.

A similar approach is adopted in Freebairn's edition of *The Wallace*. Again, the underlined words and phrases are in roman type.

Text (5.6) Freebairn ('1715'/'1758'b: 1)

Our Ancestors, of whom we should oft read,
And hold in mind their noble worthy deed,
We let overslide, through very slothfulness,
And cast us ever to other business.
To honour enjoying is set our whole intent,
Which hath been seen into these times bywent.
Our old enemies coming of Saxon blood,
That never yet to Scotland would do good,
But ever on force, and contrare haill their will,
Holy great kindness there has been kyth'd them till,

[p. 2]

It is well known on many divers side,
How they have wrought into their mighty pride,

To hold Scotland at under evermair,
But God above has made their might to pair;
Yet we should think on our bears before.
Of thir parables as now I speak no more.
  We read of one right famous of renown,
Of worthy blood, that reign'd in this region:
And henceforth now, I will my process hold
Of William Wallace, as ye have heard it told.

Freebairn's treatment of *The Wallace* is much as his treatment of *The Bruce*, although he does retain some Scottish features, e.g. *kyth'd* 'shown', and – also as in *The Bruce* – some features are obviously constrained by their occurrence in rhyme, e.g. *evirmair* (rhyming with *pair*) and *till* 'to' (rhyming with *will*). It will have been observed in terms of substantive content that Freebairn's edition returns to the old anti-English text which had been replaced by the version printed by Lekpreuik, presumably consulting Ramsay's manuscript to do so.[7] The admonition to the reader (referring to the Monk of Bury) has also gone. These changes may be because of a bias towards antiquarian correctness, but are more probably made because of Freebairn's own Jacobite, anti-Unionist views at the time. Jacobitism was in many ways an assertion of the superiority of traditional ways of doing things; it was also 'catholic', and an attack on monks would have thus been inappropriate. Freebairn's reversion to blackletter in both texts seems to have been part and parcel of this attitude. To print this edition with these features in the context of early eighteenth-century Scotland was, pragmatically, a political act to which his intended discourse community would have been sensitive, and Freebairn was clearly too ideologically committed to have been insensitive as to how his version of the text could be interpreted. It is possibly for this reason that the circulation of these texts had to wait.

The final version of *The Bruce* to be examined here is that by John Pinkerton, published in 1790. Pinkerton was, for all his notorious 'irascibility' (MacDonald 2012: 555) and the 'irregularities in his conduct' on which contemporaries enthusiastically commented,[8] a crucial figure in the transmission of medieval Scottish culture to future generations (see e.g.

[7] The consultation could be careless: we might note *enjoying* for Ramsay's *Ennymyis* in line 5.

[8] Pinkerton's turbulent personal history, as summarised in ODNB, suggests that he was yet another sufferer from *mal d'archive*. He corresponded with Percy, but ended up by quarrelling with him; and his *Select Scotish* [*sic*] *Ballads* of 1783 incurred the wrath of Ritson, who revealed in the *Gentleman's Magazine* that Pinkerton's continuation in that collection of the poem *Hardyknute* – itself an eighteenth-century pastiche – was his own work, although he passed it off as a medieval text. In 1815 Pinkerton left for Paris, dying there in reduced circumstances. It will be no surprise for attentive

Sher 2006: 125), and his text represents the first attempt at a 'modern'-style critical edition of the poem. The opening lines of Pinkerton's edition read as follows:

Text (5.7) Pinkerton (1790: 1)

BUKE I.

STORYSE to rede ar delitabill,
Suppose that thai be nought but fabill;
Than suld storyse that suthfast wer,
And thai war said on gud maner,
Have doubill plesance in heryng.
The fyrst plesance is thair carping,
And the 'tothir thair suthfastnes,
That schewys the thing rycht as it was;
And such thyngs that ar likand
Tyll manys heryng ar plesand.
Thairfor I wald fayne set my will,
Giff my wyt mycht suffice thairtill,
To put in wryt a suthfast story
That it lest ay furth in memory
. . .

In comparison with Freebairn's '1715'/'1758' edition of *The Bruce*, Pinkerton's is much closer to Ramsay's text (on which it explicitly drew), but there are some obvious differences. Pinkerton follows Lekpreuik (and not Ramsay) in dividing the text into *bukes*. However, whereas earlier printers, from Hart to Freebairn, used blackletter type as an archaic testimony of authenticity, but felt quite able to modify the linguistic features of their exemplars in radical ways, Pinkerton's edition adopts different strategies, with at least a partial return to the manuscript authority, something emphasised by the appearance – in italic capitals – on the title page of the phrase '*THE FIRST GENUINE EDITION*', but another important departure is the adoption of a roman font (see further sections 5.2 and 5.3 below). Punctuation has been introduced, of course, and we might note the apostrophe to indicate a presumed omission in *'tothir,* cf. Ramsay's *toyir*. The flourished *ß* in the manuscript is interpreted as <se> in *STORYSE*, and instead of <y> for thorn Pinkerton's edition has <th>. The

readers to discover that one of the few friends he retained was – despite his disapproving of Pinkerton's 'advanced' views on religion – Sir Walter Scott. *Hardyknute* was actually by Elizabeth, Lady Wardlaw (1677–1727); it was later included, as an additional text, in Ramsay's *The Ever Green* (see section 5.2 below), and in Percy's *Reliques*. Scott claimed that *Hardyknute* was the first poem he had learned by heart.

edition also attempted to reproduce Scots (*Scotish*) linguistic features; although the anglicised form *nought* appears in Pinkerton's edition for *nocht*, this seems a slip, since *rycht*, *mycht* appear for *right*, *might*. Other differences from the manuscript in the edition's opening lines are *Have* for *Hawe*, *schewys* for *schawys*, *was* for *wes* (despite the rhyme with *suthfastnes*), *thyngs* for *thyngis*, *manys* for *mannys*, and *Thairfor* for *Yarfor*. Forms such as *herying* for *heryng*, *thair* for *ye* and *such* for *suth* seem to be simple errors of transcription. It is likely that Pinkerton was not himself responsible for these errors, for, in 1820, John Jamieson wrote as follows in his preface to his own edition of *The Bruce*:

> The best edition of this Poem, which has yet appeared, is that of Mr Pinkerton, A. 1790. But the learned editor, though he did all in his power to obtain a faithful copy of the manuscript, is satisfied, that, as he had not an opportunity of examining it himself, the work is in many respects inaccurate. He, therefore, with laudable candour, has, in common with many other literary friends, for some years past, urged the writer of this Preface to undertake a new edition. (Jamieson 1820a: viii)

Features of the edition were designed to flag the antique setting of the work in ways which would appeal to a contemporary reader: at the head of the opening page a line-drawing of a coin from Bruce's time (always attractive to antiquarian collectors), and the 'sentimental' depiction on the title page not of a battle but of the tearful leave-taking of Bruce and his queen when she and her ladies were sent for safety to Kildrummy Castle (Book III, line 347). Such iconic objects or images were the common currency of historical memorialisation in the eighteenth century, especially favoured in Jacobite circles (see Pittock 2010), and of course prefigure the kind of antiquarianism we associate with, above all, Sir Walter Scott. Antiquarian attitudes also clearly inform Jamieson's later edition, which continued this practice: Jamieson's title page of *The Bruce* has an illustration of various weapons and coats of arms, while the title page of *The Wallace* has a fallen warrior, in re-created Highland dress, with his broadsword and targe prominently in view.

Pinkerton, interestingly, did not produce an edition of *The Wallace* – perhaps a precursor of the change in taste which saw *The Bruce* becoming the more representative text of medieval Scotland – but an edition of *The Wallace* from the same year as Pinkerton's shows a similar responsiveness to contemporary tastes, albeit with a slightly distinct cultural inflexion. The Perth printer Morison's 1790 edition of *The Wallace* offered a distinct approach to 'authenticity'. Robert Morison the younger had a reputation for fine editions of major works, including those of Fergusson's *Poems* and

Thomson's *The Seasons*; indeed, the title page of the latter places his own name at the very top of the page (*MORISON's EDITION OF Thomson's Seasons*). By 1794, the year Morison was appointed as printer to the University of St Andrews, his presses were producing between 20,000 and 30,000 volumes a year (SPAT 1996: 18). Morison's was in its time the biggest publisher in Scotland outside Edinburgh and Glasgow. And Robert Burns, a subscriber to Morison's *Wallace*, praised the book to his correspondent Mrs Dunlop as being 'the most elegant piece of work that ever came from any Printing-Press in Great Britain' (cited in Brunsden 1999: 106).

The lengthy text on the title page of Morison's edition demonstrates that there has been a step-change in editorial attitudes since Freebairn's day:

> THE METRICAL HISTORY OF SIR WILLIAM WALLACE, KNIGHT OF ELLERSLIE, BY HENRY, COMMONLY CALLED BLIND HARRY: CAREFULLY TRANSCRIBED FROM THE M.S. COPY OF THAT WORK, IN THE *ADVOCATES' LIBRARY*, UNDER THE EYE OF THE EARL OF BUCHAN. AND NOW PRINTED FOR THE FIRST TIME, ACCORDING TO THE ANCIENT AND TRUE ORTHOGRAPHY. WITH NOTES AND DISSERTATIONS. IN THREE VOLUMES. VOL. I. "A! Fredome is a nobill thing! "Fredome maks a man to have lykinge, "Fredome all solace to men gives, "He lives at ese that freely lives! BARBOUR'S BRUS. PERTH: PRINTED BY R. MORISON JUNIOR, FOR R. MORISON AND SON, BOOKSELLERS; PERTH. M,DCC,XC.

The information provided here is much more comprehensive than anything seen on the poem's title pages before. Reference is made not only to the hero but also to the author; a claim of authority is made, backed up by a reference to the validation of the text by a member of the aristocracy, with no other editor or even transcriber named; the text is eager to assert that it is printed *according to the ancient and true orthography*; scholarship is asserted (*with notes and dissertations*) and – a sign of changing taste – the motto of choice comes from another, also aristocratic, text, Barbour's *Bruce*, but with a quotation which in 1790, a year when the French Revolution was undergoing its most optimistic phase, would have had a degree of ambiguity.

The association of the earl of Buchan with the project is also in this context significant. In addition to being a major antiquary, Buchan was a slightly eccentric Whig grandee with libertarian views: he had supported John Wilkes and the American Revolution, was on friendly terms with Benjamin Franklin and corresponded with George Washington. Indeed, the year after the publication of this edition he sent Washington a snuff-box said to be made out of wood from a tree in which Wallace had hidden after the battle of Falkirk, and in 1814 he was to erect a colossal statue of Wallace – still there – on his estate at Dryburgh. He could be at times inappropriately enthusiastic: 'The story of how in 1819 he tried to storm Sir Walter Scott's sick-room to reassure him that he would personally supervise all the arrangements for Scott's funeral at Dryburgh has been retold many times as evidence of his propensity for the ridiculous' (ODNB). Back in the 1790s Buchan even went so far as to join the London Society of the Friends of the People, a group sympathetic to the ideologies emerging in revolutionary France. Like many contemporary intellectuals he combined radicalism and antiquarianism, having a claim to being the founder of the Society of Antiquaries of Scotland (King 2007: 132).

The text of the poem is, as in Pinkerton's *The Bruce*, presented in roman type: blackletter has gone. Text (5.8) is a transcription of the opening lines of Morison's edition:

Text (5.8) Buchan (1790: 1)

OUR Antecessowris, yat we suld of reide,
And hald in mynde yar nobille worthy deide,
We lat ourslide, throw werray slouthfulness,
And casst us evir till uthir besynes.
Till honour ennymys is our haile entent,
As has beyne seyne in yir tymys bywent.
Our auld ennymys cummin of Saxonys blud,
That never zeit to Scotland wald do gud,
Bot evir on fors, and contrar haile yair will,
Quhow gret kyndnes yair beyne kyth yaim till,

[p. 2]

It is weyle knawyne on mony diverss syde,
How yai haff wrocht into yair mychty pryde,
To hald Scotlande at undir evirmair,
Bot God abuff has maid yair mycht to par;
Zhit wi suld thynk one our bears befor.
Of yair parablyss as now I say no mor.
We reid of ane rycht famous of renoune,
Of worthi blud yat ryngs in yis regioune:
And hensfurth, I will my proces hald
Of Wilzham Wallace as ye haf hard beyne tald.

Like Pinkerton's edition, Buchan's (or Morison's) has made a definite effort to offer an accurate transcription of the manuscript, albeit with the imposition of eighteenth-century punctuation. The 'flourished' <s>, *ß*, has been expanded as <ss>, and other interpretations include replacing <w> with <u> in *ws* 'us', and <u> for <v> in *vthir* 'other', yielding *us, uthir*. The edition retains <y> for thorn. Some contractions have been expanded (silently) in ways which a modern scholar would do differently, e.g. *ryngs* in place of *ryngis*. There are some flaws and miscopyings even in this short passage, e.g. *yair beyne* for *yar has beyne*, *wi* for *we*, and *as ye* for *ȝhe*, but we are certainly offered something more accurate, as a transcription of the manuscript original, than hitherto. In sum, this antiquarian edition is attempting something 'authentic'.

But the paratextual title page places the whole text within a contemporary political frame. It is no surprise that Robert Burns subscribed to this edition, for, if conceived of in line with the sentiments of its framing materials, the poem correlates with Burns's own libertarian views; indeed, Burns was later to send a copy of 'Scots wha hae', his Wallace poem, to Buchan in 1794 (Crawford 2009: 369). It seems both men shared what Colin Kidd has termed, with reference to Buchan, a common 'whiggish intellectual patriotism' (1993: 214). An old text, in a new form, has taken on yet another, contemporary meaning, expressed inter alia through the pragmatic features in which it has been presented.

5.2 Jacobite Recuperations (1): Allan Ramsay

Robert Freebairn was not alone as a Jacobite conduit of medieval texts. Two other individuals offered different kinds of recuperation: Allan Ramsay the elder (1684–1758) and Thomas Ruddiman (1674–1757). Ramsay is, as shall see shortly, a figure whose wide cultural achievement 'remains both historic and underestimated' (ODNB), and a seminal editor of medieval Scottish verse, while Ruddiman – acknowledged in his time and afterwards as the leading British Latinist of his generation, most famously by Samuel Johnson – was not only a publisher in his own right but a distinguished critical editor of Gavin Douglas's Older Scots translation of Virgil's *Æneid*. Like Freebairn, both men were Jacobites, although somewhat more discreet in expression, and knew each other well; all three were members of the culture of conviviality and sociability – a distinctive discourse community – that existed in Edinburgh's cramped Old Town at the beginning of the eighteenth century, and which led to the emergence of the distinctive Scottish enlightenment.

Allan Ramsay was born in Leadhills in Lanarkshire. In 1701, he moved to Edinburgh to enter the wigmaking business, later becoming a bookseller and dealer in medals, jewellery and silver; eventually he opened a circulating library and became involved in various cultural initiatives, including the development – albeit short-lived – of an Edinburgh theatre. His son, Allan Ramsay the younger (1713–84), was to become a distinguished painter of portraits, and, like Thomas Percy, a member of Samuel Johnson's circle. However, the elder Ramsay is now best-known for his poetry, both his own compositions and – perhaps even more – for his reworkings of past texts.

One of his most influential efforts in this regard was *The Ever Green*, which appeared in 1723–4, published by Ruddiman. *The Ever Green*, subtitled *Being a Collection of Scots Poems, Wrote by the Ingenious before 1600*, is a key work in the transmission of medieval Scottish verse, introducing the works of Robert Henryson, William Dunbar and their contemporaries to later generations. Like Chaucer and Gower before him, Dunbar 'showed a concern for textual integrity, and was sensitive to the way poetry might be "magellit", or mutilated, once it passed from the author's possession' (Bawcutt 1998: 11), and, if he could have foreseen the future, it seems likely that he would have found Ramsay's approach troubling. *The Ever Green* drew upon another famous manuscript in Edinburgh's National Library of Scotland, already encountered in the Introduction: MS Advocates' 1.1.6, copied by the Edinburgh merchant George Bannatyne *in tyme of pest*. This manuscript is usually dated to 1568, but it may have been written a little earlier, perhaps relating to the marriage of Mary Queen of Scots to Henry Lord Darnley (see MacDonald 1986).

Ramsay's approach to medieval texts prefigured that of Thomas Percy, in that he clearly saw his role as an imaginative re-creator of these older writings. Indeed, in 1726 he even added a short poem, 'On the Ever Green being gathered out of this manuscript', in his own hand to the end of Advocates' 1.1.6; its purpose was to thank the book's then owner, James Carmichael, Earl of Hyndford ('The good Carmichael Patron kind'), for lending it to him (folio 374v; see Fox and Ringler 1980: xvi, but see also ODNB). He had already approached a past text in such a way, through his addition of two cantos of his own invention to his edition of the medieval ballad *Christ's Kirk on the Green* (1721); and his addition in *The Ever Green* of an extra stanza to William Dunbar's *Lament for the Makaris* to include a prophecy of himself, and of extra poems of his own composition, are further examples of such interventionist revision. However, there are also some more subtle changes that are worth closer scrutiny. The survival of the Bannatyne manuscript makes it possible for us to examine the modifications made in *The Ever Green* in some detail; moreover, we are in the fortunate position of being able to trace the transmission of this text via the manuscript version Ramsay himself prepared for the printer, now London, British Library, MS Egerton 2024.

We might, for instance, examine Ramsay's edition of a short but well-attested poem: Dunbar's *Discretioun in Taking*, one of a small cluster of verses on the giving and receiving of gifts, a crucial aspect of late medieval and early modern court culture. The poem is witnessed in two early modern copies other than the Bannatyne manuscript: Cambridge, Magdalene College, Pepys MS 2553, better known as the Maitland Folio manuscript, and Cambridge, University Library, MS Ll 5.10, known also as the Reidpeth manuscript. The Reidpeth manuscript, written in 1622–3, is a copy of the Maitland Folio.[9]

Texts (5.9) through (5.11) are, respectively, transcripts of the opening of *Discretioun in Taking* as it appears in the Bannatyne manuscript, in Egerton 2024, the copy Ramsay prepared for the printer, and in the edition that Ramsay's publisher, Thomas Ruddiman, eventually produced.

Text (5.9) Edinburgh, National Library of Scotland, Advocates' MS 1.1.6 (the Bannatyne manuscript), folio 62v

ffollowis discretioun in taking

Eftir geving I speik of taking
Bot littill of ony gud forsaiking
Sum takkis our littill awtoritie
And sum our mekle And yat is glaiking
In taking sowld discretioun be

The clerkis takis beneficis w^{t} brawlis
Sum of sanct petir and sum of sanct pawlis
Tak he the rentis No cair hes he

[folio 63r]

Suppois the diuill tak all thair sawlis
In taking sowld discretioun be

Barronis takis fra the tenne*n*tis peure
all fruct yat growis on ye feure
In mailis and gersomes rasit ouirhie
and garris thame beg fra dur to dure
In taking sowld discretioun be

[9] Both Maitland Folio and Reidpeth manuscripts deserve greater attention than offered here; I plan to discuss them further in a future study. A preliminary discussion of the Maitland Folio version of *Discretioun in Taking* appears in Smith and Kay 2011.

Text (5.10): London, British Library, Egerton MS 2024, folio 149r

ffolows Discretioun in Taking

Now After giving I speik of taking
but littell of ony gude forsaiking
Sum taks owre Scrimp autoritie
and sum owre-mekle and that is Glaiking
in Taking sould discretion be

2

SO The Clerks had benifices with Crawls
Sum of saint peter sum of saint pauls
take he the rents nae cair hes he
abeit the Deil tak all thair sauls
in taking sould discretion be

3

Barrons tak frae thair Tennants pure
all fruit that grows upon the feure
in Mails & Gersomes raist owre hie
And gars them beg frae dore to dore
in taking sould discretion be

Text (5.11) Ramsay, *The Ever Green* (1723–4: vol. II, 87)

Follows Discration in Taking.

I

NOw after Giving I speik of Taking,
But litill of ony Gude forsaiking;
Sum taks owre scrimp Autoritie,
And sum owre-mekle, and that is glaiking;
In Taking suld Discration be.
[p. 88]

II

THE Clerks tak Benifices with Brawls,
Sum of Saint *Peter*, sum of Saint *Pauls*,
Take he the Rents, nae Cair hes he,
Abeit the Deil tak all thair Sauls;
In Taking suld Discration be.

III

BARONS tak frae thair Tenans pure
All fruit that grows upon the Feure,

In Mails and Fersomes raist owre hie,
And gars them beg frae Dore to Dore;
In Taking suld Discration be.

There is no punctuation as we would understand it in the Bannatyne text. Bannatyne uses punctuation elsewhere in the manuscript, notably the virgula suspensiva to indicate a pause, or the double virgula suspensiva, which appears sporadically for a final pause (in some poems used fairly frequently). However, features of layout are used, such as an initial rubric to mark the poem's beginning, and capitals to mark sense [sense] divisions in lines 4 and 8. Capitals are also used interestingly at the beginning of lines; we might compare their presence and absence at the beginnings of lines 4 and 14.

These features are thrown into relief when compared with the eighteenth-century versions, namely Egerton 2024 and the 1723–4 edition. Both texts derive overtly from Bannatyne, something Ramsay acknowledged in the mock-up version (folio 1r) of the title page he provided for Ruddiman in the Egerton manuscript. This page includes a hierarchy of script size to represent the equivalent in typeface, careful underlining, a motto from Pope, and even the placing of such statements as 'Published by Allan Ramsay', 'Edinburgh', and 'Printed by Mr Tho. Ruddiman for | the Publisher at his Shop near the Cross'. Despite this presentational care, however, no marks of punctuation are included in the transcriptions themselves, although Ramsay was clearly able to use such in his own prose, as demonstrated by his letter of dedication to James, Duke of Hamilton, Captain General of the *Royall Company of Archers*.[10] The opening of the letter of dedication, Text (5.12), shows Ramsay's own practice (engrossed forms are flagged in the transcription by emboldening; deleted forms are marked by a single strike-through):

Text (5.12): London, British Library, Egerton 2024, folio 2r

To
His Grace James
Duke of Hamilton
Captain General of the Archers

[10] Hamilton, the fifth duke, had succeeded his 'extravagant and profligate' father when the latter died in a duel in 1712. The fifth duke, quieter in temperament than his father and now generally known for his association with the London Foundling Hospital, nevertheless seems to have shared many of his father's political views, and the Company of Archers was 'a nest of closet Jacobites' (ODNB); a list of the members of the company survives, published by David and James Adams in Edinburgh in 1715, and includes the name of Robert Freebairn in the muster. Ramsay composed a poem in praise of the Company ('On the Royal Archers Shooting for the Bowl'), which survives on folio 41v of another holograph manuscript: Edinburgh, National Library of Scotland, MS 2233; presumably the poem was written with the Archers as his intended discourse community.

and the Honourable Members
of the **Royall Company**
~~of~~
~~ARCHERS~~

~~Right Noble, Right Honourable~~ } My Lords & Gentlemen
~~and Honourable Noble Men and Gentlemen~~ }

When the more Eminent concerns of Life, or the agreeable
Diversion of ye Bow; make no demands upon your Time: the
following, **Old Bards**, present you with ane entertainment
that can never be disagreeable to any **Scots Man**, who
despises the fopery of admiring nothing but what is either
new or foraign, and is a Lover of his Countrey. Such
the Royall Company of Archers are, and such
every good man should strive to be.

By contrast, the printed version of *Discretion in Taking* is quite fussily punctuated, and italics, with no handwritten equivalent in Egerton 2024, have been used to mark the names *Peter* and *Paul*. Semicolons are introduced at line-endings, and, in place of Bannatyne's capitals marking a sense-change, the printed edition has introduced mid-line commas. Both Egerton 2024 and the printed edition deploy capitalisation in ways different from that in the Bannatyne text, but the Egerton text of *Discretion* – contrasting with Ramsay's practice in his introductory epistle – deploys capitals more sparingly, apparently to mark distinctively Scots words (*Scrimp*, *Glaiking*, *Crawls*, *Deil*, *Mails*, *Gersomes*), and words relating to the 'estates' theme of the opening (*Clerks*, *Barrons*, *Tennants*); capitals are also used to mark a few words important for the discourse structure of the verse (*Now*, *After*, *Sum*, *SO*, *And*). The printed edition, however, is in line with more conventional eighteenth-century general practice, whereby key words in discourse, usually nouns, appear with capitals: *Giving*, *Taking*, *Gude*, *Autoritie*, *Discration*. Bannatyne's connecting rubric as the italicised title for the poem has been retained in both Egerton and printed versions (though, interestingly if understandably, *Follows* is dropped in the running-head). Layout of the text has been changed to create a more interesting appearance on the page and emphasise the refrain.

Ramsay himself has also made a special intervention of a more conventionally linguistic character. Earlier in Egerton 2024, Ramsay corrected his own transcription in ways that show he was not entirely comfortable with Older Scots forms. For instance, in his transcription of *A Ballat to the scorn and derision of Wanton Women*, he originally transcribed the opening stanza thus:

Text (5.13): London, British Library, Egerton 2024, folio 53r (my lineation)

Ye Lusty Ladys luke
  the Rackles lyves ye leid
haunt not in hole or nuke
  to hurt your Womanheid
I red for best Remeid
  forbeir all place prophane
gif this be cause of feid
  I sall not fayt again

However, he then revised the text as follows:

Line 1: *Ye* is struck through, and *ȝe* written above it.
Line 3: The letters <ch> are written over *not*, indicating that is to appear as *nocht*.
Line 4: The form *your* is struck through, and *ȝour* written above it.

Such changes are numerous; later in the same poem Ramsay modifies his original *What* to read *Quhat*, strikes through *litle*, *She*, *shall* and replaces them with *Lytill*, *Scho*, *sall* etc. Ramsay was clearly increasingly interested in sustaining Older Scots spelling, and indeed made an explicit comment about the matter in his notes to the edition of *Christ's Kirk on the Green* earlier in the Egerton manuscript (folio 6r):

> Because we strictly observe the old orthography for the
> more Conveniency of the Readers, we shall note some Generall
> rules at the Bottom of the Page, as they ocur, wherin the old
> Spelling difers from the Present in words that have nothing els
> of the antique, or Difference from the English but shall refer you to
>   the Glossary at the end
> of the second vol. for the Explanation of all of that kind in particular
> and of those that are more Peculiar to the Nation

Both in Egerton 2024 and in the printed version, spellings have been partially modernised/anglicised, e.g. *giving*, but other interventions have been made to accord the text with Ramsay's own version of Scots, e.g. *Deil* 'devil' in line 9, for Bannatyne's *diuill*. In this instance, Ramsay's form is a hypercorrection in the direction of a perceived more 'authentic' Scotticism: *v*-deletion, i.e. the dropping of [v] with compensatory lengthening of the vowel, is increasingly common in Scots after c. 1450, but is clearly not reflected in Bannatyne's spellings. Other changes are similarly imposed. Inflexions which are syllabic in Older Scots are removed, e.g. *taks* (line 3) for Bannatyne's *takkis*. Further, Ramsay generally drops the characteristically Scots/Northern Middle English present plural verb-inflexion in *–s* (e.g. *The Clerks tak* for Bannatyne's *The clerkis takis* in line 6), save in line 14 (*gars*), where it is possible that he has failed to note concord between the verb and the subject (i.e. *Barons*, cf. B's *Barronis*). Finally, Ramsay has intervened too in the text's discourse grammar, pointing up the contrast with the previous poem in the series by adding *Now* at the outset of the poem.

As a community of practice, Ramsay and his printer have, then, both had distinctive inputs to the appearance of this text, producing a work which is poised interestingly between English and Scots.[11] In the production of the 1723–4 edition, Ramsay's collaboration with Ruddiman offered synergies between the creative energy of the poet and the shaping intelligence of the learned printer; Ruddiman was clearly no neutral conduit for the author's ideas. But then that is hardly a surprise, since Ruddiman himself had an earlier track record of collaboration in editing Gavin Douglas for Robert Freebairn and the older printer Andrew Symson (c. 1638–1712);[12] and the outcome on that occasion is interestingly distinct from his collaborative production with Ramsay.

5.3 Jacobite Recuperations (2): Thomas Ruddiman

Whereas Ramsay came to an interest in Older Scots texts from an entrepreneurial background, Ruddiman's was more conventionally scholarly. A prizewinning graduate of classics at King's College in Aberdeen, Ruddiman was for five years a schoolmaster at Laurencekirk, a village to the south of the city; but in 1700 he moved to Edinburgh to work as a copyist in the Advocates' Library, rising to assistant librarian. He supplemented his modest income with various other enterprises; from 1706 onwards, for instance, he worked as a proofreader and editor for Robert Freebairn. In that capacity he undertook with Freebairn and Symson

[11] See Corbett 2013 and Murphy 2015 for a further discussion of the English–Scots relationship in Ramsay's verse; Corbett's discussion draws upon the *Corpus of Modern Scottish Writing 1700–1945* project, available at www.scottishcorpus.ac.uk/cmsw/.

[12] For Symson, see ODNB. By the time of publication of the *Eneados*, Symson was over 70, with a career as a (fairly) controversial Church of Scotland minister behind him; 'licensed to preach' in 1663 by the bishop of Edinburgh, after the Restoration and the (brief) reappearance of bishops in the kirk, he had resigned his ministry when presbyterianism was restored with the Act of Settlement of 1690. In 1705 he had – in collaboration with Robert Freebairn and others – published his own English epic poem, *Tripatriarchicon, Or, the Lives of the three Patriarchs, Abraham, Isaac and Jacob, Extracted forth of the Sacred Story, and digested into English Verse*. I am grateful to Gerry Carruthers for some insightful discussion of Symson's career.

a major publishing enterprise: the 1710 edition of the Older Scots *Eneados*, a translation of Virgil's *Æneid* completed, probably in 1513, by Gavin Douglas (c. 1476–1522), poet and bishop of Dunkeld. The work seems to have been originally commissioned by the 'book-loving' (Wingfield 2016: 437) Sinclair family of Roslin, who also owned copies of John Mirk's *Festial* and *The Kingis Quair* (now Cambridge, St John's College, MS G.29 and Oxford, Bodleian Library, Arch. Selden. MS B.24 respectively). The work was subsequently printed by William Copland of London in 1553: the only edition before that published in 1710.

The 1710 edition of *VIRGIL'S ÆNEIS, Translated into* SCOTTISH *Verse* included a preface acknowledging the assistance from such luminaries as Bishop William Nicolson of Carlisle (a known enthusiast for runes; see Page 1999: 2, 4, 208), Robert Sibbald, Archibald Pitcairn, John Drummond and '*the Worthy* Mr. John Urry *of* Christ-Church, Oxon.': this last acknowledgement is the first reference to Urry's interest in medieval textual scholarship, prefiguring the work on Chaucer which was discussed in Chapter 4. All those mentioned are known to have had Jacobite or nonjuring sympathies, or to have had associations with known nonjurors; Urry had lost his Christchurch studentship in 1688 for refusing to take the oath of loyalty to William III (ODNB), while Nicolson, albeit someone who had felt able to take the oath of allegiance, was a member of the circle surrounding George Hickes and had been helpful in raising subscriptions for the *Thesaurus* (see James 1956, Harris 1992: 97). It is therefore perhaps unsurprising that there is considerable evidence that the Older Scots *Eneados* became a source of Jacobite 'code'; Allan Ramsay's cognomen as a member of the Easy Club, a group of like-minded individuals that emerged in the backwash of the rising of '15, was 'Gavin Douglas'. There were also acknowledgements for the assistance derived from standard learned authorities, including John Ray, Gilles Menage, '[Franciscus] Junius's Glossarium Gothicum', Gerardus Vossius, 'Du Fresne' (i.e. du Cange), and Henry Spelman. Two such works were singled out for special attention: '*We have received no small Aid from that Incomparable Work of the Pious and most Learned* Dr. [George] Hickes, *his* Linguarum Septentrionalium Thesaurus … *But above all we owe much to* Dr. [Stephen] Skinner's Etymologicon Linguæ Anglicanæ, *without the Assistance of which we had often remained in the dark*.' Such extensive acknowledgements do not appear in Ramsay's edition of *The Ever Green*; Ramsay simply thanks the advocate William Carmichael, the earl's brother, for assisting him with accessing the Bannatyne manuscript.

Even more effusive were the acknowledgements for Ruddiman's contribution: '*We are also obliged by all the Ties of Justice and Gratitude to acknowledge that this Work is very much indebted to the Care and Pains of the Judicious* Thomas Ruddiman, *A.M.* Under-Keeper *of the* Advocates Library, *who deserves all Respect and Incouragement from the Patrons of Vertue and Letters.*' Ruddiman's role in the production of the Douglas edition was clearly crucial, even if vaguely outlined in this preface; and although later accounts, notably in ODNB, consider him primarily responsible for the Glossary, the most thorough discussion of Ruddiman's career to date (Duncan 1965) considers that Ruddiman was responsible for the edition as a whole, a conclusion supported by the formidable level of scholarship evinced in the edition. In what follows it will be assumed that Ruddiman was indeed the editor.

The 1710 edition certainly marked a major step forward in the editing of vernacular texts. It included not only the very substantial Glossary with etymological notes and conjectured cognates (marked in blackletter typeface where Germanic forms were cited), and marginal narrative summaries, but also a grammatical section ('General Rules For *Understanding the Language of Bishop* Dowglas's *Translation of* Virgil's *Æneis*', with cross-references to such authorities as Hickes's *Thesaurus*), and a list of 'The most considerable of the *Various Readings* of the *MS* and *Old Edition*', i.e. textual notes. Certainly the care in approaching the work was explicitly outlined elsewhere in the introduction, and is worth quoting in full:

> *There is none who looks into the Edition of* Bishop Douglas's *Translation of* Virgil's Æneis, *Printed at* London, Anno. 1553, *about 30 years after the Author's Death, but may observe innumerable and gross Errors, through the Incorrectness of the Copy, or Negligence of the Printers, or probably both. Which render it difficult, if not impossible, without extraordinary Pains, to reap the least Advantage from that excellent* Version. *As it was therefore necessary to Correct those Faults, so it has been done with the greatest Care, by comparing the* Translation *with the* Original, *and narrowly observing the* Language *of our Author, and those who wrote in, or near his time. But let none think, that we have followed the Example of those bold* Criticks, *who stick not to alter in Authors, what they do not understand; and are not asham'd to substitute their own* Conjectures, *without the least Shadow of Authority: For there are few of our Amendments, which are not owing to, or at least confirmed by an old and excellent MS, belonging to the Library of the College of* Edinburgh. *And on this occasion we acknowledge our Obligations, and return our most hearty Thanks to that learned* Society, *and their Honourable* Patrons, *the Lord* Provost *and the other* Magistrates *of the* City, *who were pleas'd most courteously to allow us the use of that valuable* MS. *so long as it could be serviceable to our Design. In some*

> *places the* Printed *and* MS. *Copies have different* Readings, *both which agree very well with the Sense of the* Original; *and then we thought our selves at Liberty to choose which of the two pleas'd us best: And the other may be seen amongst the* Various Readings *at the End of the Work. It was once design'd to have given a full List of all the* Errors *of the* Printed Copy: *But that required more Labour than the thing was worth, and wou'd have swell'd the Book above measure.*

As stated in this preface, the 1710 edition was based primarily on the blackletter 1553 edition of William Copland (d. 1569). Copland specialised in romances, especially those already produced by his predecessors Wynkyn de Worde and William Caxton. Ruddiman claims to have collated Copland's edition with a manuscript, almost certainly Edinburgh, University Library, MS Dc 1.43. A note on a fly-leaf of this manuscript, ascribed by an anonymous, later, annotating librarian to the great nineteenth-century antiquarian David Laing, would support the view that Ruddiman was the editor of the 1710 text: 'This appears to be the MS. collated by Ruddiman for his edition of Gawain [*sic*] Douglas's Virgil, printed 1710.' Known as the Ruthven manuscript, the book was at one time owned by William Ruthven, fourth Lord Ruthven and first Earl of Gowrie, who was beheaded for treason in 1584 (see Wingfield 2016 and references there cited). The book then passed to Edinburgh University in the middle of the seventeenth century as the gift of a graduating class of students; at the foot of folio 2r, in an italic hand, appears the legend: 'Ego donatus sum Academiae Edinburgenae á Magisterij candi-|datis a.d.1643.' Both sources for the 1710 edition are thus available for comparative analysis.

Transcriptions from the beginning of the poem in Copland's and Ruddiman's editions appear here as Texts (5.14) and (5.15) respectively, accompanied by the equivalent passage in the Freebairn/Ruddiman edition; we will be returning to the Ruthven manuscript shortly.

Text (5.14): Copland (1553b: folio 9r)

The first Booke of Eneados.

¶ The Poete first proponyng his entent
Declaris Junois wrath, and matalent.

T He battellis and the man I will discriue
Fra Troyis boundis, first that fugitiue
By fate to Italie, come and coist lauyne
Ouer land and se, cachit with meikill pyne
Be force of goddis aboue, fra euery stede
Of cruel Juno, throw auld remembrit feid

The propo
sicion of
the hole
worke

Grete payne in batelles, sufferit he also
Or he his goddis, brocht in latio
And helt the ciete, fra quham of nobil fame
The latyne peopill, taken has thare name
And eik the faderis, princis of Alba
Come, and the walleris, of grete rome Alsua
O thow my muse, declare the causis quhy [Inuoca= cione.]
Quhat maiesty offendit, schaw quham by
Or ȝit quharefor of goddis, the drery Quene
So feil dangeris, sic trawell maid sustene
Ane worthy man, fulfillit of pietie
Is thare sic greif, in heuinlie myndes one hie

Text (5.15): Ruddiman (1710: 13)

THe battellis and the man I will discriue, [The propesition of the hole worke.]
Fra *Troyis* boundis first that fugitiue
By fate to *Italie* come, and coist *Lauyne*:
Ouer land and se cachit with meikill pyne,
Be force of goddis aboue, fra euery stede,
Of cruel *Juno* throw auld remembrit feid.
Grete payne in batelles sufferit he also,
Or he his goddis brocht in *Latio*,
And helt the ciete, fra quham of nobil fame
The *Latyne* peopill taken has thare name,
And eike the faderis princis of *Alba*
Come, and the walleris of grete *Rome* alsua.
O thow my muse declare the causis quhy; [Invocacione.]
Quhat maiesty offendit, schaw quham by,
Or zit quharefor, of goddis the drery Quene,
So feil dangeris, sic trawell maid sustene
Ane worthy man, fulfillit of pietie:
Is thare sic greif in heuinlie myndes one hie?

Ruddiman was clear about the defects of Copland's edition from the outset. The title page includes an explicit critique of the 1553 text, claiming that his was '*A new EDITION.* | WHEREIN | The many Errors of the Former are corrected, and the De-|fects supply'd, from an excellent MANUSCRIPT. | To which is added | A Large Glossary, | *Explaining the Difficult Words: Which may serve for a Dictionary* | *to the Old SCOTTISH Language.*' And, in the preface, he went even further:

> *There is none who looks into the Edition of* Bishop Douglas's *Translation of* Virgil's Æneis, *Printed at* London, Anno. 1553, *about 30 years after the Author's Death, but may observe innumerable and gross Errors, through the*

> *Incorrectness of the Copy, or Negligence of the Printers, or probably both. Which render it difficult, if not impossible, without extraordinary Pains, to reap the least Advantage from that excellent* Version. *As it was therefore necessary to Correct those Faults, so it has been done with the greatest Care, by comparing the* Translation *with the* Original, *and narrowly observing the* Language *of our Author, and those who wrote in, or near his time.*

Ruddiman also offered an explicit statement on his edition's policy with regard to punctuation:

> *Great Care hath been taken of the* Pointing, *which had been done very negligently in the first* Impression. *There is a* Comma *about the middle of each Line in the* London Copy; *which, without Doubt, was intended for a* Pause *or* Stop, *that so the Verse might run and sound more smoothly: But, tho somewhat like to this was us'd by the* Anglo-Saxon *Poets, yet it is not to be found in our* MS: *And by the Advice of the best Judges, it was thought very convenient to omit it; both because, after a small Acquaintance with our Author, none can want any such Assistance; and these* Comma's *were often misplac'd: And tho they could have been set right again, yet even then might frequently be taken for ordinary* Interpunctions, *and so destroy the Sense, and perplex the Reader.*

The reference to '*the* Anglo-Saxon *Poets*' seems likely – especially given the Preface's reference to Hickes's *Thesaurus* – to be a nod in the direction of half-lines. Of course, Old English metre, for reasons to do with the language's then grammatical structure, had a trochaic rather than an iambic metrical norm, and used alliteration rather than rhyme as a cohesive principle in verse. This principle was, as we have seen in Chapter 2 above, still not fully understood; nevertheless, it is impressive that Ruddiman is open to engaging with the issue, showing that he was in touch with the most up-to-date philological thinking.

Ruddiman's revision of Copland is in line with his discussion, as demonstrated by his approach to the text.[13] Freebairn derived his *Wallace*, for the most part, from one of Andro Hart's editions, although with the earlier introduction that presumably derives from the manuscript tradition, and demonstrated his antiquarian sentiments by deploying blackletter; by contrast, Ruddiman generally replaces Copland's blackletter typeface with a more modern-style roman font. As in Ramsay's edition of Dunbar, names are italicised, a usage found in prints of contemporary novels and plays, and Ruddiman replaces Copland's yogh with <z>.

[13] We will assume for convenience that Ruddiman is responsible for these decisions, although of course he would have been working with compositors, and 'Ruddiman' in what follows refers in reality to a community of practice.

However his edition differs from that of Ramsay in retaining the sixteenth-century printer's use of <u> and, <w> in *fugitiue* 'fugitive', *trawell* 'travail' etc. Otherwise Ruddiman retains Copland's spelling accurately, save in this passage for the form *eike* 'also', where a final *–e* has been added, presumably as an archaisticism; but this deviation is a rarity, and substantive interventions of this kind are, by contrast with Ramsay, very few.

As flagged, however, Ruddiman has been much more interventionist in '*the* Pointing'. He has replaced the mid-line comma-mark in Copland's edition, which seems to have functioned as a metrical indication of a caesura; apart from capitalisation, Copland uses no other marks in the translation itself, although he does deploy the punctus, manicules, paraph-marks and hederae in the accompanying paratextual material, and in his prefatory verses, and he replaces comma-marks with virgules in the headings printed in smaller black-letter font, e.g. on folio 10r:

> ☞ How dame Juno/ till Eolus cuntre went
> And of the storme on the Troianis furth sent.

or on folio 11r:

> ❧ How Eneas was/ with the tempest schaik
> And how Neptune his nauy/sauit fra wraik.

But Ruddiman's revisions of Copland's practice was not simply a matter of replacement; close examination shows that – unlike so many earlier editors of Older Scots texts – Ruddiman indeed took '*Great Care*' with the 'Pointing'.

Ruddiman's editorial activity in this area is, it seems, closely related to his discussion of punctuation in what was to be by far his most successful publication: his *Rudiments of the Latin Tongue*, which was published first by Freebairn in 1714 and went through fifteen editions in Ruddiman's lifetime alone. Ruddiman left his discussion of punctuation to the end of the *Rudiments* but, significantly, links it to the third part of the book, 'Of Sentences, or Speech'. In this section, he offers an interesting definition of the sentence: '*A SENTENCE is a Thought of the Mind, exprest by two or more Words put together*' (1714: 74). He goes on, in a section 'Of Exposition or Resolution (defined as 'the Unfolding of a Sentence'), to distinguish 'Simple' from 'Compound' sentences: 'A SIMPLE *Sentence* is that which hath one *Finite Verb* in it', whereas 'A COMPOUND *Sentence* is that which hath two or more such Verbs' (1714: 103). At the end of part III, he then goes on to link this discussion to punctuation (1714: 104):

> the *Parts* of a *Compound Sentence* are separated from one another by these *Marks*, called INTERPUNCTIONS. 1. These that are *Smaller*, named *Clauses*, by this Mark (,) called a *Comma*. 2. These that are *greater*, named *Members*, by this (:) called a *Colon*, or this (;) called a *Semicolon*. 3. When a *Sentence* is thrown in that hath little or no Connection with the rest, it is included within what we call a *Parenthesis*, marked thus, ( )
>
> But when the *Sentence*, whether *Simple* or *Compound*, is fully ended, if it is a plain *Affirmation* or *Negation*, it is closed with this Mark (.) called a *Point*. If a *Question* is asked, with this Mark (?) called a *Point of Interrogation*. If *Wonder* or some other sudden *Passion* is signified, with this Mark (!) called a *Point of Admiration*.

Ruddiman was in this case referring to the presentation of Latin, but it becomes clear from examining his edition of Douglas that he has adopted a similarly informed approach to the vernacular text: a text that deployed Older Scots syntax to reflect a well-known Latin work that itself had a distinct syntactic structure. We might for example take again the opening lines of his edition:

> **T**He battellis and the man I will discriue,
> Fra *Troyis* boundis first that fugitiue
> By fate to *Italie* come, and coist *Lauyne*:
> Ouer land and se cachit with meikill pyne,
> Be force of goddis aboue, fra euery stede,
> Of cruel *Juno* throw auld remembrit feid.

> [Translation: *I will describe the conflicts and the man, who, a fugitive, first came from Troy's boundaries to Italy, and the Lavinian coast: driven over land and sea with great pain, from every place, by force from (the) gods above, through the ancient remembered enmity of cruel Juno.*]

Any educated reader of the period would have been familiar with the Latin equivalent, and to account for Ruddiman's activity it is helpful to compare the Douglas version, as presented by Ruddiman, with Virgil's original. The following text appears as laid out in a widely circulated late seventeenth-century edition: *Publii Virgili Maronis Opera*, published by Evan Tyler and R. Holt for the Stationers' Company in 1679 (for Tyler, see Spurlock 2011).[14] Here are the opening lines as they appear in the edition (Virgil 1679: 74):

[14] A heavily annotated copy of the 1679 edition, now Oxford, Bodleian Library, 297.g.85, was owned by Thomas Hearne, with whom Ruddiman collaborated on the Oxford edition of Fordun's *Scotichronicon* (Hearne 1722); Hearne was, as we have seen, yet another nonjuring, Jacobite sympathiser.

Arma, virúmque cano, Trojæ qui primus ab oris
Italiam, fato profugus, Lavináque vênit
Littora, multùm ille & terris jactatus, & alto,
Vi superûm sævæ memorem Junonis ab iram:

[Translation: *Of arms and a man I sing, who first from the boundaries of Troy, exiled by fate, came to Italy and the Lavinian shores: he was thrown greatly both on land and on sea, by the power of the gods, on account of the remembered anger of savage Juno: …*]

The delayed verbs in Douglas's text are *cachit* (from *cache*, glossed 'drive, catch' by Ruddiman in his 'Large Glossary, Explaining the Difficult Words'), *discriue* 'describe' (not glossed by Ruddiman) and *come*. Their placement in Douglas is clearly a reflexion of Latin verb-final positioning (cf. *jactatus*, *cano* and *venit* respectively in Virgil's verses). Perhaps encouraged by Virgil's separation of modifying *Lavina* (usually *Lavinia* in modern editions) from its headword *Littora*, but adopting a different approach, given that he was working with a comparatively uninflected language, Douglas has placed *and coist Lauyne* after *come*. He has thus separated these words from the rest of the prepositional phrase *to Italie*, adopting an inherited Old English syntactic practice: a 'split heavy group', whereby noun or adjective phrases linked by a coordinating conjunction such as *and* are split, e.g. 'an old man and a wise', 'the woman spoke, and her daughter'. This usage eventually became archaic (as it is in present-day English), but has in this case helpfully allowed for a rhyming couplet.

In order to assist his readers, Ruddiman has replaced Copland's punctuation to flag Douglas's grammatical structure very carefully, obviously informed by his understanding of the Latin original. He relocated the comma-mark in line 3, thus separating *and coist Lauyne* from the preceding verb *come* and marking its status as a distinct phrase, albeit 'split' from the rest of the prepositional phrase *to Italie*. By removing a comma-mark between *Ouer land and se* and *cachit* he captured the close link in Virgil's Latin between the past participle *jactatus* and its modifying nouns *et terris … et alto*. However, in the case of *fra euery stede*, the addition of a final comma-mark in Ruddiman's version clarifies the phrase's parenthetical status in a way that would be acceptable – if a trifle fussy – to a present-day reader. It is noticeable that the comma-mark inserted by the modern editor of the Latin after the end of the opening *Arma virumque canō* correlates with that Ruddiman places after *discriue* in the first line. And the modern semicolon at the end of the Latin quoted above correlates with the full stop inserted by Ruddiman, after *feid*, at the end of Douglas's opening sententia (line 10). Indeed, Ruddiman clearly understands the principles of ancient approaches to the sentence, and this understanding is demonstrated where he departs from the modern editor's punctuation of the Latin; the double punctus at the end of line 3 reflects the 'major medial pause, or disjunction of sense' (Parkes 1992: 302) within the sententia, marking the division between cola.

This approach is confirmed by Ruddiman's version of the complex end of the passage, the invocation to the muse:

> O thow my muse declare the causis quhy;
> Quhat maiesty offendit, schaw quham by,
> Or zit quharefor, of goddis the drery Quene,
> So feil dangeris, sic trawell maid sustene
> Ane worthy man, fulfillit of pietie:
> Is thare sic greif in heuinlie myndes one hie?

> [Translation: *O you my muse declare the causes why; what offended majesty, show by whom, or still why, the doleful Queen of the Gods made a man filled with piety to endure so many misfortunes, such labour. Is there such misery in celestial minds on high?*]

Again the Latin in the Tyler/Holt edition offers a helpful parallel:

> Musa mihi causas memora, quo numine læso,
> Quidve dolens regina deûm, tot volvere casus
> Insignem pietate virum, tot adire labores,
> Impulerit, Tantæne animis cœlestibus iræ?

> [Translation: *Muse, recall the causes to me, for what injured godhead, or, grieving at what, the Queen of the Gods compelled a man marked by piety to suffer so many misfortunes, to come to so many labours. (Is) there such anger in celestial spirits?*]

Ruddiman's semicolon at the end of line 17 represents a brief pause, shorter than that flagged by the earlier colon-mark designed to introduce the invocation; in present-day English a colon-mark would be expected. The series of comma-marks that follow then assist readers 'to resolve structural uncertainties' by disentangling Douglas's somewhat convoluted syntax; Douglas's usage was itself driven by the complex word order of the original Latin, including the delayed verb *impulerit* 'compelled' (cf. Douglas's *maid*). Ruddiman's colon-mark after Douglas's *pietie* parallels the comma-mark in the Tyler/Holt edition of the Latin, flagging that the sententia is not completed until the question-mark (punctus interrogativus) at the end of line 22. The combination of comma-mark and following upper-case letter in

Tyler/Holt's *Tantæne* (= *tantae* 'such' + the interrogative suffix *–ne*) seems to perform the same role. In sum, Ruddiman – as we might expect from such an accomplished scholar – offers us a parsed Douglas, presented as he might have presented an edition of a major classical author, and informed by his profound engagement with the Latin original.

As a contrast to the discussion so far, we might compare the passages discussed with the parallel text in the Ruthven manuscript, which Ruddiman collated with the Copland text. A transcript appears as Text (5.16); lineation has been added to assist with cross-referencing. The engrossed words (here emboldened) at the outset of the transcription reflects the usage of the manuscript.

Text (5.16) Edinburgh, University Library, MS Dc 1.43 (the Ruthven manuscript), folio 10v

The battellis and ye man I will discrive
ffra troy boundis first yat fugitive
By fate of Itale come to coist latyne
Ouere land and sey cachit with mekill pyne
By force of goddis abof fra euery stede
Of cruell Iuno throw ald remembrit fede
Grete pane in batall sufferit he also
Or he his goddis brocht in latio
And helt fro quhom of nobill fame
The latyne pepill taken has yare name
And eik ye faderis princis of Alba
Come and ye walleris of grete Rome alsa
O thow my muse declare / ye causis quhy
Quhat maieste offendit schaw quhom by
Or ȝit quharefore of goddis ye drery quene
Sa feill dangeris s*i*c travell maid sustene
Ane wourthy man*e* fulfillit of piete
Is yare s*i*c greif in hevinly mynd*is* on*e* hie

Comparison shows that for this passage Ruddiman has clearly favoured Copland, preferring to keep the more distinctively Scots forms *quham* rather than the quasi-anglicised *quhom* (lines 9, 14), the latter a usage favoured in some 'high-style' Older Scots texts in the early sixteenth century (see Aitken 1983). He has also ignored Ruthven's obviously erroneous reading in line 3, i.e. *latyne* for Copland's *lauyne*, cf. Ruddiman's *Lauyne*. But the Ruthven manuscript's presentation is interesting in its own terms. It seems, according to Emily Wingfield's (2016) researches, to have been produced around the same time or rather later than the Copland edition, but independently.

By contrast with the printed editions, the scribe of the Ruthven manuscript uses little punctuation; the single virgule in line 13 is deployed to flag the disjunction between the initial invocation to the Muse and the set of questions which the poet is posing to her. The opening words *The battellis* appear in engrossed form, a usage that is also found in contemporary legal documents to mark stages in an argument or statement. Otherwise, the only punctuation feature used is capitalisation, assigned to some (but not all) names, e.g. *Itale*, *Iuno*, *Alba*, *Rome* beside *troy*, *latyne* (cf. Ruddiman's *Lauyne*), and to the first words in each line.

The contrast with the contemporary printed text, and even more with Ruddiman's edition, is marked, and it is worth briefly setting aside these other versions and looking at the functioning of the Ruthven text in its own terms, as a manuscript that seems to have been bespoke for a particular readership. Absence of punctuation in the Ruthven text emphasises the verse-form of the poem rather than its syntactic structure, and in those circumstances it is hard to avoid noting how many lines begin with a conjunction, a preposition, or an interrogative: *ffra*, *By*, *Ouere*, *By*, *Of*, *Or*, *And*, *Or*, *Quhat*. Other lines begin with an asseveration, *O*, determiners flagging the presence of a following noun phrase, e.g. *The*, *Ane*, *Sa*, and a copular verb *Is*. Once these closed-class words are set aside, there are only two line-initial words left in Text (5.16), both of which, being lexical, are therefore emphasised: *Grete*, *Come*. It is hard to avoid the impression that the readership (or indeed audience) of the Ruthven manuscript would – like that of the Edinburgh manuscript of Hary's *Wallace* and Barbour's *Bruce*, or the Petworth manuscript of the *Canterbury Tales* discussed in Chapter 4 – have apprehended the poem differently, guided by the function words rather than the marks of punctuation.

Comparison of the three texts of Douglas's *Eneados*, therefore, along with the other texts discussed in this chapter, reveals how their 'accidental', pragmatic features, the outcome of activities undertaken by discrete communities of practice, relate to the expectations of the distinct discourse communities for which they were prepared. The manuscript versions of Older Scots verse – the Edinburgh manuscript of *The Bruce* and *The Wallace*, the Bannatyne and Ruthven manuscripts – were all bespoke productions clearly originally designed for private reading, within an intensive reading culture where the few texts encountered were read repeatedly: Symon Lochmalony, George Bannatyne and his circle, the

Ruthven family. The printed versions by contrast needed a more sophisticated presentational apparatus, but different approaches related to different socio-cultural functions. Lekpreuik and Hart were producing copies of *The Wallace* and *The Bruce* which sought to strike a balance between the old and the new, mixing blackletter archaism with added punctuation to assist an increasingly extensive or varied readership;[15] the not-so-subtle modification of substantive features deemed roman catholic correlates with this modernisation, and offers an assertion of a particular kind of national identity. The antiquarianism of Freebairn and even more of Allan Ramsay represents an attempt to reshape the past for a distinct cultural, Jacobite agenda, reflected in their presentational choices. However, their friend Ruddiman – a rather less flashy figure – was doing something rather different and arguably even more radical: he was assigning the vernacular writings of Gavin Douglas the same status as contemporaries assigned to the classics. In that he was not only asserting the value of Older Scots culture, a discreet assertion of the historical basis of Scottish identity, but also prefiguring a new approach to the vernacular cultures of the past that was to become dominant. And the principles of advanced textual criticism within which he was working were explicitly stated in the assured apparatus which framed his edition, and – central to the themes of this book – in the presentational decisions he took. In the next, and last, chapter we will see where this development was to lead.

[15] Some evidence for the extensive – i.e. varied – literacy of early modern Scotland can be found in the wills of Edinburgh booksellers of the period, where their stock is listed. Henry Charteris's inventory records *in his Buith* (i.e. shop) numerous copies of major poets, e.g. *fyve scoir tua Wallaces . . . sevin hundreth lxxxviij Dauid Lyndesayis . . . v^{c}xlv Testamentis of Cresseid* (see Dickson and Edmond 1890: 353).

CHAPTER 6

On Textual Transformations: Walter Scott and Beyond

6.1 Walter Scott's Edition of *Sir Tristrem*

This book began with the case of Thomas Percy, and it seems therefore appropriate to conclude it with a figure who has a claim to be Percy's principal successor as an imaginative recuperator of the medieval past, and whose presence will have been noted in several places earlier. In 1804, Walter Scott published his first edition of *Sir Tristrem; a Metrical Romance of The Thirteenth Century; by Thomas of Erceldoune, called The Rhymer.* Scott was not yet Sir Walter; nor was he yet the laird of the great estate of Abbotsford, which was still a farm nicknamed Clarty (i.e. 'muddy') Hole. Abbotsford's archetypal 'Scottish baronial' chateau, its best-known physical feature, was still in the future: construction only began after Scott bought the estate in 1811.[1] So the title page of *Sir Tristrem* simply referred to the editor, modestly, as 'Walter Scott, Esq., Advocate'. *The Lay of the Last Minstrel* (published 1805), *Marmion* (1808) and *The Lady of the Lake* (1810), the great historical verse-narratives which were to secure Scott's reputation as a poet and indeed a cultural icon, had not yet appeared, and the Waverley novels were a decade in the future. It seems that Scott needed, to be sure of a hearing, to establish his *bona fides* with a professional label.

However, the specific affiliation Scott cited was actually appropriate to the matter in hand, for the source of the edition was, as also announced on the title page, a book in the Advocates' own Library, once the property of the distinguished judge Alexander Boswell, Lord Auchinleck.[2] This book – referred to in passing in Chapter 3 above – is the Auchinleck manuscript, now Edinburgh, National Library of Scotland, Advocates' MS 19.2.1: one

[1] See www.scottsabbotsford.com/, last consulted on 25 June 2019. I am grateful to Douglas Gifford, then Honorary Librarian, for an insightful guided tour of Abbotsford before its recent renovation.

[2] Better-known now as the father of James Boswell, Samuel Johnson's biographer.

of the library's best-known treasures.[3] Copied in London by no fewer than six scribes in the middle of the fourteenth century, possibly for the court of Edward III or for the family reading of a socially aspirant merchant (Doyle 1983; see also Hanna 2005: 104–47), it is arguably the most important surviving repository of medieval English verse-romances and saints' legends: in the fourteenth century the genre distinction was not precise. Its contents include such well-known Middle English works as *Sir Orfeo*, *Amis and Amiloun*, *Guy of Warwick*, *Bevis of Hampton*, *King Alisaunder* and *St Patrick's Purgatory*. Although there is no direct indication of his engagement with this particular manuscript, it seems likely from the evidence of his own writings that Geoffrey Chaucer himself either knew of the volume or something very like it.

There is moreover a strong case – notably but not exclusively supported by the analysis of rhyming practices – that the poems in the anthology were originally composed in various parts of the English-speaking world of the earlier fourteenth century before being brought together for a London audience. For instance, one of the Auchinleck romances, *Sir Orfeo*, seems to have been in origin a product of the Anglophone culture of the English–Welsh border (see the discussion in Bliss 1969 and references there cited). Scott, indeed, was attracted to *Sir Tristrem* as potentially an addition to the canon of medieval Scottish literature, and although scholars now generally agree that the poem originated in Yorkshire (see McIntosh 1989, Putter et al. 2014), there are strong indications that the Auchinleck manuscript was in Scotland some time before Boswell acquired it, possibly as early as the late sixteenth century; such a location would suggest at least some Scottish cultural capital before that claimed by Scott.

As a member of Edinburgh's august Faculty of Advocates, and from 1795 the curator of its library,[4] Scott had privileged access to the Auchinleck manuscript in a way that to a modern scholar will seem unthinkable but was then much more common. It appears that Scott simply borrowed the book for several long periods to allow him to carry out his task (Matthews 1999: 61). Like Thorkelin, and in accord with contemporary custom, Scott seemed to have worked for the most part from a transcription undertaken

[3] A facsimile and digital edition compiled by David Burnley and Alison Wiggins, including a full description and discussion of the Auchinleck manuscript, is to be found at https://auchinleck.nls.uk/, last consulted on 15 August 2017; see also Pearsall and Cunningham 1977. An important recent set of essays on the manuscript has been edited by Susanna Fein (2016), which includes a discussion of its early provenance by Fein herself. See also Connolly and Edwards 2017.

[4] The Advocates' Library formed the core of what was in 1925 to become the National Library of Scotland.

by an assistant: the philologist, orientalist and minor poet John Leyden (1775–1811), a quotation from whose *Ode on Visiting Flodden* later appeared – aptly, given the latter's subject – on the title page of Scott's *Marmion* (1808).[5]

Scott's edition of *Sir Tristrem* is by the standards of his day an accomplished and – as described in David Matthews's important account – 'unrelentingly scholarly' (1999: 67) piece of work. Production values were excellent, as were to be expected from his printer (James Ballantyne) and publisher (Archibald Constable), both then leading figures in the contemporary Edinburgh book trade. Constable, however, seems to have been, as Matthews puts it, 'wary' of the poem, and the initial edition was actually limited to 150 copies; there was no special subscription list to ensure income, as had been commonly the custom in the eighteenth century. Constable's wariness may have arisen because of certain content considered to be of a 'scandalously sexual nature': the worrying appearance of the word *queynt*, potentially interpretable as 'female genitalia', in line 2254 seems to have disconcerted poor Leyden so greatly that he refused to copy any more of the text, and the offending line was eventually omitted in the published version, despite Scott's protests (Santini 2010: 79–83).[6] However, the first edition of *Sir Tristrem* was generally well received at the time, and three further editions followed in the next decade and a half. Scott, Leyden, Ballantyne and Constable clearly formed a community of practice, focused on undertaking a mutual editorial endeavour, but it was a community whose members had slightly conflicting agendas and concerns.

[5] Details of Leyden's career may be secured from ODNB, and Walter Scott wrote a characteristically generous memoir of Leyden included in subsequent copies of the latter's verse. Leyden's poetry, now largely forgotten, had some cultural impact on contemporaries and indeed for some time afterwards. In this context students of material culture will be pleased to note that an 1858 presentation copy of his poems and ballads, bound especially in boards made from a tree in the grounds of Melrose Abbey and including Scott's memoir, exists in the Royal Collection (RCIN 1018743); see www.royalcollection.org.uk/collection/1018743/poems-and-ballads-dr-john-leyden-with-a-memoir-of-the-author-by-sir-walter-scott, consulted on 16 August 2017.

[6] Unlike Leyden, who in his career as a scholar of Indian society repeatedly demonstrated his shock at what he perceived to be the laxity of Hindu morals, Scott was no prude, as is demonstrated by his protests against the omission of the offending line. It may be relevant in this context to note that Scott owned a copy of Robert Burns's notorious *The Fornicator's Court*, probably composed in 1786 but not published (and then only privately) until 1817, well after the poet's death; Scott's copy included a tipped-in authorial holograph manuscript of Burns's equally louche poem 'Saw ye my Maggie' (see Gray 2005). For a facsimile of Scott's copy of *The Fornicator's Court*, with a useful introduction, see Carruthers and Gray 2009. Other cheerfully robust works in Scott's collection include *Benefit of farting explain'd*, undated but ascribed, entirely unsurprisingly, to Jonathan Swift. See, in addition to the Abbotsford Catalogue, the important but as yet unhappily unpublished thesis by Lindsay Levy (2014).

Despite this mild bowdlerisation, Scott seems to have been proud of what he had done, and described his edition of *Sir Tristrem* as 'A correct edition of this ancient and curious poem' (1804: iii). The claim of 'correctness' was, unhappily, overstated; a later editor, the distinguished German philologist Eugen Kölbing, referred with a somewhat scathing metaphor to 'swarms of errors and inaccuracies in [Scott's] rendering of the manuscript', which Kölbing tactfully blamed on the failings of 'some hired clerk ... in exact accordance with the usage of his day' (1878–9: 1, cited in McNeill 1886: xxx). Some of these inaccuracies were corrected in subsequent editions (even if – depressingly – new errors crept in).

The work was, however, accompanied by a substantial apparatus that was entirely Scott's. The extensive prefatory material consisted of several sections: a contextualising introduction, setting out Scott's views on the authorship, provenance and original date of the poem, a brief discussion of 'the mode in which the editor has executed his task' (1804: lxxxix), i.e. his editorial policy, and a series of appendices. The first appendix is an edition of a Latin charter granted by 'the son and heir of Thomas of Erceldoun' to the 'convent of Soltra', followed by a short anecdote about an inscribed stone in Earlston ('Erceldoun') churchyard. The inscription, still as it happens *in situ*, reads: 'Auld Rymer's race/ Lies in this place'; it is, we are told, allegedly a replacement of an original 'defaced by an idle boor, in a drunken frolic' (1804: xcviii) in 1782. The ascription to the legendary Rhymer, now no longer accepted, was central to Scott's argument about the origins of the poem.[7] Further appendices follow: an edition with parallel translation of a Welsh version of the Tristram legend; a translation of the Old French 'Lai dee Chevrefoil, by Mademoiselle Marie' [sic], i.e. Marie de France; and a description of the Auchinleck manuscript itself.[8] This last includes much of the material we would now expect in a modern edition of a medieval text, including a fairly full list of the manuscript's contents. Scott, citing the opinions of 'the most able antiquaries' (1804: cvii), also suggests a dating to the 'earlier part of the 13th century', which presumably refers to the poem rather than to the manuscript, which is now generally placed in the middle of the fourteenth century, although recent discussions agree with Scott as to the dating of the text itself (see Putter et al. 2014).[9] Again, offering a dating for the text is

[7] The afterlives of several writings ascribed to Thomas the Rhymer, notably the *Prophecies* and the *Ballad*, are the topic of a forthcoming AHRC-funded Glasgow doctoral thesis by David Selfe.

[8] Then with the shelf-mark W.4.1.

[9] It may be relevant that a pencilled question-mark, of uncertain origin and date, appears in the margin of the 1804 edition in the NLS (F.5.f.42) alongside the reference to 'the 13th century'; Scott himself

expected in modern editions. The text appears next, followed by extensive notes and a glossary; the last of these, says Scott earlier, needs little explication, since '[t]he labours of Macpherson and Sibbald have greatly removed the difficulties of such a compilation' (1804: xci). However, Scott still offers a glossary of some twenty-four pages.

'Macpherson and Sibbald' were early lexicographers of Scots, the language variety in which Scott – almost certainly erroneously – deemed *Sir Tristrem* to have originally been composed. David Macpherson (1746–1816) was a historian who published, in 1795, the first edition of Andro Wyntoun's *Chronikle*, and included in it an accompanying glossary of Older Scots. Macpherson's edition of Wyntoun was to form the basis for the much more substantial work produced by the greatest Scottish antiquarian of the nineteenth century, David Laing (1793–1878). James Sibbald (1747–1803) was a bookseller and journal editor whose *Edinburgh Magazine* had first printed Robert Burns's *Tam o'Shanter*. Sibbald's *Chronicle of Scottish Poetry: From the Thirteenth Century to the Union of the Crowns* (1802) contained what Scott himself described in a private letter as 'an uncommonly good glossary' (ODNB) of some 5,000 words; Sibbald claimed in his preface that this work could 'be considered as a Dictionary of the antient [*sic*] language of Scotland'. It should, though, be noticed that, in a later footnote, Scott is clearly aware of the need for enhanced lexicographical resources beyond those he cites. He there refers to John Jamieson, who had been 'long toiling' in such a compilation for Scots, 'and surely it is only necessary to say that such a work is in agitation, to secure the patronage of every antiquary and philologist' (1804: xcii). Such antiquarians and philologists formed the wider social network and discourse community in which the production team for *Sir Tristrem* was located.[10]

Much work has been undertaken on Scott's medievalism; a recent example, for instance, is Jerome Mitchell's *Scott, Chaucer, and Medieval Romance* (2015), which offers a useful analytic list of how Scott deployed this literary mode. The key discussion, however, remains to be found in David Matthews's *The Making of Middle English, 1765–1910*, a pioneering and authoritative study of the reception of Middle English texts in the eighteenth and nineteenth centuries (1999; see also Matthews 2000, an

donated this copy to the Faculty of Advocates. However, the early date was sustained in subsequent reprintings of his edition, which suggests that the question-mark is not in Scott's own hand.

10 Susan Rennie's biography (2012) of Jamieson discusses all three figures; for a sketch of Sibbald and Macpherson as lexicographers, see Rennie 2012: 29–31.

accompanying anthology of primary sources).[11] Matthews devotes almost a complete chapter ('The Last Minstrel') to a discussion of Scott, and unlike many critics gives *Sir Tristrem* some attention, as an important transitional text between older scholarship and more recent trends:

> *Sir Tristrem* was genuinely a departure. Scott was innovative in privileging a single poem, rather than printing an anthology. In this respect, *Sir Tristrem* can be seen as anticipating the scholarly volumes of the [Early English Text Society, henceforth EETS]. But . . . Scott's *Sir Tristrem* has its important links with the formation that produced [Thomas Percy's] *Reliques* [*of Ancient English Poetry*, 1765] . . . Scott's scholarship belonged as securely to conservative romanticism as Percy's, and his editing of the Middle Ages was, as much as the *Reliques*, a tool for self-shaping and part of the process of social advancement. (Matthews 1999: 58)

Closer analysis of editorial practice in Scott's *Sir Tristrem* confirms Matthews's assessment. On the one hand, elements of Scott's apparatus we have already noted, such as his provision of appendices containing sources and a manuscript description, a glossary and a discussion (albeit brief) of editorial principles, point forward to practices that were later to become commonplace, and his presentation of a single text also aligns, as Matthews suggests, with the later practice whereby particular texts are isomorphous with a single volume.[12] Other aspects, however, are less satisfactory by modern standards. For instance, Scott added a pastiche conclusion to the poem, remedying thereby a leaf missing towards the end of the text in the original manuscript.[13] This addition points back to the

[11] Matthews has recently taken his arguments further in 'Ideas of medieval English in the eighteenth and nineteenth centuries', one of several important essays in a collection edited by Tim William Machan (2017).

[12] Eighteenth-century encounters with texts through anthologies of excerpts from longer poems have been recently emphasised; see Williams 2017, referred to in Chapter 1 above, for an important discussion. Williams has pointed out that anthologies, or indeed such works as Scott's *Lay of the Last Minstrel* or, later, Byron's *Childe Harold's Pilgrimage* that were sectionalised into handy books or cantos, were particularly suited for communal reading – through oral delivery and aural reception – as part of a widespread culture of sociability.

[13] Scott's pastiche is worth some examination, as an attempt at Middle English. Scott's scholarship is generally admirable, although uncertainty about the morphology of the 3rd person singular inflexion is noticeable, e.g. *wepeth* beside *prepares*. Scott is moreover capable of inventing forms not historically attested to fit his rhyme scheme; a good example in rhyming position is the form *tare* 'tear(s)', not recorded in this form in the MED but clearly adopted to rhyme with more authentically northern Middle English forms such as *thare* 'there', *fare*, *bare* and *ware* 'were':

> Ysonde was sad woman,
> And wepeth bitter tare, . . .

Other unhistorical forms include *trewd* '?believed'.

kind of imaginative 'creative' responses to early works deemed defective that are a feature of Percy's *Reliques of Ancient English Poetry* (1765 – see the Introduction), or indeed of Allan Ramsay's edition and extensive continuation of *Christ's Kirk on the Green* (1721 – see Chapter 5); indeed, it is also characteristic of Scott's own earlier *Minstrelsy of the Scottish Border* (1802–3). Scott, like Percy and Ramsay, clearly saw it as his duty to (re)create texts in a form that was 'complete', in line with contemporary tastes.

Another part of this alignment with contemporary aesthetic standards was to relate *Sir Tristrem* to the writings of the one medieval English author whose canonical status – in contrast with that of his late fourteenth-century contemporaries John Gower or William Langland – was in the eighteenth century never in doubt: Geoffrey Chaucer. As is quite common in the presentation of volumes of poetry at the period, a small quotation from another writer appears as a motto on the title page. The text chosen is a stanza, the beginning of the third '*fitt*', from Chaucer's own tail-rhyme romance about a knight's relationship with an 'elf-queen', *Sir Thopas*: the reference to a fairy encounter is to the ballad of *Thomas the Rhymer* that Scott had already published in the *Minstrelsy*. However, there is no overt acknowledgement of Chaucer's notoriously burlesque intention in his only 'tail-rhyme' romance; indeed, the passage seems to be presented without any irony at all.[14] The task of the quotation is, rather, to 'place' *Sir Tristrem* in relation to a recognised cultural reference point:

> Now hold your mouth, pour charitie,
> Both Knight and Lady fre,

[14] Scott seems quite often to have inserted such excerpts from memory (I owe this point to Gerry Carruthers); if that is the case here it is interesting – and relevant to a theme returned to earlier in this book – that Scott could recall a comparatively obscure stanza from towards the end of *Sir Thopas* in this way. There is of course evidence that Scott regarded memorisation of verse as an important skill (as with *Hardyknute*, referred to in Chapter 5 above, footnote 4). For Scott's (and Tyrwhitt's) form *druerie*, Stow's edition has still-current *drerie*, presumably to be interpreted as 'dreary', which makes little sense in context even though it is an attested form in several medieval manuscript witnesses (e.g. MSS London, British Library, Royal 18 C.ii and Sloane 1686, and Oxford, Bodleian Library, Barlow 20, all dating from the middle of the fifteenth century). The Ellesmere manuscript of the *Canterbury Tales* (San Marino, Huntington Library, MS EL 26 C.9), the source for most modern editions, has *drury*, usually interpreted, as cited above, as 'love-making', 'flirtation'; *Drury Lane* in London, now the city's theatre quarter, was notoriously at one time its red-light district. Scott's spelling, *druerie*, is recorded in the MED as an acceptably medieval variant spelling. Tyrwhitt, as we have seen a highly accomplished philologist, offers a somewhat bowdlerised translation in his glossary: 'Courtship, gallantry', deriving the form from French but also citing medieval Latin *drudaria*, as recorded in du Cange's *Glossarium ad scriptores mediae et infimae Latinitatis* (1678); this etymology, still including the reference to du Cange, remains in the OED. Judging by the citations in the latter authority, the form was obsolete in English (if not Scots) by the end of the fifteenth century. Later in his introduction to the edition Scott cites *Sir Thopas* in order to compare its 'stanzas of a simple structure' with the more complex patterns of *Sir Tristrem* (1804: lxxxvii).

And herkneth to my spell;
Of battaile and of chivalrie,
Of Ladies' love and druerie,
Anon I wol you tel. – CHAUCER.

No holograph manuscript for Scott's edition of *Sir Tristrem* is known to survive, but it seems likely, given his close association with the printer and well-known interest in the transmission of his texts, that the choice of this verse for the title page was Scott's own. Scott's library at Abbotsford eventually housed several editions of Chaucer referred to in Chapter 4 above, ranging from the blackletter versions by John Stow (1561) and Thomas Speght (1602), through John Urry's much-criticised publication of 1721 and the modernised selection collected by George Ogle in 1741, to Thomas Tyrwhitt's of 1775.[15] In none of these editions, however, do these lines from *Sir Thopas* appear quite in this form. The nearest in substantive variants are Stow's and Tyrwhitt's editions (the others all intrude the word *also* after *and* in the second line), and the appearance in the fifth line of the form *druerie* 'love-making, flirtation', as in Tyrwhitt's version, suggests the latter as the primary source. The use of *Sir Thopas* as (presumably) a serious cultural reference point is perhaps surprising to a modern reader, but different views, e.g. on the 'moral' properties of the poem or on its role as an exemplary ballad, were expressed in early modern and eighteenth-century criticism. (See Burrow 1982, especially 71–2; for an especially nuanced reading, see Lerer 1993: 95.)

Other aspects of the title page of *Sir Tristrem* gesture to the past rather more subtly. Although the bulk of the title page is in a roman font, a claim of antiquity is made through the strategic deployment of blackletter typeface to reflect the 'antient' character of the poem's genre, i.e. in the apposed phrase 'a Metrical Romance of The Thirteenth Century'. It is also interesting that blackletter is picked up again when the printer is referred to ('Printed by James Ballantyne'). The deployment of a typeface that attempted to reproduce high-status medieval *textura* script by this date flags the printer's virtuosity; it certainly foregrounds Ballantyne's role in the creation of the book. Ballantyne and Scott were personal friends of some years' standing, and their close association reflected what has been described as Scott's interest 'not just in content but in books as artefacts

[15] It should be noted, however, that Scott continually added to his collections as part of his confessed bibliomania, so its appearance in the Abbotsford catalogue does not necessarily imply that he owned a particular book at the time he was editing *Sir Tristrem*.

which would articulate the "message"' (ODNB; see also Millgate 2000).[16] Scott was after all, despite his 'modern' intentions, still at heart what a later generation would call one of 'the blackletter men', something contemporaries could clearly relish, even if *Sir Tristrem* did not adopt blackletter font wholesale. Other editors did: Siân Echard has drawn attention to such publications as the 'aristocratic' Roxburghe Club's productions with their medievalizing typefaces, and Thomas Whitaker's notorious edition of *Piers Plowman* (1813), described by Isaac D'Israeli in 1841 as 'the most magnificent and frightful volume that was ever beheld in the black letter' (see Echard 2008: 12).[17] When Thomas Johnes, the wealthy Welsh antiquarian, published a modern translation of Jean Froissart's Old French *Chronicle*, he was disappointed by the criticism (anonymous, as was customary) that it attracted from the legendary *Edinburgh Review*. 'I suspect', he wrote in 1805 to an Edinburgh friend, 'your reviewer is some young man who has not read much, nor is very learned in books but, smitten with the love of Black letter, sees nothing beautiful but in that' (cited in Echard 2008: 12). The 'young man' was, we may not be surprised to discover, Walter Scott.

Whoever made the choice of blackletter in this particular case, the usage was clearly an archaic practice, inviting antiquarian reflexion. Ballantyne's name and role were similarly marked in the third edition of Scott's *Minstrelsy of the Scottish Border* (1806), although interestingly not in the earlier editions of 1802–3. It was used for the printer's name on title pages – though not for anything else – in Scott's own verse: *The Lay of the Last Minstrel* (1805), and for the subtitle ('A Tale') in *Marmion*, also printed by Ballantyne, in 1808. Wherever it was deployed on the title page, the presence of blackletter typeface was clearly – like that found in the Roxburghe Club publications, and later in EETS editions until well into the twentieth century – a statement of a particular antiquarian aesthetic, as well as making a claim for authenticity by means of a 'typographical underpinning' (Echard 2008: 33).

As flagged by Kölbing, Scott's edition of the Auchinleck text left, by later standards, something to be desired. However, a comparison of the opening lines of his edition with those of his medieval exemplar raises issues that are relevant for the larger purposes of this book. Text (6.1) is a transcription of the opening two stanzas of Scott's first edition:

[16] Scott had encouraged Ballantyne to move from his earlier career as a solicitor and newspaper publisher in Kelso, and the professional trajectories of the two men had much in common. A few years later Scott and Ballantyne broke from Constable to form their own publishing company, with unfortunate results.

[17] See Introduction above, note 6.

Text (6.1): Scott, *Sir Tristrem* (1804: 9–10)

FYTTE FIRST.
============

I.

I WAS at [Erceldoune:]
With Tomas spak Y thare;
Ther herd Y rede in roune,
Who Tristrem gat and bare.
Who was king with croun;
And who him forsterd yare;
And who was bold baroun,
As their elders ware,
Bi yere:-
Tomas telles in toun,
This auentours as thai ware.

II.

This semly somers day,
In winter it is nought sen;
This greves wexen al gray,
That in her time were grene:
So dos this world Y say,
Y wis and nought at wene;
The gode bene al oway,
That our elders have bene
To abide:-
Of a knight is that y mene;
His name is sprong wel wide.

And here for contrast are the same stanzas transcribed directly from the Auchinleck manuscript:

Text (6.2): Edinburgh, National Library of Scotland, Advocates' MS 19.2.1 (Auchinleck manuscript), folio 281r, column 1

I was at [. . . . . . .]
wiþ tomas spak y þare.
þer herd y rede in roune.
who tristrem gat and bare.
who was king wiþ croun.
& who him forsterd ȝare.
& who was bold baroun.
as þair elders ware.
bi ȝere ;

tomas telles in toun.
þis auentours as þai ware.
¶ þis semly somers day.
in winter it is nought sen.
þis greues wexen al gray.
þat in her time were grene.
so dos this world y say.
y wis and nought at wene.
þe gode bene al oway.
þat our elders have ben.
to abide ∵
of aknizt is þat y mene.
his name is sprong wel wide.

It will be observed that, with the exception of the addition in the printed text of the postulated reading *[Erceldoune:]*, to remedy a lacuna in the manuscript, there are no substantive differences in lexicon or grammatical inflexion between the two versions of these stanzas. However, there are numerous small 'accidental' ones:

(1) The edition has imposed the section heading *FYTTE* on the text, following Scott's sense of 'the action of the poem', which in his view demanded its 'division into three *Fyttes*, or Cantos' (1804: lxxxiv); Scott's usage in this context seems to have influenced Lord Byron in his use of the term *fytte* in *Childe Harold's Pilgrimage* (xciii, 1). The term was sanctioned by Thomas Percy's use (and learned note on the matter) in the *Reliques*, which Percy derived from his exemplar, the Percy Folio manuscript anthology described in the Introduction. Indeed, Percy's own pastiche of romance (published separately from the *Reliques*), *The Hermit of Warkworth: a Northumberland Ballad* (1770), was divided into 'Three Fits or Cantos'. The Percy Folio used the word *ffitt* twice to divide the poems *Death and Liffe* and *Scotish ffeilde*, both alliterative poems, and deployed the term elsewhere in internal references. The usage was in addition sanctioned for Scott by its appearance in *Sir Thopas*, the poem he used, as we have seen, for *Sir Tristrem*'s title-page motto. In manuscripts of *Sir Thopas*, '*fitts*' (as they are spelled by modern editors) are flagged not, as in modern editions of the poem, by the use of a rubric but by an internal reference: 'Loo, lordes myne, heere is a fit!/ If ye wol any moore of it,/ To telle it wol I fonde' (Benson et al. 1987: 215). In some manuscripts containing *Sir Thopas* a large initial or a *diple* ('quotation-mark') follows the end of each section so distinguished (e.g. in Oxford, Trinity College, MS D.29, folio 200v).

The term seems to have originated in the Germanic past, first recorded in the Latin preface to the Old Saxon *Heliand* (see Chapter 2, section 2.1).[18]

(2) Scott's edition numbers the poem's stanzas, whereas the Auchinleck scribe simply uses an engrossed initial for the first line of the poem at the top of each column, with paraphs or pilcrows (¶) to mark subsequent sections.

(3) Scott's edition uses present-day word division, although obsolete words sometimes present problems, e.g. *y wis* 'certainly', which usually appeared in Middle English as a single word *ywis* (cf. Old English *gewis*); the edition follows the Auchinleck scribe's comparatively unusual separation of the prefix *y* from the rest of the word. The Auchinleck scribe's word divisions are roughly comparable with those used in Scott's publication, although quite frequently the scribe, by contrast with the edition's usage, did not separate the indefinite article from the noun it modifies, e.g. *akniȝt* 'a knight'.

(4) In his discussion of how he as an editor 'has executed his task', Scott describes how he has replaced 'ancient characters' whose use 'throws unnecessary embarrassment in the way of the modern reader':

> The modern *th* has been substituted uniformly for the Saxon character, which expresses that sound; in like manner, the *z* has usually been discarded for the modern *y*, or *gh* … *Y*, when used for the pronoun *I*, is printed with a capital, to distinguish it from *y*, the usual corruption of *ge*, the Saxon preposition. (Scott 1804: lxxxix)

Scott's edition generally replaces the manuscript <u> with <v> where a consonant is needed, e.g. *greves* for *greues*, but he misses the replacement in *auentours*, possibly because he does not recognise that in this last case <u> is a consonant rather than a vowel. The edition also introduces capital letters for personal names and the personal pronoun *Y* 'I', and at the beginning of verse-lines. The Auchinleck scribe, apart from the engrossed letters at the top of each column (see (2) above), does not deploy capitals,

[18] Various versions of the line in *Sir Thopas* are recorded in the manuscript witnesses, often reflecting fifteenth-century metrical uncertainties, e.g. London, British Library, MS Sloane 1686, folio 246v: *Lo lordes myn here a fitte*. For a full discussion of the term *fitt* and its deployment in both medieval and later texts, see Hardman 1992, an important discussion of formal divisions in medieval English narrative poems; see also Chapter 2 above, note 3 and references there cited. For further discussion of the imposition of archaistic sectionalising, see the discussion of John Pinkerton's deployment of the term *BUKE* 'book' in his edition of John Barbour's *Bruce*, discussed in Smith 2013a and also in Chapter 5 above.

although the first letter in each line is shaded with red ink. The practice in Scott's edition is in line with that found in many present-day student editions, notably of Chaucer's works.

(5) Finally, Scott's edition replaces the Auchinleck manuscript's marks of punctuation. The Auchinleck scribe uses two such marks: a punctus, used at the end of most lines, e.g.

tomas telles in toun.

and a punctus elevatus used after each 'bob' in the verse-form, e.g.

to abide؛

In the punctuation of the Auchinleck manuscript, there is a close relation between its deployment and the spoken mode. The punctus is here deployed to mark both a lesser pause at the end of a line and a greater one at the end of a stanza, while the punctus elevatus is used to mark a 'silent stress' before the summary pair of lines with which each stanza ends. By contrast, the 1804 edition of *Sir Tristrem* has a much more extensive repertoire of marks of punctuation, with such symbols familiar to present-day readers as full stops, semicolons and colons, with the punctus elevatus replaced by a combination of colon and hyphen. Whether or not the final responsibility for deploying punctuation in the edition is Scott's or Ballantyne's – given his interest in the materiality of his publications, and his close association with the printer, it is hard to think that Scott was not involved in determining the matter, as part of the same community of practice in the edition's construction – it is clear that something is happening that is rather different from current 'educated' usage of the kind prescribed in present-day printers' handbooks, such as Hart (2014).

The difference is emphasised if we present the verse-format of Scott's edition in prose fashion, as in the following version of the first stanza:

> I WAS at [Erceldoune:] With Tomas spak Y thare; Ther herd Y rede in roune, Who Tristrem gat and bare. Who was king with croun; And who him forsterd yare; And who was bold baroun, As their elders ware, Bi yere:- Tomas telles in toun, This auentours as thai ware.

The first 'sentence' 'I . . . bare' is comparatively well-formed by modern prescriptive standards in terms of the deployment of punctuation, even if the presence of a colon (where present-day readers might expect a semicolon) and a semicolon in a single sentence is a little unusual. The first two clauses of the sentence, the first in subject-predicator-complement ordering, and the second with archaic reversal of predicator and subject (*spak Y*) after an initial adverbial (*With Tomas*), are linked equiparatively by the colon. A semicolon links the first two clauses to the remainder of the sentence, where a subordinate clause ('Who Tristrem gat and bare') is linked to the main clause ('Ther herd Y rede in roune') by a comma.

However, the following subordinate clauses, 'Who was king with croun;', 'And who him forsterd yare;' and 'And who was bold baroun,', all of which also depend on the main clause 'Ther herd Y rede in roune', are separated – unusually in terms of present-day approved 'educated' usage – by a full stop and further semicolons. Such usage is not 'grammatical'; rather, it is 'rhetorical', deploying marks of punctuation in line with eighteenth-century 'elocutionist' ideas about the spoken manifestation of texts. Rhetorical punctuation here aligns commas, semicolons and full stops with increasing lengths of pauses for breath in speech. In that sense, there is a perhaps unexpected continuity between the Auchinleck manuscript and the printed version: both are to a greater or lesser extent 'speech-like'.

The usage in Scott's edition does not therefore align with the prescriptivist and grammatical rules of punctuation that are the reference point for modern educators. Although in many ways his edition represented, as David Matthews stated, 'a genuine departure' and pointed forward to trends in textual editing of the vernacular that were to become dominant, in textual minutiae his work also represents a continuity, reflecting the special conditions of literacy which applied at the time of his edition's appearance. We will turn to some of these issues to do with the uses of literacy – and their implications for present-day notions of textual criticism – in what follows.

6.2 Textual Criticism

In a valuable study, Diane Scott has aptly argued that 'the gradually changing "model" of reader during the late medieval and early modern periods exerted gradual pressure on the systems of paratext and punctuation applied by editors to the chosen texts' (2015: 52): a statement that summarises well the discussions in the preceding chapters. In this context Walter Scott's edition of *Sir Tristrem* offers a fitting conclusion to the present discussion, given how culturally significant its editor was as a mediator of the medieval past to his Romantic present. *Sir Tristrem* represented a step-change in terms of the apparatus that accompanied a vernacular text, but it is also important to recognise that it emerged from practices that were becoming increasingly widespread in the late eighteenth and early nineteenth centuries – practices that remain at the core of many present-day approaches to the editing of past texts, and that were a response to the development of 'enlightened' attitudes to the past.

Certainly notions of correctness, flagged by Scott as one of the achievements of his edition, were already much in evidence in the work of earlier editors of texts which were more securely part of the Scottish literary tradition than was *Sir Tristrem*. A good example is the collection of *Ancient Scottish Poems* published in 1770 by the jurist and historian Sir David Dalrymple, Lord Hailes (1726–92), and already discussed in the Introduction. Hailes's edition of the poems of Robert Henryson, William Dunbar and other authors now regarded as canonical, drawing on the Bannatyne manuscript, was explicitly designed as an improvement of Ramsay's *The Ever Green* (see Chapter 5). Hailes appreciated the 'singular native genius' of his predecessor's work, but – as one might expect of a friend of Dr Johnson and a self-confident scholar who dared to argue with Edward Gibbon – he had nevertheless a clear sense of what he considered to be its imperfections:

> This is the MS. which the editor of the *Evergreen* used: but he has omitted some stanzas, and added others; has modernized the versification, and varied the ancient manner of spelling. Hence, they who look in the *Evergreen* for the state of language and poetry among us during the fifteenth century [*sic*], will be missed, or disappointed.
>
> The many and obvious inaccuracies of the *Evergreen*, suggested the idea of this new collection. In it the MS. has been fairly copied; no liberties in amending or interpolating have been taken. The reader will find the language, versification, and spelling, in the same state as they were in 1568. (Hailes 1770: xx)

Hailes nevertheless allowed himself, as Scott did and indeed later editors have continued to do, what he called the 'interpolation' of interpretative punctuation.

Such comments are reminiscent of Kölbing's criticism of Scott almost a century later, and it is therefore in its own terms disappointing that close analysis of Hailes's *Ancient Scottish Poems* shows that its editor's claims, like Scott's, were overstated. Percy's observations on the text have already been cited in the Introduction, while Scott himself – though muted in his public criticism in accordance with decorum as well as in line with his habitual kindliness – noted problems with Hailes's edition. Scott knew the Bannatyne manuscript well: he presided, in 1823, over the creation of the eponymous antiquarian Club whose goal was the publication of medieval and early modern Scottish texts, and he provided a 'Memoir of George

Bannatyne' as an introductory essay for a collection of papers the Club published in 1829. He refers to Hailes's edition briefly at the end of the 'Memoir':

> The publication of Lord Hailes, is entitled "Ancient Scottish Poems, published from the manuscript of George Bannatyne. 1568. Edinburgh, 1770," 12mo. It was designed to correct the many infidelities and inaccuracies of the Evergreen, and is accompanied with notes and a glossary, valuable as coming from the pen of so celebrated an antiquary. Yet *aliquando dormitat* – Lord Hailes, himself the most accurate of men, after spelling the name of our patron correctly in the title page, calls him in the first page of his preface "one Ballantine." Had he discovered this misnomer in the work while in the bookseller's hands, he would certainly have cancelled the preface. The publication is an excellent specimen of Bannatyne's Collection, though the severe delicacy of Lord Hailes's taste has excluded some curious matter. (Scott 1829: 23–4)

The missing 'curious matter' is fairly easy to determine; Hailes's extensive deployment of asterisks in such poems as *The Sweiris and the Devill* or *The Flyting* veils material of the kind that would have greatly distressed Scott's amanuensis, John Leyden (e.g. *swyfe* 'copulate with'), and Hailes himself drew explicit attention to such practices through such comments as 'This line is omitted on account of its blunt co[a]rse style' (1770: 242).

Emphasis on 'correct' editing, even if generally focused on classical authors, was already well under way in enlightened circles at the beginning of the eighteenth century, building on the insights of great early modern humanists such as Angelo 'Poliziano' (1454–94) and Pietro Bembo (1470–1547). The key figure in this regard was Richard Bentley (1662–1742), master of Trinity College, Cambridge and one of the greatest scholars – and innovative (if controversial) university administrators – of his age. It is no surprise that Scott himself owned, as well as copies of Bentley's editions of Cicero and Lucretius, two other works in which Bentley figured: an anonymously produced *The Life and Conversation of Richard Bentley* (1712) and a satirical pamphlet (?1737) whose full title is remarkably extended even by eighteenth-century standards:

> The session of the critics: or, the contention for the nettle. A poem. : To which is added, a dialogue between a player and a poet. With notes, explanatory and critical, after the manner of the learned Dr. Bentley. With the following miscellanies, viz. I. On a Thanksgiving, which happened just before Lent. By Dean Swift. II. Rules and directions for behaviour at Bath. III. The art of thriving at Bath. IV. Battle-Royal, reviv'd. A ballad. Occasioned by religious controversy. V. Verses laid on Sir Cloudesly

> Shovel's tomb, &c. VI. On Tate and Brady's Psalms. VII. On a person's pronouncing the syllable phra, in Euphrates, short. Viii. On a certain arch in Oxfordshire. IX. Verses stuck on the gate of Jesus College, Oxford, with a piece of cheese. X. The receipt. XI. On Phyllis. XII. Have you not in a chimney seen, &c. Translated. XIII. The resolution. XIV. A conflict on business. XV. The button hole. A riddle. XVI. A mad song.

The appearance of Bentley's name in such a work as *The session of the critics* is a witness to his currency as a well-known intellectual reference point.

Scott also owned a 1777 edition of Bentley's seminal *A dissertation on the epistles of Phalaris*, originally published in 1699. Bentley's study of a gross (if minor) ancient forgery, although it was to attract satirical attention from Jonathan Swift in *The Battle of the Books* (published as a supplement to *A Tale of a Tub*, 1704), established his reputation as a textual scholar of international importance and had a considerable subsequent impact: Hailes, for instance, attempted something similar in a study of the early Christian apologist Lactantius (240–c. 320 CE), part of a wider editorial enterprise that he developed as a riposte to Gibbon's notorious thesis that the fall of the Roman Empire was due to the adoption of Christianity.

Bentley's editorial activities showed him to be an important precursor of future trends. His editions of major authors such as Horace and Terence, as well as Cicero and Lucretius, attracted attention and indeed controversy through his adventurous deployment of what is now called 'conjectural' emendation. Throwing caution to the winds, he even extended his techniques to the editing of John Milton's *Paradise Lost* (1732), attempting to reconstruct the author's original intentions before presumed revisions by the blind poet's amanuenses: an 'absurdly interventionist' (Gillespie and Hudson 2013: 2) exercise that attracted considerable scorn from contemporaries, including a lengthy and robust correspondence in the *Grub-Street Journal* and *Gentleman's Magazine* (see references in Cohen and Bourdette 1980).

Bentley's edition of *Paradise Lost* may have been misconceived – his nephew, who corrected the proofs, tried to persuade him against publication (ODNB) – but it had the virtue of explicitness and an underpinning ideology of correctness; the editor was not afraid to 'show his working'. He adopted various strategies to indicate his 'corrective' interventions, deploying apostrophes to mark elisions, accents to mark the stressing of polysyllables, and numerous footnotes recording and justifying his emendations and variants. Bentley's aims are, in the context of this chapter, worth quoting:

> *These small Improvements will be found in the present Text, which challenges to be the Truest and Correctest* [of the text] *that has yet appear'd: not* ONE *Word being alter'd in it; but all the Conjectures, that attempt a Restoration of the Genuine* Milton, *cast into the Margin, and explain'd in the Notes. So that every Reader has his free Choice, whether he will accept or reject what is here offer'd him; and this without the least Disgust or Discontent in the Offerer.* (Bentley 1732: sig. a1v)

More significant for the future, however, were editions that Bentley only projected: of Homer and, above all, of the Bible. Bentley's 'Proposals' for an edition of the New Testament (1720) outline techniques of editing that were to become dominant a century later: the *collation* (line-by-line comparison) of witnesses, the creation (albeit implicitly) of a 'family tree' of manuscripts or *stemma codicum*, and the identification thereby of the relative authority of the earliest sources for the text. Bentley's aim was to restore the Bible to the form to be found at the Council of Nicaea of 325 CE (Reynolds and Wilson 2013: 188), which he regarded as the earliest recoverable version of the text, now known as the *archetype*: although suggested by humanist editors, Bentley seems to have been the first to give this notion a precise formulation.[19]

Bentley's goal in his *Proposals* is now generally referred to as *recension*, and the techniques he describes were later refracted, reformulated and developed by even more famous successors, such as Karl Lachmann (1793–1851), or B. F. Westcott (1825–1901) and F. J. Hort (1828–92). Recension was clearly part of the emerging classificatory paradigm that was to dominate scientific thinking from the late eighteenth century onwards. Recension remains dominant among modern editors, followed by the critical act of *emendation* whereby 'common-sense and judgement and taste' (Reynolds and Wilson 2013: 209) are deployed to purge the archetype from obvious errors (more correctly, 'non-original readings').

However, the processes of recension and emendation in the editorial process have not remained unchallenged. One difficulty arises from 'contaminated' traditions, whereby scribes compared two or more exemplars, not necessarily closely related, which they happened to come across and simply chose those readings that seemed to them most appealing; in such

[19] That Bentley never produced his Bible seems to have been due in part at least to the disastrous 1731 fire at Ashburnham House, Westminster, that not only destroyed or damaged a significant proportion of the medieval manuscripts in the Cotton collection but also affected his own papers, including – reported *The Gentleman's Magazine* – 'those which Dr *Bentley* had been collecting for his *Greek Testament*'. See further Chapter 2 above. For an assessment of Bentley, see also Barker 2002: 225–6.

circumstances the creation of a stemma becomes problematic. Authors themselves complicated matters by revising their own works, and, since in antiquity and during the Middle Ages they rarely had any control over the subsequent copying process, different 'authorised' versions could contaminate each other. Moreover, it is clear that scribes themselves quite frequently considered themselves to be creative partners in the textual enterprise, intervening to improve (from their own perspectives) the work they were copying. And a final point is perhaps also worth making: if the aim of textual criticism is the reconstruction of the author's original conception of the work, it is worth pondering what that work would have looked like in the author's own time. Should a modern edition of, say, Virgil's *Æneid* appear in a form that Virgil would have recognised, i.e. as a scroll, perhaps presented in *scriptio continua* with no modern punctuation and no gaps between words, with all the implications for the author–reader relationship – very different from present-day conditions – that such presentation implies?

By the end of the twentieth century such questions were increasingly worrying for scholars. Joseph Bédier (1864–1938), the great editor of medieval French romances including *Le Lai de l'ombre* (1890) and *La Chanson de Roland* (1922), had already challenged the dominance of the stemmatic method. Bédier argued that editions should be based on conjectural emendation of a 'best-text' witness, the choice being determined by evaluative literary criticism and thus emphasising the primacy of critical and humanistic (and of course Gallic) *élan* over a perceived stolid, unimaginative, Germanic scientism (see especially Bédier 1928). And such questioning became even more urgent much later as the rise of 'theory' as a distinctive academic orientation in the humanities demanded what the philosopher of science Rom Harré once called the 'explicit identification of the structure of one's conceptual system' (1972: 17). Scholars like Jerome McGann (1983) and Bernard Cerquiglini (1999), for instance, influenced by the destabilising trends brought about through postmodernism, offered critiques of textual criticism that made the whole editorial enterprise seem increasingly problematic.

Editors have over the years responded variously to such challenges. Some have sturdily refused to engage with such perceived faddism, taking the provocative view, like the poet and classicist A. E. Housman (1859–1936), that editing is 'not susceptible to hard and fast rules' (in Ricks 1988: 325), but of course such a position is itself a 'theory of editing' (*pace* the view cited by Vincent Gillespie and Anne Hudson, 2013: 6). Some have extended Bédier's insights and focused on conjectural emendation based on the analysis of variants; a good example of such an enterprise, on a grand scale, is the great Athlone edition of the fourteenth-century Middle English alliterative poem *Piers Plowman*, a work that seems to have been subjected to authorial rolling revision and that survives in over sixty medieval manuscript witnesses, many the outcome of complex patterns of contamination (see e.g. Kane 1988, the revised edition of a work first published in 1960; see Patterson 1987 for a comprehensive critique of Kane's methods). Others have used new approaches to classification, often computer-assisted, to refine and enhance or modify the stemmatic method. Such techniques have been applied by classicists (see Reynolds and Wilson 2013: 297 and references there cited), while Anglicists have employed such approaches to the complex, multi-witnessed tradition of Nicholas Love (see Sargent 2005), and indeed to the *Canterbury Tales* themselves (see e.g. Barbrook et al. 1998; for a critique, see Cartlidge 2001).

Yet others have stepped back from the traditional enterprise of conventional editorial practice altogether. There had always been an interest in the (apparently) humble transcribing of manuscript witnesses as 'diplomatic' (as opposed to 'critical') editions, and indeed some of the earliest EETS publications consisted of parallel texts of different versions of the same work. A good example here – still commonly used in teaching Middle English dialectology – is Richard Morris's rather fine edition of the various manuscripts of the *Cursor Mundi*, published by EETS from 1871 onwards and still the tenth most-cited work in the OED. Similar productions from around the same time include the Six-Text Edition (1868) of the *Canterbury Tales*, published by Frederick J. Furnivall's Chaucer Society, which offered diplomatic transcriptions of six important early fifteenth-century copies of the poem (see, for a recent discussion, Spencer 2015). Such productions reached their apogee with the EETS's printing (1944–2000) of editions of *Ancrene Wisse/Ancrene Riwle*, a text that survives not only – as we have seen – in nine Middle English versions ranging in date from the thirteenth to the fifteenth centuries but also in medieval translations into Latin and French.

Such editions are no longer commonly produced in printed form – arguably a matter for regret. Eric Dobson's diplomatic edition of the Cleopatra manuscript of *Ancrene Riwle* (London, British Library, MS Cotton Cleopatra C.vi = Dobson 1972) is a fine example of the genre: a work of formidable philological learning, not only in Dobson's words 'solving the problems' of a very complex manuscript but, in its introduction and apparatus, giving access to the equally complex processes of linguistic evolution under way in the South-West Midlands during the centuries immediately after the Norman Conquest. Such an edition proves conclusively that there is still an important role for diplomatic presentation, distinct from that afforded by the increasing availability of photographic facsimiles.

A major (and exciting) exception to such neglect, however, is in the appearance of electronic transcriptions of texts, often accompanied by facsimiles and significant bodies of accompanying material, and thus 'image-based editions'. Such editions allow not only for comparatively easy 'text-mining' but also act as interpretative tools for accompanying images. Major medieval English examples include the NLS's *Auchinleck Manuscript* online, the *Canterbury Tales Project* and the *Piers Plowman Electronic Archive*; numerous other examples could be cited. Such 'electronic editions' raise questions of what users of such editions are supposed to do with the huge amount of information that they offer. As the late Hoyt Duggan, one of the principal investigators leading the *Piers Plowman Electronic Archive*, famously asked: 'We Are Building It. Will They Come?' (cited in Millett 2013: 44). It has been argued that such editions are best thought of as – in Eric Dobson's words – '*in usum editorum philologorumque*, valuable primarily as a foundation for future research' (cited in Millett 2013: 51). However, given that *all* research is supposed to be an ongoing, collaborative dialogue, that argument seems to me open to challenge: production of 'foundations' is surely a completely valid research activity, offering new insights that can – potentially at least – be effectively shared. The academic community is clearly still thinking through the implications of rapid digital innovation.[20]

It will be clear that the business of textual criticism remains, at the beginning of the twenty-first century, as racked by controversy as it was in Bentley's time. In this context, Roy Michael Liuzza's wise comments are very much to the point:

> It is true that an edition of a manuscript is no substitute for the manuscript itself – map is not territory, as they say – but on the

[20] Useful discussions of some of the problems and opportunities involved with electronic editions include Millett 2013 just cited, and also the prescient essays in Deegan and Sutherland 2009; important insights about the manuscript/image interface are also to be found in Nichols 2017. The issue of sustainability is explicitly discussed in, e.g., McGann 2010. All such discussions, of course, tend to be overtaken by developments in a rapidly growing field; some of the challenges are discussed in further forward-looking discussions, e.g. Prescott 1997, and chapters in Carpenter et al. 1998. Incidentally, the definition of research given here, namely 'new insights, effectively shared', was that adopted for the UK's Research Excellence Framework 2014. A difficulty is that such work is sometimes dismissed as 'research enhancement', and thus not liable to attract dedicated external funding.

> other hand territory isn't map either; nor do modern readers have the same relationship to text and page that medieval readers or audiences might have had. An edition, like a map, is useful precisely *because* it is a model, a representation of a text and its history, an analytical language for reducing artifact to information. (Liuzza 2006: 276; see also Machan 1994: 72–3)

But one positive outcome of the various controversies current has been an increasing habit of reflexion on the editorial craft. With special reference to medieval studies, Tim Machan had already called for 'editorial and interpretive self-conscious[ness, and] . . . greater historical sensibility in an activity that is inherently historical' (1994: 193). Machan's and Liuzza's views have, with pithy perceptiveness, been more recently echoed by Derek Pearsall: 'the only rule that all scholarly editors and editors of critical editions *must* observe is – *Show your working*, as we used to be exhorted when we were doing maths problems at school' (2013: 205). There is above all an awareness that the editorial process is not – and never has been – 'neutral' or 'objective' but is rather a hermeneutic act constrained by contemporary conditions of publication and intended audience. As has been emphasised throughout this book, editors, along with their publishers, form a community of practice, and the formal features of the resulting editions are constrained by the socio-cultural functions such editions are expected to perform for the contemporary discourse community in which they exist. As we have seen in the previous chapters, although printers, publishers and editors regularly claim 'authenticity' for their outputs – as witnessed by such statements as Andro Hart's description on the title page of his 1616 Edinburgh edition of *The Bruce* as 'Newly corrected, and conferred with the best and most ancient Manuscripts' – in reality the notion of 'textual truth', 'correctness' or 'authenticity' is a fluid one, open for negotiation as texts are recuperated at different times.[21]

6.3 Textual Transformation

Throughout this book, the fluidity of such notions of 'authenticity' has been constantly emphasised: any recuperation of a text from the past, it has been argued, has a Janus-like relationship to both past and present, the

[21] The starting-point for all discussions of textual criticism, with currency well beyond the Greek and Latin texts on which it is focused, remains Reynolds and Wilson 2013. Relevant essays also appear in Minnis and Brewer 1992, and in Gillespie and Hudson 2013 (some of which are cited above). Machan 1994 remains foundational, as does Talbot Donaldson's classic essay (1970).

contemporary socio-cultural functions of a given text being reflected quite delicately by its formal characteristics in a particular manifestation.

It is of course a truism of many disciplines that, when a cultural artefact comes down to us from the past – a poem, piece of music, painting, sculpture, tapestry – its 'authenticity' as a witness for its own time may be remarked upon, but it is also, of course, situated within twenty-first-century culture. A piece of 'early' music is, for instance, just as much part of our contemporary cultural capital as a composition from our own time. When a gallery of medieval art is created for the twenty-first century, the pieces on display can interact with their present-day setting to produce distinctive (in many ways potentially problematic) cultural experiences, as in the Burrell Collection in Glasgow or Columbia University's Cloisters in New York, for example, where medieval elements are incorporated into the buildings' fabric. These last examples are themselves part of a great tradition: when he reconstructed his home at Abbotsford, Sir Walter Scott installed the door from the old Edinburgh Tolbooth, the city's lock-up, into one of his new mansion's sidewalls.

Thus the ways in which artefacts are presented in subsequent centuries relate dynamically to the changing ways in which the past is integrated within broader narratives and imperatives; we cannot encounter Beethoven's Fifth Symphony in the same way as those who attended the first public performance in Vienna in 1808, bringing their own socio-cultural contexts and preconceptions with them. Similarly, by tracing the transformation of a range of culturally significant texts as they were copied and recuperated and edited by distinct communities of practice, it has proven possible to track these broader shifts and relate them to the evolution of the discourse communities who encountered the texts in question in their various forms.

Throughout the book, therefore, it has been demonstrated how textual forms, in the widest sense, and however seeming-small, can be related to textual functions. The late Christian Kay and I have previously argued as follows:

> Any text can be viewed as a conversational partnership between transmitter and received. In face-to-face conversation, communication is assisted by extralinguistic features such as tone of voice or facial expression; problems of interpretation are often solved by context. For written texts, a greater range of factors may render communication problematic, not least the key role of a third participant in the conversation: the scribe or editor who mediates between the creator and the reader of the text. The further back in time the reader goes, the more problematic this role becomes. When a text has been

> copied or edited over hundreds of years, repeated opportunities are available to modify or reinterpret not only its language but pragmatic features such as layout, punctuation or capitalisation, all of which affect reception. As the edition grows more remote from its source, the importance of recognising the significance of such features increases. (Smith and Kay 2011: 212)

Since Kay and I wrote these words, I have come to appreciate two modifications to this statement, which – it may be hoped – will provoke further investigation as part of what we might call a 'reimagined philology'. First, transmitters, receivers and mediators of texts exist within a wider framework: dynamically shifting socio-cultural communities of practice and discourse communities, influenced – as we have seen – by overlapping ideological engagements with religion, social structure and national identity. In the case studies that form the bulk of this book such engagements have been constantly noted. As Norman Fairclough put it, 'language is a part of society, and not somehow external to it . . . language is a social process' (2015: 22).

Secondly, the division between 'language' and the 'pragmatic features' we identified in 2011 is, it could be argued, unhelpful. There is rather, as I hope I have demonstrated in this book, a profound connexion between all these communicative manifestations, and it is clear that the language disciplines as they have been distinguished in the later twentieth century would benefit from deeper engagement with – and might contribute powerfully to – others such as paleography, typographical studies, book history, reception studies and so on, as well as the original 'new philology's' ancient sister-discipline, textual criticism. And as I hinted in passing at the beginning of Chapter 1, there are even ways in which the approaches taken here could be extended to the analysis of 'new' modes of discourse, e.g. computer-mediated communication (though that is a task for someone other than myself). Such research across traditional disciplinary boundaries, often and necessarily highly collaborative, is attracting increasing interest, offering new insights into the dynamic dialogues that have always existed between past and present.

Appendix of Plates

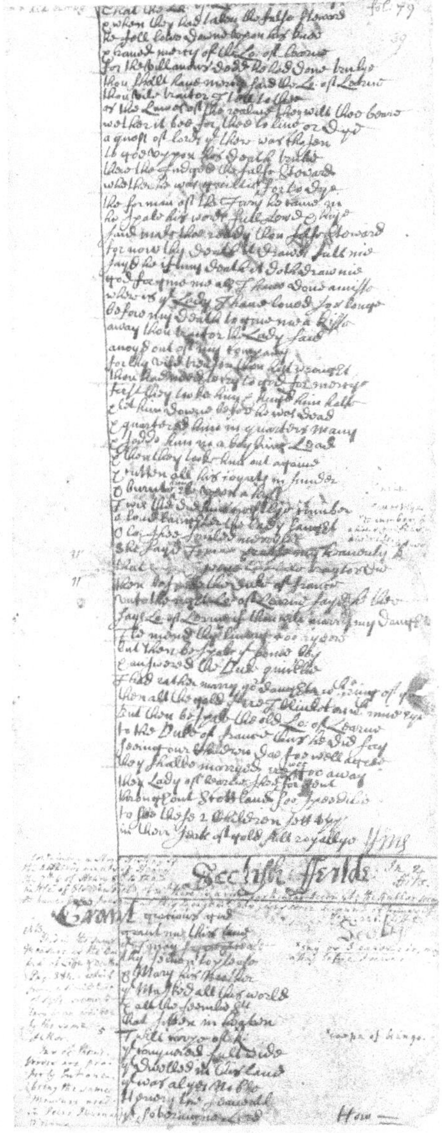

I **The Percy Folio manuscript (seventeenth century):** 'lying dirty on the floor, under a bureau in the parlour . . . being used by the maids to light the fire' (Hales and Furnivall 1867–8: vol. I, lxiv). This illustration shows Thomas Percy's annotation of *Scotish ffeilde*, including the addition by him of the heading '2 ffits' after the title of the poem (see Introduction). (© British Library Board, London: MS Additional 27879, folio 39r (modern foliation) = page 79)

J. Wale del. C. Grignion Sculp.

These venerable antient Song-enditers
Soar'd many a pitch above our modern writers:
With rough majestic force they mov'd the heart,
And strength and nature made amends for Art.

Rowe

II **Thomas Percy, *Reliques of Ancient English Poetry* (1765)**: 'a seminal work of English Romanticism' (ODNB). Samuel Wale's frontispiece appeared in volume III of the *Reliques* (see Introduction). (By permission of Glasgow University Library: Sp Coll Bd20-h.24 vol. 3, frontispiece)

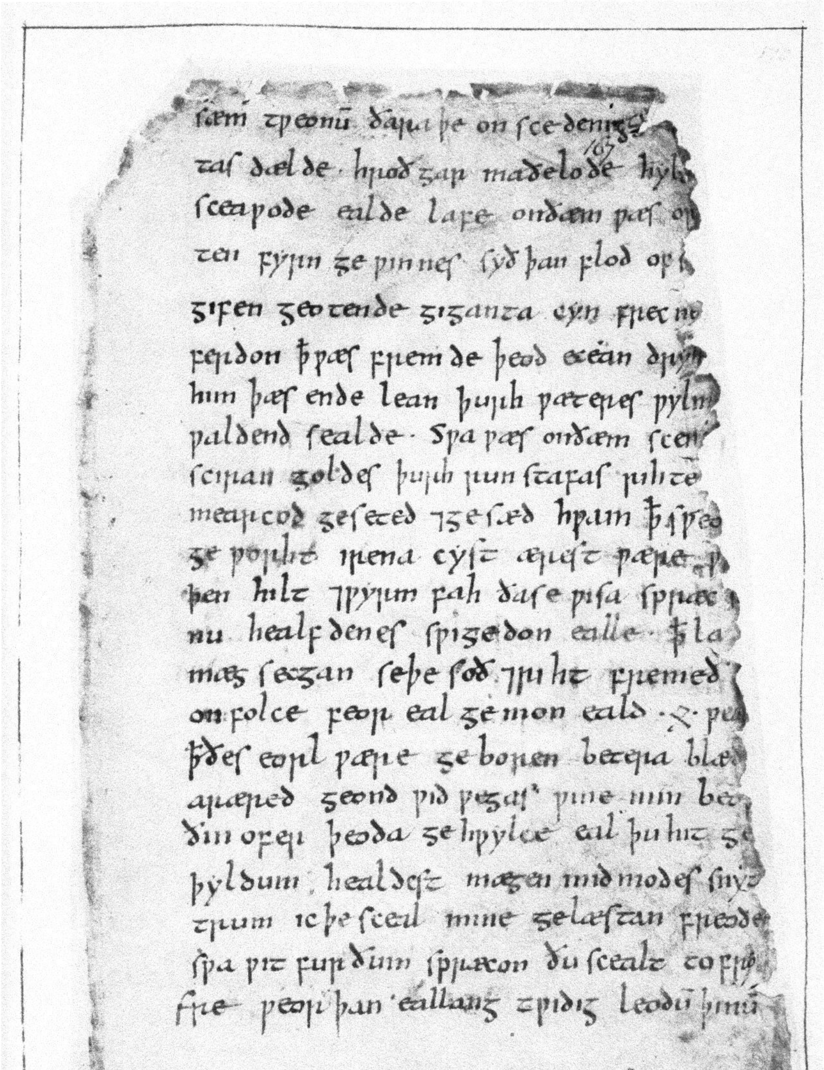

III **The *Beowulf* manuscript (c. 1000 CE)**: In three places the manuscript's first scribe uses the rune ᛟ to signify the Old English word *ēþel* 'homeland'. One example appears eight lines from the foot of this illustration (see Chapter 2). (© British Library Board, London: MS Cotton Vitellius A.xv (part II), folio 170r)

DE

D A N O R U M

Rebus Gestis Secul. III & IV.

POËMA DANICUM DIALECTO ANGLOSAXONICA.

EX BIBLIOTHECA COTTONIANA MUSAEI BRITANNICI

edidit versione lat. et indicibus auxit

Grim. Johnson Thorkelin. Dr. J.V.

Eques Ord. Danebrogici auratus. S. R. M. a Consiliis Status. Arcanis Regni Scriniis Præfectus. Regiis Legati Arna-Magnæani Curatoribus a Literis. Regiar. Societ. Scient. Havniens. et Islandicæ. Antiqvarior: Londinens. et Edinburg. necnon Academiæ Reg. Hibernicæ sodalis etc.

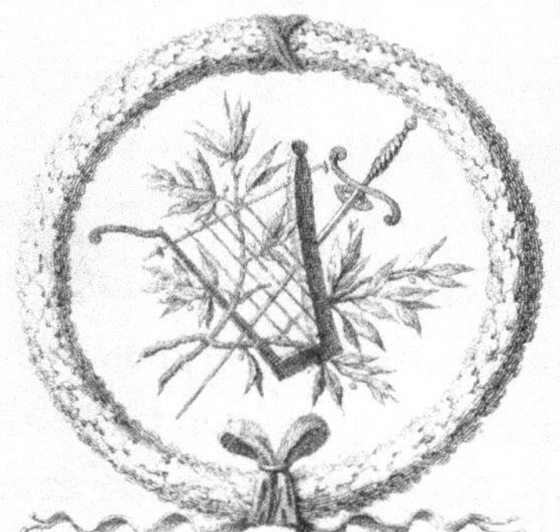

Havniæ Typis Th. E. Rangel.

MDCCCXV.

IV ***Beowulf*** **(1815):** Grimur Jonsson Thorkelin (1752–1829) published the first full printed edition of the greatest epic poem in Old English, although he claimed it as part of Danish culture. The illustration here is of the flamboyant title page (see Chapter 2). (By permission of Glasgow University Library: Sp Coll Bc30-x.16, title page)

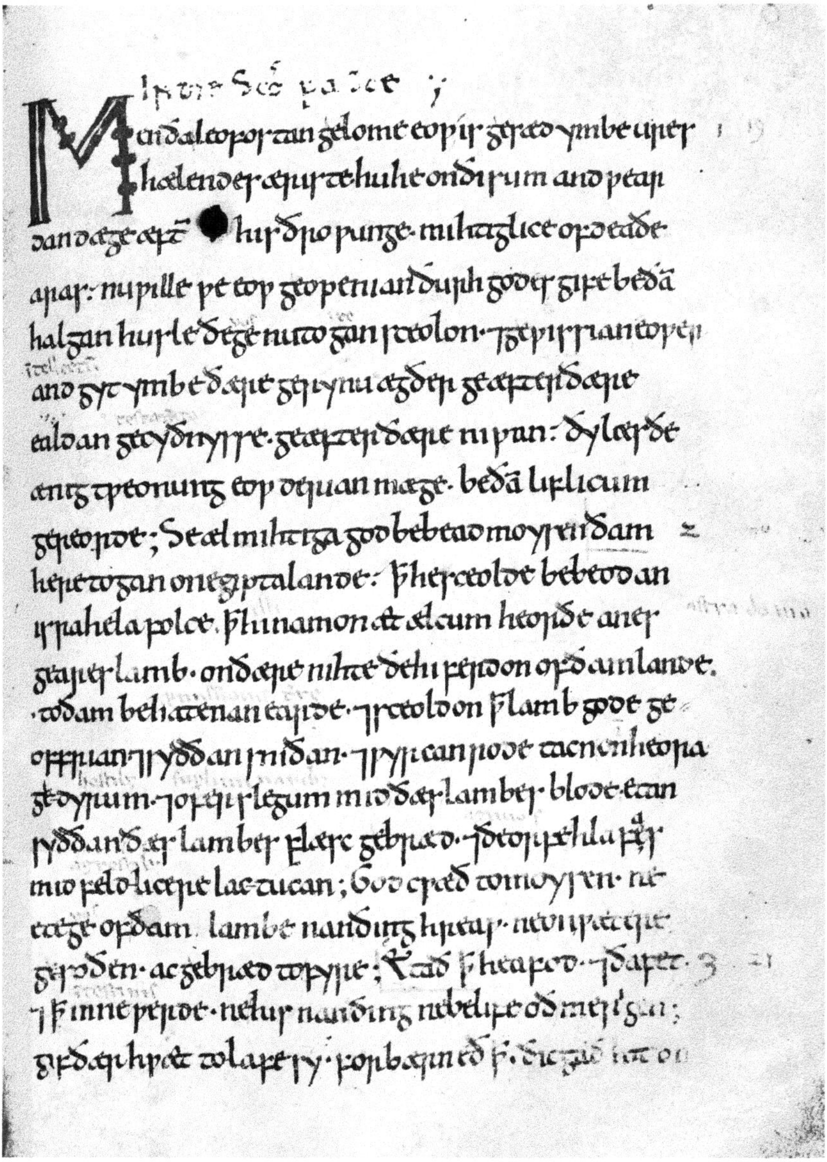

V **The opening of Ælfric's homily *In die Sancto pasce*,** in a manuscript dating from the early eleventh century. Marginalia by John Joscelyn, collating the manuscript with the printed edition of 1566 (see Plate VI), are visible, as are the annotations made by the Tremulous Hand of Worcester in the thirteenth century (see Chapter 2). (By permission of the Parker Library, Corpus Christi College, Cambridge: MS 198, folio 218r)

In die Sancto Pascæ.

Men ða leofostan. gelome eoƿ is gesæd ymbe ures hælendes æriste. hu he on ðisum andƿeardan dæge æfter his ðroƿunge mihtiglice of deaþe aras; Nu ƿille ƿe eoƿ geopenian ðurh Godes gife be ðam halgan husle ðe ge nu to gan sceolon. and geƿissian eoƿer andgyt ymbe ðære gerynu. ægþer ge æfter þære ealdan gecyþnysse. ge æfter þære niƿan. ðy læs ðe ænig tƿeonunge eoƿ derian mæge be þam liflicū gereorde; Se ælmihtiga God bebead Moyses ðam

A Sermon on Easter day. 20

Men beloued, it hath bene often sayd vnto you aboute our Sauiours resurrection, how he on this present day after hys suffering, mightely rose from death. Now will we open vnto you through Gods grace, of the holy housell, whiche ye shoulde nowe goe vnto, and instructe your vnderstandyng aboute thys mysterie, both after the olde couenaunte, and also after the newe, that no doubting may trouble you about thys liuelye foode. The almyghtie God badde Moyses C.iiij. *his*

VI ***A testimonie of antiquitie*** **(1566).** The first-ever edition of an Old English work – Ælfric's homily on Easter Sunday (see Plate V) – was printed as part of a 'pamphlet war' between evangelicals and conservatives on the vexed issue of transubstantiation. The illustration shows the opening of the work, with the Old English text, in its 'counterfeit' typeface evoking Anglo-Saxon insular script, facing a translation into early modern English (see Chapter 2). (© British Library Board, London: 695.a.31, folios 19v–20r)

VII **The antiquary Stephen Batman (d.1584)** taught himself Anglo-Saxon insular script and liked to use it even when annotating a text where it was anachronistic, such as in this religious miscellany from late fourteenth-century London. Here he has inserted a poem of his own composition on a blank space after the manuscript's glossed Psalter and before its version of *Ancrene Riwle* (see Chapter 3). The poem, though in early modern English, is written in Batman's version of insular script. (By permission of the Pepys Library, Magdalene College, Cambridge: MS Pepys 2498, p. 370)

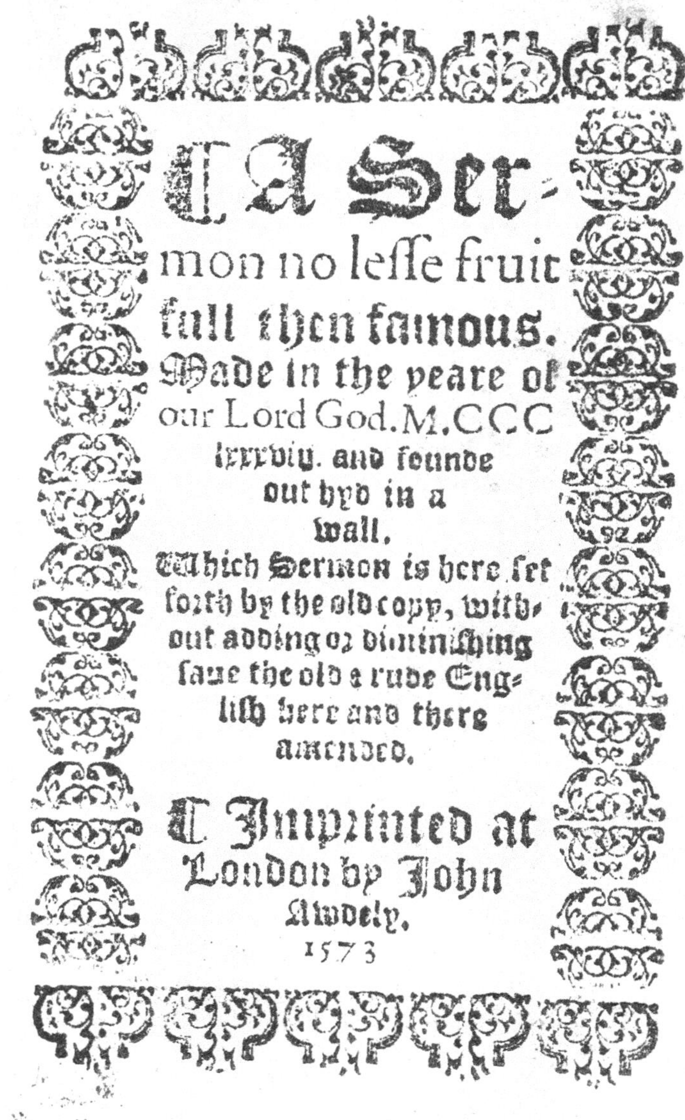

A Ser-
mon no lesse fruit
full then famous.
Made in the yeare of
our Lord God. M.CCC
lxxxviij. and founde
out hyd in a
wall.
Which Sermon is here set
forth by the old copy, without adding or diminishing
saue the old & rude Eng-
lish here and there
amended.

Imprinted at
London by John
Awdely.
1573

VIII ***A Sermon no lesse fruitfull then famous*** **(1573).** Thomas Wimbledon's fiery *Sermon*, originally delivered at Paul's Cross in 1387 or 1388, was widely circulated in manuscript format, and, because perceived to be a precursor of reformed religion, was regularly reprinted during the sixteenth and seventeenth centuries. This edition was printed by John Awdelay in 1573; in later editions Awdelay added the word *GODLY* to the title (see Chapter 3). (© British Library Board, London: 1359.a.49, title page)

Be blessed by the boke in bodye and soule.
Labores manuum tuarum.&c.
Yet I pray you ꝙ Pierce praye Charitie & ye canne,
Any leche crafte lere it me my deare
For some of my seruauntes and my selfe bothe
Of al a weke workenot, so our wombeaketh,
I wote well ꝙ Hunger, what sikenes you ayleth
Ye haue manged ouer muche, & ỷ maketh you grone,
And I hote the ꝙ Hunger, as thou thy hele wilneste
That thou drinke no day, ere thou dyne somewhat
Eatenot I hote the, ere Hunger the take,
And send the of hys sauce to sauour wyth thy lyppes
And kepe some tyll souper time, and sytte not to long
And ryse vp ere appetite haue eaten his fyll
Lette not syr Surfet syt on thy borde
Leue him not for he is lecherours & licorous of tong
And after mani maner of meat his maw is a hūgred
And if thou diet the thus, I dare laye my eares
That phisike shal his furred hodde, for his foode sell
And hys cloke of Calabrye, wͭ al his knaps of golde,
And be fayne by my fayth his phisike to lette
And lerne to laboure wͭ hond, for lyue lode is swete,
For murtherers are many leches lorde hem amende.
They do mē dye by their drinkes yer destiny it wolde
By. S. Paule ꝙ Pierce these ar profitable wordes
Wend ỷ honger when ỷ wylt, ỷ wel be thou euer
For this is a louely lesson, Lord it the foryeld,
Bihote god quod honger, hence ne will I wende
Til I haue dined by this day, and dronken both.
I haue no peny quod Pierce, polettes for to bie
Ne neither gose ne grys, but two grene cheses
A fewe curdes and creame, and an hauer cake

How Pieres prayeth hūger to teche him a lich craft for hym and for hys seruauntes

I.iii. And

IX **William Langland, *The vision of Pierce Plowman* (1550).** The poet, printer and evangelical controversialist Robert Crowley published three editions of *Piers Plowman* in 1550, perhaps as a response to the social upheavals of the previous year. This illustration is from the first edition; on the fly-leaf of this copy appears the inscription 'Robertus Burton Armiger me possidet' (see Chapter 4). Robert Burton is better known to literary historians as the author of *The Anatomy of Melancholy* (1621). (By permission of Glasgow University Library: Sp Coll 1168, folio 35r)

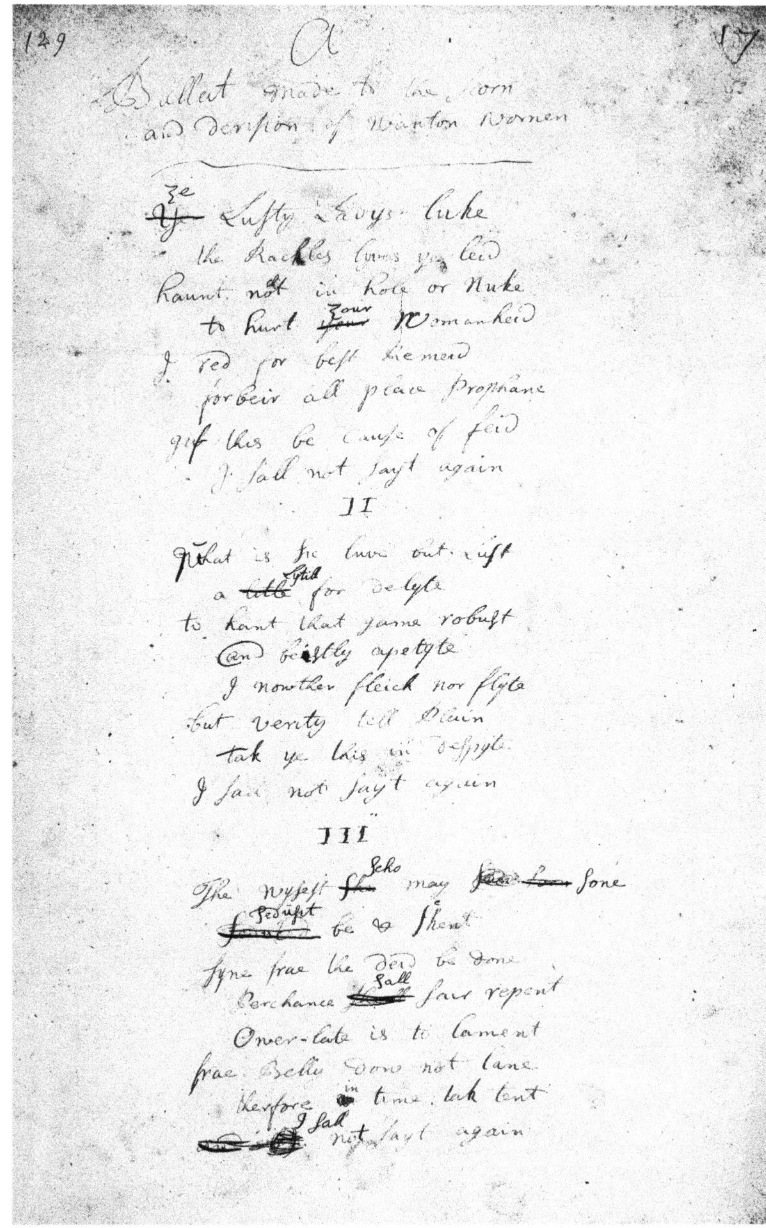

129 A 17

Ballat made to the scorn
and derision of wanton women

Ze Lusty Ladys luke
the Rackles Cums ye leid
haunt not in hole or nuke
to hurt Zour Womanheid
I red for best remeid
forbeir all place prophane
gif this be cause of feid
I sall not say't again

II

What is sic luve but lust
a Stull for delyte
to haunt that same robust
and beastly apetyte
I nowther fleich nor flyte
but verity tell plain
tak ye this in despyte
I sall not say't again

III

The wysest Scho may sone
Seduist be & shent
Syne frae the deid be done
Perchance Sall sair repent
Over-late is to lament
frae Bellie dow not lane
therefore in time tak tent
I sall not say't again

X **Allan Ramsay (1686–1758)** was one of the most important figures in the early eighteenth-century 'vernacular revival' of poetry in Scots. He prepared this handwritten text of *The Ever Green* for the use of his printer, Thomas Ruddiman, who published the work in 1723–4; the Egerton copy is itself derived from the Bannatyne manuscript, 'wrote by the Ingenious' in 1568. This picture shows some of Ramsay's corrections to his transcription (see Chapter 5). (© British Library Board, London: MS Egerton 2024, folio 53r)

VIRGIL's Æneis,

Tranflated into *SCOTTISH* Verfe,

BY THE

Famous Gawin Douglas
Bifhop of Dunkeld.

A new EDITION.

WHEREIN

The many Errors of the Former are corrected, and the Defects fupply'd, from an excellent MANUSCRIPT.

To which is added

A Large Gloffary,

Explaining the Difficult Words: Which may ferve for a Dictionary to the Old SCOTTISH Language.

By Mr Thomas Ruddiman

And to the whole is prefix'd

An Exact Account of the Author's Life and Writings, from the beft Hiftories and Records.

By the Reverend John Sage

EDINBURGH,

Printed by Mr. ANDREW SYMSON, and Mr. ROBERT FREEBAIRN, and fold at their Shops. MDCCX.

XI **Gavin Douglas, *Eneados* (1710).** Thomas Ruddiman was one of the most accomplished scholars of his age, and his edition of the *Eneados* demonstrated not only his solid grasp of Older Scots but his profound engagement with the Latin original (see Chapter 5). (By permission of Glasgow University Library: Sp Coll Bo2–b.13, title page)

SIR TRISTREM;

a

Metrical Romance

of

The Thirteenth Century;

BY

THOMAS OF ERCILDOUNE,

CALLED

THE RHYMER.

EDITED FROM THE AUCHINLECK MS.

BY

WALTER SCOTT, ESQ.

ADVOCATE.

Now, hold your mouth, pour charitie,
Both Knight and Lady fre,
And herkneth to my spell;
Of battaille and of chivalrie,
Of Ladies' love and druerie,
Anon I wol you tel.—CHAUCER.

EDINBURGH:

Printed by James Ballantyne,

FOR ARCHIBALD CONSTABLE AND CO. EDINBURGH,

AND LONGMAN AND REES, LONDON.

1804.

XII ***Sir Tristrem*** **(1804).** Walter Scott's edition of *Sir Tristrem*, derived from the fourteenth-century Auchinleck manuscript, set new standards for the presentation of a medieval romance. However, the blackletter typeface used for the subtitle and for the name of the printer – Scott's friend, James Ballantyne – reflects an older antiquarian tradition that would persist for many years to come (see Chapter 6). (By permission of the National Library of Scotland, Edinburgh: F.5.f.42, title page, under the Creative Commons 4.0 International Public License, for which see https://creativecommons.org/licenses/by/4.0/legalcode)

Bibliography

List of Abbreviations, Used Below and Elsewhere

BL	British Library
ECCO	Eighteenth-Century Collections Online
EEBO	Early English Books Online
EETS	Early English Text Society
ESTC	English Short-Title Catalogue
LALME	Linguistic Atlas of Late Medieval English
MED	Middle English Dictionary
NLS	National Library of Scotland
ODNB	Oxford Dictionary of National Biography
OED	Oxford English Dictionary
STS	Scottish Text Society

List of Manuscripts Cited

Cambridge, Corpus Christi College, MS 198
Cambridge, Corpus Christi College, MS 286
Cambridge, Corpus Christi College, MS 357
Cambridge, Corpus Christi College, MS 402
Cambridge, Corpus Christi College, MS 449
Cambridge, Magdalene College, MS Pepys 2125
Cambridge, Magdalene College, MS Pepys 2498
Cambridge, Magdalene College, MS Pepys 2553 (the Maitland Folio manuscript)
Cambridge, Pembroke College, MS 307
Cambridge, Sidney Sussex College, MS 74
Cambridge, St John's College, MS G.23
Cambridge, St John's College, MS G.29
Cambridge, Trinity College, MS B.14.38
Cambridge, Trinity College MS B.15.17
Cambridge, University Library, MS Additional 6578
Cambridge, University Library, MS Additional 6686
Cambridge, University Library, MS Ff.6.31

Cambridge, University Library, MS Gg 1.1
Cambridge, University Library MS Gg 4.31
Cambridge, University Library, MS Ll 4.14
Cambridge, University Library, MS Ll 5.10 (the Reidpeth manuscript)
Cambridge, University Library, Syn.3.50.3
Copenhagen, MS Ny kgl. Saml. AM 448 4°
Copenhagen, MS Ny kgl. Saml. 167b
Copenhagen, MS Ny kgl. Saml. 512 4° (Thorkelin B transcript of *Beowulf*)
Copenhagen, MS Ny kgl. Saml. 513 4° (Thorkelin A transcript of *Beowulf*)
Edinburgh, National Library of Scotland, MS 2233
Edinburgh, National Library of Scotland, MS 6127
Edinburgh, National Library of Scotland, MS Advocates' 1.1.6 (the Bannatyne manuscript)
Edinburgh, National Library of Scotland, MS Advocates' 18.1.7
Edinburgh, National Library of Scotland, MS Advocates' 19.2.1 (the Auchinleck manuscript)
Edinburgh, National Library of Scotland, MS Advocates' 19.2.2
Edinburgh, National Library of Scotland, MS Advocates' 19.3.1
Edinburgh, University Library, MS Dc 1.43 (the Ruthven manuscript)
Exeter, Cathedral Library, MS 3501 (the Exeter Book)
Glasgow, University Library, MS Hunter 176 (T.8.8)
Glasgow, University Library, MS Hunter 409 (V.3.7)
olim Helmingham Hall, Suffolk, MS LJ II.2 (now in an unspecified private collection; see Edwards and Griffiths 2000: 360, item 43)
Lichfield, Cathedral Library, MS 29
London, British Library, MS Additional 10053
London, British Library, MS Additional 19901
London, British Library, MS Additional 22283 (the Simeon manuscript)
London, British Library, MS Additional 27879 (the Percy Folio manuscript)
London, British Library, MS Additional 37677
London, British Library, MS Additional 37787
London, British Library, MS Additional 47967
London, British Library, MS Cotton Cleopatra C.vi
London, British Library, MS Cotton Faustina A.ix
London, British Library, MS Cotton Julius A.ii
London, British Library, MS Cotton Julius E.vii
London, British Library, MS Cotton Nero A.xiv
London, British Library, MS Cotton Otho A.vi
London, British Library, MS Cotton Titus D.xviii
London, British Library, MS Cotton Vitellius A.xv (part II) (the Nowell Codex)
London, British Library, MS Egerton 2024
London, British Library, MS Harley 874
London, British Library, MS Harley 1758
London, British Library, MS Harley 2398
London, British Library, MS Royal 8 C.i

London, British Library, MS Royal 15 B.xxii
London, British Library, MS Royal 18 A.xvii
London, British Library, MS Royal 18 B.xviii
London, British Library, MS Royal 18 C.ii
London, British Library, MS Sloane 1686
London, Lambeth Palace, MS 487
London, Society of Antiquaries, MS 134
London, University Library, V.17 (part of the Clopton manuscript)
Longleat House, Wiltshire MS 258
New Haven, Yale University Library, MS Beinecke 535
New Haven, Yale University Library, MS Takamiya 23 (olim Sion College)
Oxford, Bodleian Library, Arch. Selden. MS B.24
Oxford, Bodleian Library, MS Auct. D.2.19 (the Rushworth Gospels)
Oxford, Bodleian Library, MS Barlow 20
Oxford, Bodleian Library, MS Bodley 277
Oxford, Bodleian Library, MS Bodley 343
Oxford, Bodleian Library, MS Bodley 938
Oxford, Bodleian Library, MS Bodley 959
Oxford, Bodleian Library, MS Digby 86
Oxford, Bodleian Library, MS Digby 145
Oxford, Bodleian Library, MS Douce 25
Oxford, Bodleian Library, MS Eng. poet. A.1 (the Vernon manuscript)
Oxford, Bodleian Library, MS Eng. th. f.39 (*olim* Helmingham Hall, Suffolk, MS LJ II.9)
Oxford, Bodleian Library, MS Fairfax 3
Oxford, Bodleian Library, MS Hatton 57
Oxford, Bodleian Library, MS Junius 11 (the Caedmon manuscript)
Oxford, Bodleian Library, MS Junius 12
Oxford, Bodleian Library, MS Junius 121
Oxford, Bodleian Library, MS Laud Misc. 622
Oxford, Bodleian Library, MS Rawlinson B.203
Oxford, Bodleian Library, MS Rawlinson C.208
Oxford, Bodleian Library, MS Wood empt. 17
Oxford, Brasenose College, MS 9
Oxford, Trinity College, MS D.29
Oxford, University College, MS 97
Petworth House, Kent, MS 7
Princeton, University Library, Taylor 11 (part of the Clopton manuscript)
Reykjavík, Arni Magnusson Institute, MS GKS 2365 4° (Codex Regius)
San Marino, Huntington Library, MS EL 26 A.17 (the Stafford manuscript)
San Marino, Huntington Library, MS EL 26 C.9 (the Ellesmere manuscript)
San Marino, Huntington Library, MS HM 502
Tokyo, Waseda University Library, MS NE 3691
Vercelli, Biblioteca Capitolare, MS CXVII (the Vercelli Book)

Washington, DC, Folger Shakespeare Library, MS V.b.236 (part of the Clopton manuscript)
Worcester, Cathedral Library, MS F.174

List of Manuscripts Cited, and Destroyed in the Ashburnham House Fire (1731)

MS Cotton Otho A.xii
MS Cotton Otho B.x

List of Books Cited, and Printed before 1800

[All the following pre-1800 publications are reproduced in ECCO and EEBO, unless marked with an asterisk *]

Anderson, Andro (pr) 1666, 1673. *The Life and Acts of the Most famous and valiant Champion, Sir William Wallace* (Edinburgh: Anderson) (= Hary)
(pr) 1670. *The Acts and Life of the Most victorious Conquerour Robert Bruce, King of Scotland* (Edinburgh: Anderson) (= Barbour)
Anon. 1633. *The Psalms of David, in prose and metre* (Aberdeen: Raban)
1693. *A Specimen of the Several Sorts of Letter, Given to the University by Dr. John Fell, Late Lord Bishop of Oxford. To which is Added The Letter Given by Mr F. Junius* (Oxford: Printed at the Theater)
(ed.) 1712. *The Life and Conversation of Richard Bentley, delivered in his own words, for the most part from his own writings* (London: Morphew)*
?1737. *The Session of the Critics …* (London: Cooper)
Awdelay, John 1559. *The Wonders of England* (London: Awdelay)
(pr) 1573. *A Sermon no lesse fruitfull then famous* (London: Awdelay) (= Wimbledon)
Barbour 1571 = Lekpreuik; Barbour 1616 = Hart; Barbour 1620 = Hart; Barbour 1648 = Lithgow; Barbour 1665 = Sanders; Barbour 1670 = Anderson; Barbour 1672 = Sanders; Barbour 1737 = Carmichael and Miller; Barbour '1715'/'1758' = Freebairn; Barbour 1790 = Pinkerton
Baron, Robert 1636. *Canons and constitutions ecclesiasticall* (Aberdeen: Raban)
Bentley, Richard 1699. *A dissertation on the epistles of Phalaris* (London: Mortlock and Hartley)
1720. *Η ΚΑΙΝΗ ΔΙΑΘΗΚΗ, Graece Novum Testamentum Versionis Vulgatae* (Cambridge: n.p.)
(ed.) 1732. *Milton's Paradise Lost: A new edition* (London: Tonson)
Berthelette, Thomas (pr) 1532, 1554. *Jo. Gower de confessione Amantis* (London: Berthelette)

Blow, James (pr) 1728. *The Life and Acts of the most famous and valiant Champion, Sir William Wallace* (Belfast: Blow) (= Hary)*

Boorde, Andrew 1555. *The fyrst boke of the introduction of knowledge* (London: Copland)

Bryson, James (pr) 1640, 1645. *The Life and Acts of the most famous and valiant Champion, Sr. William Wallace* (Edinburgh: Bryson) (= Hary)

of Buchan, Earl ('overlooked by') 1790. *The Metrical History of William Wallace* (Perth: Morison) (= Hary)

du Cange, Sieur Charles du Fresne 1678. *Glossarium ad scriptores mediae & infimae Latinitatis* (Paris: Martin)*

Carmichael, Alexander and Alexander Miller (pr) 1737. *The Acts and Life of the Most victorious Conquerour Robert Bruce, King of Scotland* (Glasgow: Carmichael and Miller) (= Barbour)

Cates, Thomas (pr) 1635. *A Sermon, No less fruitfull, then Famous* (London: Cates) (= Wimbledon)

Caxton, William (pr) 1477. [Chaucer, *Canterbury Tales*] (Westminster: Caxton)

(pr) 1483a. [Gower, *Confessio Amantis*] (Westminster: Caxton)

(pr) 1483b. [Chaucer, *Canterbury Tales*] (Westminster: Caxton)

(pr) 1484, 1490. [Love, *Mirror of the Blessed Life of Jesus Christ*] (Westminster: Caxton)

Charteris, Henrie (pr) 1594. *The lyfe and actis of the maist illuster and vailzeand campioun VVilliam Wallace* (Edinburgh: Charteris) (= Hary)

Charteris, Robert (pr) 1601. *The lyfe and actis of the maist illuster and vailzeand campioun VVilliam Wallace* (Edinburgh: Charteris) (= Hary)

Chaucer 1477 = Caxton; Chaucer 1483 = Caxton; Chaucer 1492 = Pynson; Chaucer 1498 = de Worde; Chaucer 1526 = Pynson; Chaucer 1532 = Thynne; Chaucer 1542 = Thynne; Chaucer 1550 = Thynne; Chaucer 1561 = Stow; Chaucer 1598 = Speght; Chaucer 1602 = Speght; Chaucer 1682 = Harefinch; Chaucer 1721 = Urry; Chaucer 1775 = Tyrwhitt

Chepman, Walter and Andro Myllar (pr) 1509. [Hary's *Wallace*] (Edinburgh: Chepman and Myllar)*

Churchyard, Thomas 1552. *Davy Dycars Dreme* (London: Lant)

Copland, William (pr) 1553a. *The Palis of Honoure Compeled by Gawyne dowglas Bysshope of Dunkyll* (London: Copland)

(pr) 1553b. *The xiii Bukes of Eneados of the famose Poete Virgill Translatet out of Latyne verses into Scottish metir, bi the Reuerend fathir in God, Mayster Gawin Douglas Bishop of Dunkel & vnkil to the Erle of Angus* (London: Copland)

Crowley, Robert 1548. *An Informacion and Peticion Agaynst the Oppressours of the Poore* (London: Day)

1549. *The Voyce of the Laste Trumpet* (London: Grafton for Crowley)

(ed.) 1550a. *The Vision of Pierce Plowman*, 1st edn (London: Grafton for Crowley)

(ed.) 1550b. *The Vision of Pierce Plowman*, 2nd edn (London: Grafton for Crowley) (ed.) 1550c. *The Vision of Pierce Plowman*, 2nd (= 3rd) edn (London: Grafton for Crowley)

1550d. *One and Thyrtye Epigrammes* (London: Crowley)

1550e. *The Way to Wealth* (London: Mierdman for Crowley)

1551. *Philargyrie of Greate Britayne* (London: Crowley)

Descartes, René 1649. *Les passions de l'âme* (Paris: de Gras)*

Dickson, David 1635. *A short explanation, of the epistle of Paul to the Hebrewes* (Aberdeen: Raban)

Douglas 1553a = Copland; Douglas 1553b = Copland; Douglas 1710 = Ruddiman

Drummond of Hawthornden, William 1616. *Poems* (Edinburgh: Hart)

Erasmus, Desiderius 1530. *De recta Latini Grecisque sermonis pronuntiatione* (Basle: Froben)*

Foxe, John 1563. *Acts and Monuments of matters most speciall and memorable* (London: Day)

(ed.) 1571, *The Gospels of the Fower Euangelistes, Translated in the Old Saxon Tyme out of Latin into the Vulgare Toung of the Saxons* (London: Day)

Freebairn, Robert (pr) '1715'/'1758'a. *The Life and Acts of the Most Victorious Conqueror Robert Bruce, King of Scotland* (Edinburgh: Freebairn) (= Barbour)

(pr) '1715'/'1758'b. *The Acts and Deeds of the Most Famous and Valiant Champion, Sir William Wallace* (Edinburgh: Freebairn) (= Hary)

Gau, John (trans) 1533. *The richt way to the kingdome of heuine* (Malmö: Hochstraten)

The Gentleman's Magazine, October, 1731*

Gower 1483 = Caxton; Gower 1532 = Berthelette; Gower 1554 = Berthelette

Guild, William 1624. *Three Rare Monuments of Antiquitie* (Aberdeen: Raban)

Hailes, Lord (Sir David Dalrymple) (ed.) 1770. *Ancient Scottish Poems* (Edinburgh: Balfour)

Harefinch, John (?) (pr) 1687. *The Works of our Ancient, Learned & Excellent Poet, Jeffrey Chaucer* (London: J. H.)

Hart, Andro (pr) 1611, 1618, 1620b. *The life and acts of the most famous and valiant campion, Sir William Wallace* (Edinburgh: Hart) (= Hary)

(pr) 1616, 1620a. *The actes and life of the most victoriovs conquerouvr Robert Bruce, king of Scotland* (Edinburgh: Hart) (= Barbour)

Hary 1509 = Chepman and Myllar; Hary 1570 = Lekpreuik; Hary 1594 = Charteris;

Hary 1601 = Charteris; Hary 1611 = Hart; Hary 1618 = Hart; Hary 1620 = Hart; Hary 1630 = Raban; Hary 1640 = Bryson; Hary 1645 = Bryson; Hary 1648 = Lithgow; Hary 1661a = Lithgow; Hary 1661b = 'Society of Stationers'; Hary 1665 = Sanders; Hary 1666 = Anderson; Hary 1673 = Anderson; Hary 1684 = Sanders; Hary 1685 = Sanders; Hary 1690 = Sanders; Hary 1699 = Sanders; Hary 1713 = Sanders; Hary '1715'/'1758' = Freebairn; Hary 1728 = Blow; Hary 1790 = Buchan, Earl of

Hearne, Thomas (ed.) 1722. *Johannis de Fordun Scotichronicon* (Oxford: e Theatro Sheldoniano)

1726. *Johannis Confratris et Monachi Glastoniensis Chronica* (Oxford: e Theatro Sheldoniano)

Hickes, George and Humfrey Wanley 1705, *Linguarum Vett. Septentrionalium Thesaurus Grammatico-Criticus et Archaeologicus* (Oxford: e Theatro Sheldoniano)

Jaggard, William (pr) 1617. *A Sermon No lesse Fruitefull, then Famous* (London: Jaggard) (= Wimbledon)

James VI, king of Scots 1585. *Essayis of a Prentise in the Divine Art of Poesie* (Edinburgh: Vautrollier)

Jonson, Ben 1640. *The English Grammar made by Ben. Iohnson* (London: n.p.)

Joscelyn, John (ed.) 1566. *A testimonie of antiquitie, shewing the auncient faith in the Church of England touching the sacrament of the body and bloude of the Lord here publikely preached, and also receaued in the Saxons tyme, aboue 600. yeares agoe* (London: Day)

Langland 1550a = Crowley; Langland 1550b = Crowley; Langland 1550c = Crowley; Langland 1561 = Rogers

Lekpreuik, Robert (pr) 1570. *The actis and deidis of the illuster and vailzeand campioun, Schir William Wallace* (Edinburgh: Lekpreuik for Charteris) (= Hary)

(pr) 1571. *The actys and lyfe of Robert Bruce King of Scotland* (Edinburgh: Lekpreuik for Charteris) (= Barbour)

L'Isle, William (ed.) 1623. *A Saxon Treatise Concerning the Old and New Testament* (London: Haviland)

Lithgow, Gedeon (pr) 1648a. *The Life and Acts of the most victorious Conquerour Robert Bruce, King of Scotland* (Edinburgh: Lithgow) (= Barbour)

(pr) 1648b, 1661. *The Life and Acts of the most valiant Champion, Sir William Wallace* (Edinburgh: Lithgow) (= Hary)

Love, Nicholas 1484 = Caxton; Love, Nicholas 1490 = Caxton; Love, Nicholas 1494 = Pynson; Love, Nicholas 1506 = Pynson; Love, Nicholas 1517 = de Worde; Love, Nicholas 1525 = de Worde

Macpherson, David (ed.) 1795. *The orygynale cronykil of Scotland* (London: Bensley)*

Morgan, Joseph 1732. *Phoenix Britannicus* (London: Morgan, Edlin and Wilford)

Morison, Robert (pr) 1790. *The Metrical History of William Wallace* (Perth: Morison) (= Hary; see also Buchan, Earl of)

Moxon, Joseph 1683. *Mechanick Exercises, or, The Doctrine of Handy-works* (London: Moxon)

Ogle, George (ed. and trans.) 1741. *The Canterbury Tales of Chaucer, modernis'd by several hands* (London: Tonson)

Panter, Patrick 1633. *Valliados: de gestis Illustrissimi GULIELMI VALLÆ* (Edinburgh: Hart)

Percy, Thomas (ed.) 1763. *Five Pieces of Runic Poetry* (London: Dodsley)

(ed.) 1765. *Reliques of Ancient English Poetry* (London: Dodsley)

Pinkerton, John (ed.) 1790. *The Bruce; or, The History of Robert I, King of Scotland* (London: Nicol) (= Barbour)

Poyntz, Robert 1566. *Testimonies for the Real Presence of Christes Body and Blood in the Blessed Sacrament*

Pynson, Richard (pr) 1492. [Chaucer, *Canterbury Tales*] (Westminster: Pynson)
(pr) 1494, 1506. *Incipit Speculum Vite Cristi* (London: Pynson) (= Love)
(pr) 1526. *Here begynneth the boke of Canterbury tales* (London: Pynson)
Raban, Edward (pr) 1630. *The Lyfe and Acts of the most famous and valiant Champion, Sir William Wallace* (Aberdeen: Raban) (= Hary)
Ramsay, Allan 1721. *Poems* (Edinburgh: Ruddiman)
(ed.) 1723–4. *The Ever Green, being a collection of Scots Poems, Wrote by the Ingenious before 1600* (Edinburgh: Ruddiman)
Rawlinson, Christopher (ed.) 1698. *An. Manl. Sever. Boethi Consolationis Philosophiae Libri V. Anglo-Saxonice redditi ab Alfredo, Inclyto Anglo-Saxonum Rege. Ad apographum Junianum expressos edidit Christophorus Rawlinson e Collegio Reginae* (Oxford: e Theatro Sheldoniano)*
Ritson, Joseph (ed.) 1783. *A Select Collection of English Songs* (London: Johnson)
Rogers, Owen (pr) 1561. *The vision of Pierce Plowman* (London: Rogers)
Ruddiman, Thomas (ed.) 1710. *Virgil's Æneis, Translated into Scottish Verse, by the Famous Gawin Douglas Bishop of Dunkeld* (Edinburgh: Symson and Freebairn)
1714. *The Rudiments of the Latin Tongue, or A plain and easy Introduction to Latin Grammar* (Edinburgh: Freebairn)
Salesbury, William 1550. *A briefe and playne introduction, teachyng how to pronounce the letters of the British tong* (London: Grafton for Crowley)
1567. *A playne and a familiar introduction* (London: Denham)
Sanders, Robert (father and son) (pr) 1665a, 1684, 1685, 1690, 1699, 1713. *The Life and Acts of the most famous and valiant Champion, Sir William Wallace* (Glasgow: Sanders) (= Hary)
(pr) 1672. *The acts and life of the most victorious conqueror, Robert Bruce, King of Scotland* (Glasgow: Sanders) (= Barbour)
Shakespeare, William 1609. *The Late, And much admired Play, Called Pericles, Prince of Tyre* (London: White and Creede)
Sheridan, Thomas 1759. *A Discourse delivered in the Theatre at Oxford, in the Senate-House at Cambridge, and at Spring-Garden in London* (London: Millar)
Skelton, John 1545 [1554]. *Why come ye nat to Courte* (London: Copland)
'Society of Stationers' (pr) 1661. *The Life and Acts of the most famous Champion, Sir William Wallace* (Edinburgh: Society of Stationers) (= Hary)
Speght, Thomas (ed.) 1598. *The Workes of our Antient and Learned English Poet, Geoffrey Chavcer, newly Printed* (London: Islip)
(ed.) 1602. *The Workes of ovr Ancient and Learned English Poet, Geoffrey Chavcer, newly Printed* (London: Islip)
Spenser, Edmund 1579. *The Shepheardes Calender* (London: Singleton)
Stow, John (ed.) 1561. *The Workes of Geffrey Chaucer* (London: Kyngston)
1598. *A Suruay of London* (London: Windet)
Strutt, Joseph 1779. *The Chronicle of England* (London: Evans and Faulder)
Suhm, Peter 1787. *Symbolae ad Literaturam Teutonicam Antiqviorem* (Copenhagen: Horrebow)*

Swift, Jonathan 1704. *A Tale of a Tub* (London: Nutt)

Symson, Andrew 1705. *Tripatriarchicon, Or, the Lives of the three Patriarchs, Abraham, Isaac and Jacob, Extracted forth of the Sacred Story, and digested into English Verse* (Edinburgh: Symson)

Thomas, Percy, 1770. *The Hermit of Warkworth: a Northumberland Ballad* (Alnwick: Davidson)

Thynne, William (ed.) 1532. *The Workes of Geffray Chaucer* (London: Godfray)

(ed.) 1542. *The Workes of Geffray Chaucer* (London: Grafton)

(ed.) 1550. *The Workes of Geffray Chaucer* (London: Hill)

Turner, Sharon 1799–1805. *History of the Anglo-Saxons* (London: Cadell and Davies)

Tyrwhitt, Thomas (ed.) 1775. *The* Canterbury Tales *of Chaucer* (London: Payne)

Urry, John (ed.) 1721. *The Works of Geoffrey Chaucer* (London: Lintot)

Virgil 1679. *Publii Virgilii Maronis Opera* (London: Tyler and Holt)

Willich, Anthony 1798. *Elements of the Critical Philosophy; . . . to which are added: Three Philological Essays* (London: Longman)

[Wimbledon, Thomas] 1540–1. *A Sermon no lesse fruteful then famous* (London: n.p.)

1573 = Awdelay; Wimbledon, Thomas 1617 = Jaggard; Wimbledon, Thomas 1635 = Cates

de Worde, Wynkyn (pr) 1498. *The boke of Chaucer named Caunterbury Tales* (Westminster: de Worde)

(pr) 1517. *Vita Christi* (London: de Worde) (= Love)

(pr) 1525. *Vita Christi* (London: de Worde) (= Love)

List of Cited Specific Copies of Printed Books

Belfast, Queen's University Library, Percy 571 (= Crowley 1550b)
Cambridge, University Library, Syn.3.50.3 (= Chepman and Myllar 1509)†
Edinburgh, National Library of Scotland, DNS/A.5 (= L'Isle 1623)
Edinburgh, National Library of Scotland, F.5.f.42 (= Scott 1804)
Edinburgh, National Library of Scotland, Ry.III.e.8 (= Charteris 1594)
Edinburgh, National Library of Scotland, Ry.IV.f.4 (= Hailes 1770)
Edinburgh, National Library of Scotland, T.387.d (= Thorkelin 1815)
Glasgow, Mitchell Library, S.R.341201 (= Chepman and Myllar 1509)†
Glasgow, University Library, Sp Coll 1168 (= Crowley 1550a)
Glasgow, University Library, Sp Coll Bc30-x.16 (= Thorkelin 1815)
Glasgow, University Library, Sp Coll Bd20-h.24 (= Percy 1765)
Glasgow, University Library, Sp Coll Bm5-f.18 (= Berthelette 1554)
Glasgow, University Library, Sp Coll Bo2-b.13 (= Ruddiman 1710)
London, British Library, C.10.b.15 (= Caxton 1490)
London, British Library, C.37.d.4 (= de Worde 1517)
London, British Library, C.37.d.5 (= de Worde 1525)
London, British Library, C.39.d.24 (= Lekpreuik 1570)

London, British Library, C.65.l.1 (= L'Isle 1623)
London, British Library, G.18516 (= Freebairn '1715'/'1758')
London, British Library, IB.55527 (= Pynson 1494)
London, British Library, 675.f.16 (= Foxe 1571)
London, British Library, 695.a.31 (= Joscelyn 1566)
London, British Library, 1359.a.49 (= Awdelay 1573)
New York, Pierpont Morgan Library, 15586 (= Lekpreuik 1571)
Oxford, Bodleian Library, 297.g.85 (= Tyler et al. 1679)
Oxford, Bodleian Library, Douce L.205 (= Crowley 1550b)
Windsor Castle, Royal Library, RCIN 1018743 (= Leyden 1858)
For volumes still in Sir Walter Scott's library at Abbotsford, see the Catalogue of Edinburgh's Faculty of Advocates: http://voyager.advocates.org.uk/webvoy.htm
† Both sets of the Chepman and Myllar fragments of Hary's *Wallace* are most accessibly consulted by means of the rotographs in the NLS: Edinburgh, National Library of Scotland, F.6.a.8.

General Bibliography

Aarsleff, Hans 1967. *The Study of Language in England 1780–1860* (Princeton University Press)
Aitken, Adam J. 1983. 'The language of Older Scots poetry', in J. Derrick McClure (ed.), *Scotland and the Lowland Tongue: Studies in the Language and Literature of Lowland Scotland in Honour of David D. Murison* (Aberdeen University Press), 18–49
Alderson, William 1984. 'John Urry (1666–1715)', in Ruggiers (ed.), 93–114
Ambrose, Gavin and Paul Harris 2011. *The Fundamentals of Typography*, 2nd edn (Lausanne: AVA Academia)
Anderson, Wendy (ed.) 2013. *Language in Scotland: Corpus-Based Studies* (Amsterdam: Rodopi)
Andersson, Bo 2014. 'Female writing in manuscript and print: Two German examples from the cultural and political context of late seventeenth-century Sweden – Maria Aurora von Königsmarck (1662–1728) and Eva Margaretha Frölich (?–1692)', *Studia Neophilologica* 86, 9–28
Aston, Margaret 1984. *Lollards and Reformers* (London: Hambledon)
Bally and Sechehaye 1916 = Saussure 1916
Barbour 1820 = Jamieson 1820; Barbour 1870–89 = Skeat 1870–89; Barbour 1980–5 = McDiarmid and Stevenson 1980–5
Barbrook, Adrian, Christopher Howe, Norman Blake and Peter Robinson 1998. 'The phylogeny of the *Canterbury Tales*', *Nature* 394, 839
Barker, Nicolas 2002. 'Editing the past: Classical and historical scholarship', in Barnard et al. (eds.), 206–27
Barnard, John 2002. 'Introduction', in Barnard et al. (eds.), 1–25

Barnard, John, Donald F. McKenzie and Maureen Bell (eds.) 2002. *The Cambridge History of the Book in Britain IV: 1557–1695* (Cambridge University Press)

Barton, David 2007. *Literacy: An Introduction to the Ecology of Written Language* (Oxford: Blackwell)

Baugh, Albert C. (ed.) 1956. *The English Text of the Ancrene Riwle, Edited from British Museum MS. Royal 8.C.i* (London: EETS)

Bawcutt, Priscilla (ed.) 1998. *The Poems of William Dunbar* (Glasgow: Association for Scottish Literary Studies)

Bax, Marcel and Daniel Kádár (eds.) 2011. 'Understanding historical (im)politeness', Special Issue, *Journal of Historical Pragmatics* 12.

Beadle, Richard and Rosamund McKitterick 1992. *Catalogue of the Pepys Library at Magdalene College, Cambridge. V. Manuscripts i. Medieval* (Woodbridge: Brewer)

Bédier, Joseph 1890. *Le Lai de l'ombre* (Fribourg: L'Œuvre de Saint-Paul)

1922. *La Chanson de Roland* (Paris: L'Edition de l'Art)

1928. 'La Tradition manuscrite du *Lai de l'Ombre*', *Romania* 54, 161–96

Bell, Maureen 2002. 'Mise-en-page, illustration, expressive form: Introduction', in Barnard et al., 632–5

Benskin, Michael 1982. 'The letter <þ> and <y> in later Middle English, and some related matters', *Journal of the Society of Archivists* 7, 13–30

2004. '"Chancery Standard"', in Christian Kay, Carole Hough and Irene Wotherspoon (eds.), *New Perspectives on English Historical Linguistics*, volume II (*Lexis and Transmission*) (Amsterdam: Benjamins), 1–40

Benskin, Michael and Michael L. Samuels (eds.) 1981. *So meny people longages and tonges: Philological Essays in Scots and Mediaeval English Presented to Angus McIntosh* (Edinburgh: Benskin and Samuels)

Benson, Larry (gen. ed.) 1987. *The Riverside Chaucer* (London: Oxford University Press)

Bergs, Alexander 2012. 'The uniformitarian principle and the risk of anachronisms in language and social history', in Juan Manuel Hernández-Campoy and Juan Camilo Conde-Silvestre (eds.), *The Handbook of Historical Sociolinguistics* (Malden: Wiley-Blackwell), 80–99

Bergstrøm, Geir 2017. '"Yeuen at Cavmbrigg": A study of the medieval English documents of Cambridge', PhD thesis, University of Stavanger

Birkett, Tom 2014. 'Unlocking runes? Reading Anglo-Saxon runic abbreviations in their immediate literary context', *Futhark: International Journal of Runic Studies* 5, 91–134

Black, Robert and Raymond St-Jacques (eds.) 2012. *The Middle English Glossed Prose Psalter* (Heidelberg: Winter)

Blake, Norman (ed.) 1972. *Middle English Religious Prose* (London: Arnold)

Bliss, Alan J. (ed.) 1969. *Sir Orfeo* (Oxford: Clarendon Press)

Blodgett, James E. 1984. 'William Thynne (d. 1546)', in Ruggiers (ed.), 35–53

Bradley, Sidney A. J. (trans.) 1982. *Anglo-Saxon Poetry* (London: Dent)

Bray, Robyn 2013. '"A scholar, a gentleman, and a Christian": John Josias Conybeare (1779–1824) and his *Illustrations of Anglo-Saxon Poetry* (1826)', PhD thesis, University of Glasgow

Bremmer, Rolf 1991. 'Hermes–Mercury and Woden–Odin as inventors of alphabets: A neglected parallel', in Alfred Bammesberger (ed.), *Old English Runes and Their Continental Background* (Heidelberg: Winter), 409–19

(ed.) 1998. *Franciscus Junius F. F. and His Circle* (Amsterdam/Atlanta: Rodopi)

Brewer, Charlotte 1996. *Editing Piers Plowman* (Cambridge University Press)

Brewer, John 1997. *The Pleasures of the Imagination: English Culture in the Eighteenth Century* (London: HarperCollins)

Briggs, Charles 2000. 'Literacy, reading, and writing in the medieval West', *Journal of Medieval History* 26, 397–420

Bromwich, John 1962. 'The first book printed in Anglo-Saxon types', *Transactions of the Cambridge Bibliographical Society* 3, 265–91

Brown, Michael 2015. 'Barbour's *Bruce* in the 1480s: Literature and locality', in Steven Boardman and Susan Foran (eds.), *Barbour's Bruce and Its Cultural Contexts: Politics, Chivalry and Literature* (Cambridge: Brewer), 213–31

Brown, Stephen, and Warren McDougall (eds.) 2012. *The Edinburgh History of the Book in Scotland*, volume II (*Enlightenment and Expansion 1707–1800*) (Edinburgh University Press)

Brunsden, George 1999. 'Aspects of Scotland's social, political and cultural scene in the late 17th and early 18th centuries, as mirrored in the *Wallace* and *Bruce* traditions,' in Edward Cowan and Douglas Gifford (eds.), *The Polar Twins* (East Linton: Tuckwell), 75–113

Burnyeat, Myles 1997. 'Postscript on silent reading', *The Classical Quarterly* 47, 74–6

Burrow, John A. 1982. *Medieval Writers and Their Work* (Oxford University Press)

Butler, Emily 2014. 'Recollecting Alfredian English in the sixteenth century', *Neophilologus* 98, 145–59

Butt, Peter and Richard Castle 2001. *Modern Legal Drafting: A Guide to Using Clearer Language* (Cambridge University Press)

Caie, Graham D. 2008. 'The manuscript experience: What medieval vernacular manuscripts tell us about authors and texts', in Renevey and Caie (eds.), 10–27

2011. 'The relationship between MS Glasgow, Hunter 409 and the 1532 edition of Chaucer's works by William Thynne', in Pahta and Jucker (eds.), 149–61

Campbell, Alistair (ed.) 1962. *The Chronicle of Æthelweard* (London: Nelson)

Campbell, Lyle 2006. 'Why Sir William Jones got it all wrong', *International Journal of Basque Linguistics and Philology* 40, 245–64

Carpenter, Leona, Simon Shaw and Andrew Prescott (eds.) 1998. *Towards the Digital Library* (London: The British Library)

Carroll, Ruth, Matti Peikola, Hanna Salmi, Janne Skaffari, Mari-Liisa Varila and Risto Hiltunen 2013. 'Pragmatics on the page: Visual text in late medieval English books', in J. Kendall, M. Portela and G. White (eds.), 'Visual text', Special Issue, *European Journal of English Studies* 17, 54–71

Carroll, Ruth, Risto Hiltunen, Matti Peikola, Janne Skaffari, Sanna-Kaisa Tanskanen, Ellen Valle and Brita Wårvik 2003. 'Introduction', in Risto Hiltunen and Janne Skaffari (eds.), *Discourse Perspectives on English: Medieval to Modern* (Amsterdam: Benjamins), 1–12

Carruthers, Gerard and Pauline Gray (intro.) 2009. *Robert Burns: The Fornicators Court* (Edinburgh: Abbotsford Library Project Trust/Faculty of Advocates)

Carruthers, Mary 1990. *The Book of Memory* (Cambridge University Press)

Cartlidge, Neil 2001. 'The *Canterbury Tales* and cladistics', *Neuphilologische Mitteilungen* 102, 135–50

Cerquiglini, Bernard 1991. *La Naissance du français* (Paris: Presses Universitaires de France)

(trans. Betsy Wing) 1999. *In Praise of the Variant: A Critical History of Philology* (Baltimore: Johns Hopkins Press)

Chambers, R. W. and Marjorie Daunt (eds.) 1931. *A Book of London English 1384–1425* (Oxford: Clarendon Press)

Chomsky, Noam 1965. *Aspects of the Theory of Syntax* (Cambridge, Mass.: MIT Press)

Clanchy, Michael 1993. *From Memory to Written Record*, 2nd edn (Oxford: Blackwell)

Clemoes, Peter 1952. *Liturgical Influence on Punctuation in Late Old English and Early Middle English Manuscripts*. Occasional Papers 1. (Cambridge: Museum of Archaeology and Ethnology/Department of Anglo-Saxon)

Cohen, Michael and Robert Bourdette 1980. 'Richard Bentley's edition of *Paradise Lost* (1732): A bibliography', *Milton Quarterly* 14, 49–54

Coleman, Joyce 1996. *Public Reading and the Reading Public in Late Medieval England and France* (Cambridge University Press)

Colledge, Eric 1939. '*The Recluse*: A Lollard interpolated version of the *Ancren Riwle*', *Review of English Studies* 15, 1–15

Colley, Linda 1992. *Britons: Forging the Nation, 1707–1837* (New Haven: Yale University Press)

Collinson, Patrick, Arnold Hunt and Alexandra Walsham 2002. 'Religious publishing in England 1557–1640', in Barnard et al. (eds.), 29–66

Connolly, Margaret and Anthony S. G. Edwards 2017. 'Evidence for the history of the Auchinleck Manuscript', *The Library* 18, 292–304

Connolly, Margaret and Raluca Radulescu (eds.) 2015. *Insular Books: Vernacular Manuscript Miscellanies in Late Medieval Britain* (Oxford: The British Academy)

Connor, Patrick 2008. 'The Ruthwell monument runic poem in a tenth-century context', *Review of English Studies*, New Series, 99, 25–51

Cook, Brian 2017. 'Textual homelands: Reinterpreting the manuscript runes of *Beowulf*', *English Studies* 98, 351–67

Cook, Megan 2012. 'How Francis Thynne read his Chaucer', *Journal of the Early Book Society* 15, 214–43

Corbellini, Sabrina, Bart Ramakers and Margriet Hoogvliet (eds.) 2015. *Discovering the Riches of the Word: Religious Reading in Late Medieval and Early Modern Europe* (Leiden: Brill)

Corbett, John 2013. 'The spelling practices of Allan Ramsay and Robert Burns', in Anderson (ed.), 65–90

Cowan, Edward (ed.) 2007. *The Wallace Book* (Edinburgh: Donald)

Crawford, Robert 2009. *The Bard* (London: Jonathan Cape)

Culpeper, Jonathan and Merja Kytö 2010. *Early Modern English Dialogues* (Cambridge University Press)

Dahood, Roger 1988. 'The use of coloured initials and other division markers in early versions of *Ancrene Riwle*', in Edward D. Kennedy, Ronald Waldron and Joseph S. Wittig (eds.), *Medieval English Studies presented to George Kane* (Woodbridge: Brewer), 79–97

Dane, Joseph and Svetlana Djananova 2005. 'The typographical gothic: A cautionary note on the title page to Percy's *Reliques of Ancient English Poetry*', *Eighteenth-Century Life* 29, 76–97

D'Arcy, Julian and Kirsten Wolf 1987. 'Sir Walter Scott and *Eyrbyggja Saga*', *Studies in Scottish Literature* 22, 30–43

Deegan, Marilyn and Kathryn Sutherland (eds.) 2009. *Text Editing, Print and the Digital World* (Farnham: Ashgate)

Dekker, Kees 2000. '"That Most Elaborate One of Fr. Junius": An investigation of Franciscus Junius's manuscript Old English dictionary', in Graham (ed.), 301–44

Dickins, Bruce 1949. 'The Irish broadside of 1571 and Queen Elizabeth's types', *Transactions of the Cambridge Bibliographical Society* 1, 48–60

Dickins, Bruce and Raymond M. Wilson (eds.) 1951. *Early Middle English Texts* (London: Bowes and Bowes)

Dickson, Robert and John Edmond 1890. *Annals of Scottish Printing* (Cambridge: Macmillan and Bowes)

Dobson, Eric J. 1968. *English Pronunciation 1500–1700* (Oxford: Clarendon Press)

(ed.) 1972. *The English Text of the Ancrene Riwle, edited from BM. Cotton MS. Cleopatra C VI* (London: EETS)

1975. *The Origins of Ancrene Wisse* (Oxford: Clarendon Press)

Donaldson, E. Talbot 1970. 'The psychology of editors of Middle English texts', in *Speaking of Chaucer* (London: Athlone), 102–18

Donatelli, Joseph 1993. 'The Percy Folio manuscript: A seventeenth-century context for medieval poetry', *English Manuscript Studies* 4, 114–33

Doyle, A. Ian 1983. 'English books in and out of court from Edward III to Henry VII', in V. J. Scattergood and J. W. Sherborne (eds.), *English Court Culture in the Later Middle Ages* (London: Duckworth), 163–82

(intro.) 1987. *The Vernon Manuscript: A Facsimile of Bodleian Library, Oxford MS. Eng.poet.A.1* (Cambridge: Brewer)

Doyle, A. Ian and Malcolm B. Parkes 1978. 'The production of copies of the *Canterbury Tales* and the *Confessio Amantis* in the early fifteenth century', in Malcolm B. Parkes and Andrew G. Watson (eds.), *Medieval Scribes, Manuscripts and Libraries: Essays Presented to N. R. Ker* (London: Scolar), 163–210

Driver, Martha and Veronica O'Mara (eds.) 2013. *Preaching the Word in Manuscript and Print in Late Medieval England: Essays in Honour of Susan Powell* (Turnhout: Brepols)

Drout, Michael and Scott Kleinman 2010. 'Doing Philology 2: Something "Old", Something "New": Material philology and the recovery of the past', *The Heroic Age* 13 (online publication = www.heroicage.org/issues/13/pi.php, last consulted on 25 May 2019)

Duffy, Eamon 2005. *The Stripping of the Altars*, 2nd edn (New Haven: Yale University Press)

Duncan, Archibald (ed.) 1997. *John Barbour: The Bruce* (Edinburgh: Canongate)

Duncan, Douglas 1965. *Thomas Ruddiman: A Study in Scottish Scholarship of the Early Eighteenth Century* (Edinburgh: Oliver and Boyd)

Echard, Siân (ed.) 2004. *A Companion to Gower* (Woodbridge: Brewer)

2008. *Printing the Middle Ages* (Philadelphia: University of Pennsylvania Press)

Eckert, Penelope and Sally McConnell-Ginet 1992. 'Think practically and look locally: Language and gender as community-based practice', *Annual Review of Anthropology* 21, 461–90

Edwards, Anthony S. G. and Jeremy Griffiths 2000. 'The Tollemache collection of medieval manuscripts', *The Book Collector* 49, 349–64

Edwards, Anthony S. G. and Simon Horobin 2010. 'Further books annotated by Stephen Batman', *The Library* 11, 227–31

Fairclough, Norman 2015. *Language and Power*, 3rd edn (London: Routledge)

Falconer, Alexander (ed.) 1954. *The Percy Letters: The Correspondence of Thomas Percy & David Dalrymple, Lord Hailes* (Baton Rouge: Louisiana State University Press)

Fein, Susanna (ed.) 2016. *The Auchinleck Manuscript: New Perspectives* (York Medieval Press)

Fjalldall, Magnus 2008. 'To fall by ambition – Grimur Thorkelin and his *Beowulf* edition', *Neophilologus* 92, 321–32

Fleming, Daniel 2004. '*Eþel-weard*: The first scribe of the *Beowulf* MS', *Neuphilologische Mitteilungen* 105, 177–86

Fox, Adam 2000. *Oral and Literate Culture in England 1500–1700* (Oxford University Press)

Fox, Denton and William A. Ringler (intro.) 1980. *The Bannatyne Manuscript: National Library of Scotland, Advocates' MS 1.1.6* (London: Scolar Press, in association with the National Library of Scotland)

Frantzen, Allen 1990. *Desire for Origins: New Language, Old English, and Teaching the Tradition* (New Brunswick: Rutgers University Press)

Frantzen, Allen and John Niles (eds.) 1997. *Anglo-Saxonism and the Construction of Social Identity* (Gainesville: University Press of Florida)

Franzen, Christine 1991. *The Tremulous Hand of Worcester: A Study of Old English in the Thirteenth Century* (Oxford: Clarendon Press)

Fulk, Robert D. (ed. and trans.) 2010. *The Beowulf Manuscript* (Cambridge, Mass.: Harvard University Press)

Furnivall, Frederick J. (ed.) 1868. *A Six-Text Print of Chaucer's Canterbury Tales* (London: Chaucer Society)

Furnivall, Frederick J. and G. H. Kingsley (eds.) 1865. *Francis Thynne: Animadversions uppon the annotacions and corrections of some imperfections of impressiones of Chaucer's workes* (London: EETS)
Gatch, Milton 1998. 'Humfrey Wanley (1672–1726)', in Helen Damico and Joseph Zavadil (eds.), *Medieval Scholarship: Bibliographical Studies on the Formation of a Discipline*, vol. II (*Literature and Philology*) (New York: Garland), 45–57
Gavrilov, Aleksandr 1997. 'Techniques of reading in classical antiquity', *The Classical Quarterly* 47, 56–73
Geddie, William 1912. *A Bibliography of Middle Scots Poets* (Edinburgh: STS)
Genette, Gérard (trans. Jane Lewin) 1997. *Paratexts: Thresholds of Interpretation* (Cambridge University Press)
Gillespie, Vincent 2007. 'Vernacular theology', in Paul Strohm (ed.), *Middle English: Oxford Twenty-First-Century Approaches to Literature* (Oxford University Press), 401–10
Gillespie, Vincent and Kantik Ghosh (eds.) 2011. *After Arundel: Religious Writing in Fifteenth-Century England* (Turnhout: Brepols)
Gillespie, Vincent and Anne Hudson (eds.) 2013. *Probable Truth: Editing Medieval Texts from Britain in the Twenty-First Century* (Turnhout: Brepols)
Gneuss, Helmut 2001. 'Humfrey Wanley borrows books in Cambridge', *Transactions of the Cambridge Bibliographical Society* 12, 145–60
Godden, Malcolm (ed.) 1979. *Ælfric's Catholic Homilies, the Second Series Text* (Oxford: EETS)
Goring, Paul 2004. *Rhetoric of Sensibility in Eighteenth-Century Culture* (Cambridge University Press)
Graham, Timothy 2000. 'John Joscelyn, pioneer of Old English lexicography', in Graham (ed.), 83–140
(ed.) 2000. *The Recovery of Old English* (Kalamazoo: Medieval Institute Publications)
Gray [Mackay], Pauline 2005. 'Burns's O Saw Ye My Maggie', *Burns Chronicle* (spring number), 11–14
Greg, Walter W. 1950/1. 'The rationale of copy-text', *Studies in Bibliography* 3, 19–36
Gregory, E. David 2006. *Victorian Songhunters: The Recovery and Editing of English Vernacular Ballads and Folk Lyrics, 1820–1883* (Lanham: Scarecrow Press)
Groom, Nick 1999. *The Making of Percy's* Reliques (Oxford University Press)
Gunn, Cate 2008. *Ancrene Wisse: From Pastoral Literature to Vernacular Spirituality* (Cardiff: University of Wales Press)
Haarder, Andreas and Thomas Shippey 1998. *Beowulf: The Critical Heritage* (London: Routledge)
Haarländer, Stephanie 2006. *Rabanus Maurus zum Kennenlernen* (Mainz: Wissenschaftliche Buchgesellschaft)
Habinek, Thomas 1985. *The Colometry of Latin Prose* (Berkeley: University of California Press)

Hales, John and Frederick J. Furnivall (eds.) 1867–8. *Bishop Percy's Folio Manuscript: Ballads and Romances* (London: Truebner)

Hall, Joseph (ed.) 1920. *Selections from Early Middle English 1130–1250* (Oxford: Clarendon Press)

de Hamel, Christopher 2016. *Meetings with Remarkable Manuscripts* (Harmondsworth: Allen Lane)

Hammond, Carolyn J.-B. (ed. and trans.) 2014. *Augustine: Confessions, Books 1–8* (Cambridge, Mass.: Harvard University Press)

Hanna, Ralph 2005. *London Literature, 1300–1380* (Cambridge University Press)

Hardman, Philippa 1992. 'Fitt divisions in Middle English romances: A consideration of the evidence', *The Yearbook of English Studies* 22, 63–80

Harlow, C. Geoffrey 1959. 'Punctuation in some manuscripts of Ælfric', *Review of English Studies*, new series 10, 1–19

Harré, Rom 1972. *The Philosophies of Science* (Oxford University Press)

Harris, Kate 1983. 'John Gower's *Confessio Amantis*: The virtues of bad texts', in Derek Pearsall (ed.), *Manuscripts and Readers in Fifteenth-Century England* (Woodbridge: Brewer), 27–40

Harris, Richard (ed.) 1992. *A Chorus of Grammars: The Correspondence of George Hickes, and His Collaborators on the Thesaurus linguarum septentrionalium* (Toronto: Pontifical Institute of Mediaeval Studies)

Hart, Horace 2014. *New Hart's Rules for Compositors and Readers* (Oxford University Press)

Hary 1820 = Jamieson 1820b

Haugen, Einar 1966. 'Dialect, language, nation', *American Anthropologist* 68, 922–35

Heine, Bernd and Tania Kuteva 2007. *The Genesis of Grammar: A Reconstruction* (Oxford University Press)

Hellinga, Lotte 1997. 'Nicolas Love in print', in Oguro et al. (eds.), 143–62

2014. *Texts in Transit: From Manuscript to Proof and Print in the Fifteenth Century* (Leiden: Brill)

Henderson, John 2007. *The Medieval World of Isidore of Seville* (Cambridge University Press)

Henry, Avril 1990. '"The pater Noster in a table ypeynted", and some other presentations of doctrine in the Vernon Manuscript', in Pearsall (ed.), 89–113

Hines, John 2004. *Voices in the Past: English Literature and Archaeology* (Cambridge: Brewer)

Hines, John, Nathalie Cohen and Simon Roffey 2004. '*Iohannes Gower, Armiger, Poeta:* Records and memorials of his life and death', in Echard (ed.), 23–41

Hoggart, Richard 1957. *The Uses of Literacy* (London: Chatto and Windus)

Horobin, Simon 2006. 'A new fragment of the *Romaunt of the Rose*', *Studies in the Age of Chaucer* 28, 205–15

2010. 'Adam Pinkhurst, Geoffrey Chaucer and the Hengwrt manuscript of the *Canterbury Tales*', *The Chaucer Review* 44, 351–67

Horobin, Simon and Aditi Nafde 2015. 'Stephen Batman and the making of the Parker Library', *Transactions of the Cambridge Bibliographical Society* 15, 561–82

Houwen, Luuk (ed.) 1990. *The Sex Werkdays and Agis* (Groningen: Forsten)
Hudson, Anne (ed.) 1978. *Selections from English Wycliffite Writings* (Cambridge University Press)
1983. '"No newe thyng": The printing of medieval texts in the early Reformation period', in Douglas Gray and Eric G. Stanley (eds.), *Middle English Studies Presented to Norman Davis* (Oxford: Clarendon Press), 153–74
1985. 'A new look at *The Lay Folks' Catechism*', *Viator* 16, 243–58
1988. *The Premature Reformation: Wycliffite Texts and Lollard History* (Oxford: Clarendon Press)
1994. '*Piers Plowman* and the Peasants' Revolt', *Yearbook of Langland Studies* 8, 85–106
1996. '"Springing cockel in our clene corn": Lollard preaching in England around 1400', in Scott Waugh and Pieter Diehl (eds.), *Christendom and Its Discontents* (Cambridge University Press), 132–47
Hudson, Anne and Pamela Gradon (eds.) 1983. *English Wycliffite Sermons* (Oxford: Clarendon Press)
Irvine, Susan (ed.) 1993. *Sermons from MS Bodley 343* (Oxford: EETS)
Jack, Ronald D. S. and Pat Rozendaal (eds.) 1997. *The Mercat Anthology of Early Scottish Literature 1375–1707* (Edinburgh: Mercat Press)
Jajdelska, Elspeth 2007. *Silent Reading and the Birth of the Narrator* (University of Toronto Press)
James, Francis 1956. *North Country Bishop: A Biography of William Nicolson* (New Haven: Yale University Press)
Jamieson, John (ed.) 1820a. *The Bruce: Or, the Metrical History of Robert I, King of Scots, by John Barbour, Archdeacon of Aberdeen* (Edinburgh: Ballantyne)
1820b. *Wallace: Or, The Life and Acts of Sir William Wallace, of Ellerslie* (Edinburgh: Ballantyne)
Jasper, David and Jeremy J. Smith 2019. '*The Lay Folks' Mass Book* and Thomas Frederick Simmons: Medievalism and the Tractarians', *Journal of Ecclesiastical History* 70, 785–804
Johnson, Ian 2015. 'From Nicholas Love's *Mirror* to John Heigham's *Life*: Paratextual displacements and displaced readers', in Corbellini et al. (eds.), 190–212
Johnson, Ian and Allan Westphall (eds.) 2013. *The Pseudo-Bonaventuran Lives of Christ: Exploring the Middle English Tradition* (Turnhout: Brepols)
Jones, Marie Claire 2000. 'Vernacular literacy in late medieval England: The example of East Anglian medical manuscripts', PhD thesis, University of Glasgow
Jones, Michael R. 2011. '"This is no prophecy": Robert Crowley, *Piers Plowman*, and Kett's rebellion', *The Sixteenth Century Journal* 42, 37–55
Jones, Sir William 1807. *The Works of Sir William Jones*, vol. III (London: Stockdale and Walker)
Jucker, Andreas and Irma Taavitsainen 2013. *English Historical Pragmatics* (Edinburgh University Press)
Kaislanemi, Samuli 2017. 'Code-switching, script-switching, and typeface-switching in Early Modern English manuscript letters and printed tracts', in Peikola et al., 165–200

Kane, George (ed.) 1988. *Piers Plowman: The A Version*, rev. edn (London: Athlone Press)

Kane, George and E. Talbot Donaldson (eds.) 1988. *Piers Plowman: The B Version*, rev. edn (London: Athlone Press)

Karkov, Catherine 2012. 'The arts of writing: Voice, image, object', in Clare Lees (ed.), *The Cambridge History of Early Medieval Literature* (Cambridge University Press), 73–98

Kelemen, Erick 2006. 'More evidence for the date of *A Testimonie of Antiquitie*', *The Library* 7, 361–76

Kelly, Stephen and John J. Thompson (eds.) 2005. *Imagining the Book* (Turnhout: Brepols)

Kemble, John Mitchell (ed.) 1833. *The Anglo-Saxon Poems of Beowulf, The Travellers, and The Battle of Finnesburh* (London: Pickering)

Ker, Neil R. 1957. *Catalogue of Manuscripts Containing Anglo-Saxon* (Oxford: Clarendon Press)

Kerby-Fulton, Kathryn 2014. 'Confronting the scribe–poet binary: The Z text, writing office redaction, and the Oxford reading circles', in Kerby-Fulton et al. (eds.), 489–515

Kerby-Fulton, Kathryn, John J. Thompson and Sarah Baechle (eds.) 2014. *New Directions in Medieval Manuscript Studies and Reading Practices* (University of Notre Dame Press)

Keynes, Simon and Michael Lapidge 1983. *Alfred the Great* (Harmondsworth: Penguin)

Kidd, Colin 1993. *Subverting Scotland's Past* (Cambridge University Press)

2007. 'The English cult of Wallace and the blending of nineteenth-century Britain', in Cowan (ed.), 136–50

Kiernan, Kevin 1986a. 'Part One: Thorkelin's discovery of *Beowulf*: The Thorkelin transcripts of *Beowulf*', *Anglistica* 25, 1–41

1986b. 'Part Three: The reliability of the transcripts, and the conclusion: The Thorkelin transcripts of *Beowulf*',*Anglistica* 25, 97–151

1997. *Beowulf and the Beowulf Manuscript* (Ann Arbor: University of Michigan Press)

King, Elspeth (intro.) 1998. *William Hamilton of Gilbertfield: The Wallace* (Edinburgh: Luath)

2007. 'The material culture of William Wallace', in Cowan (ed.), 117–35

King, John N. 1982. *English Reformation Literature* (Princeton University Press)

Klaeber, Frederick, rev. Robert D. Fulk, Robert E. Bjork and John D. Niles (eds.) 2014 *Klaeber's Beowulf* (University of Toronto Press)

Kirk, John and Iseabail Macleod (eds.) 2013. *Scots: The Language and Its Literature* (Amsterdam: Rodopi)

Knight, Ione Kemp (ed.) 1967. *Wimbledon's Sermon* (Pittsburgh: Duquesne University Press)

Kölbing, Eugen (ed.) 1878–9. *Die nordische und die englische Version der Tristan-Sage* (Heilbronn: Henniger)

Kopaczyk, Joanna and Andreas Jucker (eds.) 2013. *Communities of Practice in the History of English* (Amsterdam: Benjamins)

Kraebel, Andrew B. 2015. 'A further book annotated by Stephen Batman, with new material for his biography', *The Library* 16, 458–66

Kretzschmar, William 2009. *The Linguistics of Speech* (Cambridge University Press)

Kytö, Merja, Jeremy J. Smith and Irma Taavitsainen (eds.) 2017. 'Interfacing individuality and collaboration in the English-language research world', *Studia Neophilogica* 89, special supplement, 1–4

Kytö, Merja and Matti Peikola (eds.) 2014. 'Philology on the move: Manuscript studies at the dawn of the twenty-first century', *Studia Neophilologica* 86, special supplement, 1–8

Laing, Margaret and Keith Williamson (eds.) 1994. *Speaking in Our Own Tongues: Papers from the Edinburgh Colloquium on Historical Dialectology* (Woodbridge: Boydell and Brewer)

Lanier, Sidney (ed.) 1883. *The Boy's Percy: Being Old Ballads of War, Adventure and Love from Bishop Thomas Percy's Reliques of Ancient English Poetry* (New York: Scribner)

Lave, Jean and Etienne Wenger-Trayner 1991. *Situated Learning* (Cambridge University Press)

Leech, Geoffrey 1983. *Principles of Pragmatics* (London: Longman)

Lerer, Seth 1993. *Chaucer and His Readers* (Princeton University Press)

Levy, Lindsay 2014. 'A life in books: Walter Scott's library at Abbotsford', PhD thesis, University of Glasgow

Leyden, John 1858. *Poems and Ballads: With a Memoir of the Author by Sir Walter Scott; and a Supplement by Robert White* (Kelso: Rutherfurd)

Lindberg, Conrad (ed.) 1959–73. *MS. Bodley 959: Genesis–Baruch 3.20 in the Earlier Version of the Wycliffite Bible* (Stockholm: Almqvist and Wiksell)

Liu, Yin 2017. 'Stating the obvious in runes', in Peikola et al., 125–39

Liuzza, Roy M. 2006. 'Scribes of the mind: Editing Old English, in theory and practice', in Hugh Magennis and Jon Wilcox (eds.), *The Power of Words: Anglo-Saxon Studies Presented to Donald G. Scragg on His Seventieth Birthday* (Morgantown: West Virginia University Press), 245–77

Lowe, Kathryn 2000. '"The Oracle of His Country"? William Somner, Gavelkind, and lexicography in the seventeenth and eighteenth centuries', in Graham (ed.), 281–300

Lucas, Peter 1997. '"A Testimonye of Verye Ancient Tyme"? Some manuscript models for the Parkerian Anglo-Saxon type-designs', in Pamela R. Robinson and Rivkah Zim (eds.), *Of the Making of Books: Medieval Manuscripts, Their Scribes and Readers: Essays Presented to M. B. Parkes* (Aldershot: Scolar), 147–88

2016. 'The earliest modern Anglo-Saxon grammar: Sir Henry Spelman, Abraham Wheelock and William Retchford', *Anglo-Saxon England* 45, 379–417

Macaulay, George C. (ed.) 1900. *The English Works of John Gower* (London: EETS)

MacCulloch, Diarmaid 1996. *Thomas Cranmer* (New Haven: Yale University Press)

2013. *Silence: A Christian History* (Harmondsworth: Penguin)

2018. *Thomas Cromwell: A Life* (Harmondsworth: Allen Lane)

McDiarmid, Matthew P. (ed.) 1968. *Hary's Wallace* (Edinburgh: STS)

McDiarmid, Matthew P. and James Stevenson (eds.) 1980–5. *Barbour's Bruce* (Edinburgh: STS)

MacDonald, Alasdair 1986. 'The Bannatyne manuscript: A Marian anthology', *Innes Review* 37, 36–47

2012. 'The revival of Scotland's older literature', in Brown and McDougall (eds.), 551–60

McDougall, Warren 2012. 'Developing a marketplace for books: Edinburgh', in Brown and McDougall (eds.), 118–31

McGann, Jerome 1983. *A Critique of Modern Textual Criticism* (University of Chicago Press)

(ed.) 2010. *Online Humanities Scholarship: The Shape of Things to Come* (Houston: Rice University Press)

McIntosh, Angus 1989. 'Is *Sir Tristrem* an English or a Scottish Poem?', in J. Lachlan Mackenzie and Richard Todd (eds.), In *Other Words: Transcultural Studies in Philology, Translation, and Lexicology Presented to Hans Heinrich Meier* (Dordrecht: Foris), 85–95

Mackay, Francesca 2012. 'The development of reading practices as represented in the textual afterlife of Nicholas Love's *Mirror of the Blessed Life of Jesus Christ*', MPhil thesis, University of Glasgow

2017. 'How the page functions: Reading Pitscottie's *Cronicles* in manuscript and print', in Peikola et al., 41–65

McKenzie, Donald F. 2002. 'Printing and publishing 1557–1700: Constraints on the London book trades', in Barnard et al. (eds.), 553–67

McKitterick, Rosamund 1989. *The Carolingians and the Written Word* (Cambridge University Press)

McLoughlin, Kate 1994. 'Magdalene College MS Pepys 2498 and Stephen Batman's reading practices', *Transactions of the Cambridge Bibliographical Society* 10, 521–34

McNeill, George (ed.) 1886. *Sir Tristrem* (Edinburgh: STS)

Machan, Tim William 1994. *Textual Criticism and Middle English Texts* (Charlottesville: University of Virginia Press)

2003. *English in the Middle Ages* (Oxford University Press)

2011. 'The visual pragmatics of code-switching in late Middle English literature', in Herbert Schendl and Laura Wright (eds.), *Code-Switching in Early English* (Berlin: De Gruyter), 303–33

(ed.) 2017. *Imagining Medieval English* (Cambridge University Press)

Mack, Frances (ed.) 1963. *The English Text of the Ancrene Riwle*, edited from Cotton MS. Titus D.xviii (London: EETS)

Macy, Gary 1994. 'The dogma of transubstantiation in the Middle Ages', *Journal of Ecclesiastical History* 45, 11–41

Magennis, Hugh 2005. 'Ælfric's *Lives of the Saints* and Cotton Julius E.vii: Adaptation, appropriation and the disappearing book', in Kelly and Thompson (eds.), 99–109

Marcus, Imogen 2017 'Whose letters are they anyway? Addressing the issue of scribal writing in Bess of Hardwick's Early Modern English letters', in Peikola et al., 219–47

Matthews, David 1999. *The Making of Middle English* (Minneapolis: University of Minnesota Press)

(ed.) 2000. *The Invention of Middle English: An Anthology of Primary Sources* (Turnhout: Brepols)

Mele-Marrero, Margarita 2012. 'A *testimonie*'s stance: Editorial positioning in Ælfric's *Sermo in die Pasce*', *Studia Anglica Posnaniensia* 47, 81–95

Millett, Bella 2005. 'The discontinuity of English prose: Structural innovation in the Trinity and Lambeth Homilies', in Oizumi et al. (eds.), 129–50

(ed.) 2005. *Ancrene Wisse* (Oxford: EETS)

2007. 'The pastoral context of the Trinity and Lambeth Homilies', in Scase (ed.) 2007a, 43–64

2013. 'Whatever happened to electronic editing?', in Gillespie and Hudson (eds.), 39–54

Millgate, Jane 2000. 'The early publication history of Scott's *Minstrelsy of the Scottish Border*', *Papers of the Bibliographical Society of America* 94, 551–64

Minnis, Alastair and Charlotte Brewer (eds.) 1992. *Crux and Controversy in Middle English Textual Criticism* (Woodbridge: Boydell and Brewer)

Mitchell, Bruce 2005. 'Some reflections on the punctuation of Old English prose', in Oizumi et al. (eds.), 151–62

Mitchell, Jerome 2015. *Scott, Chaucer, and Medieval Romance* (Lexington: University Press of Kentucky)

Mohrmann, G. P. (Jerry) (intro.) 1969. *Thomas Sheridan: A Discourse, Being Introductory to His Course of Lectures on Elocution and the English Language, 1759* (Los Angeles: William Andrews Clark Memorial Library)

Momma, Haruko 2013. *From Philology to English Studies* (Cambridge University Press)

Mooney, Linne 2006. 'Chaucer's scribe', *Speculum* 81, 97–138

Mooney, Linne and Estelle Stubbs 2013. *Scribes and the City: London Guildhall Clerks and the Dissemination of Middle English Literature 1375–1425* (York Medieval Press)

Moore, Colette 2014. *Quoting Speech in Early English* (Cambridge University Press)

2017. 'Discourse variation, mise-en-page, and textual organisation in Middle English saints' lives', in Peikola et al., 23–40

Morris, Richard (ed.) 1871. *Cursor Mundi* (London: EETS)

Morrison, Stephen 2013. 'Scribal performance in a late Middle English sermon cycle', in Driver and O'Mara (eds.), 117–31

Murphy, Michael 1969. 'Religious polemics in the genesis of Old English studies', *Huntington Library Quarterly* 32, 241–8

2015. 'Allan Ramsay's poetic language of Anglo-Scottish rapprochement', *Études écossaises* 17, 13–30
Murray, Kylie 2009. 'Dream and vision in late-medieval Scotland: The epic case of William Wallace', *Proceedings of the Harvard Celtic Colloquium* 29, 177–98
Nichols, Stephen 1990. 'Introduction: Philology in a manuscript culture', *Speculum* 65, 1–10
2017. 'Codex as critic: One manuscript's dialogue with *The Romance of the Rose*', *Digital Philology* 6, 90–120
O'Keeffe, Katharine O'Brien 1990. *Visible Song: Transitional Literacy in Old English Verse* (Cambridge University Press)
Ogburn, Vincent 1936. 'Thomas Percy's unfinished collection, *Ancient English and Scottish Poems*', *English Literary History* 3, 183–9
Oguro, Shoichi, Richard Beadle and Michael Sargent (eds.) 1997. *Nicholas Love at Waseda* (Cambridge: Brewer)
Oizumi, Akio, Jacek Fisiak and John Scahill (eds.), *Text and Language in Medieval English Prose: A Festschrift for Tadao Kubouchi* (Frankfurt am Main: Lang)
Okasha, Elizabeth 1992. 'Literacy in Anglo-Saxon England: The evidence from inscriptions', in *Medieval Europe 1992: Art and Symbolism*, vol. VII (pre-printed conference papers, University of York), 87–8.
Otten, Willemien 2000. 'Between Augustinian sign and Carolingian reality: The presence of Ambrose and Augustine in the eucharistic debate between Paschasius Radbertus and Ratramnus of Corbie', *Nederlands archief voor kerkgeschiedenis* 80, 137–56
Page, Raymond I. 1999. *An Introduction to English Runes* (Woodbridge: Boydell)
Pahta, Päivi and Andreas Jucker (eds.) 2011. *Communicating Early English Manuscripts* (Cambridge University Press)
Parkes, Malcolm B. 1991. 'The literacy of the laity', reprinted and updated in *Scribes, Scripts and Readers* (London: Hambledon), 275–97
1992. *Pause and Effect: A History of Punctuation in the West* (London: Scolar)
1997a. 'Archaizing hands in English manuscripts', in J. P. Carley and C. G. C. Tite (eds.), *Books and Collectors 1200–1700: Essays Presented to Andrew Watson* (London: British Library), 101–41
1997b. 'Stephen Batman's manuscripts', in M. Kanno, H. Yamshita, M. Kawasaki, J. Asakawa and N. Shirai (eds.), *Medieval Heritage: Essays in Honour of Tadahiro Ikegami* (Tokyo: Yushodo), 125–56
1997c. 'Punctuation in copies of Nicholas Love's *Mirror of the Blessed Life of Jesus Christ*', in Oguro et al. (eds.), 47–59
1999. 'Medieval punctuation and the modern editor', in A. Ferrari (ed.), *Filologia classica e filologia romanza* (Spoleto: Centro Italiano di Studi sull' alto Medioevo), 337–49
Patterson, Lee 1987. *Negotiating the Past* (Madison: University of Wisconsin Press)
Pearsall, Derek 1977. *Old English and Middle English Poetry* (London: Routledge)
1984. 'Thomas Speght (ca. 1550–?)', in Ruggiers (ed.), 71–92
(ed.) 1990. *Studies in the Vernon Manuscript* (Cambridge: Brewer)

2013. 'Variants vs variance', in Gillespie and Hudson (eds.), 197–205
Pearsall, Derek and Ian B. Cunningham (intro.) 1977. *The Auchinleck Manuscript* (London: Scolar Press)
Peikola, Matti 2003. 'The Wycliffite Bible and "Central Midlands Standard": Assessing the manuscript evidence', *Nordic Journal of English Studies* 2, 29–51
2008. 'Aspects of mise-en-page in manuscripts of the Wycliffite Bible', in Renevey and Caie (eds.), 28–67
2011. 'Copying space, length of entries, and textual transmission in Middle English tables of lessons', in Thaisen and Rutkowska (eds.), 107–24
2015. 'Manuscript paratexts in the making: British Library MS Harley 6333 as a liturgical compilation', in Corbellini et al. (eds.), 44–67
Peikola, Matti, Aleksi Makilahde, Hanna Salmi, Mari-Liisa Varila and Janne Skaffari (eds.) 2017. *Verbal and Visual Communication in Early English Texts* (Turnhout: Brepols)
Perry, Ryan 2007. 'The Clopton manuscript and the Beauchamp affinity: Patronage and reception issues in a West Midlands reading community', in Scase (ed.) 2007a: 131–59
2013a. 'Editorial politics in the Vernon manuscript', in Scase (ed.) 2013b: 71–95
2013b. '"Some sprytuall matter of gostly edyfycacion": Readers and readings of Nicholas Love's *Mirror of the Blessed Life of Jesus Christ*', in Johnson and Westphall (eds.), 79–126
Pittock, Murray 2010. *Material Culture and Sedition 1688–1760* (Basingstoke: Palgrave)
Plumer, Danielle Cunliffe 2000. 'The construction of structure in the earliest editions of Old English poetry', in Graham (ed.), 243–80
Powell, Susan 1997. 'What Caxton did to the *Festial*', *Journal of the Early Book Society* 11, 48–77
(ed.) 2009. *John Mirk's* Festial (Oxford: EETS)
2011. 'After Arundel but before Luther: The first half-century of print', in Gillespie and Ghosh (eds.), 523–41
Prescott, Andrew 1997. 'The electronic *Beowulf* and digital restoration', *Literary and Linguistic Computing* 12, 185–95
Pulsiano, Philip 2000. 'William L'Isle and the editing of Old English', in Graham (ed.), 173–206
Putter, Ad, Judith Jefferson and Donka Minkova 2014. 'Dialect, rhyme, and emendation in *Sir Tristrem*', *Journal of English and Germanic Philology* 113, 73–92
Ratia, Maura and Carla Suhr 2017. 'Verbal and visual communication in title pages of Early Modern English specialised medical texts', in Peikola et al., 67–93
Raven, James 2002. 'The economic context', in Barnard et al. (eds.), 568–82
Renevey, Denis and Graham D. Caie (eds.) 2008. *Medieval Texts in Context* (London: Routledge)
Rennie, Susan 2012. *Jamieson's Dictionary of Scots* (Oxford University Press)
Reynolds, Leighton and Nigel G. Wilson 2013. *Scribes and Scholars: A Guide to the Transmission of Greek and Latin Literature*, 3rd edn (Oxford University Press)

Ricks, Christopher (ed.) 1988. *A. E. Housman: Collected Poems and Selected Prose* (Harmondsworth: Penguin)

Riddy, Felicity 2007. 'Unmapping the Territory: Blind Hary's *Wallace*' in Cowan (ed.), 107–16

Robinson, Pamela 1990. 'The Vernon manuscript as a "Coucher Book"', in Pearsall (ed.), 15–28

Rogers, H. Leslie 1985. '*The Battle of Maldon*: David Casley's transcript', *Notes and Queries* New Series, 32, 147–55

Ruggiers, Paul (ed.) 1984. *Editing Chaucer: The Great Tradition* (Norman: Pilgrim Books)

Saenger, Paul 1997. *Space between Words: The Origins of Silent Reading* (Stanford University Press)

Salter, Elisabeth 2015. *Popular Reading in English c. 1400–1600* (Manchester University Press)

Salter, Elizabeth 1956. 'Punctuation in an early manuscript of Nicholas Love's *Mirror*', *Review of English Studies*, New Series 7, 11–18

Samuels, Michael L. 1963. 'Some applications of Middle English dialectology', *English Studies* 44, 81–94

1981. 'Spelling and dialect in the late and post-Middle English periods', in Benskin and Samuels (eds.), 43–54

1985. 'Langland's dialect', *Medium Ævum* 54, 232–47

Samuels, Michael L. and Jeremy J. Smith 1981. 'The language of Gower', *Neuphilologische Mitteilungen* 82, 295–304

Sandved, Arthur 1981. 'Prolegomena to a renewed study of the rise of standard English', in Benskin and Samuels (eds.), 31–42

Santini, Monica 2010. *The Impetus of Amateur Scholarship: Discussing and Editing Medieval Romances in Late Eighteenth- and Nineteenth-Century Britain* (Berne: Lang)

Sargent, Michael 1997. 'The textual affiliations of the Waseda manuscript of Nicholas Love's *Mirror of the Blessed Life of Jesus Christ*', in Oguro et al. (eds.), 175–274

(ed.) 2004. *The Mirror of the Blessed Life of Jesus Christ: A Reading Text* (University of Exeter Press)

(ed.) 2005. *Nicholas Love, The Mirror of the Blessed Life of Jesus Christ: A Full Critical Edition* (University of Exeter Press)

Saul, Nigel 2001. *Death, Art and Memory in Medieval England* (Oxford University Press)

de Saussure, Ferdinand (Charles Bally and Albert Sechehaye eds.) 1916. *Cours de linguistique générale* (Paris: Payot)

Scanlon, Larry 2007. 'Langland, apocalypse and the early modern editor', in Gordon McMullan and David Matthews (eds.), *Reading the Medieval in Early Modern England* (Cambridge University Press), 51–73

Scase, Wendy 1992. 'Reginald Pecock, John Carpenter, and John Colop's "Common-Profit" books: Aspects of book ownership and circulation in fifteenth-century London', *Medium Ævum* 61, 261–74 (ed.) 2007a. *Essays in Manuscript Geography* (Turnhout: Brepols)

2007b. *Literature and Complaint in England, 1272–1553* (Oxford University Press)

2013a. 'Some Vernon analogues and their patrons', in Scase (ed.) 2013b: 247–68

(ed.) 2013b. *The Making of the Vernon Manuscript* (Turnhout: Brepols)

2013c. 'The patronage of the Vernon manuscript', in Scase (ed.) 2013b: 269–93

Scott, Diane 2015. 'Silent reading and the medieval text: The development of reading practices in the early prints of William Langland and John Lydgate', PhD thesis, University of Glasgow

Scott, Walter (ed.) 1802–3. *Minstrelsy of the Scottish Border* (Edinburgh: Cadell and Davies)

(ed.) 1804. *Sir Tristrem; a Metrical Romance of The Thirteenth Century; by Thomas of Erceldoune, called The Rhymer* (Edinburgh: Constable)

1805. *The Lay of the Last Minstrel* (London: Longman)

1808. *Marmion* (Edinburgh: Constable)

1829. 'Memoir of George Bannatyne', in Anon (ed.), *Memorials of George Bannatyne* (Edinburgh: Bannatyne Club), 1–24

Sebba, Mark 2009. 'Sociolinguistic approaches to writing systems research', *Writing Systems Research* 1, 35–49

Senra Silva, Inmaculada 1998. 'The rune "ēþel" and scribal writing habits in the *Beowulf* manuscript', *Neuphilologische Mitteilungen* 99, 241–7

Sharpe, Kevin 2000. *Reading Revolutions* (New Haven: Yale University Press)

Sher, Richard B. 2006. *The Enlightenment and the Book* (University of Chicago Press)

Sherman, William 2008. *Used Books* (Philadelphia: University of Pennsylvania Press)

2013. 'Punctuation as configuration; or, how many sentences are there in Sonnet 1', *Early Modern Literary Studies* (online publication = https://extra.shu.ac.uk/emls/si-21/04-Sherman_Punctuation%20as%20Configuration.htm, last consulted on 25 May 2019)

Sibbald, James 1802. *Chronicle of Scottish Poetry: From the Thirteenth Century to the Union of the Crowns* (Edinburgh: Sibbald)

Simpson, Grant 1998. *Scottish Handwriting 1150–1650* (East Linton: Tuckwell)

Sisam, Kenneth 1953. 'Humfrey Wanley', in *Studies in the History of Old English Literature* (Oxford: Clarendon Press), 259–77

Skeat, Walter W. (ed.) 1870–89. *The Bruce, or, the book of the most excellent and noble Prince, Robert de Broyss, King of Scots, compiled by John Barbour* (London: EETS)

Smith, Jeremy J. 1988a. 'The Trinity Gower D-Scribe and his work on two early *Canterbury Tales* manuscripts', in Smith (ed.), 51–69

1988b. 'Spelling and tradition in fifteenth-century copies of Gower's *Confessio Amantis*', in Smith (ed.), 96–113

(ed.) 1988c. *The Language of Chaucer and His Contemporaries: Essays by M. L. Samuels and Jeremy J. Smith* (Aberdeen University Press)

1996. *An Historical Study of English* (London: Routledge)

2000a. 'The letters *s* and *z* in South-Eastern Middle English', *Neuphilologische Mitteilungen* 101, 403–13
2000b. 'Standard language in Early Middle English?', in Irma Taavitsainen, Terttu Nevalainen, Päivi Pahta and Matti Rissanen (eds.), *Placing Middle English in Context* (Berlin: Mouton de Gruyter), 125–39
2004. 'John Gower and London English', in Echard (ed.), 61–72
2008. 'Issues of linguistic categorisation in the evolution of written Middle English', in Renevey and Caie (eds.), 211–24
2010. 'Scots and English in the letters of John Knox', in Kevin McGinley and Nicola Royan (eds.), *The Apparelling of Truth: Literature and Literary Culture in the Reign of James VI: A Festschrift for Roderick J. Lyall* (Cambridge Scholars), 1–10
2012a. *Older Scots: A Linguistic Reader* (Woodbridge: STS)
2012b. 'The historiography of the English language', in Alexander Bergs and Laurel Brinton (eds.), *English Historical Linguistics* (Berlin: Mouton de Gruyter), 1295–312
2013a. 'Mapping the language of the Vernon manuscript', in Scase (ed.), 49–70
2013b. 'Punctuating Mirk's *Festial*: A Scottish text and its implications', in Driver and O'Mara (eds.), 161–92
2013c. 'The language of the letters of Archibald Campbell, Lord Ilay (1682–1761)', in Anderson (ed.), 27–44
2016. 'Scots and English across the Union', *Scottish Literary Review* 8, 17–32
2017a. 'From *secreit* script to public print: Punctuation, news management, and the condemnation of the Earl of Bothwell', *Huntington Library Quarterly* 80, 223–38
2017b. 'The afterlives of Nicholas Love', *Studia Neophilologica* 89, 59–74
2019. 'Chaucer and London English', in Ian Johnson (ed.), *Geoffrey Chaucer in Context* (Cambridge University Press), 35–42
Smith, Jeremy J. and Christian J. Kay 2011. 'The pragmatics of punctuation in Older Scots', in Pahta and Jucker (eds.), 212–25
Smithers, Geoffrey V. (ed.) 1957. *Kyng Alisaunder* (London: EETS)
Somerset, Fiona 2013. *Feeling like Saints: Lollard Writings after Wyclif* (Ithaca: Cornell University Press)
SPAT = Scottish Printing Archival Trust 1990. *A Reputation for Excellence: A History of the Edinburgh Printing Industry* (Edinburgh: Merchiston Publishing)
SPAT = Scottish Printing Archival Trust 1996. *A Reputation for Excellence: A History of the Dundee and Perth Printing Industries* (Edinburgh: Merchiston Publishing)
Spencer, Helen 1993. *English Preaching in the Late Middle Ages* (Oxford: Clarendon Press)
2004. 'Sermon literature', in Anthony S. G. Edwards (ed.), *A Companion to Middle English Prose* (Cambridge: Brewer), 151–74
2015. 'F. J. Furnivall's Six of the Best: The Six-Text *Canterbury Tales* and the Chaucer Society', *Review of English Studies*, New Series, 66, 601–23

Spurlock, Scott 2011. 'Cromwell's Edinburgh press and the development of print culture in Scotland', *Scottish Historical Review* 90, 179–203

Stanley, Eric G. 1969. 'Laȝamon's antiquarian sentiments', *Medium Ævum* 38, 23–37

Stenroos, Merja forthcoming. 'A variationist approach to Middle English dialects'

Stock, Brian 1983. *The Implications of Literacy: Written Language and Models of Interpretation in the Eleventh and Twelfth Centuries* (Princeton University Press)

2001. *After Augustine: The Meditative Reader and the Text* (Philadelphia: University of Pennsylvania Press)

Suhr, Carla 2011. *Publishing for the Masses: Early Modern English Witchcraft Pamphlets* (Helsinki: Mémoires de la Société Néophilologique)

Summit, Jennifer 2008. *Memory's Library: Medieval Books in Early Modern England* (University of Chicago Press)

Swain, Larry J. 2011. 'Whose text for whom? Transmission history of Ælfric of Eynsham's *Letter to Sigeweard*', in Thaisen and Rutkowska (eds.), 31–52

Swales, John 1990. *Genre Analysis: English in Academic and Research Settings* (Cambridge University Press)

Swan, Mary 2007. 'Mobile libraries: Old English manuscript production in Worcester and the West Midlands, 1090–1215', in Scase (ed.), 29–42

2010. 'Reading for the ear: Lambeth Palace Library, MS 487, Item 10', *Leeds Studies in English* 41, 214–24

Swan, Mary and Elaine Treharne (eds.) 2000. *Rewriting Old English in the Twelfth Century* (Cambridge University Press)

Thaisen, Jacob and Hanna Rutkowska (eds.) 2011. *Scribes, Printers, and the Accidentals of Their Texts* (Frankfurt am Main: Lang)

Thomson, Ann 1995. 'Joseph Morgan et le monde islamique', *Dix-huitième Siècle* 27, 349–63

Thompson, John 2004. 'Bishop Thomas Percy's contributions to Langland scholarship: Two annotated *Piers Plowman* prints in Belfast', in Takami Matsuda, Richard Linenthal and John Scahill (eds.), *The Medieval Book and a Modern Collector: Essays in Honour of Toshiyuki Takamiya* (Cambridge: Brewer), 451–60

2013a. 'Preaching with a pen: Audience and self-regulation in the writing and reception of John Mirk and Nicholas Love', in Driver and O'Mara (eds.), 101–16

2013b. 'Reading miscellaneously in and around the English pseudo-Bonaventuran tradition', in Johnson and Westphall (eds.), 127–50

2014a. 'Foreword to Part III', in Kerby-Fulton et al., 159–64

2014b. 'Love in the 1530s', in Carole Meale and Derek Pearsall (eds.), *Makers and Users of Medieval Books: Essays in Honour of A. S. G. Edwards* (Woodbridge: Brewer), 191–201

Thorkelin, Grimur Jonsson (ed.) 1815. *De Danorum rebus gestis secul. III & IV. Poëma danicum dialecto anglosaxonica* (Copenhagen: Rangel)

Thorne, J. R. and Marie-Claire Uhart 1986. 'Robert Crowley's *Piers Plowman*', *Medium Ævum* 55, 248–54

Tolkien, J. R. R. (ed.) 1962. *The English Text of the Ancrene Riwle: Ancrene Wisse, edited from MS. Corpus Christi College Cambridge 402* (London: EETS)

Treharne, Elaine 2012. *Living through the Conquest: The Politics of Early English 1020–1230* (Oxford University Press)

Turville-Petre, Thorlac 1990. 'The Vernon and Clopton manuscripts', in Pearsall (ed.), 29–44

Tyrkkö, Jukka 2017. 'Quantifying contrasts: A method of computational analysis of visual features on the early printed page', in Peikola et al. (eds.), 95–122

Varila, Mari-Liisa, Hanna Salmi, Aleksi Mäkilähde, Janne Skaffari and Matti Peikola 2017. 'Disciplinary decoding: Towards understanding the language of visual and material features', in Peikola et al. (eds.), 1–20

Verweij, Sebastiaan 2016. *The Literary Culture of Early Modern Scotland* (Oxford University Press)

Wakelin, Daniel 2018. *Designing English* (Oxford: Bodleian Library)

Walker, Greg 2005. *Writing under Tyranny* (Oxford University Press)

Walsh, Brian 2013. '"A priestly farewell": Gower's tomb and religious change in *Pericles*', *Religion and Literature* 45, 81–113

Walsham, Alexandra 2007. 'Inventing the Lollard past: The afterlife of a medieval sermon in early modern England', *Journal of Ecclesiastical History* 58, 628–55

Warner, Lawrence 2014. *The Myth of Piers Plowman* (Cambridge University Press)

2015. 'Scribes, misattributed: Hoccleve and Pinkhurst', *Studies in the Age of Chaucer* 37, 55–100

2018. *Chaucer's Scribes: London Textual Production, 1384–1432* (Cambridge University Press)

von Wartburg, Walther 1946. *Evolution et structure de la langue française* (Berne: Francke)

Watson, Nicholas 1995. 'Censorship and cultural change in late-medieval England: Vernacular theology, the Oxford translation debate, and Arundel's *Constitutions* of 1409', *Speculum* 70, 822–64

Whitaker, Thomas (ed.) 1813. *Uisio Willi de Petro Plouhman* (London: John Murray)

White, Hugh (trans.) 1993. *Ancrene Wisse* (Harmondsworth: Penguin)

Williams, Abigail 2017. *The Social Life of Books* (New Haven: Yale University Press)

Windeatt, Barry 1984. 'Thomas Tyrwhitt (1730–1786)', in Ruggiers (ed.), 117–43

Wingfield, Emily 2016. 'The Ruthven manuscript of Gavin Douglas's *Eneados* and a new manuscript witness of Julius Caesar Scaliger's *Epidorpides*', *Renaissance Studies* 30, 430–42

Wittig, Kurt 1958. *The Scottish Tradition in Literature* (Edinburgh: Oliver and Boyd)

Wood, Andy 2007. *The 1549 Rebellions and the Making of Early Modern England* (Cambridge University Press)

Wormald, Patrick 1977. 'The uses of literacy in Anglo-Saxon England and its neighbours', *Transactions of the Royal Historical Society* 27, 95–114

Wright, Cyril E. 1960. *Humfrey Wanley, Saxonist and Library-Keeper* (Gollancz Lecture) (London: Oxford University Press)

1972. *Fontes Harleiani* (London: British Museum)

Zettersten, Arne (ed.) 1976. *The English Text of the Ancrene Riwle, Edited from Magdalene College, Cambridge MS Pepys 2498* (London: EETS)

(ed.) 1979. *Waldere* (Manchester University Press)

Zettersten, Arne and Bernhard Diensberg (eds.) 2000. *The English Text of the Ancrene Riwle: The Vernon Text* (Oxford: EETS)

Zumthor, Paul 1972. *Essai de poétique médiévale* (Paris: Seuil)

Index of Manuscripts and Early Prints

Subject Index

For EU product safety concerns, contact us at Calle de José Abascal, 56–1°,
28003 Madrid, Spain or eugpsr@cambridge.org.

www.ingramcontent.com/pod-product-compliance
Ingram Content Group UK Ltd.
Pitfield, Milton Keynes, MK11 3LW, UK
UKHW020358140625
459647UK00020B/2539

* 9 7 8 1 1 0 8 4 1 4 8 5 2 *